Ralph Bunche

X

Ralph Bunche

Model Negro or American Other?

Charles P. Henry

NEW YORK UNIVERSITY PRESS
New York and London

NEW YORK UNIVERSITY PRESS
New York and London

Library of Congress Cataloging-in-Publication Data
Henry, Charles P., 1947–
Ralph Bunche : model Negro or American other? / Charles P. Henry.
p.   cm.
Includes bibliographical references and index.
ISBN 0-8147-3582-7 (acid-free paper)
1. Bunche, Ralph J. (Ralph Johnson), 1904–1971. 2. Statesmen—United
States—Biography. 3. Afro-Americans—Biography. 4. United
Nations—Biography. 5. Racism—United States—History—20th
century. 6. Afro-Americans—Intellectual life—20th century. I. Title.
E748.B885 H46 1998
973'.0496073'0092—ddc21   [B]   98–25482
                                                    CIP

New York University Press books are printed on acid-free paper,
and their binding materials are chosen for strength and durability.

Manufactured in the United States of America

10 9 8 7 6 5 4 3 2 1

For Loretta

Contents

Preface

This book began in the late 1970s when I was fortunate enough to teach at Denison University with historian John "Jack" Kirby. Kirby gave me an article he had written entitled "Ralph Bunche and Black Radical Thought in the 1930s." It opened a whole new world of Black intellectual and political leadership to me. I had suspected that Black leaders and intellectuals existed between the heyday of Booker T. Washington, W. E. B. Du Bois, and Marcus Garvey and my own generation raised with Martin Luther King, Jr., and Malcolm X, but somehow these figures were largely absent from my education. I quickly asked Kirby where I could find some biographies of Bunche and he informed me that there were none.

I immediately decided to write a Bunche biography, in part because he was the first African American political scientist and his work had been ignored, and in part because his radical views of the thirties had moved to the center by the forties. I wanted to know why.

Little did I know how difficult writing political biography could be or how complex a subject Ralph Bunche is. On the personal level, Bunche is an almost unbelievable figure for those who did not know him. Brilliant, handsome, hardworking, gregarious, he was universally loved and admired by those who worked with him. Yet at home, Bunche himself recognized, some of those qualities he shared outside the family were lacking. Paternalistic toward his wife, Ruth, and a rigid disciplinarian with his children, Bunche was willing to sacrifice time with his family for his career.

And what a career it was! In its eulogy of him, *Time* magazine gave him its highest compliment: he was "a man without color." This was the same compliment paid to him by his high school principal when he became class valedictorian but was not permitted to join the citywide honor society. And, therein lies the problem. Bunche's achievements were so great that White society could not credit them to a Black man. Yet he had not really transcended race because those same accomplishments were used to suggest that all Blacks could achieve "success" within the American system just as

Bunche had. Thus this is a biography that focuses on Bunche's accomplishments and how he dealt with the burden his success thrust on his shoulders. But it is also a political and cultural biography of America and how it dealt with someone whom it could not ignore but who did not fit its stereotypical representations of the American "other."

Over the years, many people have assisted me in trying to understand Ralph Bunche. First, I want to acknowledge my debt to Bunche's family, friends, and colleagues who were kind enough to share their recollections with me. These include the late Ruth Bunche, Benjamin Rivlin, John Hope Franklin, Hal Baron, William Bryant, Vincent Browne, the late Robert Martin, the late St. Clair Drake, Kenneth Clark, Robert Weaver, Harvey Mansfield, Sr., Bruce Stedman, John A. Davis, Herbert Aptheker, Maxwell Finger, James E. Jackson, and Glenn Seaborg. A very special note of appreciation to Sir Brian Urquhart and his late research assistant Barbara Nelson, who generously shared memories of Bunche and research materials with me.

A number of friends and colleagues have also read and commented on various sections and drafts of this manuscript. They include William Greaves, Dianne Pinderhughes, Earl Lewis, Francis Foster, Jack Kirby, Brian Urquhart, Harold Cruse, William Little, William Nelson, Robert Edgar, and Matthew Holden. The manuscript benefited from their insights, although I must take final responsibility for the end product.

Among the archives and collections consulted were the Ralph Bunche Papers Collection at University of California, Los Angeles, and the Ralph Bunche Papers at the Schomberg Center of the New York Public Library. Jeff Rankin, Anne Caiger, and the staff of the Department of Special Collections at the UCLA Research Library have been especially helpful over the years. Secondary collections include the National Archives, the Rayford Logan Papers at the Library of Congress, the E. Franklin Frazier Papers at Howard University, the National Negro Congress Papers, the Ralph Bunche Oral Documentation Project at Howard University, and the University of Michigan Library. Government documents on Bunche were obtained through the Freedom of Information Act from the Federal Bureau of Investigation, the Department of State, and the Department of the Navy. Polly Pagenhart did an exceptional job in compiling the FBI documents. Support for this research came from various grants from the University of California at Berkeley. Tim Barlett and Jennifer Hammer at New York University Press were especially supportive of this project.

As usual, my wife, Loretta, and my children bore my absences with their typical good grace. In a project that has taken nearly two decades to complete, they have come to think of Ralph Bunche as a member of the family.

When I started this work, I hoped to rescue a legacy in danger of being lost. As a fellow African American political scientist who has taught at Howard University and worked at the State Department, as well as being a part of several U.S. delegations to the United Nations, I believed Bunche's role as a pioneer was instructive and needed to be saved. Having never met Bunche, I thought I might be more objective in my views than his close friends and colleagues. As I worked on this project over the years, however, it became increasingly difficult not to be charmed by his personality and awed by his intelligence and energy. And, in fact, I discovered a personal link in our past. My great uncle, Charles P. Henry I, worked as a barber in the same small town—Coshocton, Ohio—and perhaps in the same barbershop as Bunche's father, Fred, during a brief period at the turn of the century. Moreover, Fred Bunch (the name was later changed to Bunche) was born in the same town as my mother, Zanesville, Ohio.

I am pleased that there are now a number of younger scholars examining the Bunche legacy, as well as a documentary film produced by William Greaves. In addition, we have excellent books looking at Bunche's life by Brian Urquhart, Robert Edgar, and Benjamin Rivlin. This work is my own contribution to these ongoing efforts.

Prologue

My plans for the future are rather definitely formed. In recognition of
my work Harvard University has granted me a scholarship, good for
next year and I intend to take advantage of this opportunity. Which
brings me to the reason for this letter. Since I have been sufficiently
old to think rationally and to appreciate that there was a "race problem" in America, in which I was necessarily involved, I have set the
goal of my ambition service to my group.
   —Ralph Bunche, in *Ralph Bunche*, edited by Benjamin Rivlin

On the eve of his graduation from UCLA in 1927, Ralph
Bunche wrote to the most distinguished Black scholar/activist of the day,
W. E. B. Du Bois, asking for the opportunity to be of service to his race.[1]
Du Bois did not provide the young scholar with a summer assignment, but
Bunche would embark on a career as distinguished as Du Bois's. Du Bois
would be remembered as the ultimate "outsider" who challenged the system
for nearly a century and eventually gave up his U.S. citizenship. Bunche, on
the other hand, was the ultimate "insider" who was absorbed by the system
and is virtually forgotten today.

Despite their diverging careers, both spent their lives studying and acting
on the same problem. Du Bois posed the dilemma in the very year Bunche
was born (1903):

After the Egyptian and Indian, the Greek and Roman the Teuton and Mon-
golian, the Negro is a sort of seventh son, born with a veil, and gifted with
second-sight in this American world,—a world which yields him no true self-
consciousness, but only lets him see himself through the revelation of the
other world. It is a peculiar sensation, this double-consciousness, this sense of
always looking at one's soul by the tape of a world that looks on in amused
contempt and pity. One ever feels his twoness,—an American, a Negro; two
souls, two thoughts, two unreconciled strivings; two warring ideals in one
dark body, whose dogged strength alone keeps it from being torn asunder.[2]

In this, the most famous paragraph in African American letters, Du Bois presents the struggle that would engage the best minds in the Black community for the next century. How can the Negro attain true self-consciousness and self-knowledge while surrounded by a sea of whiteness? How can the Negro attain self-respect and dignity when all that is reflected back are degrading stereotypes and amusing caricatures. How can the Negro achieve equality and become a first-class citizen when the very definition of American depends on the exclusion of the Black "other"?

Du Bois made the struggle infinitely more complex and ultimately more satisfying by positing the notion of Black cultural difference. That is, Du Bois is the first important Black figure to suggest that the Negro has a culture worth preserving. That the Black soul and the White soul are both spiritually and psychologically different. That African Americans are simply not European Americans in a black skin—or more accurately for the era—are not in a state of evolution toward the White ideal. In doing so, Du Bois created two warring camps in the Black community that remain even today.

Du Bois's famous challenge to Booker T. Washington and the Tuskegee machine in his 1903 essay *The Souls of Black Folk* is widely seen as establishing a radical Black beachhead from which to attack Washington's "philosophy of accommodation" that had swept the country—with the help of Northern White philanthropists—after his 1895 Atlanta Exposition speech. In that speech, Washington had publicly accepted limitations on Black suffrage, social segregation, and the withdrawal of liberal arts education in exchange for technical and vocational training that would lead to factory jobs for Black peasants in the emerging American industrial system. Washington fully embraced the dominant White mainstream values of the day: optimism, materialism, and individualism. Moreover, he linked Black progress to the newly developing corporations that he believed would transform the Southern economy.

While fully accepting the need for vocational and industrial training among Blacks and even complimenting Washington on his Atlanta address, Du Bois had become increasingly concerned about Washington's usurpation of power in the Black community. Washington's control over external financial resources in the North as well as the South, had begun to strangle Black higher education and therefore threaten Black leadership. Du Bois believed that "man" did not live by bread alone and that if the spiritual side of African American existence were to be nurtured, it must come from the "talented tenth." The major Black artists of the day—poet Paul Lawrence Dunbar, writer Charles Chesnutt, and painter Henry O. Tanner—were in the Du Bois camp. If Blacks were to attain a true self-consciousness and not merely physical survival, it would come from a Black elite educated in liberal arts at Black universities.

Du Bois wanted only "to make it possible for a man to be both a Negro and an American without being cursed and spit upon by his fellows, without having the doors of Opportunity closed roughly in his face."[3] Yet by promoting the development of Black culture, Du Bois would make this possibility infinitely more difficult to achieve. Unlike the "blue vein" societies of free Blacks in the antebellum period that strove for total assimilation of White elite culture or the accommodating Black middle-class that rose to serve the segregated communities of the Jim Crow era, Du Bois wanted inclusion on Black terms. For him, full equality meant not just the acceptance of Black physical difference but also the acceptance of Black cultural difference.

The most influential modern interpretation of this tension or duality came in Harold Cruse's *The Crisis of the Negro Intellectual*. In that 1967 work, Cruse identifies "nationalist" and "integrationist" schools of thought and criticizes Black intellectuals for failing to fashion a way of thinking and acting that fuses the ethnic sentiments of the Black community and the individualism of American social life.

Today's Black public intellectuals mirror Cruse's crisis.[4] Black neoconservatives and Black postmodernists, for entirely different reasons, call for African Americans to abandon racial identity. Afrocentrists, on the other hand, take the position that positive, non-Eurocentric values can be found in the classical civilization of Egypt (ancient Kemet). One can argue that the appearance of a variety of viewpoints among Black intellectuals is a healthy development. Yet the enlargement of the Black public sphere does not seem to have advanced the issue of racial justice that Du Bois and Bunche were centrally involved in promoting.

Over the past two decades the issue of racial justice has disappeared from the public sphere and African Americans have been neutralized as a constituency in national politics. One can date the demise of a civil rights agenda with the landslide reelection of Richard Nixon in 1972.[5] Nixon's "Southern Strategy" successfully drove a wedge between Black and White Southern Democrats. Attacks on Lyndon Johnson's Great Society programs served as potent but covert racial rallying points. White racial identity and White racial anxieties were and are being translated into successful political campaigns. Prior to the 1970s, neither welfare nor crime was associated in the public mind with African Americans. By 1988, Republicans could run the Willie Horton ads in *Massachusetts* without seriously exposing their candidate to the taint of racism.

President Clinton based his successful 1992 campaign on recapturing the same White Democratic voters who had gone to Bush in 1988 and Reagan in 1984 and 1980. Andrew Hacker remarked that "for all practical purposes, the 1992 contest was staged before an all-white electorate."[6] Clinton focused on the economy directing his only real comments on race to Black cultural proponents and Black rappers like Sister Souljah. Obviously, Clinton had listened to Democratic pollster Stanley Greenberg, who in 1984 reported the following:

> These white Democratic defectors express a profound distaste for blacks, a sentiment that pervades almost everything they think about government and politics. . . . Blacks constitute the explanation for their vulnerability and for almost everything that has gone wrong in their lives; not being black is what constitutes being middle class; not living with blacks is what makes a neighborhood a decent place to live.[7]

Of course, many Republicans had already identified with these views. Thus, in the past two decades large parts of the White electorate have defined their existence in terms of the Black "other."

How can Colin Powell emerge as a popular noncandidate for president among all segments of the electorate when issues of racism and racial justice have been largely excluded from the public policy arena? Precisely because support for Powell assures Americans that they are indeed not racist or, put more positively, they are color-blind, just as Bunche's success in the 1950s Cold War proved that the United States was indeed the land of opportunity despite what the Communists said. Yet if this is the case, then why didn't Powell's supporters elect Jesse Jackson president when they had the opportunity? Obviously, Powell's appearance, style, military background, language, and friends are not threatening to Whites. They reflect sameness. Jackson's appearance, style, religious background, language, and friends are threatening. They reflect difference. But surely their position on the issues is different—or is it? We have very little to judge Powell on, and on some key issues—affirmative action and abortion for example—he is close to Jackson.

The politics of identity are easily manipulated. Using an exceptional individual as the standard-bearer for an entire race has its dangers. While the Willie Hortons and welfare queens are used to deny the utility of liberal programs, the Ralph Bunches and Colin Powells are used to promote the utility of conservative programs. In short, if they made it, why can't all members of the group make it?

Using any one individual or stereotype to represent a group does a gross injustice to the complexity of the group and of intragroup relationships. As Harold Cruse said, "The problem of Negro cultural identity is an unsolved problem within the context of an American nation that is still in the process of formation."[8] In a country where corporate logos on clothing are often used by individuals of all races to define their status, Cruse's statement seems to ring as true today as it did in the sixties.

Cruse believed that only intellectuals and artists could rise above ethnic and racial separation (identification). He was disturbed that White scholars such as Daniel Bell and C. Wright Mills, who believed in the special role of intellectuals, ignored Black intellectuals in their work. Following Cruse, much of the current work on Black intellectuals focuses on their isolation from the Black community and from White intellectuals. Moreover, a recent work on Black intellectuals suggests that all intellectuals should be isolated from power because their function is to clarify ideas and issues not to act. Sociologist Troy Duster contends that "when you assume power, the function changes." Intellectuals in this country, says Duster, "have a history of not ever having to deal with the allocation of resources. They often don't understand that you have to make enemies. Once you are in a position of authority, you are going to make enemies. That's why I don't trust intellectuals."[9] Bunche was not isolated from the academy nor the community nor power, thus from this perspective alone his life would be instructive.

Bunche avoided marginality by attempting to synthesize the duality or dichotomy set forth by Du Bois. Like Du Bois, he chose neither assimilation nor nationalism.[10] Instead he accepted the challenge of redefining the concept of American to include the African American experience. This attempt had two major components.

First, Bunche identified "race" as a social construction and "racism" as a worldwide phenomenon. Although he emphasized the economic roots of racism, he did not view himself as a Marxist, which would again have marginalized his racial identity, just as mainstream political science marginalized racial identity. Drawing on recent work in anthropology that challenged biological notions of race, Bunche and some of his colleagues at Howard challenged the intellectual status quo and searched for alternative paradigms.

Second, Bunche recognized that claims to knowledge are also claims to power. In addition to his education at such major educational institutions as University of California, Los Angeles, and Harvard, he studied with Melville

Herskovits, Bronislaw Malinowski, and Isaac Schapera. He was a colleague of Gunnar Myrdal and enjoyed friendly relationships with a number of leading White social scientists. Yet Bunche realized that neither he nor his colleagues at Howard possessed the power to change the rules of discourse. No matter how cogent the analysis, Black intellectuals lacked the power to validate knowledge. That is, they could not redefine the discourse on "race" or "otherhood."

Decades before, Du Bois had recognized that education alone would not lead to the elimination of racism. As a consequence, he helped establish the National Association for the Advancement of Colored People (NAACP) and devoted himself to a life of "propaganda" and agitation. Bunche was presented with a different opportunity. World War II opened the doors of government service for a number of Black intellectuals. Bunche seized this opportunity to avoid the marginality of the academy and to influence public policy.

The founding of the United Nations gave Bunche the opportunity to avoid the marginality imposed on African American government officials. By moving to the United Nations, he achieved international recognition that surely would have been denied to him had he remained in the U.S. State Department or returned to Howard University. At the UN, Bunche gained such fame that *Ebony* magazine proclaimed him as perhaps the most influential Negro of the first half of the twentieth century. For nearly a decade, he was the most celebrated African American of his time both here and abroad. Today he is more than marginalized—he is virtually forgotten.

Bunche's rise and fall as a public symbol tells us as much, if not more, about ourselves as about Bunche. Charisma rests more in the eye of the beholder than in the qualities of the leader. And while the quality of leadership is widely assailed in this era—as in all eras—we bear the responsibility for following those we choose to lead or represent us. Personal, group, and national identity is not static. As they change, symbols of the day become historical footnotes. By understanding the process of symbol formation, we can understand not only our leaders but also ourselves. Perhaps in doing so we can demand more of our leaders and ourselves.[11]

1

1903

I'm goin' to Detroit, get myself a good job, [twice]
Tried to stay around here with the starvation mob.

I'm goin' to get me a job, up there in Mr. Ford's place, [twice]
Stop these eatless days from starin' me in the face.

When I start to makin' money, she don't need to come around [twice]
'Cause I don't want her now, Lord, I'm Detroit bound.

Because wild women lives in Detroit, that's all I want to see, [twice]
Wil' women and bad whisky would make a fool out of me.
> —Blind Blake, "Detroit Bound Blues,"
> in Paul Oliver, *The Meaning of the Blues*

Blacks had been living in Detroit from the time it was a small frontier town, but it was the tightening of Southern Black Codes in the 1830s and 1840s that led to the first substantial migration of Blacks to this Michigan city. Most of these migrants were free Negroes from the Virginia cities of Richmond, Fredericksburg, and Petersburg. Mostly mechanics and tradesmen, they were roughly equal in social and economic status and quickly united to work for the removal of the second-class citizenship placed upon Michigan's Blacks. Symbols of this inferior citizenship included disfranchisement, exclusion from juries, exclusion from militia service, prohibition of intermarriage between Blacks and Whites, and an 1827 act designed to exclude fugitive slaves as well as the Negro migrants who could not post a $500 bond guaranteeing good behavior.[1]

Despite such laws, the Black population in Detroit grew from 193 in 1840 to 587 in 1850. During the post–Civil War period, Detroit's small Black professional class, which numbered fewer than 100, or 2 to 5 percent of those working, was extremely concerned about White public opinion. For example, none of Detroit's leading Black citizens would participate in the 1871 commemoration of the Fifteenth Amendment to the U.S. Constitution lest their doing so offend White citizens. A few years later, a Black meeting approved a resolution recommending the discontinuance of celebrating "all days that are only celebrated by them [Blacks], as the tendency is to perpetuate caste feeling, and that in the future, they recognize only the national days of the country."[2] For similar reasons, Detroit's Black elite rejected the formation of separate professional societies and business leagues until after World War I. Thus, long before the birth of Ralph Bunche, Detroit's Black elite was denying the existence of an American "other."

By 1900, the old Detroit that had been a commercial city dominated by Yankee peddlers who sold New York custom goods and supplied the vast Midwest had disappeared. In its place rose an industrial city of freight-car shops, stove works, and related metal crafts, including marine engineering.[3] All of the elements were present to supply an industry that would reshape the country.

Nationally, there were eleven thousand cars, more than one million bicycles, and seventeen million horses providing transportation. But events unfolding in Detroit and elsewhere would mark the end of the horse and bicycle as modes of common transportation. In 1900, there were seventy-two American firms manufacturing cars. Thirty-eight were added in 1901; forty-seven in 1902; and fifty-three in 1903, the year of Ralph's birth, but they took a backseat to events in Kitty Hawk, North Carolina, where two bicycle mechanics named Wright who had benefited from improvements in the internal combustion engine took flight.[4] Within a very few years, then, the base of the modern American industrial economy had been laid, with Detroit playing a leading role.

The revolutionary changes in industry had an equally dramatic effect on demographics. In 1900, the population of Detroit was 285,000; in 1910, 465,766; and in 1925, well over 1,200,000. The new jobs in auto factories and their suppliers served as a powerful magnet drawing immigrants from abroad. The foreign-born population grew from roughly one-third of Detroit's population in 1904 to one-half by 1925. Leading the list were Poles, followed by Russians, Italians and Hungarians. Because of the dominance of a single heavy industry with semiskilled job requirements, Detroit was much more a working-class city than were other rapidly expanding urban centers like Los Angeles. The industrialization of Detroit and the influx of foreign workers had several important consequences. One was the early suburbanization of the area; many of the wealthiest families moved to places like

Grosse Pointe. Another consequence was a business-led effort to "Americanize Detroit." Members of the Board of Commerce working with the Board of Education opened night schools where foreigners could learn English and also adopt acceptable and respectable middle-class attitudes and habits.[5]

The composition and character of Detroit's Black community was as radically affected by the changing economy as the White community. However, the changes were well under way before the explosion in the Black population during World War I. As with many Northern urban centers at the turn of the century, the small Black elite dependent on upper-class Whites for jobs and status was disappearing in Detroit. Many trades Blacks had once dominated, such as barbering, were passing into the hands of immigrants. Replacing such tradespeople was a more Black-oriented, business-minded elite bound to the Black community by external discrimination. Yet unlike the new elites in other Northern cities, Detroit's new Black leaders followed the old caste in identifying with the native-born White groups and rejecting the ethnocentrism of the immigrant groups. They stressed the individualism and self-help of the American middle class rather than the cooperation and communalism of the tightly knit immigrant groups. Thus, while immigrant groups and the growing industrial order were changing the American way of life, Black Detroiters remained rooted in the old Washingtonian notions of optimism and accommodation. Blacks shared deeply in the American dream of individualism, hard work, and success, yet the gap between Black and White prosperity grew wider.[6]

Ralph Bunch was born at 434 Anthon Street in Detroit on August 7, 1903.[7] His twenty-one-year-old mother, Olive, had no job but was supported by an extended family that was headed by her mother, Lucy Johnson. Ralph's father, Fred, was a barber who worked in downtown Detroit. Fred was from Zanesville, Ohio, and had been raised by elderly foster parents in Mechanicsburg, Ohio, since the age of seven. At seventeen, he left home to join the circus, and it was while traveling with the circus that he met Olive in Michigan City, Indiana, in 1900.[8] Handsome, jealous of his wife, and restless, Fred was something of an outsider to the Johnson family.

The Johnson family traced its roots back to Ralph's great-grandfather James H. Johnson, a Baptist preacher and freedman from Virginia. In the mid-1830s he married Eleanor Madden in Missouri. Eleanor's mother had been a house slave and her father a White plantation owner. The Johnsons purchased a two-hundred-acre farm near Alton, Illinois, in 1842. There they raised five daughters and six sons. The farm remained in the family.[9]

The Johnson children, including Ralph's grandfather, Thomas Nelson Johnson, had the advantage of attending school. After helping on the farm, he was able to attend Shurtleff College in Alton. As one of the few Black college students in the area, he organized literacy classes for former slaves and taught night school. At a night school in the Salem Baptist Church, he met and eventually married his student Lucy A. Taylor. Lucy had been born in Sedalia, Missouri, in 1855 to a house slave, Emmaline, and an Irish landowner. Moving to Alton at the end of the Civil War, Lucy worked as a maid. After waiting until Thomas graduated in 1875, Lucy and Thomas married.

The couple moved to Fort Scott, Kansas, where Thomas taught in a small school for Black children. Lucy bore ten children in fifteen years; only five lived into adulthood, including Ralph's mother, Olive, who was born in 1882. Three years later, the family moved to Waco, Texas, where Thomas was principal of a school for Black children and edited a weekly paper, the *Texas Baptist Star*. In 1890, at the young age of forty, Thomas died of malaria and the fortunes of the family changed.

With five children and no money, Lucy sold her husband's possessions for train fare back to the Johnson farm in Alton. After two years, Lucy moved her family to Michigan City, Indiana, and purchased a house with the proceeds from her husband's share of the Alton farm. Working at a variety of jobs, including chambermaid in the Vreeland Hotel, Lucy reared Ethel, Olive, Tom, Charlie, and Nelle. Olive met Fred Bunche at a local baseball match, and they were married in 1900 when the Johnsons moved to Detroit in search of better jobs and schools.

The Johnson family was not part of Detroits' Black elite but did present an interesting mix of occupations and statuses. Tom and Charlie, the chief sources of income, worked at the Diamond Match Company. (Skilled and semiskilled jobs accounted for roughly 20 percent of the positions held by Black males in the Detroit economy of 1900.) Later they worked in service jobs at the Tullar Hotel in downtown Detroit, where Fred Bunche worked as a barber. These service jobs made up roughly half of all positions held by Black males in the city. For Black females, service jobs, which included domestic labor, comprised more than 80 percent of all female-held jobs in 1900.[10] Thus, the Johnson/Bunche family held neither the best nor the worst jobs in the Black community. Moreover, their family history and the home they owned gave them middle-class aspirations even if they sometimes lacked middle-class means.

Reading Ralph's recollections of his boyhood it is difficult to get a sense of any Black community or any discrimination:

I didn't know anything about prejudice against the Negro, had no experience with anti-Negro prejudice in Detroit between 1904 and 1914. There were mixed YMCAs in Detroit at that time. The prejudice in Detroit, and there was prejudice in Detroit, in those years was not against Negroes at all, because there weren't many Negroes then. The Negro migrations occurred during and after the first World War. The prejudice in Detroit in my youth was against the Italians, against the southern Europeans, and against the Italians especially, who were coming in at that time as immigrant populations competing with the indiginous [*sic*] workers.[11]

Bunche goes on to say that ironically he shared that prejudice against the Italians, as well as the accompanying stereotypes.

What are we to make of Ralph Bunche's assertion that there was no discrimination against Negroes in Detroit? He admits that he sometimes could not visit his father at work in a barber shop "because Negro barbers could and did work in barbershops which were for white clients only."[12] The Detroit YMCA was openly segregationist, although it found a few openings for the Black elite on its board. Bunche often declared that they lived next to Whites in Detroit. It is true that semiskilled and unskilled immigrant workers frequently lived next to Negro families, but there were also areas of high Black concentration. In fact, the last residence of the Johnson/Bunche family on Macomb Street had one of the highest and oldest concentrations of Negro residences in the city.[13]

Ralph's tendency to stress the integrated nature of his childhood reflects the old Black elite's optimism about race relations. Moreover, his acceptance of native White prejudices against Italian immigrants reveals the family's drive to be accepted as part of the "American Middle Class."[14] This positive outlook is again seen in Ralph's recollection of his childhood experiences.

The entire Johnson/Bunche family attended a Black Baptist church where his aunts and uncles all sang in the choir. Many years later, while attending a performance of *Carmen* at the Metropolitan Opera in New York, Ralph would recall what a central role music had played in the life of the family:

Tom especially stood out in my memory—a rich baritone voice, mellow and with good volume. I could see him standing beside the old upright piano. . . . My recollections of the family scenes around the old piano bring the family warmly to life. Ethel, always dramatic, lively, laughing and blushing, fast-talking in her distinctly contralto tones. Nelle, the soprano and perfectionist—deadly serious about her singing and very proud of her ability to hit above high C; Charlie, the tenor and a good one, but an even better drummer. Mama was the accompanist, but I'm not sure she could read a note.[15]

In fact, the family's musical ability led them to form the Johnson Quartet. The quartet's singing in various locations in the Detroit area received good reviews, and a sketch performed in Sandwich, Ontario, even included a part for young Ralph.

Baseball and "shinny"—street hockey with tin cans and sticks—competed with music for young Ralph's attention. He sold newspapers at Navin Field and rooted for the Tigers, especially Sam Crawford, Hughey Jennings, and Ty Cobb.

Bunche described himself as a shy and reticent youngster with a skinny build. He must have become less reticent, for he was disciplined in the fifth grade for being a chatterbox. Bunche attended Barstow Grammar School in Detroit, where, according to him, he was a student with average intelligence.[16]

Although the Johnson/Bunche family attended church regularly and Ralph was a member of the Sunday school at 2nd Baptist Church, the church and traditional religion had little influence on his life. As he explained in 1927 when he visited Detroit and was reluctantly baptized, "the Baptism didn't take hold."[17]

The pleasant days of picnics on Belle Island, circuses, ball games, and family musicals seemed to disappear when Fred Bunche moved his wife and son to Cleveland, Ohio, around 1907. Fred had been something of an outsider living with the Johnsons, but his new independence did not improve the situation of his family. Little is known of the period spent in Cleveland because the Bunches soon moved on to Knoxville, Tennessee.

As Ralph remembered Knoxville, the family spent only one winter there:

> I have only two memories of this community. One, that there were great banks of red clay and apparently it was in this red clay that the fine yams, large sweet potatoes, grew, I remember that. And the only other recollection I have of Knoxville is that there was a park not far from the house in which we lived. And soon after we moved there I wandered into this park one day and was promptly ordered out by the guard of the park because the park was not open to Negroes of any age, not even those of six or seven. That stuck in my mind. When I hear Knoxville, Tennessee mentioned I think of this park and this experience.[18]

This first experience with "Jim Crow" segregation was used by Bunche to demonstrate the power of racism to dominate all other recollections of a community.

From Knoxville the family moved to Toledo, Ohio, where Ralph's sister,

Grace, was born in 1909. Fred had no better luck finding work in Toledo, and it was while the family was living in a single, cold room that Olive came down with tuberculosis. When Olive's sister Ethel found the Bunches in such dire conditions on a visit to Toledo, she insisted they move back to Detroit. Grandmother Lucy Johnson, called Nana by the family, cared for the children while Olive was confined to a sanitarium for two years. Fred Bunche visited the family frequently, but there was no room for him in the house the Johnsons now occupied.

When Olive's brother Charlie came down with tuberculosis, his and Olive's sister Ethel decided he could best recover in Albuquerque, New Mexico. He left in May 1914, and was followed three months later by Olive, whose condition had deteriorated. Lucy and Olive and Fred's children—Ralph and Grace—moved to Albuquerque in October 1915, to be followed later by Fred, who, in order to get there, was forced to "ride the rails." After a year of concerts in the Midwest, Olive's brother Tom moved to Kansas City and sister Nelle moved to Corsicana, Texas.[19]

Albuquerque's history was vastly different from that of Detroit. Founded in 1706 by Don Francisco Cuervo y Valdes, the twenty-eighth governor and captain-general of New Mexico, the site in the Rio Grande Valley had been inhabited for centuries by Indians. The villa grew steadily during the 1700s, serving as an important military post for first the Spanish and then the Mexicans. Upon its military occupation in 1846, it became an important United States military outpost. During and after the Civil War the town was host to repeated conflict between Union and Confederate forces and sympathizers. With the coming of the Santa Fe Railroad in 1881, a new town began to grow rapidly two miles east of old Albuquerque. Between 1890 and 1915, the Albuquerque area went from a settlement of four thousand to a city of nearly twenty thousand. It served primarily as a health resort for those suffering from asthma and tuberculosis.[20]

Despite the ill health of Olive and Charlie, Ralph's recollection of the time spent in Albuquerque was mostly pleasant. Because of his mother's rheumatic condition, he would place her on a trolley headed toward the Sunday afternoon band concerts in Old Town, then race the trolley to the park on foot to save the nickel car fare. With his grandmother firmly in charge of the household and his father only an occasional visitor, Ralph was free on many days to swim in irrigation ditches and roam the mesa hunting with his Uncle Charlie.

There were few Negroes in Albuquerque in 1915. Ralph recalls that most of the discrimination was directed toward Spanish Americans, Indians, and

Mexicans; however, Blacks were not exempt. Soon after their arrival, Olive took Ralph to a nickelodeon. As Ralph recalls:

> We took a seat in the middle of the theater on the aisle, and soon after we sat there an usher came and tapped my mother on the shoulder and told her that we should move to the rear seat. My mother knew what he meant but she had no intention of moving and did not move and she told him very politely, and she took him aback some, that she appreciated his courtesy and his consider-ation, but really, these seats were quite perfect for us and she intended to sit right there, but she thanked him for being so kind, and she did not move, nor did he pursue the matter any further, but I remember this very well.[21]

This quiet, diplomatic way of dealing with problems must have made an im-pression on young Ralph.

The public schools of Albuquerque, unlike the movie theaters, did not discriminate. Ralph made many friends among his Indian and Mexican classmates. Of his having been one of two Black students in a group of thirty-six, he later said, "There was no differentiation, no outsiders."[22] Yet perhaps the major influence in Albuquerque was not his classmates but, rather, his teacher. Emma Belle Sweet, a young, White woman, who taught him English and geography in the sixth grade at the Fourth Ward School was the first person to open up the world beyond Albuquerque to his young mind. Although she sometimes had to discipline the talkative boy with a rap on the knuckles or by directing him to stand in the corner, Ralph never for-got the inspiration she supplied. At a ceremony honoring her with the Gold Key Award of the American Association of School Administrators in 1962, Bunche said:

> From elementary to graduate grades, I learned with readiest facility not nec-essarily from the teacher who may have demonstrated greatest mastery of his material but very definitely from the teacher who made [me] feel that he knew me and was concerned about me and who gave me encouragement by recognizing achievement and stimulating my pride and zeal.[23]

Ralph was to need all the love and support he could get during his days in Albuquerque.

After school, Ralph earned money by working, stripped to the waist, in a bakery. He was to say in later years that he was self-supporting from the age of fourteen. Working hard was to be a lifelong characteristic.

Despite the warm, clear climate, a cloud hung over the family residence at 621 North Street as Olive's and Charlie's health continued to decline. Olive seemed to take a turn for the worse when Fred left Albuquerque to look for regular work in 1916.[24] By February 1917, Olive was dead. Years later Ralph would remember with regret that on the night she died, "she had asked for milk and there was none in the house because I had drunk it up."[25]

Three months later, Uncle Charlie, despondent over his health, his sister's death, and his inability to provide a house for his own mother, put a shotgun to his head and pulled the trigger. Within the space of a year, thirteen-year-old Ralph had lost his mother, his favorite uncle, and contact with his father. Responding to the crisis, Tom and Nelle moved quickly to Albuquerque, but Nana decided the family should head further west.

When W. E. B. Du Bois toured Southern California on behalf of the NAACP in the spring of 1913, he waxed eloquent about the possibilities for African Americans: "Los Angeles is wonderful. Nowhere in the United States is the Negro so well and beautifully housed, nor the average efficiency and intelligence in the colored population so high." Du Bois concluded that "[o]ut here in this matchless Southern California there would seem to be no limit to your opportunities, your possibilities."[26] White Angelenos apparently agreed with Du Bois's assessment. An entire section of the *Los Angeles Times* for February 12, 1909, was devoted to the Negro. An article entitled "The Emancipated" by John Steven McGroarty states:

> However it be that the black man has fared or is faring in other parts of the country and the world, his voice in this Lincoln Day issue of the *Times* is not tremulous with defeat or querulous with despair. Instead it is the voice of people who have traveled far and well with the vibrant march of progress; and who look out on life with level gaze from victories won.[27]

Perhaps the confidence of Black Angelenos was rooted in the city's past.

Twenty-six "Negroes and mulattoes" had joined two Whites and sixteen Indians in founding Los Angeles in 1781. Blacks soon lost their majority and did not represent a significant percentage of the population until the land boom of 1887 brought more than one thousand Black immigrants to the city. Within a decade the number of Los Angeles Negroes had doubled to more than two thousand, but the Black percentage of the total population actually declined from 2.5 percent in 1890 to 2.08 percent in 1900.[28]

Although Blacks resided in scattered parts of the city, a small Black business district had developed at Second and San Pedro Streets by 1894. After the turn of the century, small Black businesses began appearing along Central Avenue. Other Blacks were doing personal service work, selling real estate, and farming. Los Angeles grew 211.5 percent between 1900 and 1910 and another 80.7 percent the following decade. The decade of 1910 to 1920 welcomed 7,890 new Black Angelenos. However, Asian newcomers totaled 7,938 during the same period, and Mexican immigrants, who were classified as "Whites," numbered 9,027. In fact, the threat of more imported Chinese labor in 1917 led to a major campaign by the Black-oriented Los Angeles Forum. The organization wrote to the State Labor Council of Defense that Black workers, many of whom had been attracted to Los Angeles by the 1917 labor shortage, were perfectly capable of meeting the existing farm-labor needs.[29] Yet it was not farm or industrial jobs that employed Los Angeles Blacks. More than half the Black labor force worked in domestic and personal service. The second leading source of employment, with only 20 percent of the total, was the manufacturing and mechanical industries.[30]

When the Johnson family arrived in Los Angeles at the height of Black migration in 1917, race relations were changing. Los Angeles was becoming more a working-class city and less a health resort. By the 1920s there were five Black areas in the city: the Boyle Heights area, the West Side neighborhood on Jefferson Street between Normandie and Western Avenues, the Temple Street area, the Furlong Tract, and the Central Avenue community.[31]

Tom, Nana's remaining son, who was light-skinned like her, had preceded the family and rented a small house on Griffith Avenue on the east side. When the White owner saw Ralph and Aunt Nelle and realized the family was Black, he changed the locks on the door before the moving van arrived. Not deterred, on moving day Tom broke down the door and the family stayed for the full period for which the rent had been paid. The Johnsons then bought a house on East 37th Street. When some of the neighbors complained, Nana pointed out that they were only renting, and that the Johnsons owned their home.

With Fred Bunche gone and Olive dead, Nana was in full charge of Ralph and Grace's upbringing. In later years, Ralph would often cite this tiny women as the major influence in his life. In a 1954 "Person to Person" interview with Edward Murrow he listed some of the guiding principles she laid down:

- no false pride, be humble but never lose self-respect and dignity;
- never pick a fight but never run from one if you are sure you're right;
- be honest always, live by your conscience, you can never be happy otherwise;
- the United States is a democracy and you can surmount barriers of race.[32]

To a remarkable extent, Bunche embodied these principles throughout his life.

Lucy Johnson was so pale in appearance she could have passed for White, as did her twin brother, Frank. However, she was quite proud of her African American heritage, and when combined with her appearance, this pride led to a number of amusing incidents. On one occasion a door-to-door sales-man attempted to sell her a family plot in a cemetery. He assured her that they would not have to be worried about being buried next to Blacks be-cause his company "never sold burial plots to niggers." Lucy asked the sales-man to repeat himself and then excused herself and went to the kitchen. She came back at full charge with a broom in her hand and chased him out of the house shouting, "I am a Negro and proud of it!!!!"[33]

Ralph, too, had his share of racial incidents. He recalled one early expe-rience in Los Angeles:

> I was a newsboy, had a paper route in the morning. The paper took us all on an outing down to the beach. Went on all of the rides, had quite a good time. And then in the middle of the afternoon they took us to the bath house and there the good time of myself and the other Negro newsboy ended, because we were not admitted to the bath house and I remember very vividly having to sit out and wait for a couple of hours until the other boys had done their swimming and had come out. We had to wait because we had no other means of transportation home. The humiliation of it, the resentment at the injustice of it.[34]

Bunche felt that discrimination against "the oriental" and the Japanese was even more intense at that time.[35]

Although Bunche would always assert that his lifelong struggle against racial bigotry had left him with no feelings of bitterness or hate toward Whites, his childhood friend, Charlie Matthews, had a different recollection: "I recall on one occasion while Ralph was working at the City Dye Works and was required to lay carpets in the SS *City of Los Angeles* (it may have been the SS *City of Honolulu,* I'm not sure which) Ralph worked hard in order to make the deadline before sailing time and when he finished, stood out on the pier and wished 'that the damned boat would sink in the middle of the ocean.' The ship set sail and never did arrive in Honolulu; it burned and sank in the middle of the ocean."[36]

The house in which the Johnsons settled on 37th Street (now 40th Place) and Central Avenue was in a White middle-class neighborhood in 1919. Ralph attended the Thirtieth Street Intermediate School (now John Adams

Junior High School) and later Jefferson High School, which was only a half block away. Both schools were predominately White, and Ralph recalled that there was little discrimination, although he remembered being locked in a cloakroom during the last month of school so that his deportment record would be satisfactory.[37] Ralph did not remember any overt discrimination, but Lucy discovered that most Black students were tracked in vocational classes on the assumption that they would not be going to college. She immediately confronted the principal and insisted that Ralph be placed in classes that would prepare him for college.

Ralph's interest in school grew with the more challenging classes. Nana instilled in him the confidence to compete, especially against Whites. She told him to "let them, especially white folks, know that you can do anything they can do."[38] This self-confidence must have been perceived in various ways. Ralph, for example, states that he was "a chip on the shoulder type of person in high school."[39] Yet a former teacher, Dr. Cecilia Irvine, provided a quite different portrait in a 1959 letter to Bunche:

> I would like to picture you the boy you were. You were distinctly a thorough-bred who walked with a springy step, always you seemed completely at ease with the world and always looked up. I think, more than anything, I remember you with your head held high. I remember your grandmother. I met her just once. She was dressed in black with a Queen Mary black hat, and I have never forgotten the emanation of power from that tiny figure.[40]

Of course, at the time Dr. Irvine wrote her letter, Bunche was internationally known, which may have influenced her memory.

What emerged from Ralph's early educational experience was a talkative, energetic student only mildly interested in schoolwork who was disciplined on more than one occasion. If young Ralph had been permitted to remain in vocational classes, he more than likely would have pursued a skilled trade at best. With his grandmother's guidance, he became an outstanding student at Jefferson High School.

At Jefferson, Ralph was exposed to classic authors like Shakespeare and Dickens and often listed them as favorites when asked in later life. A class in civics stimulated his interest in law, which led him to major in political science when he entered college. Si Tipton, his basketball coach, taught Bunche how to relax when the pressure was on, and Ralph had many opportunities to apply it during his diplomatic career.

Everyone seemed to like Ralph at Jefferson High and he did excellent work in his courses. Despite his record of accomplishment, Ralph was excluded from the Ephebian Society, the citywide student honor society. Even though some of his teachers protested, the injustice was not corrected until 1955, when he was given honorary membership. At the time, Ralph was so hurt he contemplated leaving school. Only the memory of his mother's admonition, "Ralph, don't let anything take away your hope and faith and dreams," persuaded him to stay and graduate.[41]

Graduation provided a lesson in racial invisibility rather than visibility. Chosen to give the valedictory address, Ralph was congratulated by the school principal, as was his grandmother. In one version of the story, Bunche relates the events as follows:

> The principal was a very fine man. I'm citing these things merely to show that oftentimes these things happen by people of real good will, because the principal of Thomas Jefferson High School from which I graduated in Los Angeles, was a fine man but he had never done much thinking on the racial question. He had never given much attention to it obviously. And so on the evening of my graduation he came to me and said he was sorry I was leaving, congratulated me on graduating, and then said this, "You know, we've never thought of you as a Negro." Well, I knew that this was wrong. At this time I didn't know how to answer him, but fortunately my grandmother, my maternal grandmother, was at my side and she knew what to say. She was a little woman but a woman of great character and spirit. And in a very quiet way she explained firmly to the principal of Thomas Jefferson High School what it meant for a person to have pride in his origin, that we had no shame of being Negroes, that we were Americans like everyone else, that we had pride in our origin, and therefore it was insulting even if he did not mean it that way, for him to say what he said. And he understood and was very polite, as I recall, he unwound an apology which took about five minutes.[42]

There are other versions of this story in which Ralph's grandmother is not so quiet and polite in her response. However, the event was a symbolic one in Bunche's life. He would spend the rest of his days denying that his pioneering accomplishments somehow set him apart from or were not representative of his race. For the rest of his life, White Americans could not seem to accept him fully unless he transcended his racial roots, which he steadfastly refused to do. Instead, he chose to define *American* in a way that included his race and all others.

2 | Reverse Migration

G'way an' quit dat noise, Miss Lucy—
    Put dat music book away;
What's de use to keep on tryin'?
    Ef you practise twell you're gray,
You cain't sta't no notes a–flyin'
    Lak de ones dat rants and rings
F'om de kitchen to de big woods
    When Malindy sings . . .
         —Paul Laurence Dunbar, "When Malindy Sings,"
                in *The Book of Negro Folklore*,
        edited by Langston Hughes and Arna Bontemps

If we must die—let it not be like hogs
Hunted and penned in an inglorious spot,
While round us bark the mad and hungry dogs,
Making their mock at our accursed lot,
If we must die—oh, let us nobly die,
So that our precious blood may not be shed
In vain; then even the monsters we defy
shall be constrained to honor us though dead!
Oh kinsmen! We must meet the common foe;
Though far outnumbered, let us show us brave,
And for their thousand blows deal one death blow!
What though before us lies the open grave?
Like men we'll face the murderous cowardly pack,
Pressed to the wall, dying but fighting back!
        —Claude McKay, "If We Must Die," in Kinfe Abraham,
                Politics of Black Nationalism

The move north and west by African Americans represented more than a demographic change. It was also a psychological break with the past. The "new" Negro was more in tune with the defiance of Claude McKay[1] than with the dialect poems of Paul Lawrence Dunbar so popular at the turn of the century.[2] Defiance, in fact, reflected a real need for urban self-defense; 1917 and 1919 witnessed extensive riots in places like East St. Louis and Chicago.

But the very urban centers that created the setting for racial conflict also created never-before-seen opportunities. A former Black farmer from the rural South might walk down the street in Harlem or Cleveland and hear Communist agitators or Black Nationalist organizers or Pentecostal prose-lytizers. These former peasants might go to a jazz club or a cultural pageant. Along with fellow Southerners they might sit with Blacks from the Caribbean or Africa. If they encountered problems, the NAACP and Urban League were there to help, along with the local precinct captain who actually encouraged political participation.

With Booker T. Washington's death in 1915, Marcus Garvey assumed the mantle of self-help. However, in the place of Washington's accommodations, he inserted a fierce new racial pride and the call "Africa for the Africans." The door of cultural pluralism, opened ever so slightly by Du Bois in 1903, was flung wide as the "Jazz Age" was born.

The new issues were migration, urban self-defense, independent Black politics, and Pan Africanism. The Bronx and Manhattan Non-Partisan Leagues were bold enough in 1921 to ask President Harding to appoint a Black attorney general. And W. E. B. Du Bois, now the most prominent African American leader, used his new influence to convene the Pan African Congress in Paris in 1919. In fact, the major issue of the congress concerned the administration of the former German colonies then being debated at the Versailles Peace Conference. Although none of the leaders of the Pan African Congress had expertise in colonial administration or trusteeship, it was a subject that would involve Ralph Bunche for the major portion of his life.[3]

When he went to the University of California, Los Angeles (UCLA) in 1922, Bunche had no plan to major in international relations or African politics. After all, there were no Black role models in this area and little practical incentive to pursue it. In fact, he once said that there was never any planning or aspiring in his career—"I only sort of fell into what came naturally."[4] What came naturally after graduating from high school was having a wild summer cruising Central Avenue in the old jalopy he had acquired while working as a carpet layer. The Central Avenue group—Bunche, George Duncan, Charles "Sandy" Saunders, Wilalyn Stovall, Melvin Thistle, and Erskin and Charlie Ragland—frequented Doc Nelson's Bluebird Cabaret (making Bunche a lifelong jazz buff); Maybelle's Café, which was open late; and Thistle's Restaurant. He recalled they once turned over Thistle's father's open roadster on Central Avenue.[5] Bunche even tried his hand at boxing in the 12th Street Y.

"There'll be some changes made" was the theme song of what Bunche referred to as his gang of "new Negroes."[6] Despite their companionship, he felt

> some inner feeling of resentment about not being "Negro" enough, compared to my Negro chums. I envied Chuck Matthews for his ability to play the sax and ukelele and to whistle jazz tunes so much better than I could. and dance better, too. I felt the same about Charlie Sanders. I saw their musical ability and sense of rhythm as "Negro" traits. Similarly, I envied George Duncan's ability at buffoonery. Sometimes sly, sometimes uproarious, but always, as I thought, distinctly Negro. By contrast, I felt something like the interlocutor in a minstrel show and somehow racially short changed.[7]

Coincidentally, Bunche had served as the interlocutor of a minstrel show put on by the graduating class of the Thirtieth Street Intermediate School in Los Angeles, and two of his Negro classmates were the end men.[8]

What are we to make of this feeling of being "racially shortchanged?" Does it reflect class differences? Without knowing more about Bunche's friends, it is hard to know. We do know that the Johnson family had a middle-class background, and even though Lucy Johnson had fallen on hard times, she had a college education planned for her grandson. In fact, the family scrimped and saved to help him attend UCLA.

The Johnson/Bunche family had lived in mixed neighborhoods in Detroit, Albuquerque, and Los Angeles, places where Bunche had had playmates of all races. His cultural background seems equally diverse. Late in life he recalled that among his favorite ballads learned from his mother were "Down by the Old Mill Stream," "I Wonder Who's Kissing Her Now," "After the Ball Was Over," "Santa Lucia," "I Dream of Jeannie with the Light Brown Hair," "Comin' Thru the Rye," and "Put on Your Old Gray Bonnet." Yet Bunche indicated that he loved all spirituals, as well as these mainstream classics. Even later in life he admitted a preference for Billy Daniels, Ella Fitzgerald, and Louis "Satchmo" Armstrong. Of course, by the 1950s these artists had become part of the cultural mainstream.

In ascribing racial traits to African Americans, Bunche was only following the course of America's leaders, both Black and White. W. E. B. Du Bois and Booker T. Washington had agreed that such racial traits existed.[9] Usually the focus was on the aesthetic sense or emotional temperament of the Negro. Whites, tending to view these traits as largely negative, emphasized laziness, immorality, and lack of intelligence. Such sentiments fueled the eugenics movement and led to a peak in Klan activity (even in Los Angeles) in the twenties.

If young Bunche felt anxiety about his racial identity, it was compounded by the uncertainties of college life. Would he be able to hold his own with some of the brightest White students in Southern California?

In 1919, the regents of the University of California, for the furtherance of the educational interests of the state took over the Normal School at Los Angeles. In addition to the curriculum for training teachers certain lower-division classes in several subjects taught on the main campus at Berkeley were established. By the time Bunche enrolled in 1922, the Southern Branch of the University, as it was called, was offering a full university curriculum. Some 3,600 students were crowded into the Vermont Avenue campus (now Los Angeles City College).[10]

On this relatively small campus Bunche was remarkably active and well known. He joined the Blue C Society, Pre-Legal Club, Cosmopolitan Club, Forum, and Agenda. He also wrote articles for the campus newspaper, the *Daily Bruin*, and was assistant sports editor for the yearbook. When the campus debating club refused to accept Bunche as a member, he and some friends formed the Southern Branch Debating Society and he became its president. These extracurricular activities were added to a busy social schedule that had initially included the Kappas, a Black fraternity. However, once he enrolled at UCLA, Bunche turned in his pledge pin with the explanation that he saw no necessity for a separate fraternal organization at integrated schools such as the one he was entering. Moreover, he joined a group of independent students who had set out to break the hold of fraternities on the social life of the campus.[11]

Friendly and outgoing, Bunche loved parties and excursions. Many of his friends, both male and female, stayed in touch with him long after their college days had passed. His first White girlfriend, Eugenie Gehrke, who was from Whittier and had met him at Cosmopolitan Club meetings, was at the airport with her husband to greet him on a 1966 trip of his to Los Angeles.[12]

It was on a hayride with one of his girlfriends that Bunche suffered the first of two physical setbacks that would affect him the rest of his life. After he began to complain of severe headaches, the problem was eventually traced to a piece of barley straw in his left ear that had festered. A mastoid operation to correct the problem was incorrectly performed, leading to a second operation, which left him permanently deaf in his left ear. He withdrew from school and returned only upon Nana's urging in the fall of 1923.[13]

Athletics, not academics, had won Bunche a scholarship to UCLA. His football career, however, ended abruptly with a leg injury that caused a blood clot to form in his left calf. His leg had to be tightly bandaged with cotton gauze for a protracted period of time. The condition would remain with him the rest of his life, often causing him to have to work in bed. As a young man, however, he simply switched from football to basketball. At 5 feet, 9 inches, he played guard on the varsity team that won three consecutive Southern Conference basketball championships. Although some later writers would lead one to believe that Bunche was the prototype for Kareem Abdul-Jabbar, he was a defensive specialist and not a standout. The three miniature golden basketballs he received as a champion were his most treasured possessions.[14] But his basketball experience at UCLA also delivered a lesson in race relations that he always remembered and frequently recounted.

Caddy Works was Bunche's basketball coach at UCLA. At the first practice of the freshman basketball team, a White teammate from Louisiana complained to Works that his parents would never permit him to play with a Black teammate. Works said he understood the problem and offered a simple solution: "Just go over and turn in your suit."[15] The Louisiana student decided to stay and teamed with Bunche to form the backcourt. They became friends, and Bunche often used the story as an example of the friendship that could develop when artificial lines of separation are overcome.

The athletic scholarship did not cover all of Bunche's expenses and he held a variety of part-time jobs. He and his friend Charlie Matthews ran a little store-cleaning business. Later in his first year he worked as a janitor in the women's gymnasium and also trimmed ivy off the school buildings. For a time he was a houseboy for the silent-screen star Charles Ray. To save boarding expenses, he lived with his family on 37th Street.

Although Bunche's punctured eardrum kept him out of the ROTC (and later out of World War II), he was permitted to attend the summer session at Camp Lewis in the Pacific Northwest. Bunche hitchhiked to Seattle for the camp but stowed away on a coastal liner—at a friend's urging—for the return trip to Los Angeles. The crew of the *H. F. Alexander* soon discovered him and put him to shelling peas. They were so impressed with his work that he was hired for the rest of the summer and invited back the next summer as a busboy and petty officers' messman. Bunche would remember the cama-raderie of the crew for the rest of his life.[16]

C. H. Rieber, a philosopher from Berkeley and the dean of the College of Liberal Arts, was Bunche's favorite professor at UCLA. Rieber kept a box of cards on which he wrote memorable sayings, like "doing what I tell you to do" as the definition of cooperation. Rieber became an adviser as well as intellectual mentor. Bunche's life on campus contrasted sharply with his life on 37th Street.

Two speeches that Bunche delivered during his college years reflect his bicultural existence. In a speech to a predominantly Black business audience in Los Angeles, titled "Across the Generation Gap," he called for total resis-tance to mounting instances of racial discrimination—in this case swim-ming-pool segregation:

> Whatever may be the attitude of you older people toward this dastardly prac-tice of insolently slapping the Race in the face, I can tell you in all sincerity, that there is a violently smouldering fire of indignation among those of us who are younger in years and who have not yet become inured to such in-sults. . . . I want to tell you that when I think of such outrageous atrocities as this latest swimming pool incident, which has been perpetrated on Los An-geles Negroes, my blood boils. And when I see my people so foolhardy as to patronize such a place, and thus give it their sanction, my disgust is trebled. Any Los Angeles Negro who would go bathing in that dirty hole with that sign "For Colored Only" gawking down at him in insolent mockery of his Race is either a fool or a traitor to his kind.
>
> If we accept this can't you see that we will only too soon have separate, in-ferior schools, parks, and who knows, perhaps even *jim-crow cars* forced upon us?[17]

Ironically, at this point in the speech, Bunche tells a story about Teddy Roo-sevelt, Booker T. Washington, and a Southern "darky." He closes by calling for more racial pride, more education, and more youthful optimism about the future.[18]

The concrete reality of race relations in Los Angeles stood in sharp con-trast to a speech the young orator had at the debating society, entitled "That Man May Dwell in Peace":

> The proposal which I would present as an antidote for world "war-poison-ing" is centered about *two basic principles*, essential, I believe, to any rational peace plan. These are *International Organization*, involving *every* nation of the world; and the full development of the "*International Mind* or *Will.*" . . .
>
> Indeed, the League of Nations and its World Court are quite indispensable

as initial steps in the inevitable banding together of all national entities into an international body-politic, whose interests shall hold precedence over and above those of the individual national groups.[19]

Bunche then draws an analogy with the thirteen original colonies and their initial unwillingness to unite. Revealing his tendency toward social engineering, he contends that universal political society is possible if man is shaped to cultivate a spirit of brotherhood.

> Why can we not, by means of *social education*, centering about a new concept of the human self as a member of a *world society*, turn thorny, unproductive, shirking, exploiting, cross-grained human natures into co-operating members of a *great united human brotherhood*.... Hatreds are superficial—based upon fear, ignorance, blind prejudice or a desire to dominate for selfish ends. They are simply mental attacks upon others, perchance calling for a physical attack or war in self-defense and retaliation. . . . Let us call a halt to all ethnocentric chauvinism.[20]

According to the young scholar, education leads to understanding, which eliminates the mental fault of prejudice.

To a remarkable extent these two speeches delivered within a year of each other capture the principles that would guide Bunche's career except for brief periods in the 1930s and late 1960s. The principles included the capacity of social science to construct a better social life, the superficiality of racial prejudice combined with an intense racial pride, and the necessity of a world organization that would peacefully resolve international conflict.

UCLA had a dramatic effect on Bunche. It sharpened his intellectual curiosity and let him know he could compete with the best and the brightest. As he says, "It was the genesis and the catalyst."[21] Although Dean Rieber and everyone else assumed he was going to be a lawyer, Bunche's interest in philosophy and international organization pushed him toward graduate study in political science. Winning a fellowship for graduate study in political science at Harvard helped seal his fate. As the top student in his graduating class, he was selected by Dean Rieber to be the commencement speaker. Inspired by a book of Edna St. Vincent Millay's poems, Bunche entitled his remarks "The Fourth Dimension of Personality." The theme of the speech recalls the internationalism of his 1926 speech:

> Man professes strict moral codes; promulgates them through great educational systems; and solidifies them in his law. But invariably his subsequent deeds belie and pervert his original intent. He conjures up bitter prejudices, petty jealousies and hatreds against his fellow-men. The world is periodically scour-

aged and scarred by fiendish wars. Man *learns* and *knows* but he does not *do* as well as he *knows*. . . .

The socially valuable individual is he whose personality is *fully grown*. Ordinarily, personality is considered individuality, whose component elements are reason, self-consciousness, and self activity. Yet these elements of themselves suffice only to make a man, not the *socially valuable* man. If we are to develop our personalities to their fullest, we must add a fourth dimension to this ordinary self, that we may expand up and out from our narrow immediate world. This fourth dimension, call it "bigness," soulfulness, spirituality, imagination, altruism, vision, or what you will—is that quality which gives full meaning and true reality to others. . . . My fellow graduates I commend to you the lines of Edna St. Vincent Millay:

> The world stands out on either side
> No wider than the heart is wide.
> Above the world is stretched the sky
> No higher than the soul is high.[22]

This valediction recalls the spirituality of Du Bois's *The Souls of Black Folk* in its rejection of materialism. It also resembles an important first sermon the young Martin Luther King would deliver some twenty-five years later entitled "The Three Dimensions of Life." Although Bunche asserted that he did not understand all that he had said, a member of the university's Board of Directors was so impressed that he gave Bunche one hundred dollars to help with his graduate education.

Another member of the commencement audience was Mrs. Alice Patton. Impressed by the young graduate's speech, she led the members of the Iroquois Friday Morning Civic and Social Club of Los Angeles in raising more than one thousand dollars to assist Bunche with his living expenses while attending Harvard.[23]

Before leaving for Cambridge, Bunche wrote to Harvard's most famous Black alumnus, W. E. B. Du Bois, asking for his help in being of service to the race during his summer vacation—a sharp contrast to cruising the streets after his high school graduation.

> Since I have been sufficiently old to think rationally and to appreciate that there was a "race problem" in America, in which I was necessarily involved, I have set as the goal of my ambition service to my group. . . .
>
> But I have long felt the need of coming in closer contact with the leaders of our Race, so that I may better learn their methods of approach, their psychology and benefit in my own development by their influence. That is why I am anxious to come east and anticipate enjoying the opportunity extremely.[24]

Du Bois responded that he didn't have an opening just then but would keep Bunche in mind.

Harvard was in social ferment when the young Californian arrived. Largely because of the conservative policies of Harvard president A. Lawrence Lowell, Black students at Harvard protested publicly for the first time in 1922. They, as well as a number of faculty and alumni, were upset with Lowell's ban on Negroes living in the freshman dormitories. Of course, Lowell distinguished between the equal education all were to receive and social commingling, which was a different matter. Thus only Black freshmen had to live in segregated quarters off campus.[25]

Lowell's policy was in keeping with a long Harvard tradition: inviting Black students but isolating them socially. Although it took the university well over two hundred years to admit Blacks, some of the nation's most distinguished African Americans had attended Harvard beginning in the late nineteenth century. Among them were George Ruffin (1869), the first Black judge in Massachusetts; Robert Terrell (1884), the first Black municipal judge in Washington, D.C.; William Monroe Trotter, the leading Black militant at the turn of the century; Martin Delany, the highest-ranking Black in the military during the Civil War and a Reconstruction politician; and Du Bois (1890), the foremost Black intellectual of his time.

These distinguished Americans must have shared a love-hate relationship with the university. As the home of some of the leading "scientific" exponents of Black racial inferiority, Harvard gave its Black students status while attacking their place in civilization. In Du Bois's words, "I was at Harvard, but not of it."[26]

By the time Bunche arrived, separate dormitories were available for Black students who chose to reside on campus. Only thirty to forty Black students were enrolled at Harvard in 1927. Bunche chose to room off campus, at Ma Clark's, with two Black classmates. William Hastie, who became the first Black federal judge and was in his second year of law school, and Robert Weaver, a junior who would later become the first Black American to hold a cabinet position, secretary of housing and urban development under Lyndon Johnson. As Weaver tells it:

> His advance notices were rave and he lived up to them. We lived in close proximity and had almost daily contact, both in playing cards with a strict time schedule, discussing what university students talk about, and reserving the weekends for serious bull sessions, where race relations and strategies for attacking the color line were the dominant themes. . . . Bunche was extremely attractive, quite vocal, articulate and approachable. He made male and female

friends with ease and charm, and he had a well-developed sense of humor, which embraced the capacity to laugh at himself. What impressed me most about Ralph in those days was his optimism, I soon realized that it was not rooted in wishful thinking, as was often the case, but rather based on a long history of overcoming obstacles and an uncanny ability to produce stupendous amounts of work over long sustained periods of application. I watched this capacity grow in proportion to the critical nature of the issues. It maximized the impact of his knowledge, the brilliance of his personality, and was in my opinion the chief factor in his spectacular career.[27]

The threesome was often joined by John P. Davis, a first-year law student, who later cofounded the National Negro Congress with Bunche and published *Our World*, a leading Black magazine. Although Bunche won some money playing blackjack with his Harvard buddies, his main source of spending money came from working at a store on Harvard Square that dealt in secondhand books.

How Bunche got the job in John Phillips's bookstore may be described as the first instance of "Bunche luck." Before leaving Los Angeles, in the hope of obtaining a discount on his textbooks, he had obtained a letter from a UCLA professor introducing him to Phillips. When Bunche arrived with the letter, Phillips, who had been looking for help, assumed Bunche was a job applicant and offered him ten dollars a week, part-time. Bunche happily accepted. Later the myopic Phillips told Bunche that had he known at their first meeting that Bunche was black he probably would not have hired him, but now the young student had proven himself invaluable.[28] Bunche often related this story because it provided another example of how the superficiality of racial prejudice could be overcome by hard work—and a little luck.

Shortly after arriving at Harvard, Bunche had written to Dean Rieber at UCLA explaining his decision to study political science rather than law. He had made up his mind,

> to cast my lot in the realm of the scholarly rather than the purely legal, and from now on [I] will bend every effort toward the attainment of the Ph.D. The conversations which I was fortunate enough to have during my trip this summer with some of the leaders of my race, influenced me considerably in making the decision. That trip was an education in itself to me and it has revealed to me the tremendous amount of work there is for each of us to do during our stay on earth.[29]

Bunche would remain in the East for the rest of his life.

Bunche's decision to study political science (still called government at Harvard) was a bold one, demonstrating again his independence. Law was often seen as a lucrative field for bright young Blacks like Hastie and Davis and even his best friend from Los Angeles, Charlie Matthews. Certainly, young Bunche had no contact with Black professors at UCLA or Harvard, and he had grown up far away from the Black colleges of the South. The prospects for a rewarding academic career were limited to a few top Black schools—Fisk, Howard, and Atlanta University—which Bunche had no contact with. Thus, his decision to pursue a doctorate in political science must have been based primarily on his intellectual interests and desire to serve "his group" through education.

Three professors were central to his work in government at Harvard. Rupert Emerson, who only after Bunche left Harvard began to focus his scholarship on Africa, remained a good friend throughout the younger man's life, eventually persuading him to accept a position at Harvard in 1950. Arthur Holcombe directed Bunche's dissertation, although his own principal expertise was in American government. John Freeman Sly, who was in public administration, was the closest to Bunche. Still, Bunche would state that his best teacher at Harvard had been Charles Howard McIlwain, who taught political philosophy. It was undoubtedly McIlwain's influence that led Bunche to chose as his master's thesis topic "The Political Theory of Sir Robert Filmer."

The primary question Bunche posed in his thesis is "Why do people submit to authority?" In examining this question through Robert Filmer, who defended the divine right of kings, Bunche revealed two basic aspects of his own thought. First, he argued that although Filmer's theory was not "marketable," he should be appreciated for his contribution to the development of the rationalistic and historical method in the science of political thought. Second, Bunche argued that Filmer, unlike Hobbes, was unwilling to adapt to the new dogma of freedom and equality of man. According to Bunche, "If there is any divine law in our political theory today, it is a divine law of adaptability—of mutability and progress."[30] For his efforts, Bunche received an A+ and demonstrated both his pragmatism and his belief in the power of rationalistic social science to shape progress.

Two papers written in Bunche's first year at Harvard offer some insight into the young scholar's development. "The Negro in Chicago Politics" is primarily a descriptive work covering the increasing participation of Blacks in Chicago politics. It was accepted by the *National Municipal Review* and is Bunche's first published article. It concludes that the growing influence of the negro electorate portends a new era of negro political development. The twelve millions of negroes in this country, approximating one-tenth of the total population, must inevitably wield a more proportionate and equitable degree of influence in the political affairs—local, state, and national—of the nation. Perhaps not in this generation nor in the next, but ultimately.[31]

In the article, Bunche refers to the innate gregarious instinct of the American Negro, thereby revealing the continuing influence of biological theories of race on his thinking. He also praises the present Black politicians in Illinois as "among the best and most intelligent members of the group." He commends their service as "both efficient and capable in their respective offices."[32]

These views on innate racial traits and Black leadership would quickly change. Another freshman paper, "Negro Political Philosophy," suggests a transition to a more radical position. In it Bunche focuses on the domestic political philosophy of American Negroes, labeling it conservative. This conservatism, he says, may be attributed to most Blacks' peasant background, along with their ties to the long-dead Republicanism of Lincoln. What is needed is an emphasis on local elections, where Black votes might be "the balance of power," rather than the current focus on national elections.[33] The young scholar concludes that Blacks must become more opportunistic and less idealistic than in the past. Negroes must open their minds to liberal political philosophies and even socialism and Bolshevism. Thus, in a remarkably short time, Bunche had moved from the idealism and spirituality expressed in his UCLA commencement address to a position critical of Black leadership and pragmatic in its location and openness. The transition would be made complete with his move to Howard.[34]

When Bunche graduated with his master of arts degree in July 1928, he received a Thayer Fellowship for doctoral study at Harvard. However, word of his accomplishments had reached Howard University where the distinguished chemist Percy Julian persuaded the administration to offer him a position. The temptation to move to Washington, D.C., and to establish the first political science department at the foremost Black university in the nation proved irresistible, and Bunche declined the fellowship. His joy in starting his professional career was saddened only by the death of Nana in November 1928. Her last words were in a letter he received six days before her death: "Will you be finished at Harvard this year?"[35]

3

The New Deal's "Black Yard"

> If a colored man is ambitious to be in hell, let him be elected to the presidency of Howard University.
>
> —Howard trustee, quoted in Raymond Wolters,
> *The New Negro on Campus*

One of the positive aspects of Reconstruction often ignored by mainstream historians is the creation of a number of institutions of higher learning primarily for the benefit of former slaves and other destitute persons. Preeminent among such institutions is Howard University, established on May 1, 1867, in the nation's capital. Funded by the Bureau of Refugees, Freedmen and Abandoned Lands (Freedmen's Bureau) and led by Union Army general Oliver O. Armstrong, the university was initially open to students from all classes, conditions, and nationalities. However, as Reconstruction wound down and Jim Crow rose up, Howard's White enrollment declined, and by the time of the Supreme Court's *Plessy v. Ferguson* decision in 1896, the school was virtually all Black.[1]

Even with the closing of the Freedmen's Bureau and a shrinking budget, Howard managed to expand its curriculum from the high school level to become the country's first and only Black university. Largely due to the efforts of White Northerners connected to various churches and a small band of talented Black professors barred from teaching in White colleges, Howard developed programs in law, medicine, theology, education, and agriculture.

In 1879, Congress made the first of its annual appropriations to the university, $10,000.[2] A science center was added to the campus in 1909, when Howard's ninth president, Wilbur Thirkield, persuaded the federal government to fund it. Thirkield envisioned Howard as the Tuskegee of the North. Located in an urban area with a large concentration of Blacks, Howard could perform the kind of educational service that Tuskegee accomplished for rural Southern Blacks. Indeed, with Thirkield's fund-raising success with the federal government and private philanthropists, Howard became what its alumni called "the capstone of Negro education."[3]

When James S. Durkee took over as Howard's eleventh and last White president in 1918, he attempted to centralize the power of the university in his office. Traditionally, presidents of Black colleges had exercised virtually dictatorial powers on their campuses, but because of congressional funding, Howard had enjoyed some independence from the kind of authoritarian president-trustee control that came with the church-based funding of other Black schools. Power at Howard had been distributed among the university deans since 1880.

Durkee, a Congregationalist pastor, also stressed the importance of inculcating Christian morality, as had Howard's other White clergyman-presidents. In fact, like Booker T. Washington, Durkee declared that character building was infinitely more important than scholarship. Daily chapel attendance was compulsory, and Durkee began to crack down on those who would neglect the moral welfare of the students.

Increased authority and increased emphasis on moral training over intellectual development was an explosive mixture. By 1925, Howard had more than two thousand students, almost one-sixth of all African American college students in the nation. They were the "New Negro" generation that emerged after World War I, not the freed slaves that submitted to Booker T. Washington's morality training. Moreover, the only Black multiversity had more than 150 professors—some trained at the best universities in the United States. Among the Black faculty were Alain L. Locke, a philosopher, Harvard graduate, and the first Black Rhodes Scholar; William Leo Hansberry, one of the early specialists in African history; Dwight O. W. Holmes, author and administrator; Carter G. Woodson, historian and creator of Negro History Week; Benjamin Brawley, writer and professor of English; Kelly Miller, sociologist and administrator; E. Ernest Just, Dartmouth graduate and biologist; Charles Wesley, historian and administrator; Charles H. Houston, *Harvard Law Review* editor and founder of Howard's Law School; and chemist Percy Julian.[4]

As early as 1901, the Board of Trustees had turned down Miller's request for a university subsidy to publish the proceedings of the American Negro Academy. Locke's request for a course in "interracial relations" and a general faculty appeal for a course in "Negro problems" were denied by the trustees in 1915–1916. Woodson, even as dean, did not receive permission to develop a course in Afro-American history. After a struggle, William Leo Hansberry was permitted to offer courses in African history but was never given tenure despite decades of distinguished service. Scholars of accomplishment, such faculty were not to be dominated and confrontations increased. Miller and Locke were fired after disputes, and Woodson lost his position as dean of arts.[5] Administrative arbitrariness, a student ROTC strike, and Durkee's own racial insensitivity (he had directed a Whites–only school in Boston) led to congressional concern that threatened Howard's annual federal appropriation. Alumni pressure and a publicity campaign forced Durkee's resignation in 1926.[6]

Mordecai W. Johnson, a thirty-six-year-old Black Baptist pastor in Charleston, West Virginia, with academic degrees from Morehouse, Chicago, and Harvard became Howard's twelfth president in 1926 by a vote of 12–2. Although he was not the trustees' first choice, everyone concerned with Howard was pleased that the university had a Black leader for the first time in its history. Charismatic and frank, and with Howard as a platform, Johnson became one of the country's great preachers and remained president for thirty-four years.

Johnson moved quickly to heal the wounds of the Durkee administration. He immediately rehired the faculty fired by his predecessor, including Alain Locke. He demonstrated his respect for faculty and department chairpersons by giving them control over their budgets and a voice in making new appointments. Most important, he was able to push the Cramton bill through Congress in 1928, which guaranteed annual federal financial support for the university.[7]

In bringing Locke back to the faculty, Johnson demonstrated that he did not fear outspoken intellectuals with unorthodox lifestyles. The dapper Locke was an avowed homosexual. With the help of Locke, Just, Julian, and other nationally known faculty, Johnson began to solicit foundation support for hiring young, Black faculty—Howard's faculty was 60 percent White—and financing their research. They especially wanted scholars who viewed race from an international as well as a national perspective. Among their prize recruits were Abram Harris in economics, E. Franklin Frazier in sociology, Sterling Brown in English, and Ralph Bunche in political science. Bunche, who had been recruited by Percy Julian, was considered the star of the group.[8] All would become close friends of Bunche, with Locke serving as an intellectual mentor.

Bunche spent part of the summer of 1928 in California and then moved to Washington. Early in the fall semester, Bunche and Mortimer Weaver, a colleague at Howard and a brother of Robert Weaver (secretary of housing and urban development in the Johnson administration), dropped by the home of Ruth Harris, who was entertaining some friends, all schoolteachers. Talk soon turned to an upcoming dance. Mortimer was planning to escort Ruth, and it was suggested that Bunche take Thelma, one of the guests. Without a word to Ruth, Bunche announced that he was going to take "that quiet little girl sitting back there on the piano bench" (Ruth).[9] Everyone fell silent, and Ruth made no objection. Neither would seek another partner for the rest of their lives. However, the premarital relationship suffered at least one shaky moment after Ruth enrolled in one of Bunche's political science classes. She received a B and challenged Bunche over the grade in his office. Apparently his defense was successful because the grade went unchanged and the two were married in Ruth's brother's house in Washington on June 23, 1930.[10]

Ruth Ethel Harris was one of ten children born in Montgomery, Alabama, to Ellen and Charles Oscar Harris. Her father, although educated at Oberlin and Howard, worked as chief mail clerk in the Montgomery post office. The family moved to Washington, D.C., after Ruth graduated from Alabama State Normal School. She taught school and took night classes at Howard to meet the requirements for the bachelor's degree.[11]

The year before their marriage was especially trying and filled with passionate correspondence. Bunche had decided to return to Harvard in the fall of 1929 to complete his preliminary course work for a doctorate in political science. The pressures to compete at Harvard were so great that Bunche began to smoke and developed a number of health-related problems, including headaches, indigestion, and respiratory and dental problems. In May 1930, he entered Stillman Infirmary for a tonsillectomy, an operation on his sinuses, and a serum injection for the blood clot in his left leg. Still, he wrote to Ruth that he would "rather pass out than let one or two of them [his fellow students] in particular beat me."[12]

The racial pride that drove Bunche to compete with and even surpass his White peers had its downside. Bunche's workaholic tendencies were exacerbated by the academic workload, and he developed a sensitivity that could become self-absorbing:

> I sometimes wonder if I am too broad for my age, or in advance of it, or whether I have misinterpreted what I have thought to be the moral standards of my fellow-men, as I have seen them portrayed by my fellow class-men. It may be that my experiences and contacts at white schools have injured my moral fibers.[13]

Ruth was generally understanding when Bunche entered one of his critical or pompous moods. However, she could bridle when he treated her as a little schoolgirl, which he sometimes did. Bunche seldom if ever displayed these traits in public, but Ruth lived with them until Bunche's death.

At Harvard, Bunche grew closer to Rupert Emerson. Arthur Holcombe and John Sly, a protégé of Charles Beard, remained supportive. Classes in government exposed Bunche to theories of racial equality, and he read extensively in communist and socialist literature. His notes reveal that for him *Das Kapital* was Marx's least important work; that Bukharin's *Historical Materialism* was the best exposition of an economic interpretation of history; that Max Eastman's *Marx to Lenin* was the best critique of the economic approach; and that Harold Laski provided the best brief introduction to socialist thought.[14]

The Great Depression was not a propitious time to start a marriage. When Bunche did get a break from his studies, he played blackjack with his friends at Ma Clark's to make trainfare to Washington. He refused to live in Ruth's mother's house in Washington, and only through the miracle of a $400 scholarship to work on his dissertation was the couple able to afford to pay rent elsewhere and to make a down payment on a blue Ford coupe with a rumble seat. Having passed his general examinations at Harvard, Bunche was now ready to give Howard its due.

While Bunche was on leave Acting Dean Davis wrote him suggesting that he might form a separate political science department once he returned. Arriving back on campus, Bunche was appointed acting chair of the newly constituted department, whereupon he proceeded to hire Emmett "Sam" Dorsey, a former research assistant of Du Bois's, and R. J. Webster. S. McKee Rosen of the University of Chicago declined a position, and Paul Lewinson—who had just finished his book *Race, Class and Party*—wrote Bunche asking for work but none was promised.[15]

Over the next several years Bunche taught a wide range of courses, including

- Constitutional Law
- American Constitutional Law
- Advanced Constitutional Law
- Contemporary Political Thought
- American Political Thought
- History of Political Theory
- Freedom of Speech
- Popular Government in the United States
- Municipal Administration

- Governments of Europe
- International Law
- Leading Decisions of International Tribunals
- Feudalism and the Feudal State
- Imperialism and the World Today
- Colonial Policy
- Status of Dependencies
- Graduate seminars:
    Constitutional Law
    International Affairs
    Colonial Government and Administration in Africa and the Dutch
        East Indies [16]

By all accounts Bunche was a tough but fair grader, demanding the best from his students. Not a dynamic lecturer, he was nonetheless convincing and thorough in presentation.

Bunche constantly fought the administration for increased departmental resources and salaries. He liked to recount one of many encounters with Dean Davis over a raise for himself. Davis said, "Now you just wait and bear this in mind, Ralph, when I was at your stage and your age in the profession, I was getting only $500 per year." Bunche responded bluntly, "Well, Dean, I think that is fair, because I am becoming convinced that was all you were ever worth."[17] In a 1936 letter to Davis, Bunche complained that the Department of Political Science had no typewriter, no secretaries, and no research assistants, even though it served some two hundred students.[18]

Popular among the students, Bunche played basketball and tennis with them and wrote numerous letters of recommendation. He lived in a house on the campus for most of his time at Howard and was readily accessible. Among the students he taught who went on to distinguished careers were political scientists Robert Martin, William P. Robinson, and Vincent Browne; psychologist Kenneth Clark; attorney Hobart Taylor; former D.C. mayor Walter Washington; H.E.W. secretary Patricia Harris; former D.C. councilwoman Wilamenia Rolark; federal judge William Bryant; and Francisco Corneiro and James A. Washington, whom Bunche described as two of the best students he had ever taught.[19]

In the fall of 1931, Mordecai Johnson, president of the university, recognizing Bunche's talent and energy, appointed him assistant to the president. Bunche accepted this position as two-thirds administrator, one-third teacher, largely because of the increase in annual salary to $3500.[20] At the time he was making less than his wife's $2000. Although it was a perfect position from which to put himself in line to succeed Johnson, Bunche had no stomach for ingratiation. He often stood up for students in their conflicts with the administration.

Kenneth Clark credits Bunche with saving his academic career. When Clark was arrested for leading a group of students picketing the segregated restaurant in the U.S. Capitol, Johnson wanted him expelled lest the university's appropriation fall victim to congressional disapproval. Clark was brought before the faculty disciplinary committee, where Bunche won over a majority, contending that Clark and the students should be rewarded rather than punished for their action.[21]

Faculty disputes were also dealt with by the young presidential assistant. Bunche was asked to mediate a particularly sensitive matter in the Chemistry Department. It seemed that Professor Thompson had discovered departmental chair Julian in Julian's apartment with Thompson's wife. Before Thompson took legal action against Julian, he wanted the university to guarantee him security of employment in light of the status differential between the two men. Bunche recommended withholding action until some formal charge was made against Julian. It was not the first time that the Chemistry Department had been embroiled in controversy.[22]

Bunche's brief career as an academic administrator ended in 1932 when he accepted a $2000 Rosenwald Fellowship to complete his dissertation, a comparison of colonial administration in the French colony of Dahomy and in the French-administered League of Nations mandate of Togoland. The grant called for Bunche to do fieldwork in Africa and Europe. He sailed for Europe on June 15, 1932, six months after the birth of his first child, Joan, in December 1931.

Howard's president was not pleased to lose his young assistant and publicly criticized him at a faculty meeting: "Bunche is going all the way to Africa to find a problem."[23] Bunche would later use the statement as an example of the provincial nature of Black colleges. In truth, he was delighted to escape Johnson's autocratic style and the oppressive discrimination of Washington.

On his return to Howard, Bunche remained a faculty leader in restructuring the work of the university. In 1934, the Division of Social Science was created; it comprised six departments: history, economics, philosophy, sociology, political science, and commerce and finance. This reorganization made it possible for the division to sponsor conferences such as the one on the New Deal in 1935. Speaking at an alumni meeting, Bunche noted the doubling of the university's assets since 1926 and stated that Howard was in the forefront of all Negro institutions.[24] Several years later he proposed to his colleagues that the faculty committee on discipline, rather than the various deans, should exercise the power of expulsion. His concern about the deans' arbitrary decisions and students' rights of appeal prompted the proposal. Bunche also proposed that Howard establish a National Negro Library and Museum and was appointed to the committee to oversee the project by Johnson.[25]

Bunche did not limit his activities to the Howard campus. Speaking before a wide variety of audiences in Washington and across the country, he took firm positions on a number of controversial issues. In "Gandhi and the Future of India in 1930," he fully supported the independence movement, saying it was the "acid test for imperialism."[26] The socialist-leaning Capital City Forum invited Bunche to speak in 1935. His talk, "Academic Freedom," was initially canceled by the "red squad" of the D.C. Police because of the lack of an occupancy permit and because there was no third-floor fire escape. After the obstacles were finally overcome, Bunche launched a vigorous defense of the rights of students: "The student, in his continuing quest for knowledge and understanding, has a *fundamental right* to be led along the path of *free, unrestrained* investigation of the world in which he lives and of *every consequential idea in it.*"[27]

Early in 1936, at a mass meeting in Washington in support of the Scottsboro Defense Committee, Bunche spoke in opposition to the NAACP position. The Howard professor favored mass pressure to save the Black defendants. Most Blacks cited the Scottsboro case as a prime example of the lynch mob mentality of Southern Whites, but Bunche contended that in other parts of the South some poor Whites served as allies.[28]

Two weeks later Bunche had an opportunity to challenge segregation himself. The Black singer Todd Duncan wrote to his old friend Bunche asking him to intervene so that Negroes might be seated at the National Theater to see his production of *Porgy and Bess.* Bunche rallied Howard faculty and students to form one of the first picket lines in the nation's capital. Some of the pickets were from Local 440 of the American Federation of Teachers (AFT), which Bunche had recently joined. The effort was successful in forcing the integration of the theater, but for that production only.[29]

By preferring to struggle through the mechanism of interracial alliances, Bunche came into conflict with some of his best friends. In 1933, a group of his friends and acquaintances had established the New Negro Alliance to fight for the jobs of three Blacks who had been fired and replaced by three

Whites at the Hamburger Grill in Washington, D.C. Among the activists were John A. Davis, William Hastie, Belford V. Lawson, and M. Franklin Thorn. The picket line in front of the restaurant quickly led to the rehiring of the Blacks and helped establish the tactic as effective in gaining and protecting jobs for African Americans.

Bunche, however, had reservations about such tactics because of their adverse consequences for White workers. He felt that its continued use would drive a wedge between Black and White worker solidarity. As the alliance continued its activities, its defenders argued that they "didn't see an awful lot of white people who were interested in getting in the struggle with us, except those who had communist leanings, and they were more interested in advancing their own cause than ours."[30]

The debate reached a peak in 1935, when Bunche publicly attacked the alliance at one of its own events. In a speech at the New Negro Alliance Forum in March 1935 entitled "The Tragedy of Racial Introversion," Bunche declared that "racialism [is] an interpretation of all social, political and economic phenomena in terms of racial interest [that] develops a social romanticism which leads to a distorted picture of society, which puts race as the basic factor in social causation." On the other hand, Bunche believed that the latest social science research indicated that "race is not the basic factor in social causation . . . it is economic."[31] He went on to strongly denounce the NNA for the futility of its racial policy approach, calling the organization "opportunistic" and shortsighted in its focus on "immediate relief." The charges were widely reported in Washington's Black press, and Hastie responded that "the impact of events makes policies of immediate relief necessary and desirable and their haphazard occurrence makes opportunism inevitable."[32]

In many ways 1935 marks the zenith of Bunche's radicalism. However, the break with his friends and past views expressed at UCLA and Harvard did not come in a vacuum. To understand his new radicalism, it must be seen in the context of the great changes occurring in American society.

As the optimism of the "Roaring Twenties" subsided, a new reality set in. Black voters had begun to leave the Republican Party in 1928,[33] but even the onset of the Great Depression did not move them fully to the Democratic side. The presidential election in 1932 still found a majority casting their ballots for the Republican candidate. It was not until the early 1930s that the NAACP began to emphasize the importance of voting, and the Urban League moved from private negotiations with business to the public lobbying of government through Workers Councils.

Of course, this new interest in public policy was prompted both by the great hardship inflicted on the Black community and the larger federal response to the Great Depression. What was known about Franklin Roosevelt was largely negative in regard to Blacks. In his prior career he had referred to Blacks as niggers, helped segregate rest rooms in government buildings, supported the U.S. occupation of Haiti and claimed to have written that country's constitution (he did not), and denied having entertained Blacks at an official luncheon in New York (he did). It was not until an address at Howard in October 1936 that Roosevelt spoke to a Black audience.[34]

Beyond these personal actions, a number of the early New Deal programs not only excluded Blacks from coverage but had a negative impact on Black workers. Agricultural Adjustment Act crop-reduction payments were to be passed on to sharecroppers and tenants by landowners who received the payments, but the recipients often chose not to distribute them. Accordingly, the number of Black tenants was reduced by a third (192,000) and the number of sharecroppers by nearly 25 percent from 1930 to 1940. The Wagner bill (The National Labor Relations Act) omitted an antidiscrimination clause for fear of offending the South, and the administration trimmed the costs of Wagner's Social Security bill by excluding agricultural and domestic employees from unemployment compensation and old-age insurance—two-thirds of Blacks worked in these areas. Initially, the National Recovery Administration (NRA) supported lower minimum wages for Black workers. The National Industrial Recovery Act provided for collective bargaining, a tactic often used by unions to force employers to fire Blacks.[35] A basic problem was that New Deal administrators believed that centralized policy planning at the federal level could be combined with decentralized administration at the state and local levels. Although the aim was to make democracy effective without creating a leviathan state, the result was increased Black expectations with continued racial discrimination by local administrators.

In the absence of a body of White liberal opinion to pressure the administration to address continuing discrimination, a number of Black organizations were formed to change federal policy. Along with the expanded programs of the NAACP and Urban League were the new programs of organizations like the Negro Industrial League, the Joint Committee on National Recovery, and the National Negro Congress. Two of Bunche's Harvard buddies, Robert Weaver and John P. Davis, founded the Negro Industrial League in the summer of 1933 "to insure the protection of the interests of the race in such measures as are taken" by the New Deal administration. Weaver and Davis began to pressure a number of prominent African

American leaders and organizations to join them in lobbying for Black representation on New Deal commissions and for equal treatment for Blacks under New Deal programs. By the fall of 1933, Davis had secured an agreement with the NAACP, and eventually twenty-three other organizations, that led to the birth of the Joint Committee on National Recovery. This loose alliance collected information on the social and economic conditions of Blacks, presented the data to the relevant New Deal agencies, and generated public pressure for "remedial action" by the government. Its greatest victory came when it succeeded in persuading the NRA not to sanction lower wage-and-hour standards for Black workers.[36]

Although the Joint Committee enjoyed some success, the conditions under which African Americans lived continued to worsen. Laundry workers, who were mainly Black, earned a minimum wage of fourteen cents an hour. Domestic and personal service workers fared even worse; some took home as little as $2.75 a week for as much as fourteen hours of work in a day.[37] Howard University's Division of Social Science, led by Ralph Bunche, was planning the conference "Position of the Negro in the Present Economic Crisis" for May 1935. Davis, the Joint Committee's executive secretary, decided the time was right to advocate a national Negro congress. He joined Bunche in cosponsoring a conference that would not only report on economic and social conditions but act on them as well. James W. Ford of the Communist Party had been actively promoting a national Negro congress throughout that spring. Thus the call for a national conference also became a call for a national congress.

The conference idea received an overwhelmingly positive response in the African American community, despite the criticism of a few who felt that the general good done by the New Deal outweighed the problems faced by Blacks. To such criticism, Bunche responded that we are being told to "stay in our own BLACK yards."[38] As might be expected, defenders of the New Deal came under severe attack at the conference.

Three themes seemed to emerge from the conference. First, New Deal efforts to reform the economic system did not begin to address the misery and poverty caused by capitalism. In his paper, later published in the *Journal of Negro Education*, Bunche contended that the New Deal would only "crystallize those abuses and oppressions which the exploited Negro citizenry of America have long suffered under laissez-faire capitalism."[39] Second, existing Negro organizations were inadequate to meet the challenge of the Urban League; a federal representative suggested that the cause of discrimination by White workers against Black workers was psychological rather than economic. The Urban League along with the NAACP, Garvey, and Black churches and lodges were attacked for pursuing middle-class goals. Third, the overwhelming majority of conference participants saw unionization as a solution for all Black workers, including those in agriculture and domestic service. When Du Bois put forth his program of voluntary economic segregation, it was strongly rejected.

That Howard University would host a conference so critical of the federal government and established Black leadership was remarkable and a testament to Mordecai Johnson's presidency. In addition to a number of prominent administration officials who addressed the conference, James Ford discussed the Communist solution to the status of the Negro, and Norman Thomas spoke on the Socialist view. A number of workers, domestic servants, and agricultural laborers also made presentations. The radical speeches caused a good deal of trouble for Howard's President Johnson. Kelly Miller, who had been unhappy with the Johnson administration for some time, charged that the university had been used to promote communism and that Johnson himself had spoken favorably of the "Russian experiment." Moreover, a Southern sharecropper had been quoted on the floor to the effect that "by the shedding of blood, shall sins be stored"—Miller interpreted this biblical admonition as a call for revolution. He asked for the resignation of Johnson and the Board of Trustees chair, General John Shelburne, for misusing a public institution.[40]

Johnson stood on the grounds of academic freedom and defended the conference from its detractors. He argued that radicals represented no more than 5 percent of the conference participants and that there had been no mention of revolution by force. When Congressman Arthur Mitchell raised the issue with the House Appropriations Committee, Johnson said he believed free speech was more important than money from Congress.[41] Joining him was Albert Bushnell Hart of Harvard in a letter to Colonel Theodore Roosevelt, who had been a trustee of Howard: "The talk about his [Johnson's] being a Communist is all rubbish and is principally due to intense jealousy felt by Kelly Miller for a long time professor at the university." Hart went on to state that Miller had charged the university an excessive price for a house Hart occupied on the university campus and that he was part of a clique that used to complain to Secretary of the Interior Ickes, who no longer listened.[42] The storm passed with Johnson rooted more firmly than ever at Howard.

Bunche would see a controversy develop around his own participation in the conference. It involved a meeting at his house on the campus during the conference with some of its key organizers. The meeting to chart the future of a national Negro congress included John P. Davis and James W. Ford. Bunche's participation in the meeting would not become an issue until the McCarthy era.

In the months following the conference, the congress movement gained the endorsement of the National Urban League, the Fraternal Council of Negro Churches in the United States, the Order of Elks, the National Alliance of Postal Employees, the National Association of Colored Women, many local labor unions, and Black civic, professional, and fraternal organizations. Black newspapers and journals promoted the idea, as did such notables as Langston Hughes and Arna Bontemps. Conspicuously absent was the NAACP.

Concurrent with the congress movement, momentum was developing on the racial issue in the labor movement. The American Federation of Labor, spurred by A. Philip Randolph and the new Congress of Industrial Organizations led by John Lewis of the United Mine Workers, began a concerted attack on segregated unions. These events helped put labor issues at the top of the agenda of a national Negro congress. In his pamphlet "Let Us Build a National Negro Congress," published in October 1935, Davis declares that "the only way out for Negroes is through widespread labor organization."[43] With Randolph's selection as president of the congress, the labor orientation of the movement was solidified.

When the first National Negro Congress convened in February 1936, in Chicago, more than 817 delegates (both Black and White) from 585 organizations representing more than 1.2 million people were in attendance. In addition, there were several hundred visitors and official observers. The three general sessions held at night drew from five to eight thousand persons at each session. The Presiding Committee was chaired by Adam Clayton Powell, Jr., and included Bunche, Lester Granger, William Hastie, James W. Ford, Ben Davis, Angelo Herndon, and Manning Johnson. Randolph's keynote address took note of the rise of fascism in the United States, France, and England, as well as Germany and Italy. The congress denounced Italy's subjugation of Ethiopia, and such figures as Huey Long and Father Coughlin were also criticized. Delegates saw the New Deal as placing property rights before human rights as they called for an end to lynching and the enforcement of civil rights. The primary solution was the right of Blacks to have jobs at a living wage and to join trade unions as equal members.[44]

Bunche had lost an internal struggle with Davis to limit the delegates to persons associated with the labor movement and was already developing a critical attitude toward the congress. This orientation is best reflected in his appraisal of the events in Chicago entitled "Triumph? Or Fiasco?" which appeared in *Race* in the summer of 1936. According to Bunche, the smorgasbord of Negro groups and organizations led to a program aimed at everyone from White philanthropists to revolutionary Communists. Profound labor resolutions were passed side by side with equally strong resolutions supporting religion and Negro business. Yet Bunche also understood that a more narrow and effective program directed only at labor solidarity would have trouble reaching the Black masses.

> Perhaps a Congress composed only of representatives of organizations actively engaged in the labor struggle could achieve more—but could it effectively reach the greater masses of the Negro people? To do so it would still have to contend with the black demagogues, the professional Uncle Toms, and the socially ignorant ministers of the gospel. . . . Its [the NNC's] fundamental purpose should be to make Negroes socially conscious, to give them a realistic understanding of their mass position as workers in society, to promote labor orientation and to stimulate the enrollment of the Negro masses in the ranks of organized labor.[45]

Bunche argued that the congress had proceeded on the assumption that the common denominator of race was enough to weld together diverse elements of the Black community in an effective campaign of action. He challenged that assumption and by 1940 had abandoned the congress.

Because of his travels in Africa, Bunche missed the second National Negro Congress meeting in 1937.[46] By the time the third National Negro Congress convened in the Department of Labor Auditorium in Washington, D.C., on April 26–28, 1940, Bunche was viewed as a hostile outsider and Davis tried to prevent him from attending. Eventually, Bunche was permitted to attend as an observer working for the Carnegie-Myrdal study and in that capacity, he wrote a blistering critique of the meeting for Myrdal. Nine hundred Negro and nearly four hundred White delegates from twenty-eight states and the District of Columbia were in attendance. Bunche immediately noted that the congress had dropped its oft-stated assertion of nonpartisanship. John Lewis delivered the first address of the opening meeting and invited the congress to affiliate itself with Labor's Non-Partisan League (LNPL, which many saw as partisan).

Following Lewis, President A. Philip Randolph made the most anticipated address. Knowing that his audience was hostile, Randolph proceeded to accuse the Soviet Union of pursuing its own national interests, which were not necessarily in the interest of world peace or democracy or American Negroes. He cautioned the congress against a too-close relationship with any organization and stressed the need for independence and nonpartisanship built up by Black effort alone. By the time Randolph finished attacking the House Un-American Activities Committee, known as the Dies Committee, and emphasizing the loyalty of American Negroes to their country, most of the audience had walked out.[47]

Randolph's assault on Communist influence in the NNC led to his resignation and replacement as president by Max Yergan. Yergan, John P. Davis, and other congress leaders laid down a pro-Soviet line that opposed American participation in the "imperialist" war abroad and focused on democracy at home. Those who had fought fascism in Spain so vigorously ignored German Nazism while attacking French, English, and U.S. imperialism. Reporting about a former student of his who saw him at the meeting but was not aware of his disgust at the proceedings of the organization he had helped found, Bunche wrote down the student's almost religious confessional statement:

> Oh, Mr. Bunche, I am no longer naive and uninformed now. I have a point of view and I will never be unprogressive again. Don't you think it's grand?

"I didn't know what to reply," said Bunche, "but started to say, 'peace sister, it's wonderful'!"[48]

Bunche's assessment of the meeting was that the NNC had reduced itself to a Communist cell. This meant its end as a force in the Black community, and Bunche held Davis personally responsible: "What Davis did was not prompted by ineptitude, nor by anger. He coolly allied the interests of the American Negro with the foreign policy of the Soviet Union as reflected in the line of the American Communist Party."[49] Bunche also believed that John Lewis was attempting to build up his own power for a run at the presidency of the United States in 1944.

In concluding his critique of the National Negro Congress, Bunche states that it never had a mass following anyway. His denigration of the accomplishments of the congress movement has been repeated by a number of scholars. Such views did a disservice to the activities of many local chapters and the thousands who participated in national campaigns.[50] Credit for much of the progress in race relations in the labor movement of the late thirties is given to the CIO. Ignored in this important shift are the pressures exerted by the only independent, Left-oriented, Black-led organization of the period: the NNC. The NNC retained its independence even after it established a working relationship with the CIO and LNPL.

Despite its labor orientation the congress has been portrayed by some as a nationalist organization. Given Bunche's orientation, this view of the NNC is fantastic. In fact, it was a remarkable collection of Blacks and Whites, Communists and non-Communists, workers and the middle class. By the time the NNC was dominated by the American Communist Party in 1940, it had made historic progress in building Black and White solidarity in the labor movement and the Left in general.

Bunche's political activities were not confined to the National Negro Congress. He attended meetings of the Scottsboro Defense Committee and the Washington Committee for Democratic Action, and supported the Loyalists in Spain. He was a member of the International Committee on African Affairs (later the Council on African Affairs) and the Joint Committee for Brazil. In the summer of 1936, he codirected the Institute of Race Relations at Swarthmore College and was an active member of Local 440 of the American Federation of Teachers. Yet despite his political activity, during the thirties, Bunche produced an outstanding body of scholarly work.

4

The Black Intellectual

Democracy in America decisively separates the intellectual from
everyone else. The intellectual in America is a radically alienated personality, the Negro in common with the white.

>—Saunders Redding, in Kinfe Abraham,
>*Politics of Black Nationalism*

Good-bye,
Christ Jesus Lord God Jehova,
Beat it on away from here now.
Make way for a new guy with no religion at all
A real guy named Marx Communist Lenin Peasant
Stalin Worker Me.
I said, ME

>—Langston Hughes, in Kinfe Abraham,
>*Politics of Black Nationalism*

America!
Land created in common,
Dream nourished in common,
Keep you hand on the plow! Hold on!
If the house not yet finished,
Don't be discouraged, builder!
If the fight is not yet won,
Don't be weary, soldier!
The plan and the pattern is here.

>—Langston Hughes, in Kinfe Abraham,
>*Politics of Black Nationalism*

The National Negro Congress experience showed Bunche and
his Howard University colleagues fully engaged in the struggles of the Black
community. In the midthirties, Bunche had played a primary role in orga-

nizing two Howard conferences aimed at affecting public policy toward Africans in 1936 and African Americans in 1935. The latter conference was remarkable in its inclusion of mainstream politicians, radical leftists, and Black workers, in addition to academics. The resulting National Negro Congress marked a highpoint in Bunche's activism and in his association with the Left.

For most of the twentieth century, Black intellectuals had been socially marginal to both the White and Black communities. Prohibited from teaching in White colleges and universities, Black scholars were isolated on a few predominantly Black campuses. Although this usually brought them closer to the Black community, it set them on the periphery of the great intellectual debates of the day.[1] There were several ways of dealing with this enforced social marginality. Some Black scholars left the country; others opted for bohemia. However, in the thirties the preferred way for a significant number was to become a member of the Communist Party.[2] As Carter Woodson told Bunche in Paris, any Black intellectual worth his salt was either overtly or covertly a Marxist.

Membership in the Communist Party was useful for several reasons. First, it broke the isolation of Black scholars and Black writers. Second, it offered the resources to hold meetings, travel, and get published. Third, it helped facilitate a redefinition of Black identity vis-à-vis African American victim status. That is, it fundamentally redefined the relationship between the oppressed and the oppressor in such a way that the dependency of the oppressed was no longer an issue.[3]

It was the last factor that attracted Bunche, along with Abram Harris and E. Franklin Frazier, to Marxism but not to the Communist Party. After all, they might be isolated from the elite White schools each of them had attended, but Howard University during the 1930s was home for the most distinguished group of Black scholars ever assembled on one campus. In 1932, Bunche reported that of the 271 Howard faculty members (including Whites), 211 were Howard graduates.[4] As late as 1936, more than 80 percent of all Black Ph.D.'s were employed by Howard, Atlanta, and Fisk Universities. By the 1940s, government service and elite White universities began luring away many of Howard's most noted faculty members.

Bunche was able to find funding for travel and meetings without turning to the Communist Party. In addition, the establishment of such journals as the *Journal of Negro Education* and the *Journal of Negro History* (he served on the latter's initial editorial board) gave scholars like Bunche a friendly and stimulating place to publish their research. Although the National Negro

Congress became increasingly dependent on Communist Party resources, the initial impetus was an attempt to link the Black community to the larger protest community, including White workers. In fact, Harris, Bunche, and Frazier had earlier tried to steer the NAACP in a new, more-inclusive direction.

In late August of 1933, thirty-three young black intellectuals gathered at the estate of NAACP president Joel Spingarn in Amenia, New York, to discuss the problems of race in the midst of a depression. The meeting was planned by W. E. B. Du Bois, who, like other officers of the NAACP, was feeling increased pressure to adjust the organization's traditional legal and political approach to the economic reality of the times. In fact, longtime race leaders like Du Bois and James Weldon Johnson would receive the brunt of the criticism coming from the young intellectuals.

Leading the attack were Harris, Frazier, and Bunche. Charging the older men with racial provincialism, the young radicals advocated Black and White labor solidarity to force through the necessary reform legislation. The older "race men" and the NAACP, they stated, were caught up in the middle-class needs of the Black business elite, ignoring the economic needs of the Black masses.[5]

Harris, Frazier, and Bunche were appointed to a special committee to follow up the Amenia Conference with specific recommendations for the NAACP; their report was debated but ultimately rejected. The young radicals went on to distinguished careers in academia and public service and their views began to diverge over the years. However, during the thirties they and other colleagues at Howard University diverged not only in their activism but more significantly in their scholarship from the previous generation of Black intellectuals.

Sitting astride the Black academic world was the figure of Du Bois. All Black intellectuals would read his work, and those in the social sciences would have to deal with his influence whether they agreed with his views or not. And, of course, his views changed over the years. A few years after the Amenia meeting, Du Bois himself would split with the NAACP over some of the same issues raised by the young radicals. Du Bois had been greatly influenced in his early years by Alexander Crummell, an Episcopal priest educated at Cambridge University. Crummell had searched from the 1840s through the 1890s for the "innate" characteristics of races. Like his ideological opponent, Booker T. Washington, he tended to see Blacks as an aesthetically gifted people, strongly enthusiastic but lacking in discipline. Crummell acquired the reputation of championing Blacks against mulattoes. His emphasis on race pride and race destiny led him to organize the Black cultural and intellectual elite into the American Negro Academy in 1897.

It was at the first meeting of the academy that its vice-president and social historian, Du Bois, read his paper "The Conservation of Races." In it, Du Bois sets forth a mystical notion of race, interchanging it with "nation." He believed that racially, growth was historically characterized by "the differentiation of spiritual and mental differences between great races of mankind and the integration of physical differences." The German nation stood for science and philosophy; the English nation stood for "constitutional liberty and commercial freedom"; but the racial ideal of the Negro race had yet to be fulfilled.

Only two years later in *The Philadelphia Negro*, Du Bois introduced social science into his defense of the race. And in a critical review of Frederick L. Hoffman's *Race Traits and Tendencies of the American Negro*, which asserted that Negroes were doomed to decline as a race because of weak genetic material, Du Bois cited relevant comparative data from European cities with which Blacks compared favorably in terms of health and crime statistics.[6] His intellectual peers Kelly Miller and Carter Woodson continued to focus on the primacy of race (prior to World War I only fourteen black Americans had Ph.D.'s from recognized universities), but Du Bois began to give class increasing consideration. Thus while Miller and Woodson quarreled with the younger generation of Black intellectuals, Du Bois supported them and invited dialogue. In so doing, Du Bois represents a transitional figure in the break from the biological paradigm.[7]

The push of the Great Depression and the pull of new anthropological evidence marked the end of the dominance of the biological explanations for Black subordination.[8] Du Bois now recognized the importance of economics and encouraged the NAACP to change its focus, yet he disappointed the "young radicals" by suggesting self-segregation in economic cooperatives as a viable economic strategy. Although Du Bois was "convinced of the essential truth of the Marxian philosophy," he asked is there any automatic power in socialism to override and suppress race prejudice?

> There are those who insist that the American Negro must stand or fall by his alliance with white Americans; that separation in any degree, physical or social, is impossible and that either, therefore, the Negro must take his stand with exploiting capitalists or with the craft unions or with the communists.[9]

Du Bois said the question was already settled because Negroes already constituted a separate nation within a nation. What remained was to be organized along economic lines that benefit the great majority of Blacks. At the same time, Blacks would continue the fight for political and civil equality.

The overthrow of the biological paradigm removed the major obstacle to racial assimilation. Robert Park, a transitional figure who worked for Washington early in his career and trained Frazier and Charles S. Johnson late in his career, provided a theory of assimilation based on urban racial contact. Although the young Black intellectuals, like Harris and Bunche, who opposed Du Bois assumed a Marxist posture throughout the thirties, by the early forties they had helped shape a new dominant paradigm based on the social psychology of Gunnar Myrdal. The paradigm was assimilationist at its core and therefore never acceptable to Du Bois.

Older than Bunche, Abram Harris was the first of the three to arrive at Howard in 1927. A native of Richmond, Virginia, Harris had graduated from Virginia Union and then attended the New York School of Social Work. While in New York, Harris worked as a research assistant for the National Urban League, came into contact with the city's left-wing intellectual community, and developed an interest in Black workers in the labor movement. By 1924, he had earned an M.A. in economics from the University of Pittsburgh with a thesis entitled "The Negro Laborer in Pittsburgh." Around this time, Harris developed a warm friendship with Du Bois that lasted until their separate splits with the NAACP in 1935. After teaching for a year at West Virginia Collegiate Institute (now West Virginia State) and spending a year as executive secretary of the Minneapolis Urban League, Harris began his doctoral studies in economics at Columbia. At the same time, he began teaching at Howard, commuting regularly between the District of Columbia and New York. Harris's best-known work, *The Black Worker* (1931), was written collaboratively with Sterling Spero and frequently cited by Bunche.

Du Bois had written an enthusiastic review of *The Black Worker* for the *Nation*, calling it "one of the first attempts in the economic field to make a synthesis of the labor movement and the Negro problem so as to interpret each in the light of the other and show them to be one question of American economics."[10] In his own journal, *The Crisis*, Du Bois "strongly recommended [*The Black Worker*] for reading, particularly by those American Negroes who do not yet realize that the Negro problem is primarily the problem of the Negro working man."[11]

In *The Black Worker*, Harris takes Booker T. Washington to task for emphasizing the old notion of the self-made man to the exclusion of the "problems peculiar to the wage earner in modern industry." Middle-class Negro leadership in general, Harris notes, always sides with capital and against organized labor, but urges Blacks to try not to set up separate unions, even if expedient, because doing so would hinder the development of class consciousness. Harris preferred the radical ideology of industrial unionism over more conservative trade unionism because the former must be more concerned about neglecting any large section of workers.[12]

As early as 1927, Harris made clear that class, not race, was the dominant force in Black oppression. Writing in *Social Forces*, he declared that "[s]lavery was an economic system which involved white freemen as masters and black men as slaves. The Negro was not enslaved because his complexion, and nose and lip formation differed from the white man's." He added that "both the lower white and black classes were weak. . . . For a short period White and Black bondsmen were on the same indefinite legal footing." This brief equality in status among the poor changed because "Negro labor being cheaper (more plentiful) than cheap white labor was more desired."[13]

Harris's sharpest attacks on the racial paradigm came in response to Du Bois. In 1935, Du Bois published what some considered his finest scholarly work, *Black Reconstruction in America*. Despite Du Bois's earlier praise of *The Black Worker* and Harris's stated admiration of Du Bois as the Negro intellectual to whom his generation owes the most, he launched a fierce attack on the work. Du Bois, said Harris, is too bound by the racial paradigm of his generation to absorb Marxism:

> Dr. Du Bois concedes the inevitability of socialism and even the desirability of it, but is at the same time distrustful of white workers. He cannot believe that a movement founded upon working-class solidarity and cutting across racial lines can afford any immediate relief to the Negro's economic plight or have any practical realization in the near future. By temperament and habituation to the Negro equal rights struggle he is wholly unfitted to join, to say nothing of initiating, such a movement. He is a racialist whose discovery of Marxism as a critical instrument has been too recent and sudden for it to discipline his mental process or basically to change his social philosophy.[14]

Du Bois's ideological confusion, according to Harris, led him to convert the wholesale flight of Negroes from the plantations into a general strike against the slave regime, while in fact the slaves had no real class consciousness nor any idea of what impact their "escape to freedom" would have on the outcome of the war. Moreover, had they pursued a truly radical agenda during Reconstruction, said Harris, their plans would never have been supported by Thad Stevens and Charles Sumner, who were members of the capitalist class.[15]

Harris would extend his criticism of Du Bois's racial chauvinism in the latter's other major economic study of the decade, *The Negro as Capitalist* (1936), which came out just after Du Bois had proposed a program for a Negro economic nation within the nation. Harris argued that Du Bois had not explained how a separate economy could function in the face of persistent industrial integration, business combinations, and the centralization of capital control. In fact, Harris linked Du Bois's proposal to those of the pre–Civil War proponent of a separate Black economy, Martin Delany, whom he called a "black Benjamin Franklin." The Black businessman emerged as the villain who encourages Black enterprise at the expense of White and Black labor solidarity. Even groups like the New Negro Alliance, which promoted "Don't Buy Where You Can't Work" campaigns, were categorized with Du Bois as middle-class Black chauvinists.[16]

Throughout the thirties, then, Harris consistently rejected interracial conciliation as the strategy of Booker T. Washington and civil libertarianism, and rejected as well militant race consciousness as the program of middle-class Blacks. The first actively supported capitalism; the latter left untouched the material basis for racial inequality. While maintaining that White trade unions must change their racial practices, he promoted class consciousness and class unity. In fact, Blacks should pursue no actions that would inflame racial antagonism. Harris, unlike contemporary radical economists such as Michael Reich, argued that "if race prejudice is not accompanied with competitive activities or the subjugation of one group by the other it is soon removed through association."[17] However, as Blacks become more competitive with White workers, hostility between the races will increase. Harris never fully explained how this cycle of competition and hostility can be overcome, but perhaps, like Bunche, he believed that the growing class consciousness of the White proletariat was inevitable.

The dramatic radicalization of Bunche's views as a result of his experiences and study at Harvard and then Howard is revealed in his essay "Marxism and the 'Negro Question,'" written around 1929. Only three years after his speech "That Man May Dwell in Peace," the essay replaced the call for peace through social education with "the overthrow of capitalist democracy thru the concentration of political power in the hands of the proletariat." Bunche, once the young race leader in Los Angeles, now regards the destruction of any "racial unity" among all classes of Blacks as "profoundly progressive and revolutionary phenomena."

"Marxism and the 'Negro Question'" foreshadowed several central themes that the radical Bunche would put forward in his writings in the

1930s. First, although Bunche used the then-fashionable language of the Communist movement, he demonstrated his independence by rejecting the Sixth World Congress's "national minority" thesis.[18] Asserting that American Negroes had none of the characteristics necessary for the formation of a nation, he states, "[T]he fundamental falsity of the 'national minority' orientation comes to erase expression in the obvious inappropriateness of the slogan of 'self-determination' . . . in a situation where every force of bourgeois law, custom, and public opinion to maintain and widen the breach between the races, is an objective support to jim-crowism."[19] According to Bunche, a truly Marxist theory of the "Negro question" or even a truly Marxist analysis of its main features had not yet been made: "The general backwardness and sterility of socialist theory in America and the traditional American Socialist 'nihilism' on the Negro Question as an indirect expression of the 'white supremacy' ideology are partly responsible for this condition."[20] Yet he proceeded to supply some of the core elements for such an analysis—an emphasis on the caste status of Blacks and the superexploitation of Black labor, the hegemony of bourgeois ideology through the incorporation of race prejudice, and the organization of Negro society along the lines of an internal colony.

Despite the fact that the young Howard scholar would consistently argue against Black nationalism throughout his life, in the late 1920s and early 1930s he retained some of the racial sentimentality he so strongly attacked in Du Bois. For example, in his lecture notes from the early years at Howard he states:

Fundamentally, the Negro is a being most sensitively sentimental; a being endowed with the most natural of artistic talents . . . (which historically leads to two very obvious truths)—one is that any distinction so far won by a member of our Race, here, has been invariably in some one of the arts . . . —the other is that any influence so far exerted by the American Negro upon American civilization has been primarily in the realm of art [cites Douglass's oratory, Dunbar, Tanner] . . . the Negro Race of all races, whether it be generally known or not, is endowed with that greatest of racial blessings,—a *soul* (which might be poetically traced back to Africa) . . . —no race has ever,—nor race *shall* ever, rise to the heights of artistic achievement until it has suffered and mourned and received deliverance . . . (Given that every race has its outstanding trait of genius)—Then it appears from past indications that the American Negro is destined to attain his greatest heights of successful achievement in the realm of art—just as he has in the past [cites folklore, dances, spirituals, composers].—The final measure of the greatness of any people of whatever creed or race, religious or political affiliation, is the amount and standard of the artistic production of that people [cites Coleridge-Taylor in England; Dumas in France; Pushkin in Russia; and Robeson, Gilpin, and Roland Hayes in the United States].[21]

Thus we see in the young Howard scholar, a Black intellectual still rooted in the biological paradigm of an earlier generation yet straining to overcome its limitations by looking at economic reality.

In his 1935 *Journal of Negro Education* article "A Critical Analysis of the Tactics and Programs of Minority Groups," Bunche laid the foundation of much of his work for the next five years and with it some of the central issues for the field of Black politics. He repeated his earlier attacks on Black nationalism, economic separatism, Black Republicanism, and middle-class Black leadership. More important, new critiques of "economic passive resistance" and civil libertarianism that would flower in his work on the Myrdal project were first presented here. Yet, unlike the Myrdal memoranda, in which Bunche criticized the NAACP and Urban League strategies, here he rejected the entire framework of the "moral dilemma" thesis as likely to lead to "genteel programs of interracial conciliation." "The only hope for the improvement in the condition of the masses of any American minority group," said Bunche, "is the hope that can be held out for the betterment of the masses of the dominant group."[22]

By the midthirties, E. Franklin Frazier had joined Harris and Bunche at Howard, and his influence is evident. In his 1936 booklet *A World View of Race*, Bunche exhibited a perspective on race decidedly different from that shown in his Howard lectures. Race, he said, first appeared in the English language in the sixteenth century and had become an effective instrument of national politics. However, existing racial divisions are arbitrary, subjective, and devoid of scientific meaning. Thus, according to Bunche, all existing human groups are of definitely mixed origin.[23]

Bunche contended that although much conflict was labeled as racial, its real causes are social, political, and economic. Racial attitudes are primarily social inheritances based on stereotypes. Like Frazier, Bunche saw racial prejudice and conflict existing as long as easily identified groups are forced into economic competition. Once society guarantees economic security to all peoples, the chief source of group conflict will be removed. Bunche implied that race war might be averted by transforming it into class war:

> If the oppressed racial groups, as a result of desperation and increasing understanding, should be attracted by the principles of equality and humanitarian-

ism advocated by the Soviet Union (and it is both logical and likely that they will) then racial conflict will become intensified. In such case, however, racial conflict will be more directly identified with class conflict, and the oppressed racial groups may win the support of oppressed, though previously preju-diced, working-class groups within the dominant population.[24]

Drawing on his dissertation, Bunche cited Africa as imperialism's greatest and most characteristic expression. He condemned the "extreme egoism" of British and French culture as expressed in their colonial policies, yet he saw West Africans as culturally in a transition stage between primitivism and civ-ilization.[25] He ended the section on Africa by comparing Lord Lugard's views on "equality in things spiritual" but "agreed divergence in the physical and material" to Booker T. Washington's famous "separate as the fingers of the hand" analogy and the familiar legal fiction of "separate but equal rights."[26]

In the last chapter of *A World View of Race*, Bunche asks, "Is the plight of the Negro the plight of a 'race'?" He contended that the policies of Wash-ington, Garvey, Kelly Miller, and others represented a plea for conciliation with the White moneyed class and at least a tacit acceptance of group seg-regation. "Dr. Du Bois," said Bunche, "has differed from these gentlemen chiefly in the militancy of his tone in his insistent demand for fair and con-stitutional treatment of the Negro as a *race*." However, Du Bois's attack was based on Washington's retreat from civil and political equality and not on Washington's economic philosophy or his misleading racialism. According to Bunche, "[R]ace to Du Bois, to Douglas, Booker T. Washington and Gar-vey, remains more important than class—despite the evident conflicts and contradictions."[27] On the positive side, "[T]he depression, ably abetted by the policies of the New Deal, has made the American population white and black, increasingly class-conscious."[28]

The same year that *A World View of Race* appeared, Bunche published two articles sharply critical of the status quo. The first was perhaps the best cri-tique of early New Deal social planning and its impact on Blacks. Bunche contended that the New Deal represented "merely an effort to refurbish the old individualistic—capitalistic system and to entrust it again with the eco-nomic destinies and welfare of the American people."[29] "Relatively few Negro workers were even theoretically affected by the labor provisions of Nation Recovery Administration," stated Bunche, "and the Agricultural Ad-justment Act deprived Negro tenants of . . . benefit from the crop reduction program."[30] In short, the New Deal was a program to benefit the middle-class, which barely existed in the Black community.

The second article in this very productive year asks the question whether separate schools for Blacks raise any separate educational problem in terms of course content. In the second article, which spoke of many of the issues that would arise after the Supreme Court's *Brown* decision, Bunche writes:

> The fact is that under our present system it is impossible to achieve educational equality for all members of any group in the society. Public schools for example, are supported by taxation. The revenue derived from taxation will depend largely upon the relative prosperity of the propertied interests in the particular locality. Since wealth is unequally distributed in the country, the present glaring inequalities in the distribution of funds for the support of education will persist even for "White Education." The basic question for all schools is not one of copying the "white man's education," but one of developing a system of education which will afford both white and black students a sound basis for understanding the society in which they live and for attacking the problems confronting them. White as well as Negro schools are woefully deficient in this respect.[31]

For Bunche, the culture of capitalism controlled Negro education as well as White education, and although Negro schools could be much more progressive than at present they would never be permitted to reconfigure the social order.[32]

If anything, Frazier was more critical of the romanticism of "race men" like Du Bois than were Harris and Bunche. In "The Du Bois Program in the Present Crisis," Frazier not only joined Harris in attacking the legitimacy of Du Bois's conversion to Marxism, but went on to state that Du Bois remained the "genteel" aristocrat who had no real conception or "sympathetic understanding" of the plight of the Black proletariat. As for Du Bois's ideal Black society, Frazier gratuitously added that "nothing would be more unendurable for him than to live within a Black Ghetto or within a black nation—unless perhaps he were king, and then he probably would attempt to unite the whites and blacks through marriage of royal families."[33] Like Harris and Bunche, Frazier was concerned that Du Bois's program would split Black workers from White workers and create false hope among Blacks for their survival in a capitalistic system. Still, the bitterness of the attack is remarkable in that Frazier's early work on the family was much indebted to Du Bois's 1908 report on the Black family, and Du Bois had hired Frazier in the early 1920s to do fieldwork in the Deep South.[34]

Frazier had been reared as one of five children in a stable and race-conscious family in Baltimore. Although his father was a bank messenger, three of the sons became professional men. Franklin won a scholarship that permitted him to enroll at Howard, from which he graduated cum laude in

1916. He did not take any formal courses in sociology, even though Kelly Miller was offering them at Howard as early as 1903. He did read Gidding's *Principles of Sociology* at Howard and became a member of the Intercollegiate Socialist Society. He taught secondary school in Virginia and Baltimore during World War I and privately published a tract he wrote opposing the war entitled "God and War." In 1919, he won a scholarship for graduate study at Clark University in Worcester, Massachusetts, where he came under the influence of Professors Frank H. Hankins and G. Stanley Hall. He appreciated the objectivity of Hankins's statistical approach to sociology but disagreed with his racism. Both Hankins and Hall were a part of the mainstream of scientific racists who supported benevolent social reforms.[35]

After receiving his master's degree from Clark, Frazier became a research fellow at the New York School of Social Work and was influenced by the psychological work of Bernard Glueck. Frazier's 1921 study of Negro longshoremen in New York City broke new ground in looking at the effects of migration at work and at home. These Southern migrants, Frazier reported, experienced problems in their families and failed to understand the nature of union organization in industry. Frazier was attracted by the socialists of *The Messenger*, supported the first Pan-African Congress, and attended the second congress in 1921. The following year he spent in Denmark as a fellow of the American Scandinavian Foundation. Influenced by Washington's praise of Danish Folk Schools, he studied them and their role in the cooperative movement (by 1928 he had given up on cooperatives). Returning to the United States, Frazier became professor of sociology at Morehouse College and later helped set up and then direct the Atlanta School of Social Work. It is during this Atlanta period that Frazier began writing on the disorganization of the Negro family and on the Black middle-class. In 1927 he wrote:

> The first fact that makes the Negro family the subject of special sociological study is the incomplete assimilation of western culture by the Negro masses. Generally when two different cultures come into contact, each modifies the other. But in the case of the Negro in America it meant the total destruction of the African social heritage. Therefore, in the case of the family group the Negro has not introduced new patterns of behavior, but has failed to conform to patterns about him. The degree of conformity is determined by educational and economic factors as well as by social isolation.[36]

Among the businessmen of Durham, North Carolina, Frazier found more stable family lives and disciplined individuals than among the poor of Atlanta.

Another work of Frazier's during the Atlanta years demonstrated the influence of psychology on his work. In "The Pathology of Race Prejudice" he compared the mechanisms that operate in prejudiced behavior with those that characterize mental illness. Frazier boldly referred to the operation of projective mechanisms in White women who accuse Negro males of attempted rape. The response to this 1927 article was so emotional among Whites that Frazier's life was threatened and he was forced to leave Atlanta almost immediately after the article appeared.[37]

By the time Frazier moved to the University of Chicago for two years of graduate study, his research focus was firmly fixed. Nonetheless, he came under the influence of distinguished teachers and fellow graduate students, including Robert E. Park, Ellsworth Faris, Earnest W. Burgess, William F. Ogburn, George H. Mead, Louis Wirth, and Herbert Blumer. Frazier's dissertation, published in 1932 as *The Negro Family in Chicago*, was clearly reflective of the Chicago tradition of empirical study of one aspect of community life to illuminate larger aspects of social reality.[38]

Park, like Du Bois, was a transitional figure who often intermixed biology and sociology. As late as 1931, he was still attempting to provide a definitive statement on the issue of whether the superior achievement of mulattoes was due to their biological or cultural inheritance. Frazier disagreed with Park's contention that the two groups differed in temperament. In his writing on the Black family, Frazier accounted for the deviation of the great majority of Black families from the normative type of family behavior through environmental factors created by the experiences of slavery, emancipation, and urbanization. Older works on the Black family insisted that racial or cultural differences in Black families were African survivals. Using the recent anthropological work of Bronislaw Malinowski and Robert Briffault on the sexual behavior of primitive peoples, Frazier contended that there was no scientific basis for the belief that Blacks and other primitive peoples had strong sexual impulses that could not be controlled by custom.[39] In short, Frazier denies the possibility of African survivals in order to refute the biological claims that Black deviance from the middle-class family norm was due to the less-evolved status of the Black race. By charging that slavery and urbanization had left the poor rural peasant with a folk culture unable to cope with city life, Frazier's view eventually won out over the biological determinists but at the price of accepting conventional White standards of behavior.

For Frazier, Park's race-relations cycle of contact, conflict, and competition would more quickly lead to acculturation or even assimilation if the

Negro became an industrial worker receiving an adequate wage that would enable the father to assume his position as chief breadwinner at the head of a stable, conventional family. At this stage, Frazier did not see any role for a unique Black culture. In fact, his condemnation of the lifestyle behind the blues revealed more than a little of the capitalist ethos he condemned in others: "[T]he Negro has succeeded in adopting habits of living that have enabled him to survive in a civilization based upon laissez-faire and competition, it bespeaks a degree of success on taking on the folkways and mores of the white race."[40]

In the early sixties, Frazier would write that it was the responsibility of the Negro intellectual to produce a new self-image or new (positive) conception of the Negro. Moreover, he would contend that he had spent his entire career at Howard trying—in vain—to explain the difference between integration and assimilation to his students. The latter, he said, "leads to complete identification with the people and culture of the community in which the social heritages of different people become merged or fused."[41] The fault may have lain not entirely in the students. Having argued that slavery had destroyed the American Blacks' African heritage and urbanization had destroyed their folk traditions, his students were left with no foundation on which they could construct an alternative to assimilation.

Harris confirmed Bunche's preference for class analysis over race analysis; Frazier pushed him toward environmental explanations for Black behavior rather than cultural explanations. Bunche ranged across a greater number of issues than did his two colleagues, but all three gave primacy to class over race, thus breaking with the racial paradigm of the preceding generation of Black intellectuals. Yet one of their own colleagues at Howard could have provided a basis for a new paradigm had they chosen to incorporate his work.

A major intellectual leader of the Harlem Renaissance was philosopher Alain Locke; his *New Negro* had defined the intellectual parameters of the era. Locke believed that African Americans, as the closest American equivalent to a peasant class, were the defining influence in the creation of a genuinely American culture. Moreover, as a student of William James and Josiah Royce at Harvard, Locke had developed a cultural pluralism that challenged the "melting pot" idea as another form of absolutism. For Locke, the solution to the problems of community life was not to change minorities from the top down through cultural domination but, rather, to develop cultural tolerance and reciprocity from the bottom up.[42]

This early "multiculturalism" criticized the natural scientific and anthropological definitions of race as incomplete and overgeneralized. According to Locke "the best consensus of opinion . . . seems to be that race is a fact in the social and ethnic sense [and not] in the physical sense." From his perspective, culture sought to be inclusive, and race operated to exclude. Thus cultural assimilation and development, rather than a reinforcement of racial distinctiveness and separation, were the keys for ultimate aesthetic beauty and humanism.[43]

Locke insisted that the "New Negro Movement" of the 1920s had been much misunderstood as a racialist project. Instead, he preferred to compare it to the Irish Renaissance, which was a "revival of very admirable folk values" and "folk culture."[44] Locke constantly warned his students to avoid "racial isolationism" by continually moving beyond narrow racial boundaries toward cultural reciprocity and universality. In fact, he criticized his own teacher, William James, for not going far enough: "For the complete implementation of the pluralistic philosophy it is not sufficient merely to disestablish authoritarianism and its absolutes; a more positive and constructive development of pluralism can and should establish some effective mediating principles for situations of basic value divergence and conflict."[45] In today's terminology, Locke sought to move from the negative of desegregation to a more positive integration but not so far as assimilation. His views paralleled those of Du Bois in many ways.[46]

It seems that the antiauthoritarian, pluralistic pragmatism of Locke would have a lot to offer a young social scientist like Ralph Bunche. After all, Locke was a major figure on Howard's campus, influencing Bunche's close friends, like Sterling Brown, and even Bunche himself. Moreover, Locke had praised works uncovering the economic components of the race question, while Bunche had been attracted to philosophy professors at UCLA and Harvard.[47] Yet Bunche never adopted the immigrant analogue perhaps because he saw that ethnic and national factionalism had destroyed the unity of the Communist Party in the United States.[48]

As the second generation of Black scholars, the young men of the Howard School were eager to break with the biological conceptions of race that so influenced their predecessors. They were also eager to demonstrate that they were modern social scientists who relied on empirical evidence, quantitative methods, and rational thought. However, Harris and Frazier had a distinct advantage over Bunche. Marxian theory had given Harris a radical alternative to mainstream economics and a "scientific" way to view the race problem. Frazier was also able to draw on the new thinking of the Chicago school of sociology, which had moved away from Social Darwinism and "custom" to view racial conflict as a product of urban contact and economic competition. Unfortunately, for Bunche, political science as a discipline had little to say about race and no radical alternatives.

Donald Matthews stated that "[d]espite the fact that the Negro problem was the most important unresolved domestic problem confronting the nation, exactly six articles containing the word 'Negro' in their titles were published in the *American Political Science Review* between 1906 and 1963."[49] Another four articles included the word *race*, and three titles contained the term *civil rights*, making a grand total of thirteen articles on this issue out of a total of 2,601 other articles in the profession's leading journal.[50]

Seeking a broader approach to race than the parochial views of his discipline, Bunche retrained himself in cultural anthropology over a period of two years with the help of a grant from the Social Science Research Council.[51] New approaches to race problems included the Chicago school of sociology's, Donald Young's comparative analysis of minority groups; Howard Odum's regional sociology; Melville Herskovits's cultural anthropology; and the "caste and class" approach, including the work of John Dollard, Allison Davis, St. Clair Drake, Horace Cayton, and W. Lloyd Warner. Perhaps the most challenging new approach from Bunche's perspective was the "immigrant analogue." This approach would gradually evolve into an ethnic analogy in politics that suggested that African Americans shared an experience and a destiny similar to that of recently arrived ethnic immigrants. In fact, during a period of immigration restrictions, Blacks had moved in record numbers to the urban North, occupying the cultural and social space that twenty years earlier had been claimed by the immigrant. According to Charles S. Johnson of Fisk University, who like Frazier had been a student of Robert Park's, "both the theory and the machinery which has been developed for dealing with the immigrant are being transferred to the Negro."[52] For Johnson, the Harlem Renaissance provided evidence of the newfound sense of "group respect" that Jews, Poles, and other oppressed groups had acquired.

For Bunche, Frazier had confirmed that African Americans were unlike any other ethnic group. Their past had been obliterated. Moreover, as a rational social scientist, he refused to accept the irrationality of racial chauvinism—even for the sake of group respect. Even the inclusive cultural pluralism of Alain Locke was seen as a hindrance to the organization of groups around their "real" and "rational" class interests. Thus Bunche was more likely to favor a Deweyan melting pot, with science and technology fulfilling the community's aim. Locke viewed race as a socially defined reality;

Bunche saw it as a collection of discredited biological theories. This view led at least one writer to declare that "if Frazier wanted to see the end of the race in the future, Ralph Bunche often ignored its existence in the present."[53] Locke saw himself as a cultural leader, but the younger Howard scholars (including Howard's famous law students and professors) viewed themselves as social engineers. Old primordial ties must give way not to the "New Negro" but to the new "rational man," and not just in the Black American community but in Africa as well.

5

The New Africa

Here is one place in a troubled world where mistakes previously
committed may be corrected; where, indeed, a new and better civilization may be cultivated, through the deliberate application of
human intelligence and understanding.
— Ralph Bunche, "French Administration
in Togoland and Dahomey"

From what I know of colonial students in Britain and America, few
university professors have had a greater influence on their political
development than Professor Harold J. Laski of the London School of
Economics and Political Science and Professor Ralph J. Bunche, head
of Howard University Department of Political Science, although both
of these teachers are too modest to claim such a distinction.
— George Padmore, *Pan Africanism as Communism?*

When Howard president Mordecai Johnson commented sarcastically to his faculty that "Bunche is going all the way to Africa to find a
problem,"[1] it was easy to understand his frustration with his young assistant.
After all, it was 1932 and the Great Depression was hitting the Black community hard. Bunche and his social science colleagues at Howard had played
a leading role in documenting the impact of the economic collapse on
Blacks. T. Arnold Hill of the Urban League concluded that "[a]t no time in
the history of the Negro since slavery has his economic and social outlook
seemed so discouraging."[2] Thus at a time when the specter of mass starvation haunted Black America for the first time, Bunche turned his attention
toward Africa for the first time.

Actually, Bunche's first dissertation topic shows the influence of Du Bois
as well as his own interest in international organizations. In a letter to Dean
Davis at Howard in December 1930, Bunche indicated that his topic would
be "The League of Nations and the Suppression of Slavery."[3] Apparently

within a year, Bunche had changed his proposed topic to a study of the mixed races in Brazil that would contrast racial assimilation there with continued segregation in the United States. However, in a letter to Professor John Sly at the University of West Virginia in February 1931, Bunche stated he believed Edwin R. Embree, president of the Rosenwald Fund, would not approve a grant to study the Negro in Brazil. He was therefore leaning toward a suggestion made by Professor R. L. Buell: a comparative study of the protectorate and mandate systems in Dahomey and French Togoland.[4] In letter to his dissertation chair at Harvard, Professor Arthur Holcombe, Bunche indicated his unhappiness with Embree and the narrow topic of Blacks in West Virginia politics, which had apparently been suggested by the foundation president. Bunche said, "I am fully persuaded that the Negro of all scholars must first develop a broad international background if his contribution to the solution of our own domestic problems are to make much impress."[5] Holcombe had already indicated he would approve a study of either Brazil or West Africa.[6]

In any case, the Rosenwald Fund offered Bunche a $2000 fellowship to do a comparative study of the impact of French colonial administration of Togoland, a territory under a League of Nations mandate, and of Dahomey, an adjoining French colony. Holcombe urged him to accept the grant to "do the African study and hope for funds from independent sources [for] 'freer play' in the scientific pursuit of the truth [about the Negro] in Brazil."[7] Ten years later, in a letter to W. C. Haygood, Embree would deny having turned down Bunche's proposal to do a comparative study of race relations in Brazil and the United States. And many years later, in delivering the Edwin R. Embree Memorial Lecture at Dillard University, Bunche diplomatically thanked Embree for funding his work on colonialism.[8] Bunche accepted the grant and became one of only six Blacks to receive research grants from the Rosenwald Fund in the 1930s. More important, he set in motion a course of study that would direct his life for the next forty years.

Bunche requested a delay in his African trip until 1932 so that he could accept an appointment, with an increase in salary to $3500, as special assistant to Mordecai Johnson. The next year also marked the birth of his first child, Joan, who, he boasted to friends, "at the moment is my great achievement."[9]

The extra year gave the new father additional time to prepare for his sojourn. He wrote to a number of colleagues who had visited Africa, soliciting information on hygiene, medical care, and living arrangements. Professor H. A. Poindexter, an assistant professor of medicine at Howard, advised vaccinations against smallpox, typhoid, cholera, malaria, and yellow fever. He also gave Bunche a long list of dos and don'ts. Another colleague, Charles Johnson, offered Bunche his mosquito net, boots, a sun helmet, and a dinner jacket with cummerbund—a substitute for a tuxedo vest used in Africa for special occasions.[10]

These preparations for the physical side of the visit were complemented by several initiatives to facilitate his research. Bunche sought letters of recommendation to assure authorities in the United States and European colonial officials in France and Switzerland of the scholarly nature of his upcoming research. He was now an established figure in the Black intellectual elite; a Department of State official in 1932 described him as "one of the few American Negroes who has a scientific interest in international and inter-racial affairs," someone who "will make a real contribution to political sciences and to inter-racial understanding."[11] Other recommendations came from Professor Melville Herskovits of Northwestern University; Carter G. Woodson, editor of the *Journal of Negro History;* and NAACP head Walter White.

Sailing on the *Europa* for Paris in June 1932, Bunche was joined by a number of distinguished Black passengers, including poet Langston Hughes, who were on their way to the Soviet Union. There were also a number of American passengers with whom Bunche was less impressed, especially "a crude group of Georgetown fellows who are continually drunk."[12]

Once in Paris, Bunche began collecting information from the French Colonial and Mandates Office, but before a week was out he began asking Ruth to join him with baby Joan. In the meantime, he was the typical foreign sightseer, even taking in the races at Longchamps. The American thought French food didn't live up to its reputation and that the French people—although well dressed—were very ordinary in appearance. Bunche enjoyed the Black American intellectuals and artists he found in the city, including the legendary nightclub owner and singer Bricktop, who became a lifelong friend. On one visit to the Latin Quarter, Bunche came across a Communist rally protesting the Scottsboro case.

> Mrs. Wright, the mother of two of the Scottsboro boys, was on exhibition and gave what appeared to be a memorized and well-rehearsed version of the affair. I met her afterwards and found her to be exceedingly ignorant. She doesn't seem to know what it's all about. . . . [T]he French are excitable, wild, woolly.[13]

Although the Bunches were on a tight budget, Ruth and Joan were able to join him on July 22. After three months' work in Europe, Bunche departed alone for West Africa on November 5, leaving his family in Paris. Bunche spent most of his time in Africa in the offices of the colonial regime, but he greatly enjoyed his few excursions to the markets of Dakar and to the interior. His overall impression of colonial Africa was expressed in a letter to Robert Weaver written while he sat on the veranda of the Hotel de France in Lomé:

> This is a marvelous country and after seeing a bit of it and its people, one is apt to become more puzzled than ever as to what is to become of it, or even what should become of it. . . . One may suggest, but easier than all is to criticize—the problem being so grand and the men fiddling about it so small.[14]

Bunche returned from Dahomey via Accra, Monrovia, Freetown, and Dakar, rejoining his family in Paris in mid-January 1933. Altogether, he spent nine months in Europe and three in Africa.

Bunche was back at Howard for the spring semester of 1933. A second daughter, Jane, was born in May 1933. That summer was spent in Cambridge, trying to piece together the puzzle that was colonial Africa.

"The study herein recorded is stimulated by a deep interest in the development of subject peoples and the hopes which the future holds for them."[15] Thus Bunche began his four-hundred-plus-page dissertation with a statement of commitment to the people he was studying. The introductory remarks are soon followed by this chapter's first epigraph, which describes Africa as a place where "a new and better civilization" may be cultivated. In a few, short years, Bunche had moved from Chicago as a political laboratory to the entire continent of Africa. While repeatedly expressing his concern for the *African* and criticizing colonial powers for losing sight of their subjects in the rush for profits, Bunche sees Africans as a people to be led—perhaps more benevolently—but still led. This creates an ambivalence in his analysis of colonialism and its demise.

In setting up his analysis, Bunche says the basic problem is twofold in any of the colonies. First, what is "the immediate effect of the impact of a capitalistic, industrial civilization upon the primitive African," and second, "what are the specific objectives of the native policy and the native welfare measures applied by the colonizing power" (3). The use of the term *primitive*, although generally accepted by scholars at the time, is symbolic of Bunche's approach to the problem. He views Africa as an opportunity to cultivate "a new and better civilization" precisely because it is relatively undeveloped or virgin. Therefore, it needs an educated elite, including social engineers like himself, to guide it into the modern age. Bunche is extremely critical of the lack of vision on the part of the colonial administrators he has met. Accordingly, it is up to the international community to assist and to insist on the training of the African elites that will guide their countries to independence.

This social engineering approach gives Bunche's analysis of the impact of colonialism a much more "balanced" or "conservative" tone than the one he would adopt two years later in *A World View of Race*.

> It has been this brief but unsavory early history of Europe in Africa which has impelled some writers to indict the general effects of European policy as "almost wholly evil," and to regard the process in its entirety as one of fraud and robbery. In the light of present policies generally operative in the West African colonies and mandates however, such statements are undoubtedly rash and ill-advised. Neither can it be ignored that the recognition of this problem of developing a sound policy for the administration of culturally primitive native races is comparatively recent, and that the policy itself must be evolved through slow and careful experimentation. If there is assurance of sincerity of purpose, sympathetic approach, and intelligent application, great progress has been made and the future holds promise. (4)

Both the gradualism of the the policy as well as its sympathetic application are questioned in *A World View of Race*.

British Prime Minister Lloyd George and President Woodrow Wilson were given credit by Bunche for preventing the division of former German colonies as outright spoils of war after World War I. However, after an extensive examination of the French administration of Togoland under the League of Nations and the administration of the French colony of Dahomey, Bunche found little difference between the two. He did find, however, a major difference between French rule and British rule. The difference, said Bunche, revolved around the relatively new policy of preparing "Africans for membership in the community of the civilized world" (82). Both policies were being implemented while economic exploitation continued and control was being indefinitely prolonged.

According to Bunche, French colonial policy grew out of the early rigid doctrine of the Pact Coloniale, under which colonies existed solely for the benefit of the mother country. The policy evolved into a less severe form of assimilation that was also totally opposed to colonial autonomy. Assimilation, also called the "policy of the Latin races," was based on the notion that nothing in the native civilization was good. This meant, in the words of Napoleon, "wherever the flag is, there is France." More recently, stated Bunche, the French "have found it expedient to abandon their pretensions at wholesale assimilation in favor of the less ambitious, utilitarian, and decidedly more liberal policy of 'association'" (89). The new policy took into account native mores and customs and even maintained them when they furthered native development. Bunche attributed this progress toward liberalism to (1) the legacy of the French Revolution; (2) the quite genuine freedom of the French mentality from race prejudice in its vulgar forms; and (3) the influence of highly skillful and scientifically oriented French administrators and scholars (93–94).

The British were just as confident as the French that Africa needed their civilizing influence. They also believed in the superiority of their culture, "to such a great extent that they have never supposed that primitive peoples could ever become sufficiently elevated to absorb it," wrote Bunche (110). In fact, he saw much in the English racial attitude to remind him of the doctrine of accommodation advanced in some sections of the United States. He compared Lord Lugard's views with the "separate as the fingers" analogy of Washington.

> Here, then, is the true conception of the inter-relation of colour: complete uniformity in ideals, absolute equality in the paths of knowledge and culture, equal opportunity for those who strive, equal admiration for those who achieve; in matters of social and racial a separate path, each pursuing his own inherited traditions, preserving his own race-purity and race pride; equality in things spiritual, agreed divergence in the physical and material. (116)

The practical result of these views moved away from any type of assimilation or even association and toward a policy of "indirect rule." Under British colonial policy many native institutions and traditional rulers were preserved to assist in colony governance. Bunche thought the French undoubtedly went too far toward the rapid disintegration of African culture and that the British went too far toward the preservation of native culture, to the detriment of Africa's development.

Change was the major theme of the Bunche dissertation. The African is in a transitional state somewhere between the "primitive" and the "civilized." Bunche emphasized that the problems encountered in modernizing are not so different from those encountered in the Western world. He seemed to agree with A. Victor Murray that the terms *peasant, workman,* and *native* are almost interchangeable and that the race problem is simply one aspect of the class problem (128–29). Yet the examples Bunche offered of this transitional stage were hardly ones most of his readers could identify with.

> In Cotonou, Porto Novo, Lomé, Lagos or Accra will be found many natives who wear fine European clothing, speak polished French or English, con-

struct beautiful homes and send their children to school. Yet they may worship fetishes, marry several wives, eat without cutlery and sleep on the floors
in bare bedrooms despite elaborately furnished parlors. They will scorn the
authority of chiefs whose education is often inferior to their own. Their conception of property is private, not communal. This type is increasing. (144–45)

Bunche's training in political science had not fully prepared him to interpret
this mix of traditional and modern culture. Why did some customs persist
and others fall into disuse? Like Du Bois's famous characterization of the
African American identity, these contemporary Africans were being torn
asunder by a "twoness." By the end of the decade, Bunche had retrained
himself in anthropology in an attempt to address some of these issues.

In his dissertation the young Black scholar saw education as the key to
modernization. The growing Black bourgeoisie gathering in African capitals
was comparable to what had happened during the urbanization of England
and France some one hundred years earlier. Yet the role of the educated
African elite in these urban centers was different and represented the chief
vehicle of African nationalism and independence. Bunche was prophetic in
seeing this elite as the basis for a nationalism that rose above tribal identities.
He also saw that with no colonial plans to transfer power to native governments, this elite constituted a potentially destabilizing and even revolutionary force. At the same time he worried that Western education also had a de-
Africanizing effect on elites. In other words, he confronted the African
equivalent of Du Bois's talented tenth in the "assimilated" French Africans,
where the problem was most acute:

> These evolved natives often tend to lose contact with their people and un-
> derstanding interest in their needs. The French Diagnes and Candaces are
> often more loyal to French than native demands. It is a matter of serious doubt
> that the celebrated Senegalese Diagne now has much honest concern with
> things African extending beyond the African bric-a-brac of his elaborate and
> ornate Paris apartment. Already many of his native constituents have hurled
> the epithet "traitor" at him. For the French system to actually succeed it is
> necessary for the advanced groups of the native population to become truly
> representative of the masses. (131)[16]

Over the next few years, Bunche would abandon any hope that the French
or any other system of colonial rule could succeed.

When Bunche's dissertation was accepted by his committee (Arthur Holcombe, Rupert Emerson, and George Benson) in February 1934, it won him
the first doctorate ever awarded to an African American in political science

in the United States. In addition, he won the $200 Toppan Prize for the best dissertation written at Harvard in the field of government that year. Surprisingly, Bunche did not follow up on Holcombe's suggestion to seek its publication. Bunche complained that the writing had been a terrible grind: every word had to be carefully weighed and every statement had to be double-checked. It was during that time of strain that he had begun chain-smoking.

Most important, he was dissatisfied with the quality of the background materials he had collected in Paris, labeling them "inadequate" and "inaccurate." Bunche believed that the annual reports France submitted to the League of Nations Mandates Commission tended to paint a too-rosy picture of the actual conditions; he recommended that visits of inspection and the right of natives to petition the League were a necessary corrective. Nathan Huggins speculates that it was the top-down nature of his archival research that prevented Bunche from addressing colonialism from the African perspective rather than that of the colonial administrators.[17] Bunche was simply unwilling to exploit his research without fully presenting the African viewpoint.

The Howard professor did publish an article in the *Journal of Negro Education* drawn directly from his dissertation research. Entitled "French Educational Policy in Togo and Dahomey," it underscores his inclination toward social engineering. He expressed three basic concerns: (1) that the European education provided to Africans allow for the teaching of native customs, history, and languages; (2) that such an "adapted" education not be based on a stereotyped view of the African, e.g., Washington's Tuskegee; and (3) that the knowledge gained be used to advance the independence of the Africans rather than the interests of the colonial power.[18]

Freed from his dissertation labors, Bunche threw himself into his work at Howard and in the larger Black community with the same gusto he had brought to earlier challenges. It helped that from 1934 to 1937, he limited his travel to relatively brief trips rather than the long, extended absences from home that characterized his adult life before and after the midthirties. Thus, at the height of his radicalism, Bunche emerged as a major force on the Howard campus.

Although Bunche did not publish his dissertation, he did produce a remarkable stream of academic and popular publications during this brief period in addition to "French Educational Policy in Togoland and Dahomey": "A Critical Analysis of the Tactics and Programs of Minority Groups" (1935); "Triumph? Or Fiasco?" (a critique of the First National Negro Congress),

"Education in Black and White," "French and British Imperialism in West Africa," and *A World View of Race* (all in 1936); and numerous book reviews, speeches, and academic papers.

In April 1935, Bunche delivered "Modern Policies of Imperialistic Administration of Subject Peoples" at the Howard conference "Problems, Programs and Philosophies of Minority Groups." The paper covers many of the themes found in his dissertation but with a noticeably harder edge:

> Just as the capitalist state in its internal affairs maintains a legal and constitutional system designed to protect absentee ownership and safeguard the property rights which make the capitalist supreme, just so, in the realm of external affairs, the state's authority, by the very nature of his relationship to it, must be employed to impose that supremacy over other peoples. . . . [O]nly therefore, when there occurs a transformation of capitalist society can there be any possibility of the development of an international order and community which will promise the subject peoples of the world genuine surcease from the burdens of imperialistic domination.[19]

At the end of the year, a highly critical talk by Bunche before the Capital Pleasure Club was entitled "Imperialism in West Africa."[20]

From 1936 to 1942, the Associates in Negro Folk Education, funded by the Carnegie Corporation and later by the Rosenwald Fund, issued nine works called the Bronze Booklet series. The overall editor was Alain Locke, who also wrote three of the booklets on art and music. Two were by Sterling Brown on fiction, poetry, and drama, one each by Eric Williams (the Caribbean), Ira De A. Reid (education), and T. Arnold Hill of the National Urban League (economics, replacing one by Du Bois that had not been accepted), and one by Bunche.[21] Although Bunche later apologized for the haste with which his contribution to the series had been written (within a week) and seemed embarrassed by its militancy, it is an accurate reflection of his views at the time and their most extensive exposition.

Throughout *A World View of Race*, one senses a tension between Bunche the idealist or leftist and Bunche the pragmatist or social scientist.[22] He no longer calls those who see the unsavory early history of Europe in Africa as "almost wholly evil" rash and ill-advised. In fact, he says, "Africa is imperialism's greatest and most characteristic expression." However, he adds, "There have been significant changes in the views of peoples of the Western World toward the African since Kipling's lyrical description of him as 'half devil and half child,' and since the Frenchman, Jules Ferry, first explained the 'duty' of the 'superior' races."[23] The major factor in this revised

Western perspective on the African is the modern anthropologists, geneti-
cists, and unbiased social scientists who attempt to interpret the African in
"scientific" terms—who "draw a distinction between lack of intellect and
ignorance" and "emphasize the significance of environment," which has re-
tarded African progress (45).

The importance of social science is highlighted in two chapters of *A
World View of Race* that cover material not found in the dissertation. In the
opening chapter, "What Is Race?" Bunche states that it is impossible to understand world politics without understanding race, which "has become an
effective instrument of national politics" (3). After a brief examination of
racial theories, Bunche concludes, *"The plain fact is that the selection of any specific physical trait or set of traits as a basis for identifying racial groups is a purely arbitrary process"*; therefore *"existing racial divisions are arbitrary, subjective and devoid of scientific meaning"* (7). Above all else, he stresses the role of environment and culture in establishing "racial" traits, and the capacity of social
intervention to change such characteristics.

In the concluding chapter, "Race in the United States," Bunche cites
slavery, colonialism, and the persecution of other racial groups as stemming
from economic competition. His comparison of U.S. racial practices with
those of other countries attributes the rigid racial lines to the predominantly
poor population of Whites who fear economic competition from the large
Black population. The Negro class that developed after Emancipation "is
chiefly a hope, a prayer and a caricature" (82). Thus, says Bunche, the development of Negro business is impossible at this late stage in the country's industrial process. "Class," he declares, "will some day supplant race in world
affairs . . . then [race war] will be merely a side-show to the gigantic class war
which will be waged in the big tent we call the world" (96).

This rather ominous and orthodox Marxist ending to *A World View of
Race* tends to obscure a number of significant and controversial intellectual
points Bunche introduces in the work. First, the dissertation has been trans-
formed; it now includes a comparison of U.S. race relations with those in
West Africa and references to other "racial minorities," making it one of the
early comparative studies of race relations in the United States. Second, by
locating the source of slavery in economic competition rather than racial hierarchy, which Bunche says developed to rationalize slavery, he puts forth a
view that gained in popularity some years after the book. Eric Williams, who
was a student of Bunche's at Howard and later became prime minister of
Trinidad and Tobago, published the classic economic analysis of slavery in
1944.[24] Moreover, Bunche's views linking race relations in the United States

to various stages of economic development resemble the framework put forth by William J. Wilson in *The Declining Significance of Race*. Of course, Bunche's perspectives on the Black bourgeoisie are borrowed from Abram Harris and presage those of E. Franklin Frazier. Third, the Howard political scientist goes beyond the traditional view that explained Black lynchings in the South as a product of irrational sexual politics to target the practice as a part of the overall economic domination of the South. Finally, Bunche's emphasis on the arbitrariness of racial classifications and the role of the environment in shaping racial characteristics reflect the cutting edge of anthropological research at that time. In fact, Bunche became so interested in the then-current work in anthropology that he decided to retrain himself in the techniques of anthropological fieldwork.

The "radical pessimism" Bunche introduced in *A World View of Race* was a prototype for a later generation of Africanists who maintained that the solution to Africa's plight lay in the destruction of capitalism. However, the pessimism also owed something to Bunche's unhappiness at Howard. While extremely productive and busy sponsoring conferences like "The Crisis of Modern Imperialism in Africa and the Far East" in May 1936, he complained frequently about the burdens of teaching and administration. This led him to propose a research project on the impact of colonial rule and Western culture on Africans from their perspective to Donald Young at the Social Science Research Council (SSRC). Young indicated that the proposal stood a better chance if Bunche were to undergo training in the field methods cultural anthropologists were using to study culture contact. Bunche readily agreed because the new acculturation studies provided a method by which to examine colonialism from the eyes of the African—something he had not been able to do in his dissertation. The reformulated proposal won him an unusual two-year grant from the SSRC. Bunche became the only African American funded by a private foundation to make a research trip to Africa until the 1950s.

Young suggested a program for Bunche that included study with three leading anthropologists: Melville Herskovits at Northwestern University; Bronislaw Malinowski at the London School of Economics; and Isaac Schapera at the University of Cape Town in South Africa. In addition, Young recommended a visit to Holland to study Dutch colonial policy, six months of field research in East Africa, and a trip to the Dutch colony of Indonesia. Young's selection of Herskovits was most interesting. As a White expert on race relations, Herskovits was one of the "objective" scholars private foundations relied on to endorse African American scholars conducting research on Blacks anywhere in the world. Bunche had faced "gatekeepers" at the Rosenwald Fund and would face them again in his work with Myrdal on the Carnegie Study.

Bunche did not see his relationship with Herskovits as one of patron and client. Herskovits had taught at Howard in 1925, and Abram Harris had introduced him to Bunche in 1932. Herskovits saw Howard scholars like Harris, Bunche, and Brown as "the only group known to me among the Negroes able to approach the tragedy of the racial situation in this country with the objectivity that comes from seeing it as the result of the play of historic forces rather than as an expression of personal spite and a desire to hold down a minority people."[25] Accurate or not, this is high gatekeeper praise indeed, given the political views of all three in the midthirties.

The SSRC grant for two years of study abroad was not applauded by Ruth Bunche, who became practically distraught over her husband's plans. He was already away for the summer, managing a race relations institute at Swarthmore when she wrote to him:

> Ralph the next two years seem like a nightmare to me. I hate to think of it. It keeps me awake at night. I want you to have everything good and all the success in the world, but I do hate to see our family break up. It seems like a death to me.[26]

Ruth was still teaching first grade during the day and acting as mother and father for two young girls during the evening. Bunche continued to express his love for her and the children, and to lament the torment of separation, but pressed on with his research program. He went to Northwestern University and the University of Chicago to work under Herskovits in the fall of 1936 and January of 1937. He did encourage Ruth and the girls to join him, however, when he moved to London for the first leg of his overseas journey, and the family would travel there together.

Herskovits regarded himself as a mentor to young Black scholars, but it was not initially clear that he and Bunche would become friends. Herskovits was best known for his controversial assertions that there were many African cultural survivals in African American culture. Bunche had already determined, with the help of Frazier, that there were practically no such survivals. Despite these differences, both Herskovits and Bunche accepted the view that the behavior of members of any society are determined by cultural influences and not any innate characteristics of race or human nature. In the paper "Psychological Types in Cultures," written at Northwestern, Bunche criticized Ruth Benedicts's *Patterns of Culture* (1934) and Margaret Mead's

Sex and Temperament (1935) for lack of statistical rigor.[27] In a later review of Herskovits's *Dahomey*, he contends that the anthropologist was so concerned about reconstructing precolonial Dahomey that he overlooked the distortions introduced by colonialism. The contention illustrates a basic problem Bunche seems to have with ethnological research: its difficulty in moving from case studies to empirically valid generalizations.

A friendship did develop between Herskovits and Bunche as the latter adjusted to life at Northwestern. Herskovits entertained visitors like Ashley Montague and Katherine Dunham, and there was much socializing. Occasionally, however, peeks at Herskovits's paternalism emerge in Bunche's diary. For example, Bunche comments that after his lecture "The Mandate Togoland" before the Northwestern University International Relations Study Group, "Mel and Frances [Mrs. Herskovits] drooled all over me— Frances stating that she and Mel would have to make me a 'big man' when I returned—e.g., pres. of H.U."[28] Also, Bunche remarks that when he had lunch at the faculty club with some colleagues, Herskovits came to their table "red and shame-faced after his meal was finished"; Herskovits had never invited Bunche to dine with him at the faculty club.

On another occasion, Bunche and two colleagues had gone to A. R. Radcliffe-Brown's Chicago apartment, where they were joined by Lloyd Warner. Later Radcliffe-Brown, Bunche, and George Willard went to a French restaurant for dinner, and Bunche found the noted anthropologist "interesting, scholarly, vain."[29]

On February 5, 1937, the Bunches sailed for England on the *Berengaria*. While on board, Bunche met Ellen Wilkinson, a Socialist member of the British Parliament, who later introduced him to many of her acquaintances. The Bunches found agreeable lodgings at Earl's Court. For the coronation of George VI Bunche got prime seats near Buckingham Palace, later complaining that the whole affair was "a cheeky flaunting of excess before these poor millions."[30] Bunche found English workers to be in poor physical shape, and English racism to be far more subtle than its American cousin.

Bunche soon found friends among the Labour Party, the left-wing intelligentsia, and especially among the African, Caribbean, and African American scholars and students then in England. The Bunches spent a good deal of time socializing with Paul and Essie (Eslanda) Robeson, Arthur Davis, Eric Williams, George Padmore, and Jomo Kenyatta. (Padmore and Williams had been students of Bunche's at Howard.) A group of Africans met frequently at the Bunches' and included, in addition to Kenyatta and Peter Koinange from Kenya, Addo, Kessie, Afurata, and de Graaf Johnson from the

Gold Coast; and Myanza and Akiki Nyabongo from Uganda. Others Bunche met while in London included Ras Makonnen, C. L. R. James (who was working on *Black Jacobeans*), Arthur Lewis, Lorenzo Turner, and I. T. A. Wallace-Johnson.

The Robesons introduced Bunche to Max Yergan, who had recently left South Africa after serving fifteen years as a YMCA missionary gradually grown more radical. Of course, it was the Robesons who made the greatest impression on the Bunches. Paul was at the height of his fame and was filming *Jericho* at Pinewood Studios outside London.

> Yergan, Essie, Young Paul & I then got in their Daimler & rode out to the Denham [Pinewood] Studios (40 miles out of city) to see Paul at work on his new picture *Jericho*. Had drinks & a talk with Paul in his beautifully appointed dressing suite—all very modern & new. Paul is *anti-white & all out for the U.S.S.R.* [Bunche does not comment on the contradiction]. He was very cordial tho they are working him hard. Had long talk with Yergan re African Com., & a discussion re self-determination policy & C.P. Max seems to be very C.P. Entertained young Paul on way back with discourse on prize-fights & fighters.[31]

Robeson invited the Bunche family on a tour of the studio, and on another occasion sang Joan and Jane to sleep after a family dinner. He was difficult not to like, even if Bunche found him "anti-white and all out for USSR."[32] Essie Robeson took Ruth on shopping trips and lent Ralph her movie camera to take to Africa. Essie had spent three weeks in South Africa in mid-1936 while an anthropology student at the London School of Economics. A decade later, she published an account of South Africa and her fieldwork in Uganda.

Jomo Kenyatta was just beginning to make a name for himself. Bunche spent much time with him, in part because Kenyatta agreed to teach Bunche Swahili at 12s 6d per lesson. Bunche also learned a good deal about Kenyan social customs from Kenyatta and would later publish an article on the subject. In addition, he found Kenyatta to be anti-White and an intense racial chauvinist rather than a Marxist.[33] Kenyatta was also a student in Malinowski's seminar and was sometimes the object of Malinowski's humor because of Kenyatta's poor English. On one occasion Bunche was asked by Malinowski to mediate a dispute between Kenyatta and an English student over the rights to some research materials they had both worked on together. Bunche recalled what happened when he and Kenyatta approached the English student outside Malinowski's office.

Latter in half [o]f Malinowski's office and walked up to Kenyatta, called him a shit & threatened him if he should say anything to Malinowski. Tried to keep Kenyatta out [o]f office when he went in. I came on in; Malinowski scared. G. [the English student] called Kenyatta a swindler & unable to substantiate it had to withdraw the statement. They finally agreed that the material should be turned over to Malinowski & nothing should be written on the subject without due acknowledgement. G. stuck close to Mal. when Kenyatta & I left.[34]

The diary suggests that a mutual girlfriend might have been at the root of the dispute.

Kenyatta was part of a core group of Pan Africanists and nationalists with whom Bunche spent time in London. On meeting Wallace Johnson—who was out of jail on bond pending appeal of a case concerning an article attacking the white man's god that he had written for a Gold Coast paper—and C. L. R. James from Trinidad at the Padmore home, he reports on his impressions and discussions with the group.

Johnson is a vigorous, vociferous, voluble fellow, very much self-confident even to point of bragging no little, but has apparently done some good organizational work among youth of Gold Coast. He is at least middle left-wing. From Sierre Leone. Has been kicked out of Nigeria. Has been to U.S.S.R. I think (like Kenyatta) up here to start a W. Africa Bureau & Journal to further nationalist movement of Gold Coast. He says their organizational motto is "Liberty or Death." The arrests have greatly stimulated membership. Also met James, tall, nervous brillant young W. Indian writer. His book "World Revolutions" is just out. Trotskyist, now working on a study of Negro revolutions centered around Toussaint L'Ouverture. Graaf (Ras Makonen) & Nyabongo also at Padmore's—they are in the *lackey* role. Discussion centered on Africa & raised question whether Africa should be a *republic* basis of a U.S. of A. or a U.S. of Europe. I suggested that U.S.S.R. would be a better model—since African culture coustomes [*sic*] etc. were more significant & *deep*-seated than they seemed to believe. All are agreed that (1) African liberation must depend on socialization thru revolution of Europe & (2) socialization of Africa. They lapped up my denouncement of the C.P.'s doctrine of self-determination for black belt.[35]

Bunche got along well with this group of expatriate radicals. He opposed their Pan Africanism, which he saw as a distraction from the primary goal of changing the structure of the imperialist nations themselves. What is remarkable in this group of Africans is his defense of African customs, contending that a U.S.S.R.-type system would protect them. This perspective might have been influenced by his new anthropological training and/or his conversations with Paul Robeson.

London was alive with rallies and concerts focusing on the Spanish Civil War and the Italian invasion of Ethiopia. Yergan offered to arrange for Bunche to go to Spain (strongly opposed by Ruth), and he actually attempted to get an Italian visa to go to Ethiopia. Bunche noted sarcastically in his diary that a visit to Madame Tussaud's Wax Museum revealed only one Black—Haile Selassie—who was placed in a section with Hitler, Mussolini, and Stalin.[36] He sometimes worried that his attendance at rallies and his radical contacts might prevent him from gaining access to Africa for his research, and indeed British intelligence kept track of him because of the company he was keeping. On one occasion, Bunche went to a meeting protesting Addis Ababa massacres at which E. W. Gallagher (a Communist M.P.), Sir Stafford Cripps, and Eric Williams spoke. Padmore was its chair. According to Bunche, "I contributed 6s to collection and Padmore read out my name—to my chagrin, since gov't. detectives were assuredly on hand."[37]

Despite this anxiety, Bunche went to fervent Socialist rallies addressed by Clement Attlee and Norman Thomas where clenched fists were raised and the "Internationale" was sung. He was entertained by left-wing activists C. R. Buxton, Ethel Mannin, Lady Rhondda, and Julius Lewin, who introduced him to Harold Laski. Professor Hugh Jones of Oxford invited Bunche for a weekend visit where he met Greek historian J. L. Myres, colonial expert Margery Perham, and historians Sir Alfred Zimmern, A. L. Rowse, G. D. H. Cole, and Sir Arthur Salter, who had devised the convoy system in World War I. Ellen Wilkinson, the Bunche's shipboard acquaintance, took them to parties and to debates in the House of Commons.[38]

Bunche's early education on colonial systems of racial classification began when he applied for a required landing permit by filling out a South African immigration form. The form asked that Bunche declare whether he was "European, Hebraic, Oriental or African." Bunche wrote in "American." Given his attitude, it was fortunate that Malcolm McDonald at the Dominions Office, son of former prime minister Ramsay McDonald, helped smooth the way with the South African authorities. Lord de La Warr at the Colonial Office was equally helpful, giving Bunche complete access to the Colonial Office library and writing in Bunche's behalf to the governors of each African colony Bunche was scheduled to visit. Knowing that South African officials were reluctant to admit Black Americans, Bunche had come to London heavily armed with letters of recommendation from U.S. government officials and scholars. Charles Loram, a leading South African educator teaching at Yale, wrote, "I realize that [it] is not wise to encourage all and sundry of the American Negroes to visit South Africa, but I have every reason to believe that Dr. Bunche will . . . refrain from saying or doing anything which might make the position of the South African Government in any way more difficult than it is."[39] However, Loram's letter was not used because he had developed a "liberal" reputation with the South African government. For his part, Bunche agreed not to address any meetings in South Africa or do anything other than collect research materials.

On July 27, 1937, the Bunche family sailed to the Netherlands, where Bunche interviewed some Dutch colonial officials. They spent his thirty-fourth birthday in Brussels and then three weeks in Paris, where they visited the World Exhibition and saw all the sights, including Josephine Baker at the Folies-Bergère. Finally, it was time for Ruth and the girls to sail home on the *Queen Mary*. At Cherbourg, Bunche was on the dock an hour waving to his young girls as they shouted, "Goodbye, Daddy."[40]

When Bunche left on the boat train for South Africa, Jomo Kenyatta, Peter Koinange, and Julius Lewin were at Victoria Station to see him off. Lewin had helped him avoid any conflict over integrated cabins by alerting the travel agents to the fact that their "American" passenger was a Negro; they discreetly reassigned him to a better cabin with a ship-line employee. However, it was impossible for Bunche to avoid the derogatory racial terms some of the White South African passengers used in their normal conversations. Curbing his usually blunt response to such terms, he noted in his diary, "A nigger is a nigger even in the middle of the ocean."[41] His usual competitive nature did surface during Ping Pong matches, in which he bested everyone on board except the national table tennis champion of Kenya. Despite his skill, he was not asked by the purser to join the tournament until his playing partners complained. Actually, Bunche preferred the company of the passengers in steerage and spent a good deal of time with them.

After paying a £5 deposit to immigration authorities to ensure his "good behavior," Bunche was permitted to disembark at Cape Town. He stayed with the "colored" family of Dr. A. H. Gool, his wife Zairunnaissa (Cissie), and their daughters Marcina and Shaheen. Bunche thought the Gool children were beautiful and later helped bring Marcina to school in the United States. Cissie Gool's father, Dr. Abdullah Abdurahman, had been a leader in the fight for the rights of the Indian and "colored" population and the first president of the National Liberation League. Cissie herself was elected to the Cape Town City Council in 1938 and eventually joined the Communist Party. In general, however, Bunche observed a real class division among the

Indians, with the commercial class exploiting both Indian workers and natives.[42]

In his research proposal, Bunche had stated that he would be studying the political, economic, and social status of the non-European groups in South Africa. Professor Isaac Schapera at the University of Cape Town was his adviser while in South Africa. Bunche attended his seminar on "African Social Organization" and had a high opinion of him. Schapera called himself a comparative sociologist rather than an anthropologist. He didn't devote himself to aspects of native culture in which he had no interest, such as music. He also preferred Radcliffe-Brown to Malinowski, views that Bunche found "very realistic."[43]

During October, Bunche visited Lesotho, Alice, Thaba' Nchu, Bloemfontein, Mafeking, Johannesburg, Benoni, Pretoria, and Durban. Traveling was an adventure for Bunche because his status as a "colored" person who was also a distinguished visitor did not fit neatly into South Africa's rigid color hierarchy. On trains he often had a first-class compartment to himself, and he at first thought the reservation sticker "Col. Male" meant he would be riding with a military man!

On the road, he broke with the pattern of foreigners who generally stayed with White liberals; he preferred to stay in Black homes, although he found officials regarded White liberals as acceptable escorts for "outsiders" entering the Black community. Bunche attempted to assume the role of detached chronicler but soon discovered that he was a subject of much curiosity and interest to Black South Africans. Despite promises to the South African government that he would avoid public speaking, he found it impossible to refuse the demands of Black audiences that he make extemporaneous remarks. Ironically, given his distaste for racial chauvinism, his remarks tended to emphasize race pride and the notable accomplishments of African Americans despite discriminatory barriers. When this theme failed to evoke a response at Fort Hare College, Bunche concluded that his listeners looked negatively on their past in much the same way as many African Americans viewed their slave experience. Indeed, at the same Fort Hare meeting, Professor D. D. T. Jabavu held that Africans should emulate African Americans precisely because they had discarded their African cultural traditions and thus were more open to new ideas, trends, and leaders (a position Bunche might have agreed with in a different context).

Perhaps the best example of Bunche's failure to remain "above the fray" comes from his attendance at the Silver Jubilee of the African National Congress (ANC). On the second night the gathered delegates split sharply over the issue of the report on the three-sided factional dispute in the Cape Province. Bunche said that chaos reigned for one half hour: "Finally ... I decided to try my hand at restoring order and succeeded, by pointing out that white men pass oppressive laws in orderly bodies and that black men can only overcome these by themselves conducting orderly and calm bodies."[44] In general, Bunche found fault with the ANC for being more intent on celebrating its silver jubilee than in addressing serious issues. He was as critical of the ANC's dependence on White outsiders as he had been of African Americans' reliance on liberal White support. Bunche directed his sharpest remarks at the inaugural meeting of the Native Representative Council (NRC). It is a rare behind-the-scenes account of an NRC proceeding and such eminent African leaders as John Dube, R. V. Selope-Thema, Richard Godlo, T. M. Mapikela, A. M. Jabavu, and C. K. Sakwe. It also affords a rare glimpse into Bunche's personal views, which are impossible to ascertain once he became a UN official. For example:

> [The White] Chairman asked if any other member of the Council wished to speak. One of the Councilors arose (speaking in Sesuto) to second suggestion of Dube's. Thanked speakers for their speeches; assured them that the Councillors, representatives of entire native population of South Africa, will always be loyal to the government. Apologized for Vereeniging—said it was not representative of native attitudes. Expressed shame for it. Said he didn't know how natives would wipe it off, but they could only hope it would not happen again. He appealed that Vereeniging should be forgotten by Europeans and natives alike. (This ass-licking speech was made by Chief Poto).[45]

The 1937 meetings were a low point for Black political organizations in South Africa. Bunche's criticism of the ANC's inertia and reliance on Whites began to be shared by others, especially younger members. In 1940, the ANC elected Dr. Xuma president, and he brought in a younger generation of activists that included Nelson Mandela, Oliver Tambo, and Walter Sisulu.

Without his family at Christmas and on New Year's Day 1938, a lonely Bunche boarded the SS *Tasman* at Durban, bound for Mombasa. The trip was dull, giving him time for a much-needed rest. One exciting and near-tragic event occurred at a stop in Lourenço Marques when Bunche stepped between two empty and unattached train cars to light a cigarette. "Just as I brought the match to the cigarette, I was hit a terrific blow on the forehead—and the two cars came together & moved ahead just as I leaped out to safety."[46] Bunche records that had he been knocked down on the tracks he would have been killed. As it was, the blow to his head caused his jaws and teeth to ache for some time.

On the night train from Mombasa to Nairobi, Bunche dined with Captain Neil-Stewart of the Criminal Investigation Department. When Neil-Stewart said that he himself would be receiving reports on Bunche's activities while in Kenya, Bunche asked, "What good will a lot of blank reports do you?"[47] One wonders what the captain's reaction was when a large delegation from the Kikuyu Central Association—arranged by Kenyatta—met him in Nairobi and planned much of his program. He stayed with an Indian, R. P. Dass, and ate and played tennis at the Indian Gymkhana Club. Bunche met with a wide variety of Indians, Africans, and government officials. He took hundreds of notes on every subject, twelve thousand still photographs, and fourteen thousand feet of film with Essie Robeson's camera.

Chief Koinange, father of Peter Koinange, was Bunche's host at Kiambu, ten miles outside Nairobi. Although Bunche's Swahili was poor, he gave eloquent speeches emphasizing his African ancestors and was treated royally. At Tigoni, he was given the name "Karioki," signifying in Swahili "he who returned from the dead," and a great feast was held in his honor. The Kikuyu Central Association arranged for him to witness a circumcision ceremony at Githiga. Bunche wrote that the four-and-a-half-hour ceremony was "the most gruesome, bloody spectacle I've ever seen."[48] He filmed both the male and female circumcision ceremonies and later wrote one of his most perceptive articles on the subject.

In "The Irua Ceremony Among the Kikuyu of Kiambu District, Kenya," Bunche demonstrates his recent training in anthropological fieldwork as well as his skill as a political scientist. Taking on the then and now controversial act of female circumcision, Bunche argues that insensitive European attempts to abolish it have made the rite the central symbol of tribal chauvinism and the rallying cry of their cultural loyalty. When placed in the context of governmental attempts to alienate Kikuyu lands and shift their settlements, the circumcision rites are elevated to the status of an emblem of national self-assertion and recompense for lost power. In short, the Kikuyu are trying to make up in cultural rights what they lost in economic rights.[49]

The trip to Kiambu District was only one of several safaris Bunche undertook while in Africa. He had purchased a Ford station wagon for £40 and acquired the services of a driver and cook. The insects, quinine-treated water, dubious food, and unreliable transportation often left him feeling apprehensive about trekking in the wilds. His mood was not improved by several letters from Ruth, who had a long list of complaints about the house, the children, and the long absences from her husband. She had calculated that they had been apart for more than half of the five years they had been married and was resentful of his less humdrum life.[50]

Bunche was having a fascinating time. As he set out for the Rift Valley wearing a new mustache, he wrote with "excitement in my heart, much conjecture as to whether our little old Ford would hold up on bad roads in my mind, a few pounds in my wallet and Jo Baker's record of 'I've got a message from the man in the Moon' ringing in my ears."[51] At Nakuru, he visited Dr. Louis Leakey's excavation camp and discussed Kikuyu customs with him. None of the hotels in Nakuru would accommodate him, so Dr. Leakey provided shelter.

From Kisumu, on Lake Victoria, he headed for Kampala in Uganda. Bunche was critical in his notes of many of the persons he observed. He saw the Kabaka, the king of the Baganda, arrive for a ceremony in a custom-built Buick and commented that the big chiefs don't give much assistance to the people. He found the British assistant chief of justice "an oily, grinning, intensely catholic and highly affected character" who advised him to visit "the catholic seminaries and their missionaries 'who have made so many fine studies of the Buganda [sic] people.'"[52] Bunche found, contrariwise, that students were taught to be of use only to Europeans. He also found that there were several West Indian lawyers in Uganda, "but they have not stood up and are unpopular with the natives."[53]

Bunche next drove twenty miles into the Congo's Ituri Forest to film pygmies. After several nights of sleeping in the car surrounded by lions and mosquitoes, he entered British territory again at Bukoba on Lake Victoria. Bunche was embarrassed by the royal treatment given him there by a colonial official and wrote of the "[i]rony of an American Negro 'lording' it over Africans in Africa. F.G.D.C. at Bukoba giving me a large four-room house with a long glass enclosed verandah, along the lake-front, and an Indian barber coming in to cut my hair while the natives looked on."[54] His notes contain an extensive discussion of the chief system in Tanganyika; he contended that under indirect rule, chiefs could become much more autocratic than they had been in precolonial times.[55]

From Tanganyika, Bunche returned to Kampala, where he had lunch with the British governor, then to Nairobi. After a week of storytelling with Chief Koinange, he was presented with a spear and shield at a "farewell tea" hosted by the chief. He received several more grand sendoffs from his friends and then boarded the *Boutekoe* at Mombasa on April 19, heading home. He soon found himself discussing the Dutch and British colonial systems with other passengers. At several Dutch colonies where the ship touched port, Bunche was impressed with the racial liberality of Dutch colonialism. When the ship reached Hong Kong, the thousands of Chinese sleeping on the side- walks and hundreds of women and children begging made an indelible im- pression. Although he wanted to go to Canton, he decided that the risk was too great for a family man. As "Bunche luck" would have it, the Japanese bombed the train he would have taken. From Hong Kong, Bunche took passage on the *Scharnhorst*, which docked in San Francisco on July 7. The first thing to greet him was a *San Francisco Chronicle* headline about the lynching of a Negro in Mississippi. He met Ruth and the girls in Los Angeles. Aunts Ethel and Nelle and the younger members of the Johnson family received a full accounting of his adventures as well.[56]

Howard University in the fall of 1939 must have seemed a dull place to Bunche in comparison. He had planned to sort through his vast collection of research notes and interviews to begin work on books on South Africa and East Africa, but more pressing events intervened. Bunche never did get around to publishing his African research despite winning a grant to pro- duce a manuscript. Still, his work on Africa over the thirties, which began as a less-preferred alternative to Brazil, left him with the reputation as one of the preeminent American scholars on that continent and prepared him for the rest of his life's work.

There are subtle shifts in Bunche's thinking on Africa during the decade, shifts that are best reflected in what one scholar has labeled as Bunche's three basic orientations: (1) a belief in the feasibility of the modernization of "backward" societies; (2) a normative commitment to egalitarianism; and (3) an affective commitment to African peoples.[57] These orientations are pre- sent throughout the period but vary in emphasis.

As a trained social scientist firmly believing in the Enlightenment and its principles of rational and secular thought, Bunche sought to bring his train- ing to the service of Africa. His initial view of Africa is almost one of a large social laboratory where the best minds might mold a new and better Africa. Given this orientation toward modernization, which became the dominant school of thought in African studies, it was necessary to acknowledge the positive aspects of colonialism. Such acknowledgment was common not only among European scholars, some of whom saw only the positive aspects, but African scholars as well. Ndabaningi Sithole, for example, in *African Na- tionalism* notes that "European power brought to Africa the coming together of different tribes; better communications; a new economic system; and the creation of new classes among the African people."[58] Casely Hayford, the prominent Gold Coast leader, expressed his loyalty to the empire in a 1920 speech:

> [A]ll of British West Africa . . . feel(s) that our loyalty and co-operation with His Majesty's Government is no mere matter of sentiment; for we feel and re-alise that our interests as a people are identical with those of the Empire, and we mean, as in the past, in the present and in the future, to stand by the Empire through thick and thin in every circumstance.[59]

Given the influence of Bunche's Harvard professors on his thinking and the limited materials and information available in European colonial offices, it is not surprising that Bunche's dissertation presents little that is new regarding the "modernization" of traditional societies. He invests great hope in the rise of an educated African elite that shares his rationalistic and internationalist outlook. At the same time, the sense of exclusiveness that developed in many members of this elite along with their strong opposition to traditional culture and religions cut them off from contact with the masses. Such elitism runs counter to Bunche's fundamental belief in egalitarianism and Western democracy.

This belief in egalitarianism drove Bunche to the left of mainstream colonial thought while an equally strong belief in Western democracy made him suspicious of the Communist Internationale or any type of authoritarian leadership. These competing beliefs led to the tension exhibited in *A World View of Race*, which provides a radical critique of colonialism without embracing Communism as the solution. Historically, race as a concept has been used by ruling groups to suppress subordinate (read: inferior) groups. Class, on the other hand, is a concept used by subordinate groups to attack those on top. Lawrence Finklestein has suggested that Bunche's economic views are more utilitarian than deeply held—that he used economic arguments to refute what he thought to be the myth of racial difference as the explanation of imperialism.[60]

Undoubtedly, Bunche's affective commitment to African peoples was strengthened by his contact with Africans in Europe and his travel throughout Africa. Almost all of the Pan African leaders Bunche met in London shared his leftist views. Moreover, the radical views demonstrated by Padmore, James, Makonnen, Kenyatta, and others had one thing in common: unequivocal rejection of international communism and Moscow's leadership.[61]

Bunche shared these views, but as a trained political scientist rather than a political leader, he wanted to move beyond the racial categories implied by

Pan Africanism. He found, however, that when he used the dominant methodology, which focused exclusively on the formal characteristics of institutions, he missed how people really behave. This weakness in his approach along with his affective commitment to Africans led him to retrain himself in anthropological field techniques. Bunche liked the attack of the Franz Boas school of anthropologists on the notions of biological race purity and its emphasis on the mutability of culture. Yet he still seemed more comfortable doing the kind of comparative sociology that Schapera did rather than immersing himself in the music, art, and mythology of Africa.[62]

By the time Bunche left Africa in 1938, he was faced with a "democratic moral dilemma." His political science training and his pragmatism told him that the Enlightenment concept of progress that viewed the Anglo-American forms of democracy and the rule of law as the apex of any nation's development was probably the best goal to work for under the existing international system. At the same time, his personal background and his knowledge of Africans and their institutions led him to believe that wholesale "modernization," with the West as a model, might not be appropriate for Africa.[63] Indeed, the very countries on which the "Western" model was based were by far the greatest imperialistic successes. Bunche would return home to find this democratic moral dilemma most sharply defined in the Southern United States.

6

An African American Dilemma

Since the beginning of the nation, white Americans have suffered from a deep inner uncertainty as to who they really are. One of the ways that has been used to simplify the answer has been to seize upon the presence of black Americans and use them as a marker, a symbol of limits, a metaphor for the "outsider." Many whites could look at the social position of blacks and feel that color formed an easy and reliable gauge for determining to what extent one was or was not American.

Perhaps that is why one of the first epithets that many European immigrants learned when they got off the boat was the term "nigger"—it made them feel instantly American. But this is tricky magic. Despite his racial difference and social status, something indisputably American about Negroes not only raised doubts about the white man's value system but aroused the troubling suspicion that whatever else the true American is, he is also somehow black.

—Ralph Ellison, *Shadow and Act*

Integration was practically an unknown term in 1940. The struggle for Negro rights was generally discussed as a struggle for "equality" or for "first-class citizenship." During the 1930s, the NAACP had launched a legal battle against "Jim Crow" schools; however, the focus was on the "equal" side of the "separate but equal" *Plessy* doctrine. That is, legal experts attempted to demonstrate that all-Black schools never had the same physical facilities and resources as all-White schools. Social scientists were seldom, if ever, a part of these legal debates or the more general discussion of race relations in the United States. While the Franz Boas school of anthropology was putting serious dents in the armor of White biological superiority, there was little agreement on other definitions of *race*. In fact, race and the study of racial politics were marginalized in political science. Other social sciences presented a variety of approaches to race relations, but none of them were particularly influential on policy makers.

In March 1935, a new kind of riot erupted in Harlem. Previous riots, like the nationwide outbreaks of violence in 1917 and 1919, had targeted Blacks as the victims of White violence. The violence in Harlem was not aimed at White individuals but at White property. It had been triggered by the arrest of a teenager accused of stealing a penknife at Kress's department store on 125th Street. When a rumor spread that the boy had been beaten to death by police, a crowd assembled and stores along 125th Street were looted and burned. By morning, when order was restored, the damaged was assessed: 3 dead (by police bullets), 100 stabbed or shot, 125 arrested, and 250 shop windows smashed.[1]

The new pattern of violence was not lost on Newton Baker, a trustee of the Carnegie Corporation. On October 24, 1935, Baker—who had been secretary of war during World War I and was also a former mayor of Cleveland—made a proposal that ultimately would change the way many Americans looked at race relations: that the foundation undertake a study of the condition of Blacks in Northern cities. Despite the foundation's long history of support for Black education few of its trustees had firsthand knowledge of urban problems. As a onetime mayor who still served on the boards of several Cleveland charities, Baker had become increasingly concerned about the poverty, crime, unemployment, and family breakups among Blacks as their number grew dramatically in the inner cities. Baker was also a founder of the National Conference of Christians and Jews and was afraid that the greater racism and religious intolerance then becoming evident in Germany would grow in the United States as well.

Baker's rhetorical attacks on discrimination and intolerance notwithstanding, his basic approach was a conservative one. He had opposed the New Deal's expansion of federal power and took a limited view of Negro potential. In a critique of a U.S. Office of Education report advocating a single standard in education, Baker implied that political correctness prevented an examination of biological questions involving Negro education and praised "the white people in this country who received the slaves from slave ships . . . who were practically caged animals . . . and undertook to make useful laborers of them."[2] It is not surprising, then, that some of those considered to conduct the study were former colonial administrators.

Baker died in 1937 and the task of choosing someone to carry out the proposed study fell to Carnegie president Frederick P. Keppel. Keppel, who had served as assistant secretary of war under Baker, had taken over the foundation in 1923. Having been an officer of the American Red Cross and the International Chamber of Commerce in Paris, Keppel was a skilled diplomat with important connections. Under him, the foundation emphasized support for the exceptional individual. He believed in Andrew Carnegie's maxim: "Find the exceptional man and having found him, give him a free hand."[3]

As the largest philanthropic organization in the world, the Carnegie Corporation occupied a strategic place from which to influence race relations. With the onset of the depression, requests for funding from civil rights organizations and scholars were at an all-time high, but corporation resources were at low point. Accordingly, the foundation was extremely cautious in making major grants.

The Baker proposal was not the only option available. Du Bois had proposed the *Encyclopedia of the Negro* as a major, multivolume publication to be overseen by a board of eminent Black and White scholars and reformers, and to be edited by Du Bois. The Phelps-Stokes Fund had provided some initial support and was encouraging other foundations to contribute to the project. Carter G. Woodson had his own plans to publish the *Encyclopedia Africana* and denounced the Phelps-Stokes Fund's effort as "Negro control." Melville Herskovits conducted a covert campaign to kill the Baker proposal. As a field innovator, he had his own plans about how research in race relations should develop: American scholarship could no longer concentrate exclusively on Western civilization; it must expand to include world cultures. He would later attempt to challenge Myrdal's approach to race relations through the Committee on Negro Studies of the American Council of Learned Societies (ACLS).[4]

The author of the report commissioned on the 1935 Harlem riot, E. Franklin Frazier, was available. But ultimately, Keppel decided that neither a Black nor White American could do a completely objective study. Frazier and his thirty-person staff had issued a hard-hitting report that cited racial discrimination and poverty as the chief causes of the Harlem violence. With economic inequality as the main underlying factor, the report recommended a long list of reforms, starting with a city ordinance denying contracts to any firm or labor union that discriminates against Negro workers. Coming ten years before Roosevelt's federal ban on employment discrimination, Frazier's report proved too hot to handle. Mayor Fiorello La Guardia, who had appointed the riot commission, refused to release the report to the public. However, the *Amsterdam News* obtained a copy, which it printed in its entirety.[5]

Keppel found the most appealing model was Lord Hailey's *An African Survey*, which was sponsored by the Carnegie Corporation and published in

1938. Evidently, Keppel thought Hailey, a former governor of the United Provinces in India, could be entirely objective about colonialism in Africa. That sixteen-hundred-page reformist work stressing the gradual modernization of Africa was the kind of work Keppel wanted on the United States. Consequently, his initial choice was a retired Dutch colonial administrator in the East Indies named Hendrik Mouw.

Mouw was to be assisted by a group of American social scientists who would provide the details of life in the United States. However, when Keppel approached scholars like Herskovits and Donald Young with the proposal they strongly objected. Herskovits said that African Americans would not give any credibility to a work produced by anyone from an imperialist country and that a committee of advisers should include Negro scholars. With Young, Herskovits convinced Keppel that the study should be a major research effort involving fieldwork conducted by American scholars. Keppel still believed the study should be led by a James Bryce–like figure[6] and eventually settled on Karl Gunnar Myrdal.

Myrdal had been suggested by Beardsley Ruml, a social scientist then serving as treasurer of R. H. Macy's department store. He had met Myrdal when the latter visited the United States in 1929–1930 as a Rockefeller Foundation Social Science Fellow. Now, at the age of thirty-eight, Myrdal was an internationally known scholar and successor to Gustav Cassel in the chair of social economics at the University of Stockholm. Equally important as Myrdal's scholarly reputation, for Keppel, was his experience in government as an elected member of the upper house of the Swedish parliament and his commitment to social engineering. With Myrdal on board, the Carnegie Corporation eventually approved the unprecedented sum of more than $300,000 (the equivalent of $3 million today) for what became the Carnegie-Myrdal study.

A good politician, Myrdal immediately set out to placate the American social scientists who thought that a foreigner with little knowledge of American race relations could not complete a comprehensive study in the allotted two years. On one of his first trips around the country, Donald Young introduced him to Herskovits and Bunche. While on a tour of Harlem nightclubs, Myrdal and Herskovits were so engrossed in discussing the race issue that Bunche joked that "those boys just can't break down—they don't know how to relax."[7] Both Bunche and Herskovits were favorably impressed with Myrdal.

When Myrdal began recruiting members of his research staff in the spring of 1939, Young and Charles H. Thompson, the dean at Howard, recommended Bunche. Myrdal decided that his nuclear staff should include one sociologist, one economist, one statistician, and one Negro social scientist. Choosing Bunche for the last slot, Myrdal wrote Keppel that Bunche "seems to be extraordinarily intelligent, open-minded and cooperative. . . . I think also, it would be a great advantage to have at least one Negro on the staff, who would serve as intimate contact with the Negro world."[8] Joining Bunche on the nuclear staff were Guy B. Johnson from North Carolina; Dorothy S. Thomas, a sociologist who worked with Myrdal in Sweden; Doxey Wilkerson, a sociologist and colleague of Bunche's at Howard; Paul Norgren, a Harvard-trained economist; and Swedish social statistician Richard Sterner.

In addition, Myrdal hired thirty-one independent scholars to write monographs on a wide range of topics; they retained the right to publish the monographs separately. Several of the monographs became classics in their own right, including Charles S. Johnson's *Patterns of Negro Segregation* and Melville Herskovits's *The Myth of the Negro Past*. Myrdal urged Bunche to consider publishing his memorandum "Conceptions and Ideologies of the Negro Problem" as a separate book, possibly supplemented with sections skimmed from the "Leadership" and "Programs" memoranda.[9] Other contributors included Otto Klineberg, M. F. Ashley-Montagu, Louis Wirth, Edward Shils, Arthur Raper, John Dollard, Allison Davis, Sterling Brown, E. Franklin Frazier, St. Clair Drake, T. Arnold Hill, and Ira DeA. Reid. Thirty-six assistants were also hired, including Kenneth Clark, and fifty more experts were consulted.

Myrdal's staff and the contributors of monographs were chosen with an eye toward the reception of the final report. By including representatives from all of the major schools of thought on race relations and providing rare honoraria and research assistance to young Black scholars as well as senior White scholars, Myrdal ensured not only a favorable reception of the report but a more profound response by using the probing questions of the less-established figures. In defending his use of "so many" young Black radicals, he insisted that he needed their viewpoint on the whole matter and that the mainstream view was easily accessible. Moreover, said Myrdal, "if they were intellectually advanced people, they were of course radical."[10]

Myrdal's frankness and obvious brilliance helped attract Bunche. They had the same type of personality: open and expansive yet cocky and dominating. Both were comfortable with students as well as with political leaders, with Blacks as well as Whites. Myrdal had risen to prominence from a peasant family.[11] He saw in Bunche an equally brilliant and accomplished social scientist who was prevented from similar ascendancy in the United States because of color. Bunche would become the American scholar closest to Myrdal, and a lifetime friendship was established.[12]

The relationship of the two men grew stronger on a long trip across the South in the fall of 1939. Barely back from Africa, Bunche was on the road again for his first experience in the "deep South." Loaded down with bags, Dictaphone, camera, typewriter, and questionnaires, he left for Richmond on October 17 in his Ford. Perhaps with Bunche's frankness in mind, the Bunche housekeeper, Miss Houston, advised him that he "would encounter no trouble with 'crackers' just so I said 'sir' to them."[13]

It was difficult enough for Bunche to control his natural instincts, but when Myrdal joined him in South Carolina, it became almost impossible. Unlike White liberals in South Africa, who seemed to be thought of as safe guides for visitors, White liberals in the South were regarded with deep suspicion. Myrdal's sense of humor combined with his lack of knowledge of Southern mores put the duo in real danger several times. Later Bunche wrote that Myrdal "thought he was on a lark," and "I was always on the verge of being lynched because of his playful pranks. We actually had to run for it a couple of times."[14]

One incident occurred during an interview with Mrs. J. E. Andrews, editor of the *Georgia Women's World*, when she loosed a tirade on miscegenation and the presumed sexual appetite of Black men. Myrdal intervened to ask whether she had a subconscious desire to have sexual intercourse with Blacks and whether she herself had Black blood. Mrs. Andrews later accused him of personal insult and defamation and a warrant for Myrdal's arrest was issued. Bunche didn't learn of the chain of events until the next day when Atlanta friends called them in Greensboro to warn that the Atlanta police were watching the trains for Myrdal and searching everywhere for him. Bunche drove all night to get them to the relative safety of Tuskegee, Alabama. An unrepentant Myrdal suggested that the party of three (they had been joined by white sociologist Arthur Raper) stay in a White hotel. Raper quickly found an excuse to leave the fieldwork team on grounds of illness. Bunche was experiencing serious pain in his right leg.[15]

In Montgomery, Alabama, Bunche visited some of Ruth's childhood friends and photographed her old home, but the twosome kept their usual full schedule and were soon in trouble again. Myrdal insisted on picking up a White girl on the road to Meridian, Mississippi, and then began to attack her responses to the "bitterly sarcastic questions and statements" he posed, including whether she would marry a Negro. Bunche feared she would jump from the car and then call on some "Mississippi cracker" to defend her honor.[16] It seemed to Bunche that Myrdal grew increasingly hostile to the White officials he interviewed, and it was with some relief that he bade farewell to Myrdal, who flew to New York from Birmingham on November 19.

Bunche made two other trips to the South, without Myrdal, but the bulk of the interviews were conducted by three field assistants. Wilhemina Jackson, a Howard student, interviewed many Negroes and some Whites in Atlantic states from Virginia to Florida. James E. Jackson, who had earlier worked in the labor movement, covered Virginia, Tennessee, Arkansas, Kentucky, Mississippi, Texas, Louisiana, Oklahoma, and Missouri. George C. Stoney, the only White member of the team and a recent graduate of the University of North Carolina, focused on local officials in Alabama, Georgia, and South Carolina. William Bryant, a former student of Bunche's at Howard, kept track of the fieldwork and did research at the Library of Congress.

Four of the forty-four research monographs prepared for the Carnegie-Myrdal study were written by Bunche (approximately 3,000 pages out of the total of 15,000 pages prepared for the project). The longest of the four, "The Political Status of the Negro," was the last one completed. It comprised 1,660 typed pages and was largely devoted to interviews collected by Bunche and his assistants and edited by Bunche. Almost all of the 550 interviews used were done in the South; the total collected was considerably higher.

Still writing at 5:45 in the morning on the last day of the project, Bunche complained that the final product was "terribly hurried, poorly integrated, and roughly written." He listed ten things left undone or done only superficially, including a statistical analysis of Negro voting in the North and South and the shift in party preference from Republican to Democratic; an evaluation of Southern state legislators, congressmen, and Negro leaders; and an analysis of Southern liberalism and the impact of unionization.[17]

Bunche was critical of the shortcomings of his work, but it was consulted by many scholars looking for empirical data on Southern politics. Although seldom acknowledging it, V. O. Key and Alexander Heard were among those using the interview material and influenced by Bunche's interpretation of the place of the Negro in Southern politics. Bunche was also invited to testify before Congress on Black disfranchisement.

Three themes emerge from Bunche's analysis: (1) the looseness and corruption of political practices; (2) the extent of the disfranchisement of both

Negroes and Whites; and (3) the lack of effective reform movements at the grassroots level.[18]

The extent of corruption in Southern politics is perhaps the most shocking information in "The Political Status of the Negro." Its discovery both confirms and denies the major thesis of a moral dilemma that undergirds *An American Dilemma*. Widespread corruption demonstrates the negative and eroding effects of the practice of segregation on democracy. At the same time, the broad tolerance of or indifference toward the corruption suggests the existence of a countercreed in the South that provided White Southerners with rationalizations for their illegal activities.

One of the most persistent rationalizations for Black disfranchisement was that the Black vote could easily be bought and controlled by unscrupulous Whites. Rather than penalize such Whites, it was easier to deny Blacks the ballot. One candid machine leader admitted in an interview "that Negro voting would increase too greatly the expense involved in machine control, since it is already necessary for them to pay up the poll taxes and buy the votes of many white voters."[19] According to this account, Black disfranchisement is a matter of economics rather than racism. Even a relatively liberal Southerner like Supreme Court Justice Hugo Black decried "the fact that Negro leadership is so often subservient to the 'interests' and is so easily bought."[20]

In wealthier cities such as Nashville and Chattanooga, where the machine chose to "buy" or encourage Negro voters in other ways, Negroes were demanding small concessions for their party loyalty: better sanitation and health facilities, better streets, and representation on the police force. George Stoney reports on similar demands elsewhere:

> Even in those places where the Negro vote has been brought about purely for machine purposes, however, some direct benefits in the form of streets, garbage collection, and so on, have resulted. The Miami vote is especially significant here. Despite the fact that it was an independent movement (or more properly *because* of it) direct improvements in garbage collection and other city services were seen almost immediately. Encouraged by this, similar Negro-inspired movements to register are going on in Winston-Salem, Greensboro, New Orleans, Little Rock, and—most successfully of all—in Birmingham, Alabama.[21]

Other cities were not so accommodating to Black demands.

Field assistant James Jackson wrote to Bunche that Memphis was the "first outpost of Fascism in America"; the Crump machine held "absolute authority" over the very lives of the people. "Their record of cold blooded political killings could not be equalled in Berlin," and there was no open opposition to the machine. In fact, Jackson said every family in the city had at least one member responsible to the machine for his or her livelihood. Given the circumstances, "Negroes don't vote here: they are voted."[22] Jackson did a lot of digging around and managed to interview Crump himself, but the muckraking almost made Jackson a victim of the machine.

> My field worker, Dr. James Jackson, got into difficulty in Memphis and had to flee the town. He had been there long enough to get notes for a good memorandum on the Memphis situation, however. It seems that he went in to question a big Jewish racketeer who is a political leader among the Negroes on Beale Street. This fellow became suspicious and had Jackson taken down to the police station. Jackson was in a terrible dither because he had with him at the time notes which were particularly damaging to the Memphis police chief and his henchmen. Jackson had also learned that several people, including a prominent attorney who was opposed to the dominant Crump machine there, had recently been beaten up. So while left waiting in one of the rooms of the police station, he ducked out, got a cab to his lodging place, grabbed his bags and took the first train out.[23]

Bunche decided that it would not be wise for Jackson to return to Memphis but that the situation there might warrant a quick trip by Myrdal and himself.

The second theme of "The Political Status of the Negro," the extent of the disfranchisement of both Blacks and Whites, dealt with the specific techniques used. Bunche found extremely low voter turnout and linked the disfranchisement of large numbers of poor Whites to the political disqualification of Blacks. Under one-party rule, the local political machines with their county courthouse "gangs" and "rings" controlled politics. Party minions installed as probate judges, county clerks, registrars, sheriffs, beat committeemen, members of election committees, and county party officers made up their own rules. Despite their great discretionary powers, Bunche found them "ludicrously ill-informed." Among characteristic abuses were a widespread absence of the secret ballot; frequent use of numbered ballots; severe misuse of absentee voting; extensive double voting and voting under names of the deceased; absence of watchers in polling places; frequent failure to provide polling booths; habitual aid in marking ballots; loosely kept voting lists; and devices like "chain-letter" balloting. Such practices applied equally to both races, but a range of practices applied exclusively to Negroes, including the following:

1. Exclusion from the Democratic primary....
2. Requiring one or more (usually two) white character witnesses....
3. Strict enforcement of the literacy tests against Negro applicants....
4. Putting unreasonable questions to Negro applicants in constitutional understanding or interpretation tests, as, for example, "*What is non compos mentis* when it is applied to a citizen in legal jeopardy?"
5. Severe application of property qualifications and requiring only Negro applicants to show property tax receipts.
6. Basing rejection of Negro registrants on alleged minor mistakes in filling out registration blanks, as, for example, an applicant's error in computing his exact age by years, months, and *days*.
7. Evasion, by informing Negro applicants that registration cards have "run out," that members of the registration board are not on hand, that it is "closing time," or that the applicant "will be notified" in due course.
8. Requiring Negro applicants to suffer long waits before the officials attend them.
9. Requiring Negro applicants to fill out their own blanks though those of white applicants are filled out for them by officials.
10. Deliberate insults, humiliations or threats by officials and/or hangers on.
11. Discarding only Negro applications for conviction of misdemeanors.
12. Requiring enrollment in Democratic clubs, from which Negroes are barred, for primary voting, as in South Carolina.
13. Severe application of the cumulative poll tax to Negro though not to white voters.
14. Loss of jobs or threat of loss of jobs by those Negroes who get "uppity" and insist on their right to register.
15. Warning prospective Negro voters in small towns that they will be "marked men" in the white community.
16. Intimidation through physical violence.[24]

The above-named practices supported the political oligarchy that ran Southern politics. Bunche, however, did not see this oligarchy as fascistic; it was so decentralized that it almost approached anarchy. The decentralization allowed for many exceptions to the rule of excluding Negroes from voting. On the basis of Bunche's evidence, Myrdal concluded that "the Southern conservative position on Negro franchise is politically untenable for any length of time."[25]

Myrdal's optimism was not supported by the third major theme of "The Political Status of the Negro," which suggested the lack of effective reform movements at the mass level. In an interesting interview, Supreme Court Justice Hugo Black suggested to Bunche that the Ku Klux Klan was a sort of populist, anticorporate group in Alabama. Black, who had once been a member of the Klan, portrayed himself as a champion of the working classes, Negro (which he pronounced "negra") and White. However, he and Bunche agreed that Supreme Court decisions were unlikely to mean much "unless they were in step with the mores of the dominant group."[26]

The South was not alone in the absence of mass movements. According to Bunche, the bourgeois character of the American Revolution helps account for the fact "that there has never been, in democratic America, a real movement embracing and representing the masses of the population."[27] It's ironic, given the great American emphasis on individualism, said Bunche, that the country has only two major parties rather than a plethora of parties. And neither of the major parties offers a substantive program. He suggests two factors contributing to this phenomenon. One, the frontier as a means of escape that was open primarily to Whites and only slightly to Blacks. Two, the public fascination with personalities rather than principles and issues.

Among Negroes, the Civil War did not immediately lead to any great political awakening and social consciousness. According to Bunche, they lacked "the ideological drive characteristic of any people who have fought their way through a revolutionary period."[28] Blacks' emergence during Reconstruction, however, led Whites to submerge their own class differences. Blacks, following such leaders as Frederick Douglass, P. B. S. Pinchback, and John M. Langston, saw political power and affiliation with the Republican Party as the way to Negro salvation, ignoring labor organizations and economic issues in the process.

Even with the rise of the New Deal, Bunche felt that sectional interests might still dominate over class interests. Still, he believed that such federal programs as the Agricultural Adjustment Act (AAA) Cotton Referenda, which encouraged voting and political education among sharecroppers and tenant farmers, provided a valuable stimulus for democracy. In fact, Bunche's student and assistant Robert Martin proved his mentor's view to be accurate. In his dissertation "Negro-White Participation in the AAA Cotton and Tobacco Referendum in North and South Carolina," Martin concluded that White economic participation was higher than White political participation, and that economic participation by Blacks led to an increase in their desire for and interest in greater involvement politically.[29]

Another sign of political stirrings was the election of a number of "bronze mayors" in many Black communities in the 1930s.[30] These compensatory activities for those locked outside mainstream politics provided an opportunity for citizens to develop campaigning and organizational skills. At the national level, the Northern Black vote was now being touted as a solid bloc that could determine presidential elections. Bunche declared such claims exaggerations because they are based upon the Negro proportion of the populations of various states rather than the actual percentage of registered Black voters. Moreover, said Bunche of a solid Black voting bloc, "It is not so now, and I do not believe that it should be, even assuming that it were possible to make it so."[31]

Bunche's views on balance-of-power voting were brief but curious, given the importance of this theory to subsequent Black politics. In the final report, Myrdal gives this issue more discussion and revealed a position different from his associate's. The Swedish scholar believed that internal differences in the Black community on Negro issues "have little significance" and "it would be natural for a national Negro political leadership to form itself and start negotiations with the two parties in advance of each national election."[32] He offers two reasons that such bargaining has not happened. First, the low educational and cultural level and the absence of political tradition in the Negro community. This explanation, however, contradicts evidence that Myrdal had presented earlier in the work showing Black voting in Chicago exceeding that of Whites and confounding the stereotype of Negro apathy.[33] The second reason points to the advantages of party allegiance and membership in the inner circle of one party. Myrdal's solution is "a division of labor and responsibility among Negro leaders" so that some work within the party structure while others of greater stature remain independent of close party ties. This, of course, takes a high degree of political sophistication that "might become more of a reality in the future."[34] In fact, this division of labor is what has developed in Black politics, although one can question the degree of communication between Black leaders within the Democratic Party and those who remain independent.[35]

Major shortcomings of "The Political Status of the Negro" are highlighted by Myrdal's discussion of the Black vote. Its treatment of Southern Negro disfranchisement is long, repetitious, and rambling, but the discussion of Black voting in the North is brief and superficial. Bunche had encouraged his research associates to spend at least a little time in some of the smallest Southern towns, and he left large urban centers in the North practically untouched.[36] This may reflect Bunche's belief that the importance of the "Black vote" had been overemphasized to the detriment of attention to economic issues. Myrdal, on the other hand, saw the "Negro vote" as a symbol of civic equality and contended that the major characteristics of Southern politics revolved around it.[37] Of course, Bunche would devote more attention to the North in his other three memoranda.

Harold F. Gosnell, who had written one of the few book-length studies of Black politics (in Chicago), criticized "The Political Status of the Negro" for ignoring the influence of language (symbolism) on politics and its failure to compare Blacks with other minorities. He also believed Bunche's generalization about Southern officials as incompetent was unfair; Gosnell believed they should be judged individually, as Bunche had done with Black Reconstruction politicians.[38] Dewey Grantham added that the failure to make distinctions of a subregional kind was a serious shortcoming.[39] Most of Bunche's data were drawn from the Southeast, thus rendering impossible discussion of regional patterns. Undoubtedly, Bunche would have asserted that a shortage of time and money made further analysis impossible.

If the strength of "The Political Status of the Negro" memorandum is its raw, unfiltered look at Southern politics, the weakness is its lack of integration and theoretical originality. However, the memoranda were not intended to be freestanding books and were meant to complement one another.

In "Conceptions and Ideologies of the Negro Problem," Bunche directly confronted the theoretical foundation of American political thought. This memorandum is accompanied by the much longer "Extended Memorandum on the Programs, Ideologies, Tactics, and Achievements of Negro Betterment and Interracial Organizations." The latter furnishes the empirical proof of the ideas presented in the former.

Even though Bunche meant for the two memoranda to complement each other, in many ways they are contradictory and lacking in integration. In "Conceptions and Ideologies" Bunche sets about unmasking (deconstructing) the social roots of African American thought, borrowing from Karl Mannheim's model in *Ideology and Utopia*. For Mannheim, ideologies were the views of the ruling group, and utopias represented the vision of the ruled. Bunche presents three general types of "Negro thinking" on the "Negro problem": ideologies, stereotypes, and folklore. For the Negro masses, who are conscious of race difference but lack race consciousness, folklore and stereotypes are the dominant modes of racial discourse. Like Mannheim, Bunche assigned ideologies to the exclusive realm of the Negro elite.

"The ideologies of both Negroes and Whites on the American Negro problem frequently appear to be so wildly distorted," said Bunche, that they "may continue to thrive and perpetuate themselves long after the social causes which gave rise to them have ceased to exist."[40] It is here that Bunche directly confronted the notion of the "American other" as presented in Lewis Copeland's "contrast conception": "Whatever the risk in defining the Negro as a biological entity or an ethnic group, the popular mind has created a conceptual dichotomy that is accepted with as little question as the counter-conceptions of night and day."[41] At least implicitly, then, Bunche recognized that the very definition of the concept of "American" for Whites excluded and is dependent on a "Black" other. This gave all four of Bunche's memoranda a more pessimistic tone than Myrdal's final report. Bunche, however, chose to fight the concept of the "American other" on economic rather than cultural grounds.

In constructing a conceptual defense against this negative image, Blacks have had to battle "a heavy inferiority complex." One polar response has been that taken by Woodson and Garvey; it seeks to play up the special "racial" talents of Negroes to the extent that they may even be superior in areas like music and athletics. At the other pole is an accommodating response that seeks to emulate White behavior in all its forms. Bunche labels the first category escapism or release; the second, accommodation.

Bunche characterized Black thinking in each of his categories as immature, uncertain in approach, and vague in objectives. For example, he finds that Jewish Zionism and Negro Garveyism are parallel ideologies, "but where the former is clear-cut, logical and well-formulated, the latter was vague, uncertain and largely emotional."[42] Yet having rejected Garveyism as escapism, he is no more comfortable with the accommodation of the NAACP. Bunche took issue with James Weldon Johnson's statement that "the solving of our [Negro] situation depends principally upon an evolutionary process along two parallel lines: our own development and the bringing about of a change in the national attitude toward us."[43] He saw this as typical Negro parochialism unconcerned with the larger structural issues in society at large; however, Johnson's views are closer to those of Myrdal than is Bunche's outlook.

This "Negro parochialism" dominated "Programs, Ideologies, Tactics, and Achievements." That is, "Conceptions and Ideologies" focused on the ideology/utopia or accommodation/escapism paradigm; "Programs, Ideologies, Tactics, Achievements," on the duality of African American social identity.

Negroes in America since Emancipation have been subject to a dual pull. As citizens in a democratic nation the aspirations of Negroes have been directed toward attainment of full equality, not as American Negroes but as full-fledged American citizens. Such aspirations are given encouragement by the creed of human equality which forms the ideological foundations of the American society. The wide disparity between theory and practice, however; the position of inequality and subordination arbitrarily fixed for the Negro in the political, social and economic structures, has impelled the Negro population to demand special consideration for its "own" or "Negro" problems. Thus when the Negro views any matter of broad governmental policy, he ordinarily weighs it not as an American citizen, but as a Negro American.

Thus there is a constant conflict between the Negro's unquestioned desire to be a full-fledged American citizen, and the necessity forced upon him by tradition and sentiment in the country to "think Negro" first, to demand special consideration for the Negro group and its problems.[44]

This conflict, of course, is at the heart of the contemporary debate over affirmative action. Bunche identified these competing tensions in two paradigms: one pulling between competing loyalties, and the other between conservatism and social change.

Having identified the tensions, Bunche did nothing to resolve them. He simply transcended them, refusing to accept the more complex reality that ideology often masks. For example, Bunche acknowledged that the view prevalent among upper-class Negroes in the South draws a distinction between the "better class" of Whites and "White trash." He also acknowledged that the upper-class Negro's exercise of political rights is connected with status and prestige. However, he did not support Myrdal's suggestion that the "higher" strata"—that is, the educated and better-off Negroes—be enfranchised immediately, and the "lower strata"—the poor and less educated—be granted the vote only gradually and in increments.[45] But instead of dealing with the symbolic importance of the Black vote in countering notions of the "American other," Bunche simply focused on the more pressing economic needs of the Negro sharecropper and unskilled worker.

Another example of Bunche's tendency to transcend questions of identity rather than confront them involves one of the few discussions of gender. In it Bunche attacks the frequently stated view that White women are generally much less prejudiced against Blacks than are White men.

One explanation advanced for this difference in racial attitude between white men and women, is that the white woman has traditionally had no responsibility for the creation and preservation of racial policy. She has herself been in a dependent and subordinate position and has occupied a lower position in the sex caste. It has been the white man who has shouldered this responsibility. White supremacy is the white man's burden. An important rationalization of such policy has been another stereotype, viz., "the necessity for the protection of white womanhood"—a protection which white women have frequently disdained.[46]

Bunche says this generalization breaks down when the racial views of White women toward Black women are examined: here the prestige status of White women is involved and their sympathetic racial attitude declines, according to Bunche. Yet this impressionistic view is not supported by any historical evidence from either Negro women's or White women's organizations.

Once again Bunche might have offered as a defense the hurried nature of his work. He complained in a letter to Myrdal that "Conceptions and Ideologies" was written in three weeks. In evaluating it, Louis Wirth argued that Mannheim's concepts don't add much to the analysis. Bunche had ignored ideologies that science had developed around the race question and his classification scheme needed work. Wirth suggested adding the category of militancy to those of accommodation and escapism. He also criticized Bunche's typology of ideologies, stereotypes, and folklore. "Ideologies may contain stereotypes and be the product of or result in folklore," said Wirth, and they cannot be confined to the intellectual.[47] Substantively, Wirth believed that Southerners are not always defensive about the Negro problem, and that they are able to separate their democratic beliefs from their caste ideology when it comes to the Negro. Finally, he warned, "[D]on't make the mistake of thinking that ideologies of Jews aren't confused. Zionism has many friends and varieties."[48] He asked whether Garvey's great attraction was not due in part to Black disillusionment.

Wirth's critique highlighted Bunche's failure to deal with the issue of social identity. If the identity of the American is defined as the opposite of Black identity, then it becomes impossible to incorporate or integrate Blacks into the "American Dream." The refusal to deal with this issue gives Bunche's solution the air of escapism.

> If there is any ideology which offers any hope to the Negro it would seem to be that which identifies his interests with the white workers of the nation. There is no strong labor movement now, and there seems to be little possibility that one will obtain in the near future. Nor is there any assurance that either white or black masses would give it sufficient support to build it into a real people's movement.[49]

Myrdal's solution is to recognize a category between escapism and accommodationism that Bunche referred to as civil libertarianism. Working with upper-class Whites, Myrdal believed progress can be made in resolving the American Dilemma. His obvious differences with Bunche are best seen in "The Programs, Ideologies, Tactics, and Achievements of Negro Betterment and Interracial Organizations."

The third memorandum was completed in June 1940 and comprised almost eight hundred pages, making it the second-longest of the memoranda prepared for Myrdal. In it, Bunche took the most exhaustive look at such organizations researched up to that time. He examined each, first in terms of effectiveness in meeting its own stated program, and second, effectiveness in contributing to the "ultimate welfare" of the Negro. Part I provides a simple, descriptive analysis with a specific critique; Part II, a general and comparative appraisal; and Part III, a constructive statement on ideologies, programs, and tactics. Bunche held to his general categories of accommodation and escape as introduced in "Conceptions and Ideologies" by placing all the organizations in one or the other category.

Material for the analysis was collected from detailed questionnaires sent to national and local groups. Given the widely known importance of the study, most were eager to cooperate with Bunche in supplying data and making their leaders available for interviews. A few, the National Negro Congress and its executive director John P. Davis, refused to provide information.[50]

A revealing statement about bias in scholarship opened the memorandum. Bunche declared that one can develop a case for almost any position based on the selective use and interpretation of facts. He then proceeded to describe how one could argue that there is a "double standard of merit" regarding the work of Negro scholars. Young Negro scholars benefit from foundation grants and have a virtual monopoly on faculty positions in Negro colleges. Yet, from the same beginning, says Bunche, one can demonstrate that this is a complete distortion of the actual facts. White scholars at White colleges do not have to compete with Negro professors and receive higher salaries. Moreover,

> [F]or a relatively small investment, as philanthropic investments go, the foundations have been able to exercise a maximum of control over the direction and character of Negro education. The scholarly grants doled out to Negro scholars by the philanthropies giving special attention to Negro education have passed through the hands of professional white "experts" on the Negro problem, many of whom have known well enough the game of racial politics. Every Negro scholar knows that the most effective endorsement a Negro ap-

plicant can have is one from a responsible and reputable white man. Moreover, the total picture of Negro disability in the American milieu must be considered. The *average* Negro who attains to the rank of "scholar" has performed a much greater feat than has the *average* white. This is incontrovertible.[51]

With Bunche's salary coming from the Carnegie Corporation, these are indeed bold statements and reflect not only his self-confidence but also a secure relationship with Myrdal.[52]

For his part, Myrdal used the radical views of Bunche in particular and his staff in general to elicit comprehensive and usually defensive responses from persons and organizations being studied. Bunche's analysis of the NAACP is the best example of this process. Walter White and Roy Wilkins were well aware of the potential impact of the Carnegie-Myrdal study on race relations and went out of their way to provide Bunche with data on the organization. Imagine their surprise, then, when they read the blistering two-hundred-page critique of the NAACP (nearly one-quarter of the memorandum) drafted by Bunche.

Setting the tone for what follows, Bunche emphasizes the aloofness of Du Bois and the Niagara Movement from the Black masses. Moving on to Garrison Villard's call to form the NAACP, Bunche asserts that Villard ignored economics and "fundamental causes," relying instead on faith in the tenets of American democracy. The membership (65,000 in 1940, 10 percent White) is largely upper-class, and local leadership is "often inept and self-seeking" (Bunche's assistants conducted interviews with local-branch officials). Without a mass financial base, it is dependent on White funding and middle-class volunteer leaders; Bunche advocates more paid leaders. The lag in action between substantial court cases means the average Negro is unaware of the NAACP. Bunche recommends the use of electronic media to reach the masses. Even though its main organ of publicity, *The Crisis*, is conducted as "a literary magazine with a heavy dash of racial chauvinism," Bunche sees the loss of Du Bois in 1934 as "a great blow" (his letter of resignation is reprinted).

The basic ideological problem that the Du Bois resignation underscored was that the NAACP's traditional program of civil libertarianism did not touch the fundamentally economic problems of the Negro. Of course, Bunche reported favorably on the plan he and Abram Harris, among others, had presented to the NAACP in 1935 but admitted it had had no significant effect. In addition, to its emphasis on economics and unity with labor, the plan called for decentralization in the control of the association and increased democratization.

"Blackmailing" the NAACP was how Myrdal described his technique of getting a detailed response from the NAACP by sending it a preliminary draft of his treatment of the NAACP based on Bunche's work. He also wrote that he quoted Bunche extensively only to refute him: "[T]he reason why I give so much space to defending the organization against Ralph is that I have found his attitude very much spread among Negro intellectuals and I wanted to set it right."[53] Assured of a favorable audience, White and Roy Wilkins produced lengthy point-by-point responses to the critique.

Prior to Myrdal's treatment, the NAACP leaders had responded to a draft of "Programs, Ideologies, Tactics." They contended that the NAACP had moved away from the narrow focus on legal defense that characterized its first two decades to a more offensive strategy dealing with equal pay for equal work and educational inequalities. Expressing their frustration with Bunche after the long hours spent answering questions, they launched a personal attack. White wrote:

> Unfortunately, Ralph has been too long sheltered in academic circles, I fear. This has led to his going on field trips as a social investigator instead of being able to identify himself as a member of the community who has to live there instead of dropping in for a few days' visit to look at the people there as specimens under a microscope. This makes some of his judgments either outdated or, at times, naive.[54]

White ends with the wish that Bunche could work for an organization like the NAACP long enough "to permit him to forget that he is a college professor" and "identify himself completely with the problems of the people."[55] White's comments reflect those of Wilkins, who had prepared a detailed response for White. It read, in part:

> Dr. Bunche, who conducted the survey, is a disciple of the "mass-action" school and a sort of armchair radical. That is, he is a professor in a college where his income is secure, and from this vantage point, both physical and economic, he is free to theorize on social movements. He can do this without any great danger to himself, and without the necessity of having to produce results in any program of social action.[56]

One wonders if the personal attack would have been launched had the critic not been an African American scholar. In fact, White hastens to assure Myrdal on another occasion that the "epithet academician" is being applied only to Bunche and not Myrdal "because your own approach is so completely lacking in the stuffed-shirt manner, I have never thought of you as an academician."[57]

On the substantive point that the NAACP lacked a mass base, Wilkins cited several local branches with predominantly working–class memberships but said complete branch data on the class makeup of members was lacking. He conceded that the only mass movement among Negroes was led by Garvey; however, it was intensely racial—"the very characteristic which Dr. Bunche finds so reprehensible in the NAACP."[58] Moreover, Wilkins stated that this mass of Blacks did not devote itself to the kind of agrarian and industrial revolutionary philosophy Bunche advocated. This point was reemphasized a year later in a very respectful response to Myrdal's draft in which Wilkins wrote that the "white masses of America are not radical, to say nothing of the black masses."[59]

More comfortable with the NAACP position, Myrdal defended it against Bunche's attack:

> To the younger school of more or less Marxian influenced Negro intellectuals, the N.A.A.C.P.'s policy is in the main only an evasion of the central problem, which is the economic one. Different as these critical judgments are in motivation (includes Northern sociologists and Southern liberals), they all express the fundamental defeatism in regard to the upholding of law and order which has become so widespread among American intellectuals of all colors and political creeds.
>
> This pessimism is exaggerated and, consequently, the criticism against the N.A.A.C.P. is largely unjustified.[60]

Even though he challenged the view represented by Bunche in *An American Dilemma*, Myrdal praised it as the best presentation of the radical critique. He also cites Wilkins's response to Bunche to the effect that adoption of a radical economic program would be suicidal for the organization.[61]

A similar defense is made of the work of the National Urban League by Myrdal. In an eighty-page critique of that organization, Bunche focused on the elite character of its leadership and the conservatism of its economic programs. Once again the subject of the critique is asked to respond to a draft. Eugene Kinckle Jones, the league's executive director, responded: "Dr. Bunche evidently has in his mind the type of organization he would form to correct the problems as he sees them, and he judges the National Urban League on the basis of this conception, while the N.U.L. has never announced a plan to solve all of the labor problems of the Negro."[62] He found Bunche's critique useless because it reflected "his focus on theory."[63]

In defending his critique as an honest effort to get at the facts Bunche waxed sarcastic:

From the swivel chair in which I weave the theories and spin the biases to which Mr. Jones reacts so violently I might add this gratuitous advice for Mr. Jones. His organization would perhaps become more effective if its leadership would take inventory of itself and its work, indulge in some self criticism now and then, ... [and pay s]ome honest attention to that made by others, and cease regarding the League as an end in itself, even though their own careers are molded in it.[64]

E. Franklin Frazier, in a letter to Myrdal, joined Bunche in his charge that the league was elitist and had not done educational work among Negro laborers.[65]

Myrdal published the National Urban League's defense of these charges and joined it against the radical's critique: "Generally speaking, *local Urban Leagues change with the community, and, in most cities, change as much in advance of the community as is possible while maintaining community good-will and financial support for their program.*"[66] Critics of the Negro organizations are charged with the mistake of assuming there should be only one unified Negro movement.

The Swede also defended interracial organizations from their radical critics as represented by Bunche. In "Programs, Ideologies, Tactics," memorandum, Bunche attacked the basic assumption of most interracialists, that race prejudice exists only because people are mistaken in their conceptions of other people. The assumption led to a strategy based on educational efforts and developing positive interracial feelings. He compared their objectives to the NAACP's but stated "they rarely indulge in pressure tactics." There are few Negroes in responsible capacities in this movement, and Whites are often permitted to act on behalf of the Negro. Because there are no competitive relationships between Whites and Blacks in these "little social worlds," Bunche deemed their efforts divorced from the reality of competitive working-class relationships.[67]

By contrast, for improving race relations, Myrdal put much more faith in the upper classes than in the working class. Actually, his thesis runs counter to that of Marx: "[T]he lower class groups will, to a great extent, take care of keeping each other subdued, thus relieving, to that extent, the higher classes of this otherwise painful task necessary to the monopolization of the power and the advantages."[68] Therefore, Myrdal sought to encourage the admittedly "weak efforts" of Southern liberalism. He believed groups like the Commission on Interracial Cooperation served a useful purpose even though they approached the problem indirectly.

Having devoted so much time to his analysis of the NAACP and National

Urban League at Myrdal's request, Bunche gave cursory treatment to a host of other organizations. These included the Amenia conference of 1916, National Negro Business League, Negro Cooperative Guild, National Negro Congress, Southern Negro Youth Congress, New Negro Alliance, Marcus Garvey's UNIA, Peace Movement of Ethiopia, National Movement for a 49th State, Commission on Interracial Cooperation, interracial activity of the YMCA, and the Commission on Race Relations of the Federal Council of Churches. In addition, in the lengthy appendix, he examines left-wing organizations, other minority organizations, and anti-Negro organizations.

Bunche's critique of left-wing organizations generally and the Communist Party in particular was at least as sharp as his attack on the Negro organizations. He contended that both the Communists and Socialists "pay lip-service to Marxian philosophy."[69] Declaring that the American Communist Party's interest in the Negro was dictated by political expediency, he outlined three phases in the evolution of the party's position on the Negro. Bunche concluded, "The fact is that Marxist, liberal and radical thinkers generally today, are confronted with the collapse of their hopes with respect to collectivism."[70]

Officials of Mexican-American organizations did not respond to Bunche's questionnaire, but the General Jewish Council did. This umbrella organization, consisting of the American Jewish Committee, B'nai B'rith, the American Jewish Congress, and the Jewish Labor Committee, sponsored a number of efforts studying race hatred in the United States. The China Society of America, established in 1913, promoted friendly relations between the Republic of China and the United States, and attacked stereotypic attitudes toward the Chinese. Bunche asserted that the group attempts to reach "primarily the intellectual and upper classes" and considered it "disadvantageous to the Chinese Americans to develop group consciousness."[71] Another group, the American Oriental Society, organized in 1842, was composed of scholars interested in "oriental subjects." Filipino rights, especially for laborers, was promoted by the Lejunerios Del Trabajo, formed in 1919 and based in Los Angeles. The Indian Rights Association was established in 1882 in Philadelphia by non-Indians concerned about the civil rights and general welfare of Native Americans. In general, Bunche's examination of the improvement and betterment organizations of other minorities was limited to information the organization provided on questionnaires. He made no critical analysis of these groups nor did he specifically compare them to their Negro counterparts. However, he did believe that their interests, like those of the Negro, could best be served by "allying themselves with those progressive forces which are aiming not at the solution of race problems alone" but at "real opportunity and real life for all citizens."[72]

A similar pattern prevailed in Bunche's reportage on organizations established by Negro women and Southern White women. For example, he stated that the Housewives League was an organization of Negro women formed for the purpose of increasing trade with Negro business and professional men and women and informing its members more fully on consumer matters. Bunche spared the Housewives League the sharp criticism given of the better-known National Negro Business League, which he regarded as reactionary. About the Association of Southern Women for the Prevention of Lynching, Bunche said that it had grown "out of the recognized need for a centralized agency and special machinery designed to change public opinion in the South toward the one specific evil of lynching."[73] He noted that the association opposed a federal antilynching law, preferring an educational approach over a legal approach.

Even this cursory examination of the protest and betterment organizations of these other minority groups was absent from Myrdal's final document. However, there was a fascinating appendix that compared the plight of women to that of Blacks. Entitled "A Parallel to the Negro Problem," it argued that women and children were two groups of people whose high visibility had led to their suppression. Myrdal pointed out that "the paternalistic idea which held the slave to be a sort of family member and in some way— in spite of all differences—placed him beside women and children under the power of the *paterfamilias*." Differences in the actual status of these several cohorts notwithstanding, the idea of a man's wife and children as his slaves played a role in the ideological defense of slavery. Therefore, reasoned Myrdal, "[f]rom the very beginning, the fight in America for the liberation of the Negro slaves was . . . closely coordinated with the fight for women's emancipation."[74] He then provided a brief history of the linkages between the movements, concluding, tellingly, with a quotation from the work of Alva Myrdal.

> In the final analysis, women are still hindered in their competition by the function of procreation; Negroes are laboring under the yoke of the doctrine of unassimilability which has remained although slavery is abolished. The second barrier is actually much stronger than the first in America today. But the first is more eternally inexorable.[75]

Another difference between Bunche and Myrdal emerged in their characterization of Garvey. Myrdal's treatment of the Garvey movement was of a much more redeeming nature than his younger colleague's. While admitting that Garvey organized "the only real mass movement that the American Negro has ever had," Bunche found that "[w]hen the curtain dropped on the Garvey theatricals, the black man of America was exactly where Garvey had found him, though a little bit sadder, perhaps a bit poorer—if not wiser."[76] Terming Garvey a swindler, Bunche said his call to race pride and consciousness was similar to that of Negro betterment organizations. Of course, Garvey's anti-White creed prohibited a policy of unity between Black and White labor. At best, his "feeble gestures toward Africa" afforded "a psychological escape for the black masses."[77]

Myrdal took issue with Bunche's conclusion that the Black man of the United States was left exactly where Garvey had found him: "the thinking and the feeling of the Negro masses on this point remains a mystery."[78] Recounting the extensive organizational structure Garvey developed in this country—although omitting the international chapters Garvey established—Myrdal described him as "a prophet and a visionary."[79] Still, "The Garvey movement illustrates—as the slave insurrections did a century earlier—that a Negro movement in America is doomed to ultimate dissolution and collapse if it cannot gain white support."[80]

White support was central for both Bunche and Myrdal. Bunche believed primary attention should be devoted to the establishment of alliances between Black and White workers;[81] Myrdal emphasized expansion of interracial ties and "fellow-feeling" among the middle and upper classes as a first step. Moreover, Myrdal acknowledged the utility of appeals to racial pride or "racial chauvinism" in building mass Black movements.

These differences are highlighted in Bunche's "Brief and Tentative Analysis of Negro Leadership." Slightly more than two hundred pages and dated September 1940, it was meant to complement "Conceptions and Ideologies of the Negro Problem" and "Programs, Ideologies, Tactics, and Achievements." Bunche repeated that his views were largely impressionistic because he had lacked the necessary data for a full treatment. His focus was on the social mechanisms by which Negro leaders were chosen and permitted to exercise influence. Were there "any peculiarly Negro factors" that enter into the Negro leadership equation, he asked, "which would not be found in the white leadership equation?"[82]

After a brief critical survey of the history of African American leadership, Bunche posited five categories or types of leaders: (1) the dynamic and aggressive leader; (2) the cautious, timid leader; (3) the "undercover" agent; (4) the symbolic head; and (5) the prestige personality. As a general rule, leadership among Negroes depended to a considerable degree on White acceptance. However, there was no necessary correlation between ability and prominence among Blacks or acceptance among Whites (19–26).

Under his first category of leadership, Bunche cited the case histories of a number of aggressive leaders in the South and of Northerners like Representative Oscar DePriest of Chicago, who toured the South preaching Negro rights. In general, though, Bunche did not speak positively about this type of leadership, which often depends on racial chauvinism. He gave a number of personal examples, demonstrating that such leadership limited itself to racial issues and ignoreed the wider world (62–72).

The second category of leadership had "many degrees of shading." Recognizing that the fear of economic reprisal, as well as more overt threats, had an effect on both leaders and followers, Bunche wrote that these Negro leaders may engage in trickster behavior and have "accommodated themselves to the social situation in much the same way that the Pullman porter flatters his white charge in order to get a larger tip" (34). Black college presidents were Bunche's prime example of this type of leadership.

More harmful was the "undercover" agent who performed various types of missions in the Negro community for the White bosses. Bunche included male and female machine politicians dispensing patronage and racketeers presiding over illegal empires in this category. He cited a long interview he and Myrdal had conducted with a "classic Uncle Tom" as typical. Mr. Jones, who managed the exhibits at the local "Black" fair, was proud of the influence he had among Whites. When Myrdal went in to see the fat lady on display in one of the concessions, he emerged feigning shock that a half-nude White woman would be displayed before gaping Negroes. Mr. Jones became greatly agitated about Myrdal's reaction and would not relax until a police sergeant assured him he would be protected from any adverse consequences (109).

Symbolic leadership was usually attached to the position held and was probably the most common type of Negro leadership. It included college presidents, lodge heads, and ministers. Although Bunche recognized that ministers and to a lesser extent lodge heads had the only real connection to the Negro masses, he was unsparing in his criticism of them: "The Negro ministers quite often have an unsavory reputation," and "are among the most active political leaders in many communities and are not always celebrated for their courage and integrity by any means" (125). Bunche went on to describe the corrupt activities of Negro ministers with political machines in San Francisco, Los Angeles, and St. Louis. Given the actual political power such leaders wielded, it is unclear whether the label "symbolic" was fully adequate.

The fifth category, prestige personality, included every Negro professional to a minor degree. Almost all prominent Negroes attain symbolic significance because "Negroes are still trafficking [*sic*] in firsts" (137).[83] Perhaps Bunche's own life would become the ultimate proof of this statement. At the time, however, he cited Bill "Bojangles" Robinson and Jesse Owens as "glamour"-type leaders who were often used by Whites. He noted that unlike some White leaders who have risen to great heights despite humble origins, prominent Blacks never play up their slave background or lack of formal training. In short, to be a "man of the people" is not prized.

An additional category, "Negro Leaders Designated by Whites" was tacked onto Bunche's original types. It is clear though that this type and some of the others overlap. In no category did Bunche find an "effective" leader of the Negro masses. And although he found it impossible to "type" a leader like Du Bois, he contended that there were no real ideological leaders and no effective organizational leaders. Concerning special qualities that Black leaders might possess, Bunche implied that oratorical ability and skin color were important factors in the Black community (he also found most Black leaders to be dictatorial). Yet the Black community was like the White community in its tendency to focus on the personality of leaders and to blame its problems on bad leadership.[84]

With the exception of his views on Black ministers, Myrdal's view of Black leadership was not nearly as negative as Bunche's, nor did he seem to find Bunche's categories that helpful. Using the poles of accommodating leadership and protest leadership, he profiled the history of Black leadership in two chapters. In addition to his more favorable impression of Garvey, Myrdal also defended the leadership of Booker T. Washington against his critics. "It is wrong to characterize Washington as an all-out accommodating leader," he stated, because "[h]e never relinquished the right to full equality in all respects as the ultimate goal."[85] Moreover, "it is not proven that he could have pressed the bargain he made for the Negro people more in their favor"[86] given the grim reaction of the period.

By contrast, Bunche described Washington's leadership as essentially a retreat. Asserting that it is difficult to get people to rally around a retreat, the Howard political scientist challenged the notion that Washington was a mass leader. Citing the audiences he addressed and his acclaim among Whites, Bunche declared that although Washington's appeal was "certainly on behalf of the Negro masses," he "devoted little if any attention to the Negro peasants, the sharecroppers and tenant farmers."[87]

These differing views of Washington's legacy illustrated the more fundamental divergence in strategies between the American and the Swede.

Bunche was promoting radical grassroots agitation across racial lines; Myrdal believed such actions were premature and preferred a top-down approach to race relations—Myrdal's belief and hypothesis was "that the Negro's friend . . . is still rather the upper class of white people."[88]

This difference in strategies flowed from divergent views on the strength of the American creed. Agreeing with Myrdal that racial practices in the United States, particularly in the South, were too decentralized to warrant the label "fascism," Bunche was nevertheless much more concerned than Myrdal about the potential for fascism to develop and much less sanguine over the prospects of the American creed's becoming a reality.

> It must be noted that Americans are a very opportunistic and a very materialistic people. We have no traditional political theory, despite our alleged reverence for our "traditional institutions." We have demonstrated, too often, how easily we can push law, constitution and tradition aside when it suits our purpose to do so. No other country in the world boasts such fertile soil for demagogues and crackpots.[89]

Thus Bunche's fear is that an American Hitler and an American fascist party would find favor among poor Whites. And given the history of "lily-white Republicanism," Bunche is not certain that Negroes could depend on the legends of Yankee sympathy to save them.

Myrdal's experience in the United States, on the other hand, had convinced him that this country "relative to all the other branches of Western civilization, is moralistic and 'moral-conscious'" (early memos on the project did not mention moral and psychological issues).[90] Quoting John Dewey to the effect that "[a]nything that obscures the fundamentally moral nature of the social problem is harmful" (lxxi), Myrdal chose to cast the "American Negro problem" as a moral dilemma. The ideals that he believed all Americans, including African Americans, held in common included the essential dignity of the individual human being, the fundamental equality of all persons, and certain inalienable rights to freedom, justice, and fair opportunity (4). The tension created by a belief in equality on the one hand and the practice of racial inequality on the other created a dynamic that promoted change. Yet Myrdal realized that the strong stress on individual rights and the almost complete silence on the citizen's duties led to a kind of legalistic formalism that stressed the "letter of the law" rather than its "spirit" (18).[91] Still, Myrdal argued that the Negro, as a minority, has had little strategy available other than playing on the conflicting values held in the White majority group. "In so doing, he has been able to identify his cause with broader issues in American politics and social life and with moral principles held dear by the white Americans" (lxxvi). Myrdal did not see the situation changing in the future and in that sense, "this is a white man's country" (lxxvi).

It would be difficult to overstate the impact of *An American Dilemma* on race relations or on American scholarship. Just like Franklin Roosevelt's "second Bill of Rights" speech in January 1944—which helped to redefine American liberalism—the publication of Myrdal's book was a watershed event. As with most studies, especially lengthy ones, the impact was not immediate, but within two months Myrdal was being compared to Tocqueville and Bryce. Over a period of two years the praise shifted from the popular press to academic journals. Du Bois, despite the fact that Myrdal's work had eclipsed his own *Encyclopedia of the Negro*, praised the study as "monumental" and "unrivaled." Other Black intellectuals like E. Franklin Frazier, Richard Wright, Horace Cayton, Charles H. Thompson, and even the iconoclastic George Schuyler hailed the work. The Black press also joined the chorus of support.[92]

White Southerners were naturally more restrained in commendation. The South's most prominent social scientist, Howard Odum, called it "the best thing that has been done on the Negro" but was stung by the criticism of Southern liberals. Many of the best-known White scholars working in the field had collaborated on the project and felt it would be a conflict of interest to review it. Although many of them did not accept Myrdal's emphasis on social engineering or the attack on the objectivity of social science, they lent their general support to its conclusions.

Black scholars had hoped the study would open up foundation coffers for further studies but the opposite happened.[93] What funding was available went to White scholars who were in institutional settings that could provide them with support. Nonetheless, the Myrdal focus on the moral and psychological foundations of the race problem would shape the research agenda for the next twenty years and influence the civil rights movement.

It was suggested by some scholars and some journalists in the Black press that Bunche was the secret author of *An American Dilemma*. St. Clair Drake declared that Bunche had assumed major responsibility for the study after Myrdal was forced to return to Sweden during the war, although Arnold Rose received the credit. David Southern credited Samuel Stouffer with having completed the study. Southern also reported that the Carnegie Corporation tried to prevent publication of parts of Bunche's work.[94] Fortunately, Myrdal and Bunche were open about their biases as scholars and frank about their disagreements. Ironically, those disagreements saved Bunche from some of the criticism directed at *An American Dilemma*.

There were opponents of the Myrdal study. Carter G. Woodson, the "father of Negro history," curtly dismissed it as "the impressions of a foreigner of limited and infrequent contact with Negroes."[95] Ralph Ellison, in a review that was not published until 1964, wrote that it was "the blueprint for a more effective exploitation of the South's natural, industrial and human resources." He charged that Myrdal refused to point out how the American creed is manipulated and used to deny the existence of an American class struggle. But Ellison saved his strongest criticism for Myrdal's portrayal of Black culture as pathological. Why, Ellison asks, if my culture is pathological must I exchange it for a higher culture that embraces lynching, Hollywood faddism, and radio advertising? He suggested that "it will take a deeper science that Myrdal's . . . to analyze what is happening among the masses of Negroes."[96]

Several critics on the left wrote extended attacks on the work. In a chapter entitled "An American Dilemma: A Mystical Approach to the Study of Race Relations" in his classic book *Caste, Class and Race*, Marxist sociologist Oliver C. Cox questioned Myrdal's use of *caste* to characterize race relations in modern, urban society. In a sophisticated analysis of *An American Dilemma* that recognized its importance as a source of information, Cox suggested that Myrdal's unwillingness to use the term *class* and inability to see race in any terms other than biological lead him to misapply the concept of caste. Having avoided the problem of a political-class interpretation, he must then find an acceptable moral or ethical interpretation. However, Cox asserted that the unquestioned acceptance of the American creed that Myrdal settled on is unrealistic, even for one of the originators of the creed—James Madison. Madison acknowledged the self-interest of factions, and Cox, too, thinks each group would insist on its own material or self-interested interpretation of the American creed.[97] Thus, Cox's views were closer to those expressed by Bunche in the four memoranda.

An even longer critique was published in 1946 by Marxist historian Herbert Aptheker. In a strident introduction to Aptheker's work, Doxy Wilkerson—a staff member on the Carnegie-Myrdal study—attacked "Gunnar Myrdal's ideological monstrosity" with no mention of his own role in it. Aptheker repeated in detail both Cox's charge that Myrdal overemphasizes the strength of the American creed and underemphasizes the role of economic self-interest and Ellison's contention that there was and is much that is viable in Black culture. Aptheker was a pioneer in revealing both the scope and types of resistance Blacks undertook against the institution of slavery. Although he offered a number of substantive criticisms of Myrdal's work, his rhetoric and ideological views, like those of Cox, relegated the critique to the margins of the academic world.

Eventually, even Bunche accepted Myrdal's conclusions as his own. The book exerts an influence even today. *A Common Destiny: Blacks in American Society*, published in 1989, was an attempt to update the changing position of Blacks in American society since 1940. A group of social scientists organized as the Committee on the Status of Black Americans received a commission from the National Academy of Science to conduct the study. Noting that their six-hundred-page study comes forty-five years after Myrdal challenged Americans to bring their practices into line with their ideals, editors Robin Williams and Gerald David Jaynes focus on the continuing institutional discrimination against Blacks. The study was criticized by Richard Herrnstein for refusing to consider evidence concerning racial differences at the individual level. The committee was also criticized by a number of Black scholars for not having included more Blacks.[98]

Other studies continue to use Myrdal's work as a starting point. Samuel Huntington, for example, argues that the national unity of the United States rests on the political ideas expressed in the American creed rather than the cultural traditions that underlie most nations.[99] Charles Hamilton has premised his major biography of Adam Clayton Powell, Jr., on the extent to which a major political figure can force the "system" to apply recognized standards of equal treatment to the "American other." In short, does the American creed apply to those with whose actions we disagree or was Madison right about "selfish" interpretations?[100] This "self-interest" is one of two foci Jennifer L. Hochschild drew from Myrdal in her study of school desegregation, *The New American Dilemma*. Calling Myrdal's approach "the anomaly thesis," she examines whether or not incremental policy-making combined with the *will* to make a change can bring about school desegregation.[101] A final example is Rodgers M. Smith's critical article "Beyond Tocqueville, Myrdal, and Hartz: The Multiple Traditions in America." Smith suggests that Myrdal, like Tocqueville, treats racism as mere prejudice and denies the self-contradictory elements of the American creed. Smith contends that a perspective that recognizes multiple traditions in American thought would reveal a complex pattern of conflicting traditions that makes reactionary change as likely as progressive change.[102]

Of course, such a perspective runs counter to the modernization approach that underlies Myrdal's analysis. In one sense both he and Bunche are right. Myrdal recognizes that in the short run the strength of White prejudice will prevent working class unity but that an appeal to the American creed could provide a weapon for racial progress. Thus he anticipates the civil rights movement and even helps prepare the ground for its development.[103] Martin Luther King, Jr., for example, in his first book, *Stride Toward Freedom*, casts the problem of segregation and racism in moral terms and then cites Myrdal as supporting his argument.[104] Other leaders, like Malcolm X and Jesse Jackson, also saw racism as a fundamentally moral issue.

Yet by overemphasizing the strength of the American creed among all segments of the population, Myrdal failed to recognize the importance of the power of vested economic and political interests, as well as the importance of competing ideologies. Bunche, on the other hand, foresaw the rise of intolerant demagogues like Joseph McCarthy and the Cold War ideologues of the fifties. He also recognized that the political and civil rights that could be won would not address the fundamental economic differences that continue to divide Whites and Blacks, and other minorities as well.

Unfortunately, both Myrdal and Bunche accepted Frazier's view that Black culture was either White American culture or a pathological imitation of it. Thus, Bunche accepted to some extent Myrdal's belief in a unified American culture with a single dominant set of values. From Myrdal's perspective, unlike freedom and equality, prejudice and discrimination were contradictions of the American ethos rather than central values of that ethos. In fact, they were merely highly particularistic and localized mental phenomena grossly inferior to the fundamental American ethos.[105] Of course, subsequent scholars have argued not only that a person can maintain contradictory beliefs for an indefinite period of time but also that racism may be a permanent characteristic of Western culture.[106]

Finally, although *An America Dilemma* contains an extended critique of the entire corpus of classical and Chicago school sociology, and includes an attack on American Marxism as having the same "do-nothing" or "laissez-faire" orientation as the sociological theories of Sumner and Park, it ultimately commits the same kind of errors in the name of a mechanistic, value-conscious sociology.[107] And although Bunche's bottom-up approach is more sensitive to Black agency than Myrdal's top-down approach, their overall cultural framework blinded them to the engines of racial protest that developed in Black churches and on Black college campuses, and that later challenged the very notion of an "American other."

7

From The Outside—In

Our bond with Europe is a bond of race and not of political ideology. . . . It is the European race we must preserve; political progress
will follow. Racial strength is vital—politics a luxury. If the white race
is ever seriously threatened, it may then be time for us to take our
part in its protection, to fight side by side with the English, French
and Germans, but not with one against the other for our mutual destruction.
—Charles Lindbergh, in Wayne S. Cole, *Charles A. Lindbergh
and the Battle against Intervention in World War II*

Our nation is composed of no one race, faith, or cultural heritage. It
is a grouping of some thirty peoples possessing varying religious concepts, philosophies, and historical backgrounds. They are linked together by their confidence in our democratic institutions as expressed
in the Declaration of Independence and guaranteed by the Constitution. . . . Our success thus far as a nation is not because we have built
great cities and big factories and cultivated vast areas, but because we
have . . . learned to use our diversities.
—Wendell Willkie, *One World*

Finally, Bunche was back at his desk at Howard University ready
to start the fall term. It was September 1941, and it had been almost exactly
a year since the Howard professor had turned in his nearly three thousand
pages to Myrdal. Although the two men stayed in touch, the Myrdals were
in Sweden and Bunche was trying to get back to his African field notes.
Since the midthirties, he had warned against the rising tide of militarism in
Europe and the possibility of native fascism at home. In a 1935 paper delivered at a Howard conference, Bunche attributed the policies of Italy, Germany, and Japan to the internal drive of capitalism.[1] The following year he
addressed the 27th annual conference of the NAACP. In his talk, "Fascism

and Minority Groups," he urged the NAACP to develop a working-class base in order to fight fascism at home and abroad.[2] At the same time, just as the Italian forces were steaming through the Suez Canal to invade Ethiopia, President Roosevelt signed the Neutrality Act. Congress renewed it twice, strengthening it each time.

The Italian–Ethiopian War generated intense interest in the African American community. Black newspapers like the *Chicago Defender* carried reports on the debates in the League of Nations over the invasion. Blacks raised funds, organized clubs, held mass meetings, and sent two Black pilots to fight with the Ethiopian air force. A small Garvey club in New York distributed the following prayer to be read in Black churches: "Great God, grant that no Ethiopian soldier misses when he fires and that every Italian bullet goes astray."[3] It was a sign of the lack of influence at both the national and international levels that the United States and League of Nations barely protested Mussolini's actions.

The public outcry was only slightly greater in 1936 when the troops of General Franco rebelled against the leftist Spanish Republic. Although most Americans recognized Hitler's desire to conquer Europe, 59 percent approved the Chamberlain agreement in 1938. And a year later, when Hitler signed a pact with Stalin, the two dictators controlled the greater part of the north European plain.[4]

As Hitler's army rolled triumphantly through Denmark, Norway, Holland, Belgium, and France in the spring and early summer of 1940, Bunche gave increased attention to the threat fascism posed for Black Americans. With the collapse of the National Negro Congress into a front for the American Communist Party, he sought new ways to mobilize public support for the war raging in Europe. In June 1940, he wrote to Charles Dollard at the Carnegie Corporation proposing that the Myrdal study include a new section on the effects of a totalitarian victory in Europe on the Western Hemisphere with special reference to the Negro in the United States.[5]

In speeches and newspaper articles, Bunche attacked both fascism and communism. He wrote to William Allen White's newly formed Committee to Defend America by Aiding the Allies, offering support. He contended that Negroes had more to lose than any other group of Americans in the current world crisis. Two articles published in 1940 reveal a subtle shift in Bunche's thinking. In "Africa and the Current World Conflict," he wrote that the "slow but steady" progress in Africa under European imperialism would be totally crushed if Germany and Italy were to replace France and England as colonial masters.

> Now that the Germans have conquered France, French Negroes, who for-
> merly were able to walk as men in France, who knew nothing of Jim Crow
> in Paris or elsewhere in the French nation ... find Nazi-dictated signs barring
> them from cafes, hotels, and even prohibiting them from buying railroad tick-
> ets. ...
>
> While this shocking transformation is taking place in Nazi-controlled
> France, British Africans in the British colonies are still able to present their
> grievances even while Britain is sorely beset.[6]

Even this backhanded praise stood in sharp contrast to the criticism leveled
at France and Britain in Bunche's dissertation and in *A World View of Race*.

Another article appearing in the same month asked the Black universities to assume a major role in indoctrinating Negro youth with the values
of democracy. In the same year that he called for a less subjective, less pro-
pagandistic Negro history, Bunche asked his colleagues to abandon their role
as "an objective and disinterested clearinghouse for the scientific truth."
"[T]oo often our search for 'Truth' becomes an escape device whereby we
can divorce ourselves from the tough and dangerous controversies of the
world."[7] While professors regale their students with an unrealistic dream
world, radical and lunatic-fringe organizations attract them because of their
efforts to deal with the real world. In a speech before the Association of Colleges and Secondary Schools for Negroes, the Howard professor outlined
seven points that teachers should be obligated to make with their students,
points that emphasized an international perspective that moves beyond
racial provincialism and embraces the precepts of democracy.[8]

One practical alternative to the National Negro Congress that emerged
during this period was A. Philip Randolph's march on Washington movement. As President Roosevelt began to pump enormous sums of money into
the defense industry, African Americans had found it impossible to get jobs.
Bunche—who the year before had prepared a memorandum for Mrs. Roosevelt arguing for the right to work, the right to remuneration on the basis
of merit and performance, and the right to advance in salary and rank[9]—
was quick to join forces with Randolph. He was one of seventeen signato-
ries of a letter to Roosevelt asking for action to open up defense industry
jobs to Blacks. When the president did not respond, Randolph threatened to
lead a protest march of 100,000 Negroes down Pennsylvania Avenue. Failing in his efforts to dissuade Randolph, Roosevelt signed Executive Order
8802, prohibiting employment discrimination in government and defense
industries and establishing the Fair Employment Practices Commission.
The mass action threatened by the march on Washington movement be-

came the model for the civil rights movement, especially the 1963 March on Washington. Bunche probably did not agree with Randolph's decision to make his 1941 effort an all-Black affair. Randolph, however, having learned from his experience with the National Negro Congress, feared Communist infiltration.

A group of Black professionals living in Washington in the 1940s worked closely with the NAACP and other civil rights groups in lobbying New Deal officials. They formed the informal Brookland Rod and Gun Club, which boasted that its members never went fishing or hunting. Members of the club (named after a D.C. neighborhood) included educators Herman Branson and Albert DeMond, poet Sterling Brown, attorneys John P. Davis and Bernard Jefferson, and Ralph Bunche.[10]

One day Bunche's phone rang, and Conyers Read, a history professor from the University of Pennsylvania, was on the line. Read was now working for the new Office of the Coordinator of Information (the COI, which later became the Office of Strategic Services, the OSS), in the Library of Congress, under the leadership of Colonel William J. Donovan, a Republican Wall Street lawyer. Read said an African specialist was needed and offered Bunche the job. Bunche, eager to contribute to the war effort, entered public service never to return to academia.[11]

Bunche's appointment came two months before Pearl Harbor and the formal U.S. entry into the war. Until that event American public opinion had been decidedly ambivalent on participation. Yet there was no doubt in Bunche's mind that the struggle against fascism was a life-and-death struggle for the Negro.

The irony of defending American democracy while fighting segregation at home was not lost on Bunche. Even his appointment to the COI reflected the inability of his mentors to judge him apart from his color. When the COI sought Harvard's advice on an African specialist, it was told of constitutional historian Benjamin Fielding Wright's opinion of Bunche "as one of the few—perhaps the only—Negro graduate student he has known at Harvard who [was] able to compete for fellowships on equal terms with the better white students." Professor C. H. McIlwain responded that Bunche was "the best graduate student of his race at Harvard in my time."[12] With this qualified support from Harvard, Bunche was appointed as senior social science analyst in the Library of Congress at $4,600 a year. Rejected by the army because of physical disabilities, Bunche was now fighting the war in the best way he could.[13]

The scholars and writers rounded up to serve the COI and its parallel organization, the Office of Facts and Figures, headed by poet Archibald MacLeish, had two objectives. First, they were to provide the president and key military officials with the information, progress reports, and surveys necessary to conduct the war. Second, they were to respond to the "untruths" of Axis propaganda and to conduct their own psychological warfare. Among Bunche's colleagues at the OSS were economists Charles Hitch and Emile Dupres, Russian expert Gerald Robinson, China expert Burton Faho, historians Conyers Read and Hajo Holborn, South American agent Maurice Halperin, and German expert Herbert Marcuse.[14]

Working under Conyers Read, head of the British Empire Section of the OSS Research and Analysis Branch, Bunche was called on to accumulate as much information as possible on colonial and native policies and problems, and race relations in British Africa (Kenya, Uganda, Tanganyika, Zanzibar), the Rhodesias, the Union of South Africa, the South African Protectorate (Bechuanaland, Basutoland, Swaziland), and the mandate of South West Africa. He also followed events in French, Portuguese, and Spanish Africa. He was to keep current with the international situation and anticipate important events through analysis of the most recent dispatches and reports.[15]

Finding that the existing data on Africa were limited mostly to encyclopedias, he quickly broadened his sources and established a daily routine: maintaining biographical card files; reading relevant clippings sent daily by the Press Intelligence Service; reading daily transcriptions of shortwave broadcasts; and inspecting regular reports on documents, books, and periodicals received in the Research and Analysis Branch library. Information gleaned was supplemented with firsthand reports from informants and Bunche's own network of friends.

Typical of the kind of work Bunche was doing was an extensive survey of Liberia. The development and use of Liberia's airport was important to the allies, and Bunche interviewed a number of Liberian officials and even Firestone Rubber Company employees. The report is extremely critical of the U.S.-Liberian elite that controlled Liberia along with Firestone.

> There can be no doubt that the lot of the natives in Liberia is considerably worse than that of the natives in some of the better administered British or French colonies, such as the Gold Coast, Nigeria, Uganda or Dahomey. Certainly the natives in some of the more badly administered areas, such as the Congo or the Ivory Coast are no worse off. . . .
>
> Firestone affords the main source of economic life and in return has virtually its own way with the government. . . .
>
> The Liberian government is now strongly pro-American, though a few

years ago it tended to be rather suspicious of this country due to a fear generated by American participation in the Geneva Commission which was proposing an international mandate status for Liberia.[16]

Bunche noted the impact on morale of Liberian resentment stemming from the actions and racial attitudes of White U.S. troops and from Black U.S. troops' graphic accounts of discrimination in the United States.

A report on the Pan African movement examined Jan Smuts's Pan African plan, which Bunche feared would encourage Black Pan Africanism.[17] Ironically, two years later Bunche accepted an invitation from Walter White to serve on an NAACP subcommittee on the 1945 Pan African Conference with W. E. B. Du Bois, Channing Tobias, and William Hastie. At one meeting the question of whether the term *Pan-African* is geographic or racial was raised. Du Bois was of the opinion that it was both, connecting the interest of the darker peoples in colonial problems, which center in Africa but include the West Indies as well. Bunche strongly argued that any conference on the problems of Africa as a territorial whole should include Liberia and Abyssinia (Ethiopia), as well as exploited groups not generally classified as Negro. If the gathering was not to be limited to territorial African problems, however, Bunche believed that the East Indies should be included. Hastie thought that U.S. colonial problems such as Puerto Rico should be included. The subcommittee members reached no final decision as to the name or subjects of the conference.[18]

Preparing American soldiers for the countries in which they were to be stationed was one of Bunche's major responsibilities. One guide, *Union of South Africa, Soldiers Guide: What Americans Should Know About South Africa*, compared English and Dutch attitudes toward Blacks with those of Yankees and Southerners in the United States. Bunche urged American soldiers not to express their racial views.

In addition to the South African guide, Bunche produced two other small handbooks, *A Guide to North Africa* and *A Guide to West Africa*. The work on North Africa, a new area of expertise for Bunche, became crucial as the United States prepared for an invasion of North Africa following Pearl Harbor. While Bunche and his colleagues in Washington were keeping U.S. plans secret, OSS agents in North Africa were providing economic aid, developing friendly contacts, and spreading Germany's anti-Moslem propaganda. Bunche warned, however, that American soldiers must "get rid of stereotypes as to [the Africans'] mental, physical and social conditions" because the "elite African is more sensitive on racial matters than is the American

Negro." He also noted that the U.S. military must preserve "the legend of America as a liberalizing force in the world."[19]

A host of recommendations flowed from Bunche's pen as he prepared the U.S. military for its appearance in Africa. He proposed press releases in Africa that emphasized the principles for which the war was being fought and their significance for Africans; the Nazi racial philosophy; and goals for Africa. He also thought that a thorough analysis of African nationalism would help Americans understand African attitudes toward the war. Detailed maps and charts of African transportation and communication facilities, docks, harbors, navigable waterways, airfields, economic resources, population distribution, health hazards, hospitals, and other medical facilities should be prepared. Other recommendations included sending a team of doctors to look into tropical diseases, using African students in the United States as sources of information, and using African Americans wherever possible as collaborators and soldiers because he believed Africans trusted them more than White Americans: "Carefully chosen American Negroes could prove more effective than whites, owing to their unique ability to gain more readily the confidence of the Native on the basis of their right to claim blood relationship."[20] That Bunche was now willing to use what he once would have regarded as racial chauvinism marks his complete transition from a radical critic of the government to a most efficient and professional insider.

Friends noticed the change. Bunche's characteristic bluntness was replaced by a more cautious manner. He resigned from the Council on African Affairs (formerly the International Committee on African Affairs) led by Max Yergan and Paul Robeson, and criticized some of their statements as irresponsible.[21] Bunche was not permitted to speak or write freely and had to receive special dispensation to complete his work on the editorial committee of the Committee on Africa, the War, and Peace Aims. "This fact perhaps," says Rayford Logan, "explains in part his very mild comments at the May [1942] meeting."[22] Logan was not the only one critical of the new, less radical Bunche. He quoted Du Bois as saying just before a meeting of the Executive Committee of the *Encyclopedia of the Negro*, "Ralph Bunche is getting to be a white folks' 'nigger.'"[23]

Bunche had indeed curbed his radical prewar views. However, within the government he pursued a discreet civil rights agenda. When he advocated integration of the army and the pursuit of democratic policies as an example to the world, he was reminded that the sensibilities of the colonial powers must be considered. He was urged to emphasize the importance of Negro soldiers and workers to the war effort instead of promoting such principles as justice and fair play. Thus when Bunche recommended that the Office of War Information produce documentary films on Negroes in war industries and wartime affairs, he stressed that the message should be on the indispensability of Black manpower to winning the war rather than on social reform principles. As he had with Myrdal, Bunche demonstrated a capacity to shape his own views to the more pragmatic concerns of his superiors.

His work did not go unappreciated. When Bunche finished his handbook on North Africa, Undersecretary of State Edward R. Stettinius wrote him, "The men who finished the mission course have expressed their great appreciation of your work in grooming them for their job."[24] After a year on his job, Bunche's supervisor, Conyers Read, wrote the following evaluation in recommending him for a promotion that would raise his salary to $5600:

> Bunche has done brilliant work and continues to do brilliant work. He is without much doubt the ablest man in his field in America. . . . His knowledge of Africa is unique, his diligence in research very remarkable, and his tact in personal contacts outstanding. Many attempts have been made by other agencies to secure his services which he has resisted because he feels he can make a greater contribution to the war effort where he is. He would be absolutely irreplaceable at any price and was the only man in the British Empire Section to get an A-1 rating.[25]

Read noted that Bunche was one of only four members of the agency invited to attend the conference of the Institute of Pacific Relations at Mont Tremblant in Quebec in December 1942.

Despite complaining about the amount of red tape he had to cut through to get to the Mont Tremblant gathering, Bunche found it the best international conference he ever attended. Two questions were before the participants: What steps could be taken by the allied nations to aid in the better prosecution of the war and in the establishment of conditions of racial, political, and economic justice and welfare? And, How can this discussion be made the basis of the practical program of the United Nations during and after the war? Assembled to debate these issues were some of the leading colonial and foreign affairs experts in the world, including Lord Hailey, Sir Frederick Whyte, and Arthur Creech-Jones from Great Britain; Ramaswami Mudaliar and Sir Zafrullah Khan of India and Pakistan, respectively; Lester Pearson, Paul Martin, Brooke Claxton, and Hugh Keenleyside from Canada; Paul Hasluck from Australia; Leo Pasvolsky of the United States; and Sao-Ke Alfred Sze and C. L. Hsia of China.

Assigned to the roundtable group on Southeast Asia and rapporteur of the roundtable on social and democratic matters, Bunche found the discussions stimulating. The Atlantic Charter signed by Roosevelt and Winston Churchill served as their framework. Bunche strongly believed that paragraphs 4 and 5 of the charter, which promoted improved labor standards and security, and freedom from fear and want, must apply to peoples in the colonial territories as well as those in the occupied nations of Europe. This controversial position was eloquently presented in a speech in which he said that schemes of future international organizations must be

> the realization of the hopes, if not the clamorous demands, of the vast millions who struggle tragically to eke out a meager existence. The real objective must always be the good life for all of the people. International machinery will mean something to the common man in the Orient, as indeed to the common man throughout the world, only when it is translated into terms that he can understand: peace, bread, housing, clothing, education, good health, and, above all, the right to walk with dignity on the world's great boulevards.[26]

The speech was followed by an ovation, and an excited Bunche wrote to Ruth, "I am right in my element." And "My tongue is wagging all day long and most of the night."[27]

Bunche was indeed in his element. His speech and participation in the conference served to bring attention to the fact that he was one of the few American experts on colonial issues. And as he testified, the U.S. delegation was rather short on expertise on the colonial problems of the Pacific compared to the expertise of the Atlantic allies. Even in the private sphere there were no competent groups that studied postwar African and colonial problems, as there were in England. So great was Bunche's admiration for the skills and seriousness of colonial officials like Lord Hailey, Lord Lugard, Malcolm McDonald, and Sir George Gater that he criticized his old friends on the Committee on Africa, the War, and Peace Aims for their attacks on European governments. After all, said Bunche, "Does the Committee realize that colonial matters are debated freely in the British Parliament, who, to date, are their own best critics?"[28]

Although he found fault with his friends outside the government, Bunche also complained that the United States was missing an opportunity in regard to shaping postwar colonial policy. The conference had stimulated his desire to work on postwar planning and he began to feel confined by his research duties in the OSS. Leo Pasvolsky's Division of Political and Economic Studies in the State Department was the only place in Washington where work on postwar Africa was being done. In June 1943, Phil Mosley, a member of Pasvolsky's staff, inquired whether Bunche would be interested in working on a "colonial charter" for the postwar world. Bunche was. And he noted that only Benjamin Gerig, a former member of the League of Nations Mandates Section, was working on the project and he had little knowledge of Africa. However, the OSS was determined not to let Bunche get away.

When he attended a seminar held by the Canadian Institute on Public Affairs at Lake Couchinching in August 1943, Bunche reported that allies of the United States had become more outspoken in their criticism of U.S. policies in North and West Africa. The French alleged that the Americans might be embarking on an imperialist course in the French African empire. The British countered U.S. criticisms of its colonial policies by pointing to the treatment accorded American Indians and Blacks. The conference highlighted European fears of American dominance in the postwar period and the need for planning if a return to the status quo ante was to be averted.

On September 18, 1943, Ralph Bunche, Jr., was born, and his father took two weeks off for "nurse-maiding, sterilizing bottles, making formulae, seeding lawn, etc."[29] The war had had a positive effect on domestic life for the Bunches. Ralph was not traveling as much as in the past and had weekends and evenings free for domestic affairs.

No news of the State Department prospect arrived until December when an OSS personnel officer asked Bunche why he had not been told of Bunche's transfer to State. Bunche replied, "It's news to me." Later he learned that two or three high-ranking officials at the State Department had objected to his appointment because of his race.

> My sponsors finally brought the matter to [Secretary of State] Cordell Hull. He listened to the objections, received an account of my qualifications, and then his famed Tennessee temper flamed into invective. A man's color, he insisted, made no difference to him. He wanted qualified men in the department. That was the sole consideration that interested him. And so I was appointed—the first Negro ever to hold a "desk job" in the State Department.[30]

Hull's support, however, did not mean that Bunche's views on colonization were welcomed with open arms by a rigid bureaucracy with antiquated ideas about African and Asians. He was generally considered a do-gooder whose pleas for the self-determination of colonial subjects were regarded as impractical.[31]

By the mid-thirties, about forty-five Blacks held taken posts in most of the cabinet departments and New Deal agencies. In 1936, they formed the Federal Council on Negro Affairs, which the press usually called the "Black Cabinet" or "Black Brain Trust." During the war their numbers grew. In addition to Bunche and his college friends Robert Weaver and William Hastie, other young Blacks included James C. Evans, Frank S. Horne, Rayford Logan, and William J. Trent, Jr. Their numbers were supplemented by such Black leaders as Eugene K. Jones of the Urban League, William Pickens of the NAACP, and the distinguished Mary McLeod Bethune. Bunche wrote that these positions in the federal government newly filled by Blacks marked "a radical break with the past."[32]

The State Department was one of the last of the federal departments to be integrated at the elite level. African American interest in foreign policy had long been regarded as quixotic at best and improper at worst. When Martin Luther King, Jr., decided to speak out on Vietnam, he was told by Black and White supporters alike to stick to civil rights.[33] The motivations behind such advice usually arose from different sources. Historically, the Black struggle for day-to-day survival in the United States had led many to see foreign policy as a luxury. Although there is a long history of elite concern with Africa stretching back to Paul Cuffee's sponsorship of a return to Sierre Leone in 1815 and the antebellum Black Conventions movement and missionary efforts, the masses were not involved in foreign policy concerns until the rise of Marcus Garvey in this century. More recently, Black objections to King's Vietnam stance had more to do with attaching the civil rights cause to a controversial foreign policy position than to a belief that King had no right to speak out on foreign policy.

White objection to Black participation in foreign policy springs from a more fundamental source. Historically, Whites have not accepted Blacks as full participants in the polity. How can one speak for the United States if one is regarded as the American "other?" There are numerous examples of this refusal to accept African Americans as part of the organic whole, ranging from the inability of Africans to become naturalized citizens and of free Blacks born in this country to obtain U.S. passports to more recent examples such as the refusal to name Blacks as ambassadors to non-Black nations.[34] In regard to the last point, a catch-22 is often at work. African Americans are regarded as "not objective" or "too emotional" to deal with African or Caribbean affairs but as lacking the expertise to handle policy dealing with nations outside those regions.

Given that most societies have normally assigned the making of foreign policy to an elite, Bunche's winning even a junior decision-making position in the department was a symbolic breakthrough. The objection to Bunche's appointment from within the State Department is evidence of its symbolic status because no questions were raised regarding his qualifications.

There is a constant tension between elite policy making and mass participation in a democratic society. As one scholar notes, "Historically . . . the national interest is whatever the public or the electorate wants it to be."[35] Concretely, however, especially in the area of foreign policy, some voices count more than others. Two experts on ethnic politics have concluded that the influence of immigrants or ethnics has been "the single most important determinant of American foreign policy."[36] Ironically, although the loyalty of hyphenated Americans has been questioned by Presidents Theodore Roosevelt, Woodrow Wilson, and others, the loyalty of African Americans was seldom doubted. Still, the economic, political and social status of Blacks meant that their influence on foreign policy was negligible.

Symbolically, Bunche's position was more important than it was substantively. His initial assignment at State was to the Near Eastern and African Section of the Division of Territorial Studies. Soon after, Benjamin Gerig sought him for the Division of International Security and Organization (ISO) over the objection of Phil Mosely, head of the Territorial Research Staff. In July 1944 the transfer was approved, and Bunche moved into a basement office near the incinerator with other UN planners. The hierarchy above Bunche included Gerig; division chief Harley Notter; later, office director Ambassador Edwin C. Wilson; and then Alger Hiss. Overall responsibility rested with Leo Pasvolsky, special Assistant to the secretary, who was in charge of postwar planning.

Roosevelt had instructed the State Department to begin preparation for the postwar period as early as December 1939. Two years later, after Pearl Harbor, he ordered Secretary of State Cordell Hull to establish a special postwar planning staff. Led by Pasvolsky, one section worked on postwar boundaries in Europe, another with reparations, and a third with disarmament issues. Later on, a section under Notter was added to deal with a new league of nations and a new international court of justice.

On the issues that would most concern Bunche—trusteeship and the formation of a world organization—Roosevelt was well ahead (though not in control) of the game. Less idealistic and more pragmatic than Wilson, his belief that permanent United States involvement in world affairs was necessary for stability and security was his motivation for seeking a new world league with peacekeeping powers. In a similar fashion, his commitment to trusteeship, which would eventually lead to self-determination for colonized people around the world, also assured the United States of strategic air and naval bases from which to police the world.[37]

Roosevelt's ability to blend or mask power concerns with idealism perfectly fit the public mood. Perhaps the best expression of the new internationalism was written by Roosevelt's old political adversary Wendell Willkie. *One World*, Willkie's 1943 account of his travels in the Middle East, the Soviet Union, and China and a plea for U.S. cooperation to preserve the postwar peace, was only the third nonfiction book in the country's history to sell more than a million copies. Willkie was joined by other prominent figures, such as publisher Henry Luce, Herbert Hoover, and Vice President Henry Wallace, in portraying the Soviets as just like us, with a simple, realistic man—Stalin—as their leader. Not to be outdone, FDR said the Chinese were even more like us and proclaimed China "one of the great democracies of the world."[38] The historian Robert Dallek attributes this new fellow feeling at the international level to an extension of American harmony at home. The war had brought about a heightened sense of unity, with every group contributing to the success of the effort. By early 1945, between 80 and 90 percent of Americans supported involvement in a new world league. Seventy-six percent wanted a world police force, 75 percent were willing to keep the U.S. military abroad after the war, and an astounding 82 percent were willing to continue to ration food for five years if that would feed the hungry.[39]

The British and French wanted no part of this new internationalism. To them "trusteeship" sounded like a system whereby American interests would take over their colonial empires. When Prime Minister Churchill, in his famous "First Minister" speech in November 1942, said that he had not become the king's first minister in order to preside over the liquidation of the British Empire, he was directly referring to trusteeship regimes. Churchill believed that Roosevelt's own conception of the British Empire belonged to the time of King George III.

For his part, Roosevelt treated Churchill and the question of India in much the same way he dealt with Southern senators on the issue of race relations and civil rights. He subjected them to monologues and proclaimed his liberal intentions but refused to act when it might undermine wartime cooperation. Bunche noted that the president often "tweaked" Churchill and the French on colonial questions: "He used to needle the French on Indo-China, and Churchill particularly on Gambia, which he saw once going through there, and which certainly isn't the pearl of the British Empire."[40] Roosevelt said of Gambia that "the people are treated worse than the livestock. Their cattle live longer [human life expectancy was twenty-six years]."[41] Although Roosevelt's actions did not match his rhetoric, he did insist on timetables for independence in India and in all European colonial possessions.

Similarly, Roosevelt used wartime anticolonial feeling to oppose de Gaulle's plans for taking control of France and resurrecting the French Empire. Thus at the Brazzaville Conference of French colonial administrators in February 1944 he refused to compromise with the basic French position that French Africa belonged to France and that France owed no accountability to the international community. In fact, Bunche, who attended the conference, wrote that the "French were clearly thinking in terms of strengthening the bonds of empire, of drawing the natives into closer communion with France and French institutions."[42]

The president's ideas about trusteeship reflected, in part, the work of two of Bunche's Harvard professors. Arthur Holcombe and Rupert Emerson published *Dependent Areas in the Post-War World* in October 1941. In it they call for reform and extension of the mandates system based on the legal precedent established by the Havana Convention in 1940. However, Roosevelt wanted to go beyond any plan that implied the sovereignty of one nation over another. In a Memorial Day address in 1942, Undersecretary of State Sumner Welles announced the death of the age of imperialism.

> If this war is in fact a war for the liberation of peoples it must assure the sovereign equality of peoples throughout the world, as well as in the world of the Americas. Our victory must bring in its train the liberation of all peoples. Discrimination between peoples because of their race, creed or color must be abolished. The age of imperialism is dead.[43]

Welles's views reflected those of Roosevelt, but they were in sharp contrast to those of U.S. military officials.

Just as Bunche arrived at the State Department, it was joining with the Department of the Interior in pushing to place the former German (then Japanese-held) islands in the North Pacific—the Mariana, Caroline, and Marshall Islands—under the trusteeship of a postwar world organization. James Forrestal, the secretary of the navy, and Henry Stimson, the secretary of the army, were wholly opposed to this notion for national security and strategic reasons. They wanted the United States to annex the islands. This conflict kept trusteeship off the agenda of the Dumbarton Oaks Conference in August 1944 in Washington and almost killed the concept completely. The British had already sidetracked the idea that all colonial territories should undergo a period of trusteeship under the international organization. They had also convinced Cordell Hull that the goal for dependent territories should be self-government and not necessarily independence.

Bunche suggested that Hull's views on trusteeship were similar to or even more advanced than his own.

> [A]fter I joined the Department in 1944, . . . one of the first things we had in that Committee [dependent areas] was a policy paper relating to French North Africa, and it had come to the Committee from Mr. Hull himself.
>
> I had thought that I was an advanced thinker on colonial questions, but when I sat there and read Mr. Hull's paper, I realized how conservative I was, because this paper was an incitement to rebellion in North Africa. It couldn't have been described as anything less, because it gave these people the full right, if they had aspirations, to get their freedom by hook or crook. Our job in the Committee was to tone down the paper that had come from the Secretary of State himself. That was one of my first assignments in the State Department, and it always struck me as amusing, because I thought I was going to have to go in there and fight my way; that if you mentioned liberation of peoples you would be very much in the minority.[44]

Perhaps this was the only assignment in which Bunche played a conservative role.

Outside the government, African American organizations took an active role in denouncing colonialism and pushing for self-determination for colonized people; the march on Washington movement, the National Council of Negro Women, the Council on African Affairs, and the NAACP all lobbied for the right of self-determination for colonial peoples. They were particularly interested in the Dumbarton Oaks proposals for a postwar international organization.

As an adviser to the U.S. delegation to the International Labor Conference in Philadelphia in May 1944, Bunche had helped to secure adoption of the recommendation "Minimum Standards of Social Policy in the Dependent Territories." This action pushed forward the idea that the Atlantic Charter applied to the whole world and could serve as a rationale for action on the dependent territories in the upcoming Conference on International Organization in San Francisco. Because trusteeship was bumped from the Dumbarton Oaks meeting, Bunche had been largely relegated to the role of note taker for its sessions. However, he did learn some valuable lessons in drafting and made a number of important contacts, including his future boss at the UN, Victor Hoo of China.[45]

Promoted to associate chief of the Division of Dependent Affairs under

Gerig in December 1945, Bunche worked with a group set up by Pasvolsky to prepare for the San Francisco conference. The 9th Conference of the Institute of Pacific Relations, dealing with security in the Pacific, in Hot Springs, Arkansas, in January 1945, had given Bunche an added opportunity to understand some of the colonial officials he would be working with in San Francisco. En route, he discussed the colonial question at length with Creech-Jones and Captain L. D. Gammans, M.P., British colonial officials whom he had met previously. Creech-Jones asked Bunche if the State Department's newly created Division of Dependent Affairs "would deal with the American dependencies as well as those of other countries and whether it would concern itself with the problems of the '15 million dependent peoples in the United States proper.'"[46] He was clearly on the offensive, impugning the moral superiority of the American position by reference to the status of American Negroes. The British were willing to talk about the principle of accountability, but they made it clear to Bunche that no international organization would be permitted to inspect the colonies or exercise any sanctions with respect to colonial administrations. Creech-Jones asserted that the "developing Nationalist groups in these territories [the British Empire] would much prefer to make slower but surer progress under British control than to take chances on an uncertain premise of more rapid progress under international arrangements."[47]

Creech-Jones was also negative about extending the idea of regional commissions to other dependent areas. He contended, for example, that racial attitudes prevalent in the United States made cooperation difficult on the Anglo-American Caribbean Commission. Bunche, on the other hand, saw the commission as a possible model (he was appointed to the United States seat on the commission in September 1945).

Before the war, Bunche might have joined in Creech-Jones's attack on American racism. However, in the current context it was clear to him that the colonial powers (British, French, Dutch) were now going on the offensive in order to protect their colonies from the anticolonial forces (Canada, the United States, Australia, and New Zealand) pushing for postwar change. Bunche's response to them was to delink the struggle of African Americans from that of the colonized:

> There is utterly no connection between the two problems. . . . The Negro is an American, and his struggle is directed exclusively toward one objective: the full attainment of his constitutional rights as an American citizen. Unlike the colonial peoples, the American Negro, who is culturally American, has no nationalist and no separatist ambitions.[48]

A generation later, Martin Luther King, Jr., would use a similar response in comparing the nonviolent civil rights struggle in the United States to the revolutions occurring in Algeria, Cuba, and southern Africa.

The United States was prevented from taking as forceful a role on the anti-imperialistic side as Bunche and his State Department colleagues might have wished, not primarily due to the status of American Blacks but because the military and President Roosevelt coveted Pacific military bases. Among the casualties of this position was a proposed declaration of principles to apply to all non-self-governing territories that had been a project of the United States. But at Yalta in February 1945, Roosevelt, Churchill, and Marshal Joseph Stalin of the Soviet Union agreed that the trusteeship system to be established should include only territories then held under mandate; those that might be detached from enemy states as a result of the war and might by agreement be placed under the system; and such other territories as might voluntarily be placed under it by the states responsible for their administration. Which of the specific territories in the above three categories would actually be placed under trusteeship was left for subsequent agreement.[49]

Going into Yalta, the U.S. military advisers led by Admiral Wilson had proposed to solve the problem of the strategic islands in the Pacific by ninety-nine-year lease arrangements. The Yalta agreement ruled out the lease option and just days before he died in Warm Springs, Georgia, on April 12, Roosevelt endorsed the State and Interior Departments' recommendation that the United States proceed with a proposal to establish a trusteeship system. What emerged going into the San Francisco conference, however, was a system that included two types of trust territories: strategic and non-strategic.[50]

Six days after the president's death, Bunche left for the United Nations Conference on International Organization (UNCIO) as a technical adviser to the U.S. delegation.[51] Throughout the long train trip the Pasvolsky group worked on the U.S. proposal plan for trusteeship. After the opening meeting in the Opera House, Bunche wrote to Ruth, "I did feel a bit proud this afternoon at being the only Negro who sat on the first floor. . . ."[52]

The San Francisco conference generated a great deal of African American interest. Prior to the conference, W. E. B. Du Bois and the NAACP had sponsored a colonial conference at the 135th Street branch of the New York Public Library that attracted forty-nine representatives from the Caribbean, India, Southeast Asia, and Africa. On the eve of the conference, a large Harlem rally sponsored by the Council on African Affairs, the NAACP, the

West Indian National Council, and the Ethiopian World Federation emphasized the end of colonialism and imperialism as prerequisites of world peace and security. Although the NAACP, represented by Walter White, Mary McLeod Bethune, and Du Bois, was the only Black organization of the forty-two American organizations that were official consultants to the U.S. delegation, other African American organizations sent observers. Their primary interest was the question of trusteeship.[53]

Aside from Harold Stassen, who headed the U.S. delegation assigned to work on trusteeship, Bunche thought the U.S. representatives were weak.[54] Calling it the hardest-working conference he ever attended, Bunche played a major role behind the scenes. According to his assistant Lawrence Finkelstein, Bunche seized every opportunity to exert "situational leverage." Although the U.S. government had abandoned plans to introduce a draft declaration of principles governing all dependent territories, the Pasvolsky group had developed such a draft. When the British delegation introduced a weak draft on trusteeship, hoping to forestall a stronger U.S. proposal, it was amended and greatly strengthened by an Australian proposal. The Australian proposal relied heavily on the U.S. draft declaration given to the Australian delegates "informally" by Bunche. Bunche's official account of this event reads as follows:

> Although not a member of the five-power group, Australia had also submitted to the Conference a trusteeship proposal which was very broad in some of its provisions and which at a late stage of the deliberations of the Conference Committee on Trusteeship contributed no little to the provisions of chapter XI of the Charter.[55]

Bunche also pushed for a "conservatory clause," which appears in the United States Charter as Article 80; it covers the period between the lapsing of the League mandates system and the negotiation of new trusteeship arrangements. The Americans fought to make the Trusteeship Council one of the principal organs of the UN, one that would include all the permanent members of the Security Council.

The signing of the charter was a landmark in international cooperation. It laid the basis for the decolonialization process that would occur over the next thirty years and also set the course of Bunche's career. His own work on trusteeship along with Gerig's was publicly acknowledged by Stassen. In a letter to Ruth, Bunche revealed the full extent of his involvement.

> Stassen, Gerig and I received full credit for winning the toughest fight of the Conference. We have a Trusteeship Chapter in this Charter, tho many thought

it could never be pulled off. It is not as good as I would like it to be, but better than any of us expected it could get—there were long periods here when it seemed that we would lose and would have no Chapter at all. A good part of the phraseology, inc. some of the most difficult provisions was drafted exclusively by me. It is a thrill even for your blasé old hubby to see his own writing in it—writing over which he struggled for long, long hours in a desperate effort to break what often seemed to be impossible impasses....[56]

While the pace of decolonialization would soon outrun the deliberate stages envisioned in San Francisco, much as the civil rights movement in the United States gained speed from the *Brown* decision, the charter gave the cause of independence and self-government an international legitimacy it had lacked before the war.

Mary McLeod Bethune organized the National Conference of Negro Leaders on June 23, 1945, in Washington, D.C., that was attended by fifty persons representing some thirty groups with a combined membership of more than eight million African Americans. The conference expressed support of the UN Charter with the understanding that under Article 87, the Trusteeship Council could hear oral petitions from colonized peoples. The Council on African Affairs encouraged ratification of the charter even though it did not guarantee the advancement of colonial peoples. Similarly, Du Bois endorsed the charter while questioning the absence of colonial representation on the Trusteeship Council and the right of oral petition without the consent of the specific colonial power. All agreed that the trusteeship system was an advance over the League of Nations mandates and a positive first step.[57]

The excitement, the bargaining, the drafting, and the opportunity to shape world events captured Bunche's imagination. In a letter to Ruth he said:

Many of my colleagues here are convinced that they will be working in the new intl. org. within a year. That's a decision we will have to make before long ... if things go right.... In many ways it would be great for all of us and especially the children—a new life, new surroundings, good schools, no ghettoes and no jim crow.[58]

Following the San Francisco conference, he gave several speeches in Los Angeles stressing the importance of the charter in promoting human rights. Every Negro, he said, should study it carefully.[59]

Bunche's hard work was rewarded in the fall of 1945 when he was assigned to advise Edward R. Stettinius at the Preparatory Commission of the United Nations in London. Adlai Stevenson was Stettinius's deputy and he and Bunche began a lifelong friendship. Even though many other friends from San Francisco were in the delegation, Bunche found London depressing. He was now widely known and respected among the colonial powers and actually represented the United States on subcommittees of the Executive Committee, where he continued to push the British, French, and Dutch to make the Trusteeship Council effective.[60]

Following the London meeting, Bunche was sent to Paris in mid-October as a member of the U.S. delegation to a conference of the International Labor Organization. Once again Bunche was lauded for his hard work and skill by the head of the delegation, Frances Perkins, former secretary of labor. In fact, he found himself playing a leading role in the deliberations, although the food in Paris made him constantly sick.

Then, after six weeks in Washington, Bunche was off to attend the first session of the UN General Assembly, which met in London in January 1946. Traveling on the *Queen Mary* with the other members of the U.S. delegation—Stettinius, Eleanor Roosevelt, John Foster Dulles, Abe Fortas of the Department of the Interior, Senators Tom Connally and Arthur Vandenberg, and other advisers—Bunche found the trip dull. He became critical of the delegation, praising only Mrs. Roosevelt and Fortas. Although the United States had emerged from the war as the world's most powerful nation, its leadership was "weak, vacillating and stumbling," said Bunche.[61] The only clear policy seemed to be an emerging anticommunism that would soon harden into a cold war.

For his part, Bunche wanted to see the Trusteeship Council set up and trusteeship agreements submitted for implementation. Crucial to effective international oversight of the colonies was a system of reliable information about what was happening. Under the limited obligation contained in Article 73(e) of the charter, colonial powers had only "to transmit regularly to the Secretary-General for information purposes, subject to such limitations as security and constitutional considerations may require, statistical and other information of a technical nature relating to economic, social and education conditions in the territories for which they are respectively responsible." Alarmed that this provision would leave the secretary-general with little or no reliable data on conditions in the trust territories, Bunche persuaded the Chinese delegation to introduce a proposal that created the Ad Hoc Committee on Information for Non-Self-Governing Territories, which later assumed permanent form. Thus, once again, Bunche demonstrated that he would not be constrained in his actions by the limited horizons of U.S. policy makers.

The constraints on the making of U.S. foreign policy must have run through Bunche's mind when he was approached by Ping Chia Kuo, the young Chinese secretary of the Assembly's Trusteeship Committee, about becoming assistant director of the Trusteeship Division in the future UN Secretariat. Although Bunche initially commented privately that Kuo, who knew nothing about the subject, should be working for him, when he returned to Washington he discovered that Gerig thought he should help the Trusteeship Council get off on the right foot. Consequently, on April 22, 1946, Bunche joined the UN Secretariat on six weeks' loan as acting director of the Trusteeship Division.

Each time Bunche's temporary term of service was about to expire, Victor Hoo, the Chinese UN assistant secretary-general for trusteeship, would beg to have it extended. Finally, in December 1946, UN Secretary-General Trygve Lie asked the United States to permit Bunche to assume the directorship of the Trusteeship Division. Gerig, Bunche's immediate State Department supervisor, very reluctantly agreed to the request while writing that he had never worked with anyone more congenial or helpful, and that he would always regard Bunche's move as temporary. For his part Bunche replied that he hoped to return to the department in the "not too distant" future. Yet Bunche was still a full professor at Howard and had repeatedly stated his intention to return to teaching once the setting up of the UN was complete.[62]

Two factors—a kind of push and pull—led Bunche to accept the UN post. First was the attraction of making sure that the agreements he had worked so hard to get in San Francisco were actually implemented. He had found a good deal of backtracking by figures like South Africa's Field Marshal Smuts and had encouraged Lie to set a tradition of activism in engaging member states on trusteeship issues. By November, Bunche had succeeded in getting eight trusteeship agreements—Tanganyika, Togoland, British Cameroons, French Cameroons, French Togoland, Ruanda-Urundi, New Guinea, and Western Samoa (altogether a total of 14 million people)—through the General Assembly bureaucracy. In December, the Assembly approved the agreements, finally allowing for the setting up of the Trusteeship Council. Lie's executive assistant, Andrew Cordier, wrote to Bunche, "[I]f it had not been for your superlative services it is really doubtful whether we should have a Trusteeship Council at this moment."[63]

Along with the excitement of building a new international system came the negative feelings Bunche had toward Washington. The segregation so evident in everyday life in the nation's capital had long irritated him. Ironically, he found that the situation only marginally better in New York. Two of the UN housing projects owned by New York Life and Metropolitan Life Insurance could deny occupancy to "nonwhites." Fortunately, a new development, Parkway Village, near the UN headquarters was integrated, with almost the entire population composed of UN staff and delegations. The Bunches sold their home at 1510 Jackson Street in Washington and moved to an apartment in Parkway Village.

Beyond Washington's segregation, Bunche must have felt that a career at the State Department would be both frustrating and limiting. Although he had made friends easily, his views were definitely not mainstream. It would be unlikely that he could advance much beyond the rank of a middle-level bureaucrat with marginal influence on foreign policy. The UN offered a world stage on which he knew many of the players and they knew him. The highest levels of the Secretariat were integrated, and Bunche was already being asked to serve as the principal staff person for one of the five major UN bodies. For the next twenty-five years he would work for the UN.

8

Pioneer Peacekeeper

I have a deep-seated bias against hate and intolerance. I have a bias against racial and religious bigotry. I have a bias against war; a bias for peace. I have a bias that leads me to believe in the essential goodness of my fellow man; which leads me to believe that no problem of human relations is ever insoluble. I have a bias in favor of both Arabs and Jews in the sense that I believe that both are good, honorable and essentially peace-loving peoples, and are therefore as capable of making peace as of waging war. I have a strong bias in favor of the United Nations and its ability to maintain a peaceful world.
—Ralph Bunche, American Association of the United Nations, 1949

With these beliefs, Ralph Bunche, who had never served in an armed force, took command of the first-ever global army of peacekeepers. It was, in Bunche's words, the first "army everyone fights to get into."[1] Moreover, it was an army not foreseen or mentioned in the United Nations Charter. How it came about, given the obstacles of the Cold War and the absence of any agreement authorizing its use, is a story that speaks to the heart of Ralph Bunche's skill as an international leader of uncommon dimensions.

On May 14, 1948, the British high commissioner and the last British soldiers left Palestine on a cruiser of the Royal Navy. On the very same day, the State of Israel was proclaimed. On that day, too, the UN, Soviet and United States representatives competed to see who could recognize Israel first. President Truman's recognition of Israel reversed an earlier U.S. position that had advocated UN trusteeship for Palestine.[2]

Israel's action unsettled Arab nations and prompted Egypt to enter Palestine the following day. Guerrilla violence and then war broke out as forces from Jordan, Iraq, Syria, Lebanon, and Saudi Arabia joined Egypt's. To stop the violence and work out a solution, the UN Security Council appointed the "United Nations Mediator in Palestine." The person selected was a Red

Cross official and World War II hero from Sweden—Count Folke Bernadotte. On May 28, 1948, he arrived in the Middle East with a small UN staff that included Bunche as his chief assistant and the secretary-general's personal representative. Ten days of intense diplomatic negotiation yielded a truce agreement, of which Bunche said:

> The truce applied not only to Palestine but to seven Arab States, and it meant
> that the shipment of war materials had to be checked and controlled; the in-
> flux of immigrants had to be checked and controlled; the movement of war
> supplies had to be checked; it also meant checking airfields, ports, military
> lines, and it meant defining the military lines in order that it might later be
> decided whether either side had advanced beyond the positions held at the
> time the Truce went into effect.[3]

Bunche began to assemble the elements of what would quickly become a full-fledged peacekeeping force. The military observers were recruited from the states that were members of the Security Council's Truce Commission and included French, Belgian, and American observers. Every effort was made to distinguish them as UN personnel with whatever material was available—armbands, flags, helmets, and so on.

As the observers began to function as the only link between the warring parties, Bunche began to establish the peacekeeping guidelines. For example, he decided that the military members of the mission should be integrated into the secretariat and should not be armed. This, of course, ran counter to the military training of the troops involved, but Bunche insisted that arms would be a provocation and that the observers were not trained in the use of weapons in this unique situation. It was a correct decision, but in less than a year, ten members of the mission had lost their lives, including Count Bernadotte.

Bernadotte's fate was sealed as he attempted to move the warring parties from a truce toward a settlement. In an effort to get the parties to a negotiating table at Rhodes, Bernadotte (with Bunche's help) drafted a number of suggestions having to do with, among other things, the boundaries of Transjordan, the Negev desert, the Galilee, and Jerusalem. Both sides rejected the suggestions, but the Israelis were particularly incensed that Bernadotte's proposals ignored the boundaries established in the General Assembly's original partition resolution and did not provide for a Jewish Jerusalem. Although the proposals were merely suggestions, Bernadotte became the second-most-hated man in Israel, after British Foreign Minister Ernest Bevin.

Just as the truce seemed about to break down, King Abdullah of Transjordan urgently summoned Bernadotte. He insisted that the UN "must force us" to accept the cease-fire even though his own prime minister had strongly rejected an extension of the truce. Bunche urged Bernadotte to go to New York to persuade the Security Council to extend the truce while permitting Arab nations to save face. Here Bunche's genius at pushing the limits of UN authority to accomplish the objective of peace becomes apparent. During their flight to New York, he drafted Bernadotte's report to the Security Council in which he asked the council to order a cease-fire and the demilitarization of Jerusalem, threatening the use of coercive measures under Articles 41 and 42 of the charter in case of noncompliance. The Security Council complied and its uniquely forceful action allowed Arab nations to save face while proclaiming a truce that was to last until a peaceful settlement of the Palestine issue.

With the truce firmly in place, Bunche drew up a plan for the supervision of the truce and instructions for observers that became the basis for UN peacekeeping. He commented that the second truce imposed by the Security Council, on July 15, 1948, "worked fairly well for the first few months. But we had warned the United Nations that no truce could go on indefinitely, and that some further step would have to be taken or that fighting would be inevitable."[4] Of course, fighting did break out in October and December of 1948. The UN General Assembly responded by creating the Palestine Conciliation Commission (PCC) composed of representatives from the United States, France, and Turkey.

The creation of the PCC reflected the two tracks the UN was pursuing in Palestine. On the one hand, the PCC had a mandate from the General Assembly to mediate the dispute in an attempt to find a solution to the Palestine problem. On the other hand, the Security Council had authorized the peacekeeping assignment of the United Nations Truce Supervision Organization (UNTSO), which was to supervise the truce and secure the armistice. Although there would eventually be tension between these dual missions, at the time both were seen as necessary and complementary.

The PCC pressured Bunche and his staff to speed up the armistice negotiations,[5] but his success with the armistice agreements actually enlarged the peacekeeping tasks of UNTSO. In addition, to the truce arrangements, which remained in place, the Security Council validated (Res. 73) the armistice agreements that made UNTSO an autonomous operation monitoring compliance with the armistice provisions. What was to be a transitory operation until permanent peace negotiations made them unnecessary became the peace itself.

Within a few years, the Israelis, who had initially welcomed the Rhodes agreement, began to see the armistice agreements as the major obstacle to a negotiated settlement. The 1949 Rhodes meetings had been Israel's first appearance as an equal to other states on the world stage. Its first application for admission to the UN had been denied and was granted only after three of the four armistice agreements were signed. Now, however, it believed that the agreements prevented it from applying the military pressure on the Arab states necessary to bring about a permanent settlement, that after the PCC failed to produce results, the Arabs hid behind the agreements, failing to recognize or deal directly with Israel and protracting the conflict.[6]

For his part, Bunche seemed to give the armistice agreements a character both temporary and permanent. He declared that the states involved had pledged not to resort to force; each agreement incorporating an article that was, in effect, a nonaggression pact. The agreements were to remain in effect until a peaceful settlement was reached, and to add political force, they were signed on behalf of the respective governments rather than the commanders in chief of the armies, as was accepted practice in such matters.[7]

Perhaps Bunche sensed the difficulty of reaching a permanent settlement at that time in the Middle East. His work not only stopped the fighting but also established the central role of the UN Secretariat in running peacekeeping operations. He also established the principle of the nonuse of force by UN military personnel. Remarkably, Bunche was the first—and until recently the only—international figure to bring the Israelis and Arabs together for direct negotiations. Although both sides praised him publicly at the time for his objectivity, he has received some criticism over the years by both camps for being biased. The record supplies little evidence to support such charges. Peggy Mann reported an unsubstantiated story that in the early days after a long negotiating session with the Irgun and Menachem Begin, Bunche said something to Begin that was not in his official report of the meeting: "I can understand you. I am also a member of a persecuted minority."[8] On another occasion, British M.P. Richard Crossman jokingly asked Bunche if he had managed to turn anti-Semitic yet as a result of being immersed in the Jewish question. Bunche replied, "That would be impossible." Asked why, Bunche explained, "Because I've been a Negro for forty-two years."[9]

Others thought Bunche's color gave him an advantage with the Arabs. Brigadier General F. P. Henderson, who was assigned to the UN Mediator's Mission during the Rhodes negotiations, made the following observation:

I came to believe that Dr. Bunche's color was a significant factor in his success in ending the first Arab-Israeli war. As you are aware, Mediterranean and Middle East peoples come in many shades, from pale olive to very dark brown. Dr. Bunche, who was light brown by color, could have been a native of any of the nations involved in the conflict. When he was meeting with any of them, they could feel that he was of their own kind, working with good will and honesty to resolve a tragic conflict in a manner just and fair to all. This helped establish rapport, especially among the Arabs, that a white man, such as Count Bernadotte, the first Mediator, could not likely achieve because of still vivid and bitter memories of years of colonial rule by whites. To me, it was a rare privilege to be able to work for and with this truly great man.[10]

On more than one occasion, Bunche commented that the real victims of the conflict in the Middle East were the 800,000 to 900,000 Palestinians displaced by the war. After the armistice talks were concluded, Bunche returned to his work on trusteeship and had little to do with the Truce Supervision Organization he had set up or the monitoring of the armistices he had negotiated.

In the late forties, Secretary-General Trygve Lie had suggested the need for a permanent International Guard that would perform peacekeeping functions but the idea was quickly dismissed. In part, it was a victim of the developing Cold War. The Cold War became hot when the Security Council voted for the United Nations to intervene with force against the North Korean invasion of South Korea, designating the United States as the "Unified Command" of the UN forces (the Soviets were not present for the vote). This "enforcement" action under Chapter 7 of the UN Charter was not "peacekeeping," yet it was nevertheless applauded by Bunche: "The UN is saved, and so is the world."[11] As Chinese troops were poised to enter into battle with the UN forces in Korea, Bunche declared that the UN "must have readily at its disposal, as a result of firm commitments undertaken by all of its members, military strength of sufficient dimensions to make certain that it can meet aggressive military force with international military force, speedily and conclusively."[12]

Yet the UN action in Korea made such preparedness impossible. Trygve Lie's bold public support of the Security Council action on Korea led to a Soviet boycott of the secretary-general. The UN Military Staff Committee, which depended on the cooperation of the five permanent members of the Security Council, was inoperable. Ironically, despite the strong actions of the UN in regard to South Korea (and Taiwan), Senators Joseph McCarthy and Pat McCarran were having some success in convincing the American public that "a large group of disloyal citizens had infiltrated the UN." Bunche was among those investigated (see chapter 10).

From the end of the armistice talks until late 1956, Dag Hammarskjöld, who replaced Lie as secretary-general, did not seek Bunche's advice on questions involving the Middle East notwithstanding his obvious experience. But when he reorganized the Secretariat in 1953, he demonstrated his confidence in Bunche by naming him to one of the new posts of undersecretary without portfolio (later changed to undersecretary-general for special political affairs). In this new role, Bunche served as the Swede's principal troubleshooter. Hammarskjöld, like Bunche, believed that the UN had to respond to demands placed on it and improvise when necessary. In a 1959 press conference, he remarked, "If we feel that those demands go beyond the present capacity, from my point of view, that in itself is not a reason why I, for my part, would say no, because I do not know the exact capacity of this machine."[13] Bunche and Hammarskjöld worked well together because both were willing to test the capacity of the machine. Thus, Hammarskjöld concluded that there was no question that has been put to the UN to which he would reply, "It cannot be done."[14]

The sudden and unexplained decision to cancel Western financing for the Aswan High Dam prompted Nasser to nationalize the Suez Canal Company. Despite Hammarskjöld's effort to defuse the situation, it was not until October 1956, when Israel, France, and the United Kingdom invaded Egypt to protect the Suez Canal that the idea of a readily available UN peacekeeping force was well received. Having initially been led to believe that the United States supported the action, Britain and France were surprised when the United States and other Commonwealth countries opposed them. Looking for a graceful means of exit, Lester Pearson of Canada proposed that the secretary-general be authorized "to begin to make arrangements with member states for a United Nations force large enough to keep these borders at peace while a political settlement is being worked out . . . a truly international peace and police force."[15] The Assembly agreed to the proposal and asked the secretary-general to submit a peacekeeping plan within forty-eight hours. Hammarskjöld, who was initially doubtful that such a plan could work, called on Bunche to implement it.

The United Nations Emergency Force (UNEF I) faced two major tasks. One was to negotiate with Nasser the entry and conditions under which the UN forces would replace the French, English, and Israelis in Egypt. This task was assigned to Constantin Stavropoulous, the legal counsel, and eventually taken over by Hammarskjöld himself. The second task—to assemble the actual force as quickly as possible—was given to Bunche. Hammarskjöld, noting that generals were plentiful, sent Bunche into the field with the order "Now, corporal, go and get me a force."[16] In mobilizing, equipping, and transporting a multinational force to Egypt, Bunche improvised as best he could. Helmet liners were requested from U.S. stocks in Europe and spray-painted United Nations blue to distinguish them from the four armies in Egypt. Food was requisitioned from the seventeen ships marooned in the Suez Canal at the time the Egyptians blocked it. By the time Hammarskjöld was ready to enter into negotiations with President Nasser, an advance guard of 650 officers and men had been assembled by Bunche and was in Naples awaiting orders.

Eager to forestall a Soviet initiative to send a joint Soviet-U.S. force to the area, Hammarskjöld and Bunche pressed ahead with the political and technical details of a UNEF buildup. Always conscious that they were establishing precedent even as they improvised, the two UN officials carefully developed the legal basis for UNEF presence and actions. Bunche was especially sensitive to symbolic issues and insisted that the UN troops fly only the UN flag and not the flags of their respective countries. Once the British and French saw the face-saving presence of the international force, they agreed to withdraw their troops by the end of the year.

With the withdrawal of the British and French and the beginning of the canal-clearance operation led by the U.S. general R. A. "Spec" Wheeler,[17] the most formidable task remaining was the pullout of Israeli troops from the so-called Gaza Strip. The Egyptians were willing to permit the deployment of UNEF troops in Sinai and on the west coast of the Gulf of Aquaba, but the Israelis refused to allow a similar deployment on their side of the line. Although the Israelis wanted a guarantee that Egypt would not reoccupy the area, Bunche and Hammarskjöld were in no position to furnish it. Moreover, the press tended to exacerbate the situation.

Pressure from the General Assembly and a national television address by President Eisenhower encouraging the Israelis to withdraw, finally brought about compliance.[18] When UNEF forces replaced the Israelis, the Egyptians insisted that their governor reenter Gaza amid much pomp and publicity. It was left to Bunche to calm Israeli fears and make sure that the Egyptians remained only in symbolic control.

The UN undersecretary had many factors working against him. Press accounts tended to view the UN as agents for a reassertion of Egyptian authority. For example, the *New York Post* accused Bunche of "exceeding his instructions" by permitting the Egyptians to resume rule in the Gaza Strip.

Bunche actually had little confidence that the leadership of either Egypt or Israel would abide by confidential agreements. During his shuttle diplomacy, he found both Nasser and Ben-Gurion had a distorted sense of history. Nasser, for example, insisted that the siege of Al-Faluja in 1948 had been an Egyptian victory; Bunche did not tell Nasser that he had negotiated the UN rescue of the Egyptian garrison from certain Israeli destruction in that conflict. Ben-Gurion shocked Bunche by suggesting that Count Bernadotte had brought on his own fate by drafting a proposal for the Israeli-Arab negotiations. Bunche was struck by how much Ben-Gurion had aged—mentally and physically—since their meeting in 1953.

Along with the irrationality of Ben-Gurion and Nasser and a hostile press, Bunche was receiving letters from Ruth, charging him with neglecting her and the children, pursuing fame and glory, and of irritability and aloofness at home. These missives combined with constant bouts of dysentery began to take a toll on his health. By 1958, Bunche had lost thirty-five pounds and began to show early signs of diabetes. He refused to take insulin until his condition reached a critical stage in midsummer 1958.

Still, the Suez Crisis had brought back old memories—both bitter and sweet—of his first experience in Palestine ten years earlier. He found the remoteness, antiquity, and religious history of Mt. Sinai deeply moving. Perhaps, most important, he and Hammarskjöld had created a new history. By 1958, UNEF had become an institution and was generally praised as a remarkable success. Despite all of the on-the-spot improvisation they had done, the UNEF was to become the model for all future peacekeeping operations.

The success of UNEF made possible at least a partial realization of Trygve Lie's original dream of an "international guard" policing the world's trouble spots. John Foster Dulles and the U.S. Congress were among those now calling for a permanent UN peacekeeping force. Hammarskjöld and Bunche, however, knowing the sensitivities and nuances involved in setting up such a force, were reluctant to establish a set response. Ironically, their next opportunity to use the peacekeeping skills they had acquired during the Suez crisis came in an effort to help extricate United States forces from the Middle East.

In April 1958, President Camille Chamoun of Lebanon amended the Lebanese constitution to allow for an unprecedented second term for himself. This act inspired a May uprising against the government that began in Tripoli and spread to Beirut, Sidon, and the Beka'a Valley. The rebellions were primarily the work of Muslim opponents of Chamoun and his pro-

Western policies. Many were admirers of Nasser, who had joined Egypt with Syria in the United Arab Republic earlier in the year.[19]

The Lebanese government attempted to involve the United States, Britain, and the United Nations in what was essentially a domestic dispute. Israel, Iraq, Turkey, and nations that feared Egyptian dominance joined in the inflammatory rhetoric. The Soviet Union, backing Nasser, warned against any Western intervention.

Hammarskjöld negotiated for and installed in Beirut a three-person UN Observation Group (UNOGIL) supported by a larger group of military observers. Bunche stayed behind in New York running the day-to-day operations of the UN and putting together the group of military observers. Despite a shocking deterioration in his physical condition, Bunche refused to admit he was ill and carried on with his heavy schedule. Yet everyone around him noticed his loss of energy and inability to focus.

Unfortunately, the Lebanese continued to press for a UN fighting force and when the government of Iraq was overthrown in a bloody July coup, the United States used it as a reason to land U.S. forces in Lebanon. Bunche was less involved in this crisis than he had been in any other, in part because of his failing health. The day after the marines landed in Beirut, Bunche recorded the following personal note:

> Because of my illness and irregular working hours I have sat down to meals with the family at home very seldom in the past few months. On this particular night, I got home early enough to have dinner with Ruth and Ralph— Joan was on vacation in Washington. I was very tired and cross and when Ruth said something that rubbed me the wrong way I slammed down my fork and napkin and stalked away from the table. Some days later when Joan came back and asked how I was doing Ralph Jr. piped up "Oh he's much better now; he's throwing his fork across the table again."[20]

By late August 1958, with medical treatment, Bunche's health was improving.

In the meantime, he and Hammarskjöld worked to increase greatly the number of military observers in Lebanon. This gave Eisenhower, who had immediately seen that U.S. intervention was a mistake, a chance to withdraw the marines. Hammarskjöld—who had fully supported his chief lieutenant through his illness—and Bunche were relieved when a new president was elected in Lebanon and the crisis died down. UNOGIL was withdrawn by December 1958.

The Congo crisis (see chapter 11) consumed Bunche and the UN for the first two and a half years of the sixties. While struggling to control the situation in central Africa, Bunche was equally concerned about the battle for civil rights at home. As a longtime proponent of equality and integration, he found time to give numerous speeches on civil rights and participate in the major marches.

Just when it seemed the Congo problem was stabilizing and Bunche might find more time for the struggle at home, events in the Middle East pulled him away again. Like previous conflicts in this region, it threatened to involve the superpowers.

Since September 1962, when an insurgent government replaced the imam, the traditional ruler of Yemen, Egypt and Saudi Arabia had been increasingly drawn into this civil war. Saudi Arabia was supporting the Royalists and permitted the imam's guerrilla forces to operate from Saudi territory. Nasser, in response to a plea from help from the Al-Sallal regime in Yemen, sent a large expeditionary force to support the Republicans. With U.S. ties to Saudi Arabia, Soviet links to Egypt, and British protectorates on the borders, the situation had all the ingredients for a disaster.

U Thant of Burma, who had assumed the secretary-generalship after Hammarskjöld's death in 1961, tried unsuccessfully for months to defuse the situation, finally calling on Bunche to make a fact-finding tour. It was a sign of Bunche's renown as a peacemaker that a huge, armed crowd met him at the airport in the Yemeni city of Taiz. Soldiers at the airstrip were unsuccessful in restraining the boisterous greeters, all of whom wanted to shake the UN official's hand. The welcome soon became a mob scene.

> At one point a path was cleared so that Bunche could witness the stoning and burning in effigy of King Hussein of Jordan. As they slowly approached the outskirts of Taiz, the crowd's mood changed, and the Yemeni ambassador to the UN, Moshin Al-Aini, who was escorting Bunche, explained gloomily that the crowd had been chewing *qat* and was becoming dangerous. The demonstrators began to rock the car violently, and Bunche felt that his last hour might really have finally come. To make matters worse, the car, an ancient Daimler, was overheating and was likely at any moment to spray the crowd with steam and boiling water, with unpredictable consequences. Al-Aini, as a last resort, ordered the driver to turn sharply off the main road through the crowd. They drove at breakneck speed across a field with the mob in pursuit, and escaped down a side street. Two and a half hours after leaving the airport, they arrived at the decrepit palace where Bunche was staying. Next day the same journey to the airport took eleven minutes.[21]

Demonstrative crowds also greeted Bunche in the capital, Sanaa, where he gave an enthusiastically received speech from an upper window of the palace. His conversations with President Al-Sallal were serious, yet Al-Sallal revealed no bitterness despite eight years of imprisonment and torture by the imam's government.

Marab, the legendary capital of the Queen of Sheba and a Royalist stronghold, was visited by Bunche in an Egyptian helicopter made in the United States and containing Soviet radio equipment. Bunche believed Marab was much like it must have been two thousand years ago, with dirt tracks for roads and no schools. He also spent a night in the British protectorate of Aden, where he enjoyed swimming at the British governor's private, shark-proof beach. The governor, Sir Charles Johnston, was badly misinformed about the situation in Yemen, Bunche found. His final stop was a visit to Nasser in Cairo. Nasser seemed anxious to withdraw his twenty-five thousand soldiers from Yemen, but the Saudis had turned down an American plan that would have led to that withdrawal. Nasser was particularly (and naturally) irritated that King Saud had twice offered two million Egyptian pounds to have him assassinated.

Having completed his fact-finding, Bunche proposed a plan to U Thant that would prohibit British interference in Yemeni affairs as a quid pro quo for assurances that Yemen would not intervene in Aden or the other British protectorates in the Gulf. In return for British recognition of the new Yemeni government, Yemen would not press its claim to the Gulf protectorates. The UN would give needed technical and economic assistance to Yemen, and the Americans and the Security Council would work to restrain the Saudis. Given the political and the physical conditions in Yemen, Bunche doubted that a UN peacekeeping force could be effective.

Despite misgivings by both Bunche and U Thant, Ellsworth Bunker—who had been on a diplomatic mission for the United States—succeeded in getting Security Council approval for UN observers to monitor a peace plan he had worked out with the Egyptians, Yemenis, and Saudis. Consequently, a small force of UN Yugoslav and Canadian soldiers (UNYOM) were sent to monitor the withdrawal of Egyptian forces and the disengagement of Saudi support for the Royalists. With no marked border and little cooperation from the two sides, the mission lasted only a few months. Within two years, the Egyptian army was in control of Yemen and stayed until the Egyptian defeat in its 1967 war with Israel.[22]

> Constantly rebuffed but never discouraged, they went round from state to state helping people to settle their differences, arguing against wanton attack and pleading for the suppression of arms, that the age in which they lived might be save from its state of continual war.

> To this end, they interviewed princes and lectured the common people, nowhere meeting with any great success, but obstinately persisting in their task until kings and commoners alike grew weary of listening to them. Yet, undeterred, they continued to force themselves on people's attention.[23]

These above words might well describe Ralph Bunche, even though they describe fourth century B.C. philosopher Sun Tzu and his disciples.

Bunche's last peacekeeping operation survived him. It did not end the civil war in Cyprus, but it did prevent the conflict from spreading. In fact, one measure of its success was that both sides wished it to continue—for different reasons. What 40,000 British troops had been unable to do, the 6,500-person United Nations Force in Cyprus (UNFICYP) was able to do.[24] In large part, the outcome was due to Bunche's accumulated expertise. At the same time he realized, as he admitted to the Canadian ambassador, that once installed, the UN forces might never be able to leave.

Like the Congo operation, the crisis in Cyprus involved the UN in its toughest role: peacemaker in a civil war. Fresh from the Congo experience, Bunche insisted that the UN force was not there to "assist" the government, as it had been in the case of the Congo. A more impartial formula, which was adopted in the Security Council resolution, prevented some of the problems and misunderstandings Bunche had had with Patrice Lumumba.[25] Moreover, Bunche made sure to distinguish UNFICYP from its British predecessor. The British had often become involved in the fighting, which contributed to the climate of violence.[26] The UN force, on the other hand, avoided any hint of participation. Bunche organized the force and inspected critical points on the island by helicopter but refused the role of mediator. Contending that his nationality would prove a handicap in the negotiations, he was pleased to see Galo Plaza Lasso,[27] a former president of Ecuador, take on the assignment. Unfortunately, when Lasso submitted a report and proposed solution, the Turks bitterly rejected it and the position of mediator lapsed.

Despite the failed political settlement, UNFICYP reduced the level of violence and a kind of uneasy peace prevailed. Bunche took pride in the operation, and when his secretary asked if he was bored, replied that in recent years his peacekeeping work had been "more interesting, and in a quiet way more self-satisfying and rewarding, than any I have done since becoming a member of the Secretariat."[28] Part of the satisfaction arose from Bunche's realization that he was creating a model: a nonviolent army that would become a permanent instrument of peace.

Cyprus flared up once again during Bunche's remaining time at the UN.

Incidents in March and November of 1967 prompted a threat from the Turkish mainland to invade. Arthur Goldberg, U.S. representative to the UN, asked Bunche to take on the negotiations with the Turks, Greeks, and Cypriots. Thinking that an American would be wrong for the job, Bunche demurred, insisting that UN Undersecretary José Rolz-Bennett was the best person for the job.[29] President Lyndon Johnson also sent Cyrus Vance to Ankara in an effort to halt Turkish action. Bunche, when Vance's heavy-handed technique failed, drafted an independent appeal from U Thant to the three governments. The appeal was successful and the crisis averted.

Bunche described his attitude toward peacekeeping while on Cyprus:

> I am a professional optimist. If I were not a professional optimist through 21 years in the United Nations service, mainly in conflict areas—Palestine, Congo, here, and in Kashmir—I would be crazy. You have to be optimistic in this work or get out of it. . . . That is, optimistic in the sense of assuming that there is no problem—Cyprus or any other—which cannot be solved and that, therefore, you have to keep at it persistently and you have to have confidence that it can be solved. . . . And so, personally, I am always inclined to pessimism, but professionally I am inclined towards optimism . . . that makes a good balance.[30]

Sun Tzu, almost two thousand years ago may have been one of the first professional peacekeepers; Bunche was certainly the first to institutionalize peacekeeping on an international scale.

In recent years, the peacekeeping activities of the UN have grown enormously, as has the controversy about them. Kofi Annan, a former undersecretary-general for peacekeeping operations (now the secretary-general) explains the primary factors behind the rapid increase. First, the proliferation of conflicts in areas where order during the Cold War had been maintained by the superpowers. Second, the increased degree of agreement among the permanent members of the Security Council to use the UN to try to manage and resolve these conflicts. Third, heightened public awareness, in large part due to the media, of humanitarian tragedies and a multitude of human rights abuses, and a concomitant desire to try to help.[31] The increase in demand for UN intervention has also broadened the types of international response. Whereas Bunche was usually involved in preventive diplomacy, peacemaking, or peacekeeping, peace enforcement and peace building have become common international responses to crisis situations. Peace enforcement, in particular, enforcement that includes the use of armed force under Chapter 7 of the UN Charter, has taken the UN in a different, more controversial direction than traditional peacekeeping. The UN is now involved in situations without a functioning government, as in Somalia, or in insisting that a government step down, as in Haiti. Whether Bunche would have supported the use of force in either of these situations is not known. However, it is useful to recall his principle of "self-defence" as it involves UN forces:

> When acting in self-defence, the principle of minimum force shall always be applied and armed force will be used only when all peaceful means of persuasion have failed. The decision as to when force may be used in these circumstances rests with the Commander on the spot. Examples in which troops may be authorized to use force include attempts by force to compel them to withdraw from a position which they occupy under orders from their commanders, attempts by force to disarm them, and attempts by force to prevent them from carrying out their responsibilities as ordered by their commanders.[32]

Even with such principles in mind, it was often Bunche's extraordinary attention to detail and his political judgment that saved the day. These qualities cannot be institutionalized.

9

The Model Negro

I am not unaware . . . of the special and broad significance of this award . . . in an imperfect and restive world in which inequalities among people are endemic and stubbornly persistent. From this northern land has come a vibrant note of hope and inspiration for vast millions of people whose bitter experience has impressed upon them that color and inequality are inexorably concomitant.
—Ralph Bunche, Nobel Peace Prize Acceptance Address, 1950

I've been the token Negro at too many parties for too many years. Coming home on the plane from Trygve Lie's funeral, an American sat next to me and—with all the good will in the world—began telling me how "important" I was "as an example. . . ." The point of it is that I'm not worth a damn as an example—except in a negative sense.
—Ralph Bunche, Interview, *Psychology Today*, 1969

The candidates for the Nobel Peace Prize in 1950 were Prime Minister Jawaharlal Nehru of India, former Prime Minister Winston Churchill of Great Britain, Secretary of Defense George Marshall of the United States, President Harry Truman of the United States, and the director of the Trusteeship Division of the United Nations—Ralph Bunche.[1] Bunche won and characteristically tried to give the award back.

The date was September 22, 1950, and Bunche's secretary Doreen Dorrington found him in the UN Delegates Dining Room. He had not expected to win, and when the shock wore off he began to have doubts that he should accept. After all "peace-making at the UN was not done for prizes," he reasoned and drafted a letter to that effect. When he revealed his intention to the secretary-general, however, Trygve Lie insisted that the award was also a tribute to the Secretariat and that the UN could use the prestige. The letter was not sent.[2]

It is difficult to imagine any award's having a greater impact. Within three months after the Palestine settlement, Bunche received more than one thousand speaking invitations; he accepted seventy. President Truman called Bunche at home on the evening of the announcement, and congratulatory messages flooded in, along with honorary degrees and job offers. Streets, schools, and housing projects were named after the new Nobel laureate. At one point, his seventy-plus honorary degrees were the most ever received by a living American. Job offers that neither Bunche nor any other prominent African American could get from elite universities now poured in from the University of Chicago, Stanford, the University of Pennsylvania, the University of California at Berkeley, and Harvard.[3] With the fame came requests for jobs, autographs, and money; crank mail; and a whole new set of friends.

Not that Bunche abandoned his old friends. In fact, Sterling Brown wrote that when he took Bunche into his neighborhood "joint," Brown's stock rose considerably. However, Bunche's new friends included the younger John D. and David Rockefeller. He listed Eleanor Roosevelt and Harold Stassen as personal references. Ernest Hemingway wrote that he would be highly honored if Bunche could find the time to meet him at the Ritz when in Paris. Visiting in California, he stayed with Will Rogers, Jr., and had Jack Benny offer his services. Season tickets for the Dodgers games and opening-night tickets for Broadway shows were a few of the perks he now enjoyed.

Yet Bunche was not a mere celebrity as he had defined the term for the Myrdal study. He was sought out for positions of at least some power and influence. On several occasions he indicated that he was an independent when it came to political party affiliation.[4] Practically, this meant that both the Republicans and Democrats sought him as a candidate. In 1960, Professor Alfred de Grazia of the Republican Party Planning Committee in New York County suggested Bunche as a vice presidential candidate. Robert Wagner wanted Bunche as Democratic senatorial candidate in New York in 1962, and Edward Costikyan, a Democratic county leader in New York, recommended him for the same office in 1964. At various times, Bunche was publicly and privately mentioned for appointment as ambassador to the Soviet Union and ambassador to Iran. In 1960, Senator John F. Kennedy invited Bunche to join his presidential campaign as a foreign policy adviser; as president, Kennedy explored the possibility of appointing Bunche to a position in his administration. Bunche's typical response to such approaches was that he was not a politician and that he was happy at the UN as undersecretary-general for special political affairs.

The most publicized refusal of a job offer came before the Nobel Prize. Shortly after Bunche concluded the negotiations on the Isle of Rhodes, he was contacted by Dean Rusk, who offered him the position of assistant secretary of state for Near Eastern, South Asian, and African affairs. On May 25, Bunche went to Washington and told President Truman why he could not accept the position. At a White House press conference Bunche explained that he would not return to Washington and subject his family and himself to the racial segregation there:

> There's too much Jim Crow in Washington for me. . . . It is extremely difficult for a Negro to maintain even a semblance of dignity in Washington. At every turn, he's confronted with places he can't go because of his color. . . . Washington isn't unique in this regard . . . but it is the national capital and its racial policies have a great symbolic significance.[5]

Bunche's public rejection of an unprecedented appointment for an African American in the State Department on the grounds of Jim Crow in Washington generated a great deal of debate in the capital and praise in the Black community. Typical was a letter from Mary McLeod Bethune: "You were very statesmanlike in refusing to accept the appointment as Assistant Secretary of State. It is a greater eye-opener to America and the world of the real feeling and thinking and courage of a man like you than we can ever put in words."[6]

The Nobel Prize increased Bunche's visibility and prestige exponentially. It placed him on a world stage as both a symbol of pride and progress and a symbol of international cooperation and goodwill. Hardly a day passed in the press without mention of Bunche's activities. Neither an entertainer nor an athlete, he was acknowledged by all as the best in his field and became a role model for a generation of African Americans.

Bunche appeared on the cover of the November 1955 issue of *Ebony* magazine, the lead article of which was entitled, "Bunche's Career Parallels Progress of American Negro." It asserted that the acclaim that Bunche had received over the past five years exceeded that ever accorded to any other single American, and *Ebony* concluded: "Beacon, stimulant, hero and inspiration to an entire race, Bunche will perhaps be ranked by historians as the most eminent Negro of the first half of the 20th century."[7] Indeed, a sampling of the accolades Bunche seemed to bear out their prediction:

> The public, the international recognition spontaneously accorded to you testifies to new attitudes in race relations the world over. I think it is easy for liberal and radical thinkers to underestimate this.   —C. L. R. James[8]

Despite the absence of a classic culture, the American Negro is a people. There is a tie that binds us all while yet allowing for the variegated lives we live. We call each other "brother," and we congregate together to eat "soul" food and listen to "soul" music. We are—from Muslim leader Malcolm X to the United Nations' Ralph Bunche—"Lodge Members." —Louis Lomax[9]

He is a model for all young men to follow. All parents can hold him up to their children as an example to which to aspire. All peoples the world around can see in him the great heights that the human spirit may reach—even in the face of great difficulty. —Mary McCleod Bethune[10]

The Negro in Birmingham ... knew that there were exceptions to the white man's evaluation: a Ralph Bunche, a Jackie Robinson, a Marian Anderson.
—Martin Luther King, Jr.[11]

From humble, crippling circumstances, George Washington Carver rose up and carved for himself an imperishable niche in the annals of science. There was a star in the sky of female leadership. Then came Mary McLeod Bethune to let it shine in her life. There was a star in the diplomatic sky. Then came Ralph Bunche, the grandson of a slave preacher, and allowed it to shine with all its radiant beauty. . . . —Martin Luther King, Jr.[12]

If he later became every closet racist's Negro-I-wouldn't-mind-living-next-door-to and an internationally acclaimed peacemaker, Bunche was a highly militant and decidedly pessimistic scholar of strong leftward political tilt in the Thirties. —Richard Kluger[13]

A few Negroes—among them, Ralph Bunche of the United Nations; Howard Thurman, chaplain of Boston University; John Hope Franklin, the distinguished historian; James Robinson of Crossroads Africa—have succeeded in gaining acceptance outside the ghetto not through civil rights leadership or business ventures but through their own personal efforts and accomplishments. —Kenneth Clark[14]

As the above quotations indicate, Bunche became a symbol of people's aspirations in some very different ways. For Blacks, Bunche was perhaps the first African American to achieve national and international recognition for his achievements outside the areas of sports, entertainment, and race leadership. Only George Washington Carver could challenge such an assertion, and his fame rested in part on his conforming to certain racial stereotypes.[15] Black children might aspire to be Joe Louis or Jackie Robinson, but their parents encouraged them to be Ralph Bunche. Bunche, in short, shattered a racial identity that limited Blacks to excellence in physical and artistic pursuits only. Without these limitations, Blacks now realized that they could pursue real power and influence rather than mere celebrity.

For White Americans, Bunche became a symbol of the success of democratic liberalism. His status proved that American democracy works. With the American creed and the U.S. Constitution as their operative ideology, Americans needed indicators that their system of government was valid or legitimate. In a system that glorifies self-interest, such self-transcending accomplishments as Bunche's provided a source of collective pride and assurance. At the level of the national psyche, they dramatically reduced the cognitive dissonance between the theory and the reality of American political culture so eloquently stated by Gunnar Myrdal. And it was, and is, through American political culture that citizens of all races gained, and gain, a sense of national identity.

For supporters across the globe of the UN concept, Bunche's achievements pointed to the potential of an international body and its civil servants, giving the UN a legitimacy that the League of Nations lacked. The fact that Bunche was of African descent and identified with the struggle of colonial peoples gave them hope and the UN a credibility not possessed by the league after World War I. Thus Bunche served as a bridge between the "First" and "Third" Worlds at a crucial time. Of course, the rise of the Cold War was quickly complicating the hopes of many internationalists.

Granted the crushing weight of expectations placed upon him, it is not surprising that Bunche repeatedly stated that he was not a race leader or even a diplomat. He once wrote, "I would consider fame to be fickle, fleeting and feckless."[16] Bunche's assessment would prove to be accurate in his own case; however, he was too much of a realist to think he could escape his celebrity and too much of a social engineer not to use his status to further his philosophy.

What Bunche attempted was bold, daring, and only partially successful. He attempted to redefine the American "other." For most of the history of the United States, what it is to be American has been defined by contrasting one group with another. It had often been easier to explain what an American was *not* rather than what an American was. This country has had little experience in describing what it is we all share. Bunche seized on this gap in our collective thinking to assert that his life experiences were at the same time typically American and typically Black. Moreover, his values and beliefs were typically American and typically Black.

In a 1954 *Person to Person* interview with the most famous television newsperson of the time, Edward R. Murrow, Bunche reflected on his grandmother's and, consequently, his guiding principles: one must be humble and honest but also self-respecting and willing to fight when challenged. She instilled in Bunche an optimism that in a democracy like the United States, all barriers of race could be surmounted.[17] The program included a tour of the Bunche home and an introduction to the Bunche family.

In 1953, on *This I Believe*, a popular CBS radio show, Bunche set forth his philosophical and religious views:

> I have an *implicit* belief in a Supreme Being.
> I love to visit the Grand Canyon . . . to reflect on how puny, indeed, is man.
> I believe in the worth and dignity of the individual.
> I have faith in people, in collectively, their goodness and good sense.
> I believe, also, in looking always on the brighter side of things.[18]

These views come across as a combination of Horatio Alger and Norman Vincent Peale, two of the most widely read writers ever among the American middle class.[19] However, the views also mask a significant break from the traditional religiosity of his grandmother. Bunche was now a social scientist who was uncomfortable with the explicit expressions of religion common in the Black community. In a 1963 speech before an American Baptist Convention meeting in Detroit, Bunche revealed his uneasiness about being baptized at the family church. Bunche was passing through the city on his way to graduate school at Harvard and the minister urged him to join the church as a way of pleasing his grandmother. His reluctant agreement immensely pleased his grandmother—and also subsequently benefited him financially when the congregation took up a collection for his graduate education. He later admitted, "I have had doubts that a decision motivated by expedient considerations, however compassionate the end, without real dedication to the faith, could constitute a valid and acceptable basis for baptism and Church membership."[20] Bunche concluded that although his baptism may have been suspect, he had tried to "live by the canons of his faith and walk humbly before God and man."[21]

In a commencement address at Fisk University that was widely reprinted in school textbooks, Bunche explains what it is to be an American:

> For who are they—these graduates? They are Americans, they are American citizens, and they are Negroes. . . .
> I would like to explore with them just what, at this very moment, in this great nation, it means to be an American, a citizen, and a Negro. . . . The privileges and rights of the American citizen—of all American citizens—are writ large in our constitution, in our traditions, in what has been called the American creed. . . .

> I am an American and I like the American way of life. I like freedom, and
> equality, and respect for the dignity of the individual. I believe that these grad-
> uates like them too. They like them so well that they bitterly resent being de-
> nied them because of an accident of birth.[22]

In fact, asks Bunche, who is a better American than one who demands the
fullest measure of respect for those cardinal principles of our society?

> These Negro graduates of Fisk University today are better Americans than
> they are Negroes. They are Negroes primarily in a negative sense—they re-
> ject that sort of treatment that deprives them of their birthright as Americans.
> Remove that treatment and their identification as Negroes in American soci-
> ety would become meaningless—at least as meaningless as it is to be of Eng-
> lish, or French, or German or Italian ancestry.[23]

Much of this address was revised and reprinted in the popular magazine
Negro Digest (without Bunche's permission) under the title "Nothing Is Impossible for the Negro." In both works, Bunche repeats his grandmother's
principles as the key to success. However, in a possible reference to his own
role, he states that the Negro has "not attained the goal until it is no longer
necessary to make reference to the fact that 'X' was the 'first Negro' to do
this or that, and until accomplishment by a Negro is taken by the public at
large as a matter of fact."[24] In short, until the phrase "a credit to the race" is
passé.

One of Bunche's proudest moments occurred when the NAACP presented him with the Spingarn Medal (its highest award) in his second hometown, Los Angeles. More than 15,000 people jammed traffic trying to get to
the ceremony under pennants and banners strung across the streets proclaiming "Dr. Bunche Day, July 17, Hollywood Bowl." Madame Pandit of
India introduced Bunche, and Roy Wilkins captured some of the excitement:

> The police and the Bowl's security men had to politely shove aside nearly a
> hundred photographers before he could start his speech. When it was over, six
> husky Los Angeles policemen had to battle their way to his side to protect him
> from people who wanted to tear at his coat sleeve or touch him on the shoul-
> der or yell something about his school days in Los Angeles.[25]

In his speech, the honoree once again hoped for the day when such awards
as the Spingarn would not be necessary.

Yet Bunche refused to deny his ancestry and in fact took pride in it. In a
1954 Washington speech he stated that he disliked being discriminated

against because of his race, but on the whole, "I find it feels good, very good indeed, to be a Negro, because the Negro knows that his cause is right, and that logic and justice and decency are altogether on his side."[26] He then turned the question around and asked how it felt to be a White American who discriminates against Negroes, Jews, Indians, Mexicans, and Orientals.

An article in the mainstream *American Magazine* repeats all of these themes with one significant addition. Putting a positive spin on racism Bunche acknowledged that competition with Whites had motivated him to achieve:

> In some ways, indeed, being a Negro may have been an advantage in making my way in the world. For the initial handicap put a keener edge on my competitive instinct, it has prodded me to exertions which I might otherwise not have undertaken. I don't think my case is unique.[27]

Although the quotation—when placed in the context of the entire article, which recounts many of the obstacles Bunche overcame—makes sense, Bunche was not always able to control the ways in which such statements might be used. Thus he walked a fine line between glorification of "the broad opportunities that America offers" and the continued discrimination against African Americans.

In 1951, Bunche returned to Hollywood to present Oscars to Joseph Mankiewicz and Darryl Zanuck at the Academy Awards ceremony. Bunche, who had once been denied entry to the Metro Pictures commissary, was pleased to honor two directors who had helped change the Black image in film.

That film image had come a long way since the year of Bunche's birth, 1903, which was also the year that the first Black character in American movies was introduced: Uncle Tom, in Edwin S. Porter's twelve-minute *Uncle Tom's Cabin*. At least Uncle Tom was a generous, selfless soul. D. W. Griffith's 1915 classic, *Birth of a Nation*, presented no such benevolent Black characters. The early films featured a number of stereotypes, including "the Tom," "the Coon," "the Tragic Mulatto," "the Mammy," and "the Black Buck." In the 1920s, "the Jester" was dominant; in the 1930s, "the Servant" seemed the only role in which Black actors could find steady work. Even the still photos in such mass-circulation magazines as *Life, Time, Fortune*, and the *Saturday Evening Post*, and the Sunday feature sections of newspapers portrayed Blacks as poor but contented and faithfully servile.[28] The early 1940s found a number of entertainers playing themselves on film, but the market for Black actors was expanded significantly by the advent of Black-market cinema led by directors like Oscar Micheaux.[29]

Like World War I, World War II produced the "New Negro," who had a dramatic impact on Hollywood's portrayal of Black Americans. Several general factors were influencing the film capital. First, the national rhetoric surrounding the war effort led to an upsurge of democratic ideology. Books like Roi Ottley's *New World A'Comin*, Rayford Logan's *What the Negro Wants*, and, of course, Gunnar Myrdal's *An American Dilemma* offered the possibility of a different racial future. The new attitude in race relations was generated in part by a booming economy. Rather than returning to the depressed conditions of the prewar years as some had predicted, the U.S. economy enjoyed the greatest growth in history. For the twenty years following 1948 the GNP, adjusted for inflation, grew at an annual average rate of 4 percent. Los Angeles became the fastest-growing metropolitan area. The economic momentum, pushed forward by federal programs like the GI Bill of Rights and the Federal Housing Administration program, brought confidence and optimism, and most of all a new middle class.[30]

The NAACP, which grew tremendously during the war years, pressured the film industry both to improve the ways in which Blacks were portrayed and to hire more Blacks. Walter White lunching with industry executives became a common sight. From 1945 through 1948 Hollywood produced its first crop of "message" movies. The war propaganda film *Negro Soldier* was commercially distributed, even as the Office of War Information (OWI) distributed 150 prints of it to PTAs, prisons, the Museum of Modern Art, and the CIAA, reaching perhaps three million viewers. Other groups, like the United Auto Workers and the American Council on Race Relations, acquired copies for educational use.

The growth of the television industry negatively affected the growth and prosperity of the movie industry, leading to a search for new and more sophisticated audiences. Adult themes such as anti-Semitism, juvenile delinquency, mental health, and race relations were more easily introduced to film than television audiences. Moreover, such themes attracted a greater Black audience, resulting in the demise of the Black film industry. *The Jackie Robinson Story*, *The Joe Louis Story*, and similar movies were sympathetic portrayals of the efforts of Black athletes to overcome racial barriers. The integrationist theme also appeared in a boom in documentaries, including *Boundary Lines* (IFF), *The Color of Man* (American Missionary Association), *One People* (B'nai Brith), *The Brotherhood of Man* (UAW), and *The World We Want to Live In* (National Conference of Christians and Jews). Conservatives challenged such integrationist productions as liberal propaganda but were beaten back by the new-conscience liberals and the Left.[31]

Parallel to the documentaries was a series of commercial movies that raised the issue of integration in new and occasionally provocative ways. Starring in many was a young actor named Sidney Poitier. Poitier had served an erratic apprenticeship in army training films, race movies, and Black theater. His first film, *No Way Out* (1950), launched a cycle of "problem" pictures. Centered on the race riots that broke out after World War II, it has as protagonist a young Negro doctor. The dialogue sounds as if it could have been lifted from the Bunche household:

> "You got 'em. All A's," the doctor's wife tells him. "No wonder you're tired. Even I'm a little tired. Cleaning up after parties. Eating leftovers. One day off a week to be with my husband. To be a woman. . . . We've been a long time getting here. We're tired, but we're here, honey. We can be happy. We've got a right to be."[32]

Poitier's next film was a 1952 adaptation of Alan Paton's South African novel *Cry, the Beloved Country*. Poitier played a young priest in the drama, a plea for racial harmony and conciliation.

After supporting roles in *Red Ball Express* and *Go, Man, Go,* Poitier costarred in *The Blackboard Jungle* with Glenn Ford, Anne Francis, and Vic Morrow. As an intelligent, angry student, he rebels against the oppressive system as represented by the teacher but ultimately comes to the teacher's defense when the latter is threatened by a student with a switchblade. Successive films, *Something of Value, Band of Angels, The Mark of the Hawk, Edge of the City,* and *The Defiant Ones,* all assert and reassert Poitier's goodness and humanity. In *Edge of the City* his kindness and loyalty destroy him, and he is so immersed in White culture that his color as well as his sexuality are rendered neutral. When Poitier's character in *The Defiant Ones* saves his fellow White convict, played by Tony Curtis, ghetto audiences jeered, one movie critic reported.[33]

Poitier went on to star in such movies as *A Raisin in the Sun, A Patch of Blue, Guess Who's Coming to Dinner, They Call Me MISTER Tibbs, In the Heat of the Night, To Sir with Love, For the Love of Ivy,* and *Lilies of the Field,* for which he won an Oscar. In all of these movies Poitier played the role of a hero for an integrationist age. One film scholar attributes his preeminence to three factors. First, he consistently played educated, intelligent characters who dressed conservatively, spoke proper English, and were polite; they were sexless, nonthreatening, and amenable. In short, a Black man who met White standards. Second, the characters had a link with the past that Americans cherished. Despite the intelligence and conscience of his characters, they were throwbacks to the mild-mannered "Toms" and humanized Christian servants of earlier eras; when insulted or badgered, they stood and took it. Third, Poitier rose to the top because he was talented and invested his characters with dignity, sensitivity, and strength. Yet by the time of *Guess Who's Coming to Dinner*, in 1967, the integrationist era had passed and Black and White critics attacked the movie. The *New York Times* ran a review entitled "Why Does White America Love Sidney Poitier So?"[34]

Many of the same characteristics that made Sidney Poitier a fictional hero in popular culture made Ralph Bunche a real-life hero in the United States and even abroad. Many of the same journalists and screenwriters who shaped a liberal integrationist image for Poitier were also influencing such "docu-dramas" as *The Jackie Robinson Story* and, five years later, *Toward Tomorrow: The Ralph Bunche–Lucy Johnson Story*.

Shown on the ABC television network on October 11, 1955, *Toward Tomorrow* comprised set pieces about the daily encounters with prejudice of individual Blacks and their refusal to give up the "American Dream." Opening with an integrated group of boys playing baseball on a rubble-strewn field, the scene emphasizes the youngsters' poverty and the competitive spirit of the great American pastime. Ralph hits a high, hard one, foreshadowing what is to come as the scene shifts.[35]

We next see Lucy "Nana" Johnson, Ralph's grandmother, who takes him into the Johnson family when his mother dies. She greets Ralph as he returns from the game with the news that the family is moving to Los Angeles, where Ralph can grow up right and get a college education. Nana's spiritual and physical efforts to ensure Ralph's successful future are at the heart of the story. The community support young Bunche received is glossed over in favor of the individualistic virtues of the family matriarch.[36]

From the story line it is clear that Bunche's characteristic optimism, perseverance, and belief in his own self-worth or equality come from his grandmother. It is also implied that his personal struggles against poverty and prejudice led to his public acclaim as a diplomat. In a curious twist to the "natural-born athlete" label that so many Black sports figures are burdened with, Bunche is presented as a natural-born diplomat whose early trials and tribulations somehow imbued him with tolerance and patience. "In a sense," one observer writes, "both Jews and Arabs were members of minority groups in Palestine and Dr. Bunche's personal background gave him a better understanding of their problems.[37]

These Poitier-like qualities of patience, tolerance, intelligence, and optimism in the face of adversity, when combined with Bunche's attractive appearance, impeccable English, and conservative dress, made him the "model Negro" in the era of integration. Television was not the only medium conveying the Bunche saga. In addition to stories in popular magazines like *Collier's*, *Reader's Digest*, the *Saturday Evening Post*, and *Ebony*, the United Nations radio promoted Bunche as "a new human being of the century—the citizen of the world." The Los Angeles Unified School District commissioned a short film on Bunche revolving around the theme "what makes a hero tick." Schoolchildren nationwide reading the *Senior Scholastic* were informed that Bunche was "one of America's greatest living diplomats."[38] From the national elementary school newspaper *Current Events*, students learned that Bunche's diplomatic prominence "has given a new sense of self-confidence to American Negroes." Bunche's own words were reprinted in basic textbooks like *Adventures in Appreciation* and Leonard S. Kenworthy's *Twelve Citizens of the World*, in which Bunche joined such figures as Mahatma Gandhi, Eleanor Roosevelt, and Albert Schweitzer as icons of a new internationalist future.

Many accounts of Bunche's life took liberties with the facts—often overemphasizing the poverty of his family and ignoring his radical views in the thirties—but most had his approval and cooperation.[39] In fact, Bunche was careful to try to control his image. He refused to endorse commercial products and objected to appearing at events where his presence was used to sell tickets for a profit. He once penned a strong letter of protest to John Johnson, the publisher of *Negro Digest*, for reprinting all or most of his Fisk commencement address. An unauthorized juvenile biography by Alvin Kugelmass provoked severe negative reaction from the Bunche and Johnson families despite its being a flattering portrait.[40] In a demonstration of patience and tolerance that would please the most devout Poitier fan, Bunche answered all of the voluminous correspondence he received personally and politely—even the hate mail.[41]

Controlling his image was impossible despite Bunche's efforts. In a sense, he was almost too successful in presenting himself as a Black American of achievement. For those who sought to defend the status quo in race relations, Bunche's Horatio Alger rise to the top proved that upward mobility was not out of the reach of Blacks willing to work hard. For those who sought to defend the United States against the challenges of communist ideology, Bunche was proof that American democracy was superior to Soviet and Chinese totalitarianism.

10

Loyalties

Family, Profession, Race, and Nation

Those who do not believe in the ideology of the United States, shall not be allowed to stay in the United States.

—Attorney General Tom Clark, in *Racism*, edited by Herbert Aptheker

"We the people." It is a very eloquent beginning. But when that document was completed on the 17th of September in 1787, I was not included in the "We, the people." I felt somehow for many years that George Washington and Alexander Hamilton just left me out by mistake. But through the process of amendment, interpretation and court decision I have finally been included in "We, the people."

—Barbara Jordan, U.S. House impeachment debate, 1974

Fame always comes with a price. Even as it brought Bunche the Father of the Year Award, it came at the expense of his family. Ruth complained increasingly of the loneliness she endured during her husband's long absences. While he received glory, she was home rearing a family.

During the first years of their marriage, Ralph returned to Harvard to complete his doctorate and then went to Europe and Africa to do field research. After missing their second and third anniversaries, he had written, "There'll be no more cause for any future separations."[1] When Ruth joined him in Paris in 1932, prior to his first trip to Africa, she had had to tend to Joan, who was six months old. By the time of his second trip to Africa in 1936 and 1937, Jane had been added to the family. Ruth was still teaching a class of first graders during the day.

On his return from Africa, the Myrdal report kept Bunche traveling for long periods in 1939 and 1940. In a curious way, World War II was a blessing for the Bunches. It not only launched Ralph on a new career but kept him at home more frequently. Unfortunately, this domestic period was a short one. From the organizing conference of the United Nations in San Francisco, Bunche expressed his concern about the behavior of Joan and Jane.

> As for the girls . . . we both have been at fault in being too severe with them. If it is not too late for us to change our ways, we ought to try to see if more love and less censure and nagging won't do the trick. We really never have taken them close to us. We have never really shared our own great love with them. I doubt that either of them have any deep feeling of love for us. We have been their masters rather than their loving parents. I know that in this regard I am criminally culpable. With your help, honey, I think I can change. In fact, I think we must change if we are not to be responsible for ruining their lives. Will you help to transform me?[2]

Yet only four months after this revealing letter, Ralph wrote that he had put everything he had into his job and proving the ability of "one of our group." He attributed his short-temperedness at home to Ruth's lack of trust in him.[3]

As Bunche became more involved in the work of the United Nations, family relations worsened. By 1947, he was suggesting that Joan and Jane be sent to boarding school so they could develop "a greater appreciation of you and their home that way."[4] Later that year, he agreed with Ruth that his prolonged absences had had "an inevitable effect" on their upbringing.[5] Then, Ruth's constant complaints of fighting with the girls and their lack of affection for their parents led Ralph to recommend that they be taken to a psychiatrist.[6]

Despite the birth of Ralph, Jr., in 1943 and continuing problems with Joan and Jane, Ralph expressed a desire several times for another child. Ruth, however, seemed not to be of that mind:

> I know I've been writing this to you for twenty years but still I hope that I won't have to spend as lonely a time during my later married years as I did during our younger days. Surely one has some obligations to one's family for companionship and guidance and help with the children. . . .
>
> Jane, Ralph, is a real tough problem to handle alone. It worries and worries me.[7]

Nine years later Ruth still seemed to be hoping for the "peace, harmony and love" that had eluded the family in the past few years.[8]

In the husband's long absences from home, the Bunche family is atypical. However, in many other ways the relationship between Ruth and Ralph was traditional: rigid and paternalistic. Ruth came to the conclusion that achievement and glory were his only "genuine passion" and began to balk at the supporting role she was expected to play.

> And I don't think it is fair to the hostess to be told there will be such an affair after the guest list has been made, the date set and the invitations already out. This has happened so many times and the invitations I never see or even told until I have to write the place cards who the guests will be.[9]

Bunche was not above ordering what was to be served to their guests and demanding that the girls entertain by playing the piano.

His behavior at home was in sharp contrast to Bunche's public statements promoting the equality of women and his own egalitarian and thoughtful behavior in the office. For example, William Mashler describes Bunche as "probably the most thoughtful man I have ever known," adding, "he was also emotionally generous—he gave of himself. You had the feeling you were the most important person."[10] Bunche was not unaware of this dual personality.

> Everyone out here with whom I work says I am the most liked person in the Dept. . . . Yet I don't seem to carry the same traits to my home. I know that at home I have too often been fractious, ill-tempered and even crude. I can't for the life of me figure out why, for I love my wife as life itself, and I love my children.[11]

Perhaps it was the burden of being a model Negro.

Years of family stress culminated in the ultimate family tragedy on October 9, 1966. At 2:10 A.M. that Sunday morning the police called the Bunches to tell them that Jane had been found dead at the base of her twelve-story apartment building; she had either jumped or been pushed. Burt Pierce, Jane's husband, had been at a football game and returned home to find the disaster. He was hysterical. On their way to Riverdale, Bunche's failing eyesight made night driving difficult, and they got lost. Fortunately, they found a police officer who guided them to the apartments.

Jane's death was traumatic for the Bunches. At first, Bunche refused to accept that it had been a suicide, even though a police investigation revealed no foul play. Ruth seemed on the verge of collapse and at times turned her rage on her husband, now a broken man. For weeks he barely functioned other than to search for some clue as to what had gone wrong. Jane had always been neurotic and had seen a psychiatrist when attending Radcliffe. Ultimately, perhaps out of guilt, Bunche accepted the fact that he had been a demanding and often absent parent. He painfully revisited his relations with his family, which made him appreciate Joan even more. Yet Jane's death contributed to his own decline and his health deteriorated rapidly.[12]

Earlier, Bunche had nearly given up his UN work to return to teaching at Harvard. Several elite schools offered him positions after he received the Nobel Peace Prize, but his old Harvard professor Rupert Emerson was the most persistent. Newspapers leaked the story that he had accepted an appointment at his alma mater. For half of 1950, Bunche carried a letter of resignation from the UN in his pocket, waiting for the right moment to submit it. The moment never came.

Although Bunche resisted the temptation to return to teaching, he refused to give up his links to the profession of political science. Although as a young scholar he had had no teaching offers from elite schools, he was nationally known among his peers a decade before his Nobel award. It was his work with Gunnar Myrdal that first brought him to the attention of political scientists across the country. In 1940, E. E. Schattschneider invited the Howard professor to participate in the American Political Science Association (APSA) roundtable "The Negro in American Politics." Asked to share information on disfranchisement from the Carnegie study, he gave a paper entitled "An Analysis of the Dynamics and Mechanisms of Disfranchisement."[13] The following year, Claudis O. Johnson of the State College of Washington invited Bunche to serve as a discussion leader for an APSA panel on poll taxes.

Although Bunche left the academy for government service during World War II—and never returned—he stayed involved in the profession. In fact, the 41st annual APSA business meeting in 1946 elected Bunche to a three-year term on the Council. Bunche thus became the first Black political scientist to serve on the Council. The broad range of his expertise is reflected in the two invitations he received to participate in the 1946 APSA gathering: from Robert K. Carr of Dartmouth, a roundtable on civil rights; from Pittman Potter of the American Society of International Law, the panel "Mandates and Trusteeship." Unfortunately, the panels were scheduled for the same time slots, and Bunche chose to accept the latter because it had been the first to arrive in the mail.[14]

Bunche, though very busy with UN work was actively involved with the APSA in 1947, serving on the local host committee for the annual meeting and also on the Willkie Award Committee on International Relations. At the 1949 APSA meeting, he gave a major presentation, "United Nations Mediation and Armistice."

Bunche was elected a vice-president of the APSA in the same year that he won the Nobel Prize for Peace, 1950. The postwar years marked a new stage in the development of the organization. Before World War II, APSA duties were performed by the secretary-treasurer, Professor Colgrave, who operated out of his office at Northwestern. The responsibilities of the president were limited to naming committee chairs, presiding over the annual meeting, and delivering a presidential address. Meetings at that time were held during the year-end academic break and often on a university campus.

After the war there was a general feeling among the membership that the organization needed to be more professional and consequently, more influential in national affairs. Along with other things, the transition brought a need for a Washington office, a full-time secretary-treasurer, and a new constitution. As part of a "seasoning" process for presidents-to-be the position of president-elect was created in the new constitution. Bunche was fully involved with the APSA during this transitional period.

While in Stockholm in December 1950, Bunche received a telegram from APSA executive director Ed Litchfield asking him to substitute for President Harry Truman in addressing the opening session of the annual meeting.[15] Bunche rushed back to the United States to deliver the speech on December 28. In his opening, he commented that the quality of the speech and his sore knees were the result of his decision to try out the toys he had purchased in Sweden for his seven-year-old son rather than work on what he was going to say. He then moved on to discuss the serious issues of Korea, Senator Joseph McCarthy, European attitudes, the UN, colonialism, and discrimination in the District of Columbia. In short, a typical, broad-ranging Bunche speech.

Despite the pressures of his increasing prominence, Bunche agreed in 1950 to serve on the APSA membership committee. Under the leadership of Roscoe C. Martin, the committee had increased membership by 10 percent in less than a year. Bunche was particularly helpful in recruiting among Department of State staffers and UN Secretariat professionals. At one point in 1953, Executive Director Litchfield asked for samples of Bunche's signature for mass-mailing purposes. Membership letters over Bunche's name went to all state governors, members of Congress and the White House staff, and cabinet members. Bunche's name also opened the doors of several foundations to the APSA.

When Bunche became president-elect of the APSA in 1953, it was facing a number of crucial decisions. The first involved a successor to the executive director; Bunche and President Pendleton Herring chose Professor John

Group portrait taken at Belle Isle, July 4, 1907. Ralph, age four, sits on the shoulder of his father, Fred Bunche, in the back row on the far left. Ralph's mother, Olive Bunche, stands third from the left in the back row with a hat. Photographer unknown. Courtesy of the Schomburg Center for Research in Black Culture.

The chairman of the Norwegian Nobel Peace Prize Committee, Gunnar Jahn, handing the prize diploma to Ralph Bunche, November 12, 1950. Courtesy of As Norsk Telegrambyrå.

Palestine mediator honored. Eleanor Roosevelt, U.S. delegate to the General Assembly, left, with Bunche, at the dinner given in his honor by the American Association for United Nations. Waldorf Astoria Hotel, New York, May 9, 1949. From the archives of the Ralph Bunche Institute on the United Nations of The City University of New York.

Ralph Bunche with the Academy Award winners Joseph Mankiewicz and Darryl Zanuck. Department of Special Collections, University Research Library, UCLA, 1951.

Ralph Bunche with Martin Luther King, Jr., and Coretta Scott King at the United Nations, December 4, 1964. Department of Special Collections, University Research Library, UCLA.

A partial view of the United Nations Security Council in session. As the acting
mediator for Palestine, Ralph Bunche, presents his report to the members. At
the table from left are Faris El Khouri, Syria; Vassily Tarassenko, Ukrainian SSR;
Jakov Malik, USSR; Sir Alexander Cadogan, United Kingdom; Ralph Bunche;
Secretary-General Trygve Lie; Warren Austin, United States; Arkady Sobolev,
assistant secretary-general in charge of Security Council affairs, and Dr.
Rodolfo Muñoz, Argentina. Palais de Chaillot, Paris, October 19, 1948. From
the archives of the Ralph Bunche Institute on the United Nations of The City
University of New York.

With fellow scholars at Howard University social science conference in 1935.
Beginning with the extreme left of front row are George O. Butler, professor of
economics; unknown; Ralph Bunche; Emmett Dorsey, professor of political
science; and W. E. B. Du Bois. Department of Special Collections, University
Research Library, UCLA.

Jefferson High School (L.A.) class photo, circa 1922. Bunche is at the far right end of the second row. Department of Special Collections, University Research Library, UCLA.

Becoming an icon. Bunche and Bunche sculpture. Department of Special Collections, University Research Library, UCLA.

IN THE CENTER COURT

EMPLOYMENT DISCRIMINATION

NEGRO SLUMS

HOUSING DISCRIMINATION

ANTI-NEGRO VIOLENCE

U.S.

RALPH BUNCHE

CARP

SURE IT'S TOUGH SON,
BUT SO IS ALL THAT

Above: Bunche with Dag Hammarskjöld and President Kasavubu in the Congo, July 28, 1960. Department of Special Collections, University Research Library, UCLA.

Left: Cartoon from the newspaper *New York Age* concerning the Westside Tennis Club incident, July 18, 1959.

Ralph and Ruth Bunche in San Francisco. Courtesy of the San Francisco Public Library.

At an international garden party, given at UN Guest House, to raise funds for the International School. Ralph Bunche, Jr. (third from left), and Ralph Bunche, Sr. (extreme right), take friends for a ride. Lake Success, New York, June 2, 1950. From the Archives of the Ralph Bunche Institute on the United Nations of The City University of New York.

Ralph Bunche, UN undersecretary general for special political affairs, paid a four-day visit (June 22–25, 1962) to the United Nations Emergency Force in the Gaza Strip and the Sinai Peninsula. Here, Bunche is seen inspecting the Guard of Honor upon his arrival at the Brazilian Battalion Headquarters camp at Rafah. On Bunche's right is Lt. Col. Darcy Lazaro, Commanding Officer of the Battalion. From the Archives of the Ralph Bunche Institute on the United Nations of The City University of New York.

RALPH BUNCHE
Height—5 feet, 9 inches
Weight—153 pounds
Position—Guard

Above: UCLA yearbook photo of basketball guard Ralph Bunche. Department of Special Collections, University Research Library, UCLA, c. 1926.

Right: With fellow Harvard graduate students, c. 1928. From the Archives of the Ralph Bunche Institute on the United Nations of The City University of New York.

UCLA senior, 1927. Department of Special Collections, University Research Library, UCLA.

Ralph Bunche and UN Mediator Count Folke Bernadotte in pajamas. Middle East, 1948. Department of Special Collections, University Research Library, UCLA.

Left: Reviewing a copy of the Carnegie–Myrdal study, *An American Dilemma* (1944), on which Bunche worked with Gunnar Myrdal. From the Archives of the Ralph Bunche Institute on the United Nations of the City University of New York.

Below: Taking a break from the Israeli–Arab armistice talks at Rhodes in January 1949. Department of Special Collections, University Research Library, UCLA.

Ralph Bunche and Notre Dame President Father Theodore Hesburgh. Notre Dame Commencement, June 2, 1957. At one time Bunche had more honorary degrees than any living American. Department of Special Collections, University Research Library, UCLA.

Left: Greeting an African diplomat in African dress. Department of Special Collections University Research Library, UCLA.

Below: Leontyne Price, the famous opera singer, here presents special phonograph albums of the opera *Aida* to Ralph Bunche, UN secretary-general for special political affairs, May 11, 1962. The presentation marked the opening of a special campaign to help save the Nubian monuments from inundation by the waters of the Aswan Dam Lake. From the Archives of the Ralph Bunche Institute on the United Nations of The City University of New York.

Ruth and Ralph Bunche with the basketball star Kareem Abdul-Jabbar (then Lew Alcindor) at the dedication of Bunche Hall at UCLA, 1969. Department of Special Collections, University Research Library, UCLA.

Gange of the University of Virginia to fill the position for one year. A year-long search brought Evron Kirkpatrick, then deputy director of the Office of Intelligence Research at the State Department, on board in a permanent capacity. Another important development in which Bunche was instrumental was the purchase of a building to be shared with the Governmental Affairs Institute. In January 1955, after Bunche paid a visit to David Rockefeller to solicit a contribution, Rockefeller sent Bunche a check in a letter that read:

> This kind of purchase really falls outside my general interest and the type of thing I would ordinarily do. But because of your own connection with these organizations (APSA-GAI), I am happy to make on my own personal part a modest contribution toward buying the building. I therefore enclose my check for $2,500, payable to the G.A.I.[16]

Bunche and Litchfield—now president of G.A.I.—were also successful in getting a $5,000 contribution from Marshall Field.

In June 1953, Bunche invited President Dwight Eisenhower to address the APSA annual meeting and said of the conversation, Eisenhower "keeps talking, rapid fire, but not very deeply or clearly. He told us 'You have to get away from this and see it from a distance or you go nuts.' Got impression he is not very happy in the job."[17] A year later, Bunche would present to Eisenhower the five-volume APSA study on presidential nominations.

When Bunche assumed the presidency of the APSA, he became the first African American to hold the position and probably the first African American to hold the highest office in any of the major professional societies in the social sciences. As was his custom, Bunche took his duties seriously. It was the inaugural year of the Congressional Internship Program (now the Congressional Fellowship Program) and Bunche was anxious to review and improve the selection process. He also spent a great deal of time preparing for the annual meeting. Given the "red scare" atmosphere created by Senator McCarthy and his followers, Bunche thought it appropriate to invite Meredith Wilson, president of the University of Oregon to speak to the members on academic freedom.

Bunche also asked President Eisenhower and his friend Adlai Stevenson to deliver addresses at the fiftieth annual meeting in 1954, but neither could accept. Stevenson wrote, "I would like to come to the meeting next fall here in Chicago, although I shiver at the thought of what I might say to such an austere group."[18]

At the fiftieth annual meeting in Chicago on September 9, 1954, Bunche delivered his presidential address, which characterized his lifelong commitment to peace, American democracy, applied social science, and the problems of race. He pointed out that of the more than six thousand APSA members, fewer than half were actively engaged in teaching. This great mixture of professionals contributed to breaking down the walls of overspecialization and to the diffusion of knowledge that he deemed salutary. He praised the recent development of interdisciplinary seminars, composite courses, and multidisciplinary research programs. Like most political scientists, Bunche believed that "the impact of the political scientist on thought and leadership is by no means comparable to his knowledge and potentiality."[19] At the same time he recognized that advances in political and social institutions had failed to keep pace with material and technological change. In concluding, Bunche returned to the subject nearest his heart: the problem of colonialism, especially in Africa, had been regrettably neglected by American political science. Finally, he encouraged political scientists to assist Americans in fulfilling their role as participants in the polity, to challenge those who promote demagoguery, and never to lose sight of the human factor in politics.

Bunche must have delivered his last lines with a good deal of emotion. He had just had a gut-wrenching experience with demagoguery that left him wondering if all his preaching on American democracy was falling on deaf ears. Actually, Bunche had first been investigated by the FBI in 1942 in accord with the internal-security provisions of the so-called Hatch Act—apparently as a condition of his employment in the Division of Special Information in the Library of Congress. The results showed that he had been but was no longer associated with various organizations listed by the government as Communist fronts in the 1930s and 1940s.

The major findings of the investigation included the following alleged misdeeds. Bunche had taken part in a 1934 conference of the Civil Liberties Union attended by well-known Communists. Bunche had participated in the 1935 Student Strike Against the War at Howard, which had been opposed by University officials.[20] In February 1936, he had attended a meeting of the Scottsboro Defense Committee and said that the Supreme Court was no good, that a united front by the masses was the only salvation.[21] Also in 1936, he had attended a meeting of the National Negro Congress (NNC); this played a major role in later investigations but had not been given unusual attention in the 1942 investigation. (Bunche admitted having attended a meeting of the Washington Committee for Democratic Action, WCDA, in 1939, and that he was a member of the International Committee on African Affairs, ICAA.)

Bunche's response to the allegations indicated that he opposed the pro-Communist influence in these organizations and had resigned to avoid further association with them. Specifically, he resigned from the National Negro Congress and the ICAA when Max Yergan assumed the leadership role in both.[22] Bunche said he had attended only one meeting of the WCDA, to hear a discussion of current antilynching legislation and a civil rights bill by their congressional sponsors.

In his interview with the FBI, Bunche cited his article "Triumph? Or Fiasco?" in *Race*, which pointed out the contradictions in the NNC; stated that he had been out of the country on a Social Science Research Council fellowship in 1936 and 1937 and had had nothing to do with the organization; and declared that when he attempted to attend the 1940 national meeting to gather material for the Myrdal study, NNC executive secretary John P. Davis had objected to his presence. Bunche then referred to his scathing attack on the NNC in the Myrdal study and produced a Howard University news article on an anti-Communist speech he had given on July 16, 1940.[23]

Several persons interviewed during the 1942 investigation declared that although they had had some doubts concerning Bunche's sympathies in the early or middle thirties, he was now a strong opponent of communism. The results of the investigation were given to the Librarian of Congress, Archibald MacLeish, who in May 1942 said Bunche had "received complete exoneration."[24]

At the same time that Bunche was thrust upon the world stage in 1950, another more sinister figure was making a name for himself. In January of that year, Senator Joseph R. McCarthy of Wisconsin uttered the lines "I have here in my hand a list of 205 [State Department Employees] who were known to the Secretary of State as being members of the Communist party and who nevertheless are still working and shaping the policy of the State Department."[25] The witch-hunt was on, even though Communists had been under fire in government and labor for several years.

McCarthy's movement was helped immensely on June 24, 1950, when the troops of Communist North Korea crossed the 38th parallel into South Korea. A series of mistakes by Truman and Secretary of State Dean Acheson, combined with the overwhelming popularity of Allied war leader Dwight Eisenhower, helped to bring about the ouster of the Democratic administration. According to some, a major error was inviting the UN to act in Korea.[26] Yet it was also a sign of the new internationalism that the United States requested such action.

The Korean War shifted the focus of U.S. policy from its new concern with civil rights[27] to a foreign policy centered on fighting communism. In this way Bunche and his image became a weapon in the ideological war, which had already begun in April 1950 when Paul Robeson created controversy by stating that "it is unthinkable . . . that American Negroes would go to war against . . . [the Soviet Union] . . . which in one generation has raised our people to full human dignity."[28] Much as African American leaders of today are asked to dissociate themselves from controversial views held by other African Americans, the same was expected in 1950. Immediately, Jackie Robinson was brought before the House Un-American Activities Committee to refute Robeson's statement. Bunche, too, was put on the spot and had to make his position clear. In a decidedly more balanced statement than Robinson's, Bunche declared in a *Collier's* interview:

> I've known Paul since 1927. He's had some very unpleasant experiences here, as all of us [have]. He's resentful of the injustices, as all of us are. I know that when he went to Russia he was very well received, and that may have influenced him to follow the party line. He's entitled to his opinions, of course, but I think he's radically wrong. His statements represent the attitudes of very few Negroes indeed.[29]

The Bunche comment most remembered and quoted, however, was "Paul should stick to singing."[30] Yet years earlier, Bunche had put the problem quite differently in a private conversation with his State Department colleague James Green: "You white folks just don't understand what we black folks go through. A black man like me, who has a sense of humor, can survive; a black man like Paul Robeson, who doesn't have a sense of humor, takes to wine, women, song, and communism."[31]

The noted Socialist Norman Thomas called Bunche "a conspicuous object lesson in the eyes of the world to the fact that the whole story of our American treatment of our colored fellow citizens is not written in terms of violence and discrimination." He agreed that "Paul Robeson's judgement of us can be explained in the light of undeniable facts" but said it was "too sweeping and severe against us and amazingly unrealistic in judging communist denials of freedom." It was his opinion that "the great service of Ralph Bunche, ought to inspire all Americans with new zeal in the elimination of racial prejudice and discrimination in our democracy."[32]

Bunche's old friend Montague Cobb contrasted the mainstream success of William Hastie and Bunche to the more radical paths taken by Black New York City council member Ben Davis and Robeson: "I submit that we have food for thought and tragic irony here. Out of the same milieu from which Paul Robeson has come as a socio-political warrior, Ralph Bunche has emerged as a fighting peacemaker."

Another Bunche friend, Walter White, put the debate in more global terms:

> Ralph Bunche's gallant conquest of the odds against him is not one of abstract nature. It is a part of America's most potent weapons for survival—its industrial production and moral principles. Korea and China have revealed the dismaying and even implacable hatred of white peoples by the majority of two-thirds of the world's population who are colored.[33]

White had gone beyond rhetoric in his efforts to counter foreign propaganda about U.S. racism. At the Breakneck Hill Conference in Connecticut on September 16, 1950, he had suggested the establishment of a National Committee on Race and Caste that would seek funding for efforts to promote pro-U.S. propaganda, educational conferences, and exchanges with foreign press. White, who had been struck by the amount of anti-American publicity he saw in India, proposed Bunche as chair; Eleanor Roosevelt, labor leader George Meany, food magnate H. J. Heinz II, William Hastie, and Henry Ford II as vice-chairs; pollster Elmo Roper as treasurer; and himself as secretary.[34]

The invidious comparison of Bunche to Robeson, the painting of Bunche as a "patriotic" figure, and the Horatio Alger–like image associated with Bunche would become the basis for alienating Bunche from a younger generation of African Americans. In a sense, rather than redefining the term *American* to include Blacks, as Bunche had hoped to do, Bunche himself was being redefined as White. That is, he was seen as someone who was accepted by Whites because he met their standards of evaluation. For Blacks growing up in the 1960s, those standards would be challenged and in many cases rejected. Hence, Bunche as a symbol of Black progress would be rejected, then ignored.

Perhaps this phenomenon is best seen in the views of former King aide and UN representative Andrew Young. As someone who spanned both generations, Young grew up admiring Bunche. "I really did have the UN in the back of my mind for a long time," said Young. "That's because of Ralph Bunche. He was the first black man in public life that I identified with as a kid."[35] However, Young, who was seen by many Black-power advocates as too integration-oriented, leveled the same criticism at Bunche: "James Baldwin wrote that people who have suffered from racism for a long time try to ignore it and deny it. That was true of Ralph Bunche. . . . A lot of his energy went into not being black and trying to assimilate."[36] Young's assessment of Bunche clearly ignores much of what Bunche said and did but is no doubt an accurate reflection of the views of many younger African Americans.

Bunche became a victim of his own success. Rather than promoting the opportunities available to African Americans, his career was used to justify keeping the system the way it was. Even such an ardent admirer as Martin Luther King, Jr., would admit that Bunche had—despite his best intentions—become the ultimate token: "If all twenty million Negroes would keep looking at Ralph Bunche, the one man in so exalted a post would generate such a volume of pride that it could be cut into portions and served to everyone." (King and Stokeley Carmichael agreed—you can't have Bunche for lunch.)[37]

Some went further than King to contend that the success of people like Bunche and Jackie Robinson was counterproductive to the race as a whole. Rather than being "a credit to the race," they had become "a burden on the race."

> The image of Jackie Robinson or Ralph Bunche is a threat to the young Negro. These heroes are exceptional and talented men. Yet, in a time of ferment among Negroes, they tend to become norms and models for the young people. Once again, there is a tragic gap between the ideal and the possible. A sense of disillusion, of failure, is added to the indignity of poverty.[38]

By the ends of their lives both Robinson and Bunche expressed bitterness over the ways in which their success had been used to impede the progress of fellow Blacks. Bunche found it especially ironic that his own patriotism would be seriously questioned.

At the height of the McCarthy era, a more intense and prolonged investigation of Bunche's radical past was launched. At the end of his presidential term, in January 1953, Truman had issued Executive Order 10422, which made all U.S. nationals working in international organizations subject to the possibility of loyalty investigations. The order was directly counter to the UN Charter principle of Secretariat independence, and Trgyve Lie appointed Bunche to an advisory panel to assist him on cases involving charges of subversive activity. However, within a month the FBI was fingerprinting American members of the Secretariat in the UN building, prompting *Pravda* to call Lie the "front man and agent of the State Department" who had "rushed to the aid of the Senate inquisition."[39]

The FBI almost immediately began an investigation of Bunche, and in

March 1953, he was called before the Senate subcommittee on internal security of the Judiciary Committee (the so-called Jenner Committee) where he denied any Communist Party affiliation. The results of the probe were furnished to the Civil Service Commission in April. On May 28, 1954, the investigation culminated in a sometimes heated hearing before the International Organizations Employee Loyalty Board that lasted nearly twelve hours. (Only 32 cases were heard by the board; 1700 Americans were covered by the executive order.) Bunche chose Ernest A. Gross, former U.S. deputy chief representative at the UN to represent him. Shortly after the hearing the board rendered a "favorable loyalty determination."

As with the 1942 investigation, most attention focused on the role of Bunche in cofounding the National Negro Congress, but this time the investigation included the allegations of two Black former Communists, Leonard Patterson and Manning Johnson, who placed Bunche at a meeting of the Communist faction planning the NNC. At least one source stated that Bunche had been introduced by the well-known Black Communist Harry Haywood as a fellow Communist Party member. The same source also suggested that Bunche worked undercover with top Negro leaders of the Communist Party in order to gain greater Black support and not antagonize NNC President A. Philip Randolph, a devout Socialist.

These revelations led the FBI to consider perjury charges against Bunche on the grounds that he had denied Communist Party membership in testimony before the Jenner Committee in 1953. On July 2, 1954, FBI and Justice Department officials met to discuss the perjury charge. Apparently, the testimony of John P. Davis and other former Communists supporting Bunche's denial prevented the FBI from proceeding.[40] Investigators also found it difficult to get witnesses critical of Bunche to testify before the Loyalty Board, either because they feared the reaction of friends and neighbors or they did not want to destroy Bunche's career.

Several other new charges were leveled against Bunche during the 1953–1954 investigation. He was listed as a contributing editor to the Marxist journal *Science and Society* from 1936 to 1940, although no actual Bunche contributions to the journal were produced. Bunche was a 1940 candidate for vice-president of the American Federation of Teachers local union in Washington, D.C., which was considered to be Communist influenced. However, he had run on the anti-Communist ticket against Doxey Wilkerson. A 1947 letterhead listed Bunche as a member of the District of Columbia chapter of the Southern Conference for Human Welfare. From 1942 to 1945, he was a member of the Institute of Pacific Relations, and at one time was considered for a top staff position—ironically, he had attended several of its major conferences as a representative of the State Department. All of these organizations were identified by the government as Communist fronts.

Perhaps Bunche's most damaging contacts involved persons he met in the State Department. The most well known was Alger Hiss, whom Bunche had worked under in the early forties and used as a reference when he moved to the UN. When Hiss was attacked for being a Communist in 1948, his former colleague wrote a strong letter of support. It said in part, "The gallant fight you are making is on behalf of the integrity and reputation of every decent American," and "I want you to know that I am in your corner."[41] Sources said that Bunche later criticized Hiss and the damage he had done to the State Department. In his own defense, Bunche contended that he had assumed Hiss was loyal because he had a higher secrecy clearance than Bunche himself had.

A similar guilt-by-association event occurred when a UN employee working with Bunche, Jack S. Harris, refused to answer questions concerning possible Communist ties before the Loyalty Board. Bunche had worked with Harris at the State Department and recommended him to the UN. Once again on the defensive, Bunche argued that he hired Harris solely on the basis of his expertise. Harris was fired but eventually given $10,000 to compensate for his lost salary.[42]

Despite Bunche's past associations and affiliations, most of those interviewed described him as a loyal American and a strong anti-Communist. Among those so attesting was Black Communist leader Abner Berry, who contrasted the views of Bunche in 1950 to those in the midthirties, when he had praised Bunche. In a *Daily Worker* article, he wrote, "It is almost certain that if Dr. Ralph J. Bunche had fulfilled the promise of his brilliant and honest early years he would not be the proud possessor of the 1950 Nobel Peace Prize. In earning the Nobel Peace Prize for his service to the Western imperialist war makers, he has thoroughly exposed his retreat from the struggle for world freedom." Berry goes on to cite W. E. B. Du Bois: "Perhaps then it was a counsel of perfection to have hoped that Ralph Bunche would have stood fast for justice, freedom and the good faith of nations and his race—perhaps; but God knows I wish he had."[43] Bunche did little to assuage Du Bois's lament. On the contrary, he openly stressed the anti-Communist tone of his writings. One notices a stronger anti-Communist, pro-American emphasis in his many speeches following the Loyalty Board hearing, but at the same time he remained opposed to McCarthyism and the hysteria it created.

A final investigation of Bunche was begun on December 8, 1960, by the

FBI. It had been requested by White House Assistant Lawrence O'Brien in connection with possible top-level appointments to be made by President John F. Kennedy. If Bunche had lost such admirers as Abner Berry and W. E. B. Du Bois in the fifties, he gained such notables as W. Averell Harriman, John D. Rockefeller III, and David Rockefeller—all of whom believed Bunche a loyal American capable of performing any important assignment. In fact, Harriman asserted that he suggested Truman appoint Bunche undersecretary of state. Among those interviewed was William Hastie, who had known Bunche since 1927 and stated that Bunche was very critical of the Soviets and their leadership.[44]

Another person interviewed in 1960 was Ernest Gross, who had defended Bunche at the 1954 Loyalty Board hearing. Gross contended that that hearing had been brought about by persons who were jealous of Bunche's position and success. Harry Gideonse, president and board chair of Freedom House for twenty-one years, stated that Bunche had served as vice president of that strongly anti-Communist organization several times.

No substantial new charges of Communist links were uncovered in the 1960 investigation. Paradoxically, the post for which Bunche was rumored to have been considered was ambassador to the Soviet Union. Although Bunche was highly recommended by almost all persons interviewed, Kennedy did not make the appointment. It is impossible to determine whether Bunche's past associations and activities played a role in Kennedy's decision; however, Bunche made it clear that he would not accept a Kennedy appointment even if it had been offered.

11

The Cold War and the Congo

Ralph Bunche, murderer of Katanga.
—Picket sign at Chapman College, 1960

The UN cannot receive ultimatums from anyone.
—Ralph Bunche to Patrice Lumumba,
in Brian Urquhart, *Ralph Bunche*

The most difficult experience of Bunche's professional life began at 8:00 A.M. on July 8, 1960, when Bunche was awaiting Thomas Kanza, the Congo's UN ambassador designate, at his hotel in Leopoldville to discuss the UN program of assistance to the Congo. Then Kanza called to say he was cut off from the hotel by military cordons. In fact, military vehicles and soldiers were swarming everywhere, and no Belgian officers were in sight. Bunche walked out on his balcony and observed two British journalists and three Israeli diplomats, including the Israeli ambassador, being marched along the street below. The soldiers spotted Bunche, and one fired just as the UN official jumped back into his room.

The trouble had only just started. Three armed Congolese soldiers—two of them drunk—burst into his room and ordered Bunche and his assistant, F. T. Liu, to go downstairs. Their mistaking him for a Belgian paratrooper "hurt me no little," Bunche would recall some time later. But at that moment his mind flashed back to his 1938 visit to the Kikuyu in the Kenyan highlands, where he had made a speech about his returning to the land of his ancestors. The grizzled elders of the tribe welcomed him home and gave him the Kikuyu name Karioki, which means he who has returned from the dead. Now Karioki might be joining the dead! Bunche quickly stashed his confidential papers behind the toilet bowl before the soldiers herded him and Liu to the lobby, where they joined other terrified hotel guests. Just as suddenly as the soldiers had arrived, they jumped into their vehicles and left.

Bunche wrote to his son that day:

Well, if things work out all right in the end this predicament we are all in now will later seem quite amusing. Wouldn't it be ironic, though, if I should now get knocked around here in the very heart of Africa because of anti-white feeling—the reason being that I am not dark enough and might be mistaken for a "blanc"! Well, life is full of ironies.[1]

Later he told the press that he had never been so frightened, and he confided to Ruth that "even Palestine was safe by comparison."[2]

It was in this environment that Bunche began the most complex and controversial operation the UN had ever undertaken. Its difficulty owed much to the unique characteristics of Belgian colonialism. The Berlin conference convened by the German chancellor Otto von Bismarck in November 1884 to divide African lands among the European powers and an 1885 agreement gave Britain and France the most territory in Africa; Germany, a million square miles; and King Leopold II of Belgium, as his personal holding, one of the largest, richest, and most strategically located areas—the Congo.

From the perspective of the European powers, the grant to Leopold was deserved. More than any other person, he had helped to create the scramble "atmosphere." Leopold had been interested in the commercial properties of the continent for more than twenty years, but his country was too small and its citizens too indifferent for him to actualize his dreams. In 1876, he had founded the African International Association as a cover for his commercial and scientific pursuits that ranged across central Africa from Zanzibar to the Atlantic. By the 1880s, Britain, France, Portugal, Germany, and Leopold were the big "players," and Leopold deftly maneuvered among the inevitable rivalries. Thus, the partition of Africa was essentially a projection onto Africa of the politics of Europe and bore little relation to the activities of Europeans in Africa during earlier periods.[3] The unfortunate phenomenon would recur in the 1960s as the Soviet Union and United States fought a "cold war" in tropical Africa.

Prior to the Berlin conference, Leopold had secured recognition by France, Germany, and the United States of his Congo Free State. They saw recognition as a way of curtailing Portugese influence in the Congo and establishing a free trade zone that could benefit all. Moreover, Leopold appeared to them to have the qualities of a perfect administrator, among which were using his own funds to sponsor expeditions, including those of Henry Stanley; financing protests against Arabs trading for slaves and ivory in the

Upper Congo; and seeking to protect British missionaries. Confident of his commitment to free trade and to the welfare of Africans, the conferees agreed to Leopold's request to assume the title King of the Independent State of the Congo, a territory seventy-seven times the size of Belgium.[4] The United States was the first to recognize the novel state, in a President's Order of Recognition on April 22, 1884:

> [T]he government of the United States announces its sympathy with and approval of the humane and benevolent purposes of [King Leopold's rule], and will order the officers of the United States, both on land and sea, to recognize its flag as the flag of a friendly government.[5]

Ironically, one of the prominent early supporters of the Congo's new relationship with King Leopold was an African American intellectual and soldier, George Washington Williams. However, after a fact-finding trip to the Congo, Williams changed his mind. In a report to the president concerning ratification of the General Act of the Conference of Berlin, he wrote:

> Mr. STANLEY was supposed to have made treaties with more than four hundred native Kings and Chiefs, by which they surrendered their rights to the soil. And yet many of these people declare that they never made a treaty with STANLEY, or any other white man; that their lands have been taken from them by force, and that they suffer the greatest wrongs at the hands of the Belgians. I have never met a chief or tribe or native, man, woman or child, from Banana, the mouth of the Congo River, to Stanley-Falls at its headwaters, who expressed any other sentiment towards the Congo State than that of hatred, deeply rooted in an abiding sense of injury, injustice and oppression.[6]

From 1885 to 1908, Leopold proceeded to violate every provision of the Berlin Conference applicable to the arrangements made for the Congo. In 1891, his government eliminated private trading in much of the Congo and required the natives to sell their rubber and ivory directly to a state monopoly. To pay for the moral and material welfare of the natives, the king was permitted to levy taxes (after twenty years, no improvements were visible yet the taxes had increased). Leopold decided that the best way to obtain the rubber and ivory he wanted was to order that taxes be paid in rubber. Taxes were collected from each village on a monthly basis rather than once a year, and if a village did not bring in the requisite revenue, one writer reported, "the King's cannibal soldiers raided it, carried off the women as hostages, and made prisoners of the men, or killed and ate them."[7] Leopold's agents were paid on the basis of the amount of rubber collected—no questions asked about methods used. The system of payment-by-results led to widespread torture, mutilations, killings, and forced slavery. British missionaries' accounts of mistreatment led Roger Casement, the British consul in the Congo, to conduct an eleven-week investigation. His shocking report was published in 1904, and carried descriptions such as this of horrendous brutalities:

> Each time the corporal goes out to get rubber, cartridges are given him. He must bring back all not used, and for every one used he must bring back a right hand. M.P. told me that sometimes they shot a cartridge at an animal in hunting; they then cut off a hand from a living man. As to the extent to which this is carried on, he informed me that in six months the State on the Mambogo River had used 6,000 cartridges, which means that 6,000 people are killed or mutilated. It means more than 6,000, for the people have told me repeatedly that the soldiers kill the children with the butt of their guns.[8]

The report was a confirmation of earlier criticisms of Leopold's rule and led to the establishment of the Congo Reform Association in the United Kingdom.

Adverse publicity forced Leopold to appoint his own Commission of Inquiry, which found the atrocities so great it refused to cover them up. Somewhat milder than Casement's report, the commission's report was largely ignored by the Belgian public but had an impact on the Belgian political elite. A traveler in the Congo in 1905 wrote:

> The dogs in the Kennels of my farm are better housed, better fed, and much better cared for, whether ill or well, than are the twenty millions of blacks along the Congo River. And that these human beings are so ill-treated is due absolutely to the cupidity of one man, and to the apathy of the rest of the world.[9]

Newton Leroy "Newt" Gingrich has written that many Belgians refused to admit that anything was amiss. Many, especially the specialists in African affairs, insisted that Leopold was a great man who had run the Congo as well as could have been expected. Gingrich quotes as an example of a holder of this opinion, Guy Malengrau: "No Belgian, whether he is the most fervent Christian or the most generous Socialist, sees in this matter a cause for his country to have a troubled conscience."[10]

So monstrous was Leopold's rule that when the Belgian government was forced by world opinion in 1908 to relieve him of his fiefdom after he had made at least $20 million in the rubber and ivory trade,[11] the Congolese tended to think of the change as their salvation. Yet what followed was one of the most rigid and paternalistic forms of colonialism in all of Africa. The

Belgians neither trained a native elite, as did the British, nor offered national citizenship, as did the French. What evolved over the period from 1908 to 1958 was a form of separate development, or apartheid. Aside from this almost-total segregation by race, there were three other unusual features of the Belgian Congo. First, education was left primarily to the Catholic missions, which made them a force in shaping colonial policy. By 1954, about 3.5 million Congolese were Catholics, one-quarter of all Congolese, and three-quarters of a million were Protestant. Second, the big Belgian companies with concessionary systems exercised tremendous influence. The economic power of Union Minière du Haut Katanga, Forminiere, and Huileries du Congo Belge provided the Congo with a much larger proletariat than in other parts of Africa. Third, the debate over annexing the Congo had been bitter in the Belgian parliament and the enabling legislation barely passed. Subsequently, there was little public interest in Belgium in what went on in the Congo. This left a small group of government administrators with a great deal of autonomy in setting policy.[12] The confluence of the interests of state planners, church, and business combined gave the native population more social services than were in place in the rest of colonial Africa but at the same time allowed more supervision and control than the other colonial systems.

The Belgian control was so extensive that as late as the midfifties neither the Belgians nor Congolese saw even a faint glimmer of independence. In the Belgian mind, the Congolese were simply "Black Gauls" comparable to the Bolgae of two thousand years ago. Although this position was liberal in its acknowledgment that Africans were capable of learning, it reinforced the notion of Belgian superiority and African backwardness. "Again and again," says Gingrich, "spokesmen on colonial questions used this imagery to reassure their countrymen that the Congolese were progressing as rapidly as could be expected." The corollary was that "if Africans were two thousand years behind, the Congo might have to remain a colony for a long, long time." Colonial Minister Godding reminded the Belgian parliament in 1946 that it should be reasonable and "not forget that there are laws which govern the evolution of human brains!"[13]

The timetable of the Congolese elite, or *evolues*, was shorter but by no means precipitous. Its journal, *Conscience Africaine*, in 1956 published a manifesto—the first such in Belgian colonial history—that proposed that Belgium should express its "sincere will . . . to lead the Congo to its complete political emancipation in a period of thirty years."[14] The elite was a small one; each of its members at the time, fewer than 900, held a *carte de mérite civique*, which was available, on application, to any Congolese who considered himself detribalized. For those who wanted additional privileges, the *carte d'immatriculation* had been established; in 1956 the applications of only 120 Congolese were approved out of a population of 13 million.[15]

Bunche, the UN's chief expert on colonialism, had had difficult dealings with the Belgians since the inception of the organization. Belgium, as one of the administering powers of the trust territories, was initially uncooperative and joined Britain and France in refusing to discuss self-government and gradual decolonization. When, with Bunche's help, the General Assembly established the Committee on Information (as stipulated in Article 73 of the Charter) for self-governing territories, Belgium failed to report regularly on the Congo. Its strategy was to isolate the Congolese from any liberal political thinking, whether national or international, while providing enough economic incentives to keep the masses complacent if not contented. Yet in a 1955 article, Prime Minister Wigny of Belgium admitted that "the Congo in the last decade has been dominated by the creation of the UN and the interpretation given to the text of the Charter which concerns the non-self-governing territories."[16]

Three events are generally credited with moving up the timetable for independence with a speed inconceivable to colonial administrators or the *evolues*. In 1958, the nearest center of nationalism was just across the river from Leopoldville, Brazzaville in the French Congo. On August 24, General Charles de Gaulle, while visiting that capital, made a startling offer of independence to the French colonies that wanted it or continued association with France. Of course, de Gaulle assumed all the French colonies would choose the latter. Among the Belgian Congolese who had crossed the river to hear de Gaulle's speech was Patrice Lumumba. Realizing the impact of France's offer on his own country, Lumumba immediately formed the Movement Nation Congolais (MNC).

Another event that affected the Belgian stance on the Congo was the Brussels World Fair of 1958, which provided a rare look at the fast-changing world to its Congolese visitors—who were a hundredfold more numerous than the Congolese who had come to Belgium during the eighty years of colonization. The magnificent Congolese pavilion, which displayed the wealth of the colony and had a large Congolese staff, portrayed the Congolese as happy beneficiaries of Belgian rule. In reality, the Congolese visitors and staffers were finding out just how limiting the colonial experience had been. Some stayed in Belgium as students, some to escape colonialism.[17] Those who returned home had had for the first time the experience of being on an equal footing with Europeans, Americans, Russians, Asians,

Arabs, other Africans. For all Congolese who had ventured forth, the status quo was unsustainable.

The final event to break down Belgian isolationism was the All-African People's Conference in Accra, Ghana, in December 1958. At the last minute, the Belgian colonial administration allowed three members of the MNC to attend—Lumumba, Gaston Diomi, and Joseph Ngalula—along with a Congolese businessman who spoke English, Jean-Pierre Dericoyard. Joseph Kasavubu, the best-known Congolese and head of the Abako (an association formed in 1950 to preserve the culture of the Bakongo), was denied permission to attend because the administration asserted his inoculation certificates were not in order. The decision left Lumumba free to impress upon Kwame Nkrumah, Tom Mboya, and other African leaders that he was a force to be reckoned with. Lumumba, who had a number of Belgian friends in the Congo, was also free to vent his anticolonialist and anti-Belgian feelings in a way not possible there. Moreover, the conferees appreciated his awareness of the centrality of the Congo to the struggle for freedom on the continent as a whole. He went home with the position of Congolese representative on the steering committee of the conference.[18]

After their return to Leopoldville, Lumumba, Diomi, and Ngalula held a series of mass meetings to report on the Accra conference and announce a new MNC program based on the Accra decision to form a permanent organization to work for the end of colonialism and the unity among peoples of Africa. Although nationalist fervor was beginning to reach the masses of Congolese, Belgians in Europe and in the Congo had little foreknowledge that change was in the air. The awakening came on January 4, 1959: Leopoldville was hit with violent rioting that killed more than fifty people and left two hundred injured. The immediate cause was a ban on a meeting in the Kalamu district of the local branch of the Abako at which members of the central committee were to speak. Once again Lumumba was the beneficiary of an event: members of the Abako leadership, including Kasavubu, were arrested and the movement proscribed; Lumumba moved into the vacuum and strengthened the MNC.

The colonial government was so shaken by the riots that on January 13 it announced its proposals for decolonization. This was a watershed event for the Belgians, who until a week before had planned to govern the Congo indefinitely. However, the declaration approved by the Belgian government called for only a gradual movement toward independence; major Belgian economic interests had to be given time to adapt.

Congolese unrest with the decolonization proposals, which the Congolese had had no part in shaping, and Belgian public opinion forced the government to speed up its timetable and to include Congolese leaders in the planning. One year after the January 1959 riots, the Belgian government convened a roundtable conference to devise political structures for the future state. The conference covered sixteen points, each of which became the subject of a resolution, and the sixteen resolutions constituted the provisional constitution, La Loi Fondamentale.[19] At the conference, the Belgians had the advantage of unity. The Congolese representatives were divided and overwhelmed by Belgian experts, who persuaded them to accept a system of governance modeled after Belgium's, with a head of state like the Belgian king, who could dismiss a prime minister but not govern. The prime minister would govern with the consent of a relatively powerless bicameral parliament. Most important, the colonial military/police, the Force Publique, would be a national army supervised by Belgian officers. In addition, the powers of the central government would be limited, allowing provincial authorities to challenge the national interest. Despite these concessions, a second roundtable, on economic issues, assured business interests of their continued control of the economy. Each of these decisions played a role in the havoc that followed independence.

The transition from total dependency to at least the appearance of independence took place in about one year. Inexperienced, undereducated Congolese leaders were faced with forming a government, and they had very few human resources to draw upon. Bunche described the dilemma:

> First has been this incredible lack of preparation; in a population of over 14 million people there were on independence day last June 30, only 17 men who had university education. There was not a doctor or a dentist or a lawyer or a professional man of any kind. There was not a church; there was not anyone who could qualify to be a professor. No engineers in the entire population on the Congolese side. There was a complete lack of political and administrative experience amongst the Congolese. They had not been permitted to develop any.[20]

Bunche was amazed when members of the Congolese cabinet would ask for permission to sit in the UN offices he set up so as to learn how an office functions. He was equally amazed when Prime Minister Lumumba would interrupt a cabinet meeting to answer his office phone because he had no trained secretary. It is not surprising, then, that after the Belgian king Baudouin's praise of his country's rule during Independence Day ceremonies and President Kasavubu's equally fulsome response, Lumumba chastised the Belgians for eighty years of "humiliating slavery imposed on us by force." He recalled the "contempt, insults and blows, morning, noon and night because we were 'blacks.'" "[W]e shall never forget that the black was called *tu*, not because he was a friend, but because only the whites were given the honour of being called *vous.*"[21] Lumumba's words were inopportune and discourteous but also painfully true.

After a period of intense political activity, Lumumba had emerged as prime minister but had been forced to accept Kasavubu as president. Through a special amendment to the provisional constitution voted by the Belgian parliament, Moise Tshombe had been appointed president of the province of Katanga a fortnight before independence. Joseph Mobutu was chief of staff to the prime minister.

Although Lumumba's image, like those of many martyrs, has been polished over the years, those who knew him well are remarkably consistent in their characterizations of him. Thomas Kanza, who was the first Congolese to obtain a college degree and who served as Lumumba's representative to the UN, met him in 1955. He describes Lumumba as a tall, slim man who was always well dressed and sociable, and who made instant favorable impressions. Lumumba had once been a postal clerk and was largely self-taught, but his powers of observation and oratory were such that persons better informed and educated than he deemed him capable. Totally committed to the independence struggle, Lumumba had become well known in Leopoldville because he was the sales representative for a popular beer, but he effortlessly made the transition from promoting beer to promoting nationalism. Kanza, a sympathetic witness, describes him: "A demagogue, yes, and not too scrupulous, perhaps; above all, Lumumba had a nose for business, a flair: he could win new sympathies without forgetting to make careful use of older friendships as well."[22]

Bunche's brief but intense relationship with Lumumba led to the following assessment:

> He was not a stooge nor was he the martyr that quick legend would now make him. He was a young man, thoroughly political in his thinking, and opportunistic politically rather than dedicated to any particular ideology. He was a fluent, and felicitous speaker and could wield great influence with his oratory. But he also often made bitter enemies and this was the decisive factor in the tragedy of his death.[23]

Kasavubu, by contrast, was described by observers as a small, squat man who was a poor speaker, slow in making decisions, and narrow in his ethnic rather than national interests.[24]

When Bunche arrived in Leopoldville early in the morning of June 25, 1960, to represent the UN at Independence Day ceremonies, he received a hint of things to come. No Congolese or Belgian official was at the airport to meet him and his colleague F. T. Liu (who had worked with Bunche in the Trusteeship Division and would serve as his French translator), but a member of the U.S. consulate who apparently had some idea of the disorganization surrounding the ceremonies did so. After his first meeting with Congolese leaders and Belgian officials, Bunche described the difficulties as largely formal and manageable in a long letter to UN Secretary-General Dag Hammarskjöld. His assignment was to stay a few weeks to assist Congolese officials in applying for UN membership and to ascertain what technical assistance the UN might provide to the new government.

Bunche realized that Lumumba and Kasavubu were probably headed for a showdown, and the independence ceremonies dramatized the differences between the two. The Belgians had dealt directly with Kasavubu concerning Baudouin's presence at the ceremonies, even though they knew Lumumba was the actual governmental power (the Belgian model). Lumumba was highly insulted and had not endeared himself to the Belgians with his angry speech—though he later toasted the king at a ceremonial luncheon—but his stock with the Congolese had risen as a result. Bunche found both Belgians and Americans in Leopoldville obsessed with the possibility of a Communist takeover despite the fact that Lumumba had little if any contact with Communists abroad. His ministers seemed more interested in salaries, titles, and cars than in ideology. Bunche's next letter to Hammarskjöld was much more pessimistic about the Congo's prospects.

Among those witnessing the scramble for wealth and prestige were the 24,000 Congolese privates who had been conscripted into the Force Publique by the Belgians. Commanding the soldiers, who were mainly in three regional detachments, were 1,000 White and Belgian superior officers. The commander, Lieutenant General Emile Janssens, had antagonized the soldiers by inscribing on a headquarters blackboard: "Before independence = after independence."[25] On July 5, the rechristened Armée National Congolaise, mutinied at its biggest base, at Thysville. The mutiny spread to Leopoldville, with the soldiers demanding Africanization of the officer corps, promotions, and better pay. Lumumba promised retribution against disloyal Belgian officers and promoted all members of the army one grade, leading Bunche to remark that the Congolese army was the only one in the world without privates.

By July 8, panic was spreading everywhere as Congolese soldiers began to round up Belgian officers and anyone who "looked Belgian," including Bunche in his hotel room. Kanza, who had an appointment to meet Bunche, became worried about his safety and sent a single Congolese soldier to guard him. Bunche ran into the new Belgian ambassador to the Congo, Jean Van den Bosch, who told him he had just countermanded an order by General Janssens to put down the mutiny by force. According to the new Treaty of Friendship between Belgium and the Congo, only the prime minister could request the intervention of Belgian troops. European civilians were already in full flight across the river to Brazzaville, and Lumumba knew that Belgian troops firing on the Congolese would lead to total disaster.

The situation could not be stabilized and quickly spread throughout the country. On July 9, the mutiny claimed its first European victims in Kasai and Katanga provinces. The following day Belgian troops intervened to protect Whites in both places, and Belgian warships and planes proceeded to kill more than twenty Congolese civilians at the Atlantic port of Matadi after all Europeans had been evacuated. Even this bleak situation deteriorated when, on July 11, Moise Tshombe announced the secession of Katanga. When President Kasavubu and Prime Minister Lumumba flew to Elisabethville the next day to attempt a reconciliation, Tshombe's minister of the interior, Godefroid Munongo, denied the plane permission to land.[26] Belgian troops were already in control of the Elisabethville airport.

Bunche had told the Belgians that any attempt to use Belgian troops to restore order without the consent of the Congolese government would be catastrophic, and advised them to seek Security Council action to protect the lives of Europeans with UN forces. Their unilateral action left Lumumba furious, and he turned first not to the Soviets or the UN for help but to the United States. The U.S. ambassador, Clare Timberlake, informed Bunche on July 10 that he had been talking with Lumumba and Kasavubu about help. The Eisenhower administration suggested that the Congolese seek assistance through the UN. Bunche proceeded to discuss the Africanization of the army officer corps with the government, offering to provide UN advisers and instructors as soon as possible. However, with the breakdown of law and order, Bunche recognized the need for an emergency food lift and technicians to run the basic public services that had been abandoned by the Belgians.

After Katanga's secession and the failed effort at reconciliation, Lumumba and Kasavubu wired Hammarskjöld directly from Luluaborg, where they were stranded, asking for military assistance to fight Belgian aggression—a request that came as a complete surprise to Bunche in Leopoldville. However, both Bunche in the Congo and Hammarskjöld in New York began to lay the groundwork for UN intervention. In the meantime, Belgian paratroopers took over the Leopoldville airport and the European area of the city, including the government and Parliament buildings. Lumumba informed Bunche that given this action, he had called on Ghana to provide immediate military assistance until the UN forces arrived. Bunche was disturbed by the prospect of Ghanaian intervention and even more disturbed when he discovered that Ambassador Timberlake had asked that French troops in Brazzaville be ready to intervene.[27]

It was these events that brought Bunche and the UN to center stage. Only quick action could prevent an explosion that might take hundreds of lives and might lead to a confrontation between the United States and Soviet Union. Hammarskjöld formally invoked Article 99 of the UN Charter for the first time, which permitted him to convene an urgent meeting of the Security Council early on the morning of July 14. The council agreed to his three main proposals: technical assistance to the Congo in security administration; the introduction of UN forces; and emergency food shipments. The next day the first UN troops, Tunisians, landed at Ndjili airport in Leopoldville, to be quickly followed by Moroccans, Ethiopians, and Ghanaians. Thus, two weeks after the Independence Day ceremonies, Bunche found himself in charge of an ONUC (Organisation des Nations Unies au Congo) force that would eventually reach a peak strength of 20,000 and cost more than $10 million a month.

The role Bunche's race played in his ability to function as the key figure in this historic, multinational operation is subject to debate. Lumumba himself had questioned why Hammarskjöld had sent "*ce nègre américain*" to represent the UN in the Congo. When told Hammarskjöld had sent "the best man in the world" for such an impossible job, Lumumba retreated and apologized.[28] Although Bunche was well known among the diplomats in Leopoldville, the Congo scholar Madeleine Kalb states that he was so light-skinned that the distinction was lost on the Congolese, who tended to view him as just another European and treat him accordingly.[29] Ironically, this view also seems to have been shared by Belgian officials in Brussels. Bunche reported his dismay at the paternalistic, derisive, and condescending comments made about the new Congolese leaders by senior officials in his presence and that of several Congolese. Because the comments were made at a luncheon in Bunche's honor, one can assume he was seen more as an "honorary" European than as an African American. Thomas Kanza, perhaps the most widely traveled of all the Congolese leaders, stated that he did not know what the Belgian colonial authorities thought of Bunche, but the Congolese received him with the greatest sympathy and the most profound respect. According to Kanza, "He was one of the few coloured Americans to have earned an undisputed reputation on the international level; and in his dealings with the new government of the Congo, the fraternity of race played a part that must not be underestimated."[30]

Still, it is difficult to assess the impact of Bunche's race on events. Kanza pointed out three handicaps that he thought limited Bunche's effectiveness. First, the Belgian colonial authorities saw him as just another colored man and watched him carefully for any hint of bias. Second, Bunche did not speak fluent French and had to rely on Liu for interpretation. Liu's presence had to have had some impact on the confidentiality of any talks Bunche had with Congolese leaders. Kanza goes so far as to say Liu to some extent dominated Bunche. Third, Bunche was an American and could not escape "the all-pervasive watchfulness of American agents."[31] In fact, try as he might to be an impartial international diplomat, circumstances led Bunche to rely on Americans more than he might like from the moment of his arrival in Leopoldville. Initially, he stayed at the Stanley Hotel and had no office and virtually no staff. On many occasions the only dependable source of communication and equipment was the U.S. embassy.

Bunche's status as an American, as well as the status of a number of other UN officials dealing with the Congo, would become a major source of criticism of the UN operation. This despite a historical record that showed that the United States had little interest in Africa in general and the Congo in particular until well into the crisis. As newly independent nations emerged in Africa in the fifties, the Eisenhower administration hesitated even to extend the normal courtesy of designating a separate ambassador to each one. There were more Foreign Service officers for West Germany alone than for the entire continent of Africa. The State Department was organized to deal with each region of the world except Africa. It did not establish a Bureau of African Affairs until as late as 1958 and then relegated it to marginal operations.[32] This indifference and ignorance were reflected in Congress, the business community, and institutions of lower and higher education.

U.S. foreign policy toward Africa, or more precisely the lack of it, is difficult to explain from a national security standpoint. The Congo was the largest and wealthiest of the sixteen African nations scheduled for independence in 1960. Mao Tse-tung advised Chinese leaders, "If we can take the Congo, we can hold the whole of Africa."[33] Union Minière had supplied the

United States with the uranium it needed to build the atomic bomb in World War II even though Belgium itself was occupied by the Nazis. As of 1959, Western capitalist countries were obtaining 7 percent of their tin; 9 percent of their copper; 49 percent of their cobalt; and 69 percent of their industrial diamonds from the Congo. Iron, zinc, gold, manganese, bauxite, and tantalum were other crucial minerals found especially in Katanga that Western economies depended on. In addition, NATO allies of the United States had heavy economic investments in Katanga and in the Rhodesian side of the Katanga copper belt. These investments included export crops of coffee, rubber, tea, cotton, and cocoa.[34] In short, the Congo was both a strategic area and a link to strategic areas in southern Africa.

It was not until Lumumba called on the Soviets for military assistance that the United States sprang into action. Soviet intervention was something Bunche was working to prevent. When the British chief of staff of the Ghanaian army, General Henry Alexander, had arrived in Leopoldville on July 15, he had on his own initiative and as the highest-ranking officer present assumed command of the arriving UN forces—a move that caused Hammarskjöld to appoint Bunche as the interim commander. Bunche immediately faced a conflict with Alexander, Ambassador Timberlake, and General Carl von Horn, the UN commander who arrived on July 17, all of whom believed the Congolese army (ANC) should be disarmed. Bunche agreed that that was desirable but believed that prior consent of the Congolese government was a requisite because it was the government that had invited UN intervention. Lumumba, of course, refused consent, and he and the Soviets used the issue to denounce the UN for wanting to disarm the Congolese and for not having thrown out the Belgians. Bunche was in a no-win situation on this issue and others to come. He had antagonized the Americans, the Ghanaian commander, the UN commander, the Congolese leaders, and the Soviets.

Wearing a blue UNEF fatigue cap as his insignia and operating out of a small office in the control tower at the airport, Bunche worked nonstop to welcome, instruct, and deploy the incoming UN troops. The airport was still occupied by Belgian paratroopers, and not all the incoming troops were thoroughly indoctrinated with the UN philosophy of peacekeeping. The four-star general who commanded the Guinean battalion, for example, had demanded to go immediately to Katanga, where he could drive the Belgians into the sea. Such views helped contribute to European fears and led Bunche to request the inclusion of a non-African contingent in the ONUC forces; the Swedish battalion from Gaza and an Irish battalion were quickly dispatched.

The logistical problems alone were daunting. The soldiers arriving on a daily basis spoke different languages, and many came with poor equipment and little training. More than 25,000 Belgians had fled, leaving the country virtually without basic services. Bunche and his small staff had to coordinate vehicles, airplanes, supplies, fuel, food (recognizing the religious rules governing some diets), ammunition, and the egos of various military commanders. Does a commissar outrank a field marshal? On top of it all, the political sensitivities of all the parties involved were at a peak and under a world spotlight. Upon arrival of the first UN troops, Bunche broadcast a message to the Congolese people that said, in part:

> I want to make certain points about these troops absolutely clear. They will bear arms, but will only use them in legitimate self-defence. They come here as friends of the Congolese people. Most of them come from independent African nations, sister-nations of this one. But they are made up of mixed elements, with both officers and soldiers liable to be white or black, all working together wholeheartedly.[35]

Bunche also warned the Congolese not to expect miracles and called for patience.

The UN forces were making progress in replacing the Belgian troops around Leopoldville, and after much frustration Bunche secured a promise that all would be out of Leopoldville by July 23. Just when Bunche thought he was establishing some understanding with the Congolese leadership, he was hit with the first of a series of ultimatums. On July 18, from Stanleyville, Lumumba demanded that if all Belgian troops were not withdrawn within forty-eight hours, Soviet troops would be invited to deal with the situation. Bunche's public response was: "The UN cannot receive ultimatums from anyone."[36]

Surprised and distressed by the ultimatum, Bunche immediately told the Congolese Council of Ministers of Lumumba's threat; and it reaffirmed its support of the UN and disapproval of any Soviet intervention. The Congolese Senate passed a motion of disapprobation regarding an invitation to the Soviets. At UN headquarters in New York, a secret meeting of members of the African bloc unanimously opposed Soviet intervention and sent Tunisian ambassador Mongi Slim to give this word to Soviet Deputy Minister Vasily Kuznetsov.[37] Hammarskjöld announced he would travel to the Congo.

Bunche found his meeting with Lumumba frustrating. Later, in a speech he described a typical session with Lumumba:

M. le Premier Ministre, we are here to help you to get your government set up, your courts opened, your schools running, your taxes collected, your army trained, etc., but we *won't* interfere in your internal differences. . . .

[A]fter listening absently, M. Lumumba, with a faraway look in his eye would say in impeccable French: "Sans blague. When are you and your UN soldiers going to go and get Tshombe?"[38]

At the same time Lumumba was attacking the UN for inaction and threatening Soviet intervention, he asked Bunche to replace with UN soldiers the Congolese soldiers guarding the Palais de la Nation, who, he suspected, were plotting to assassinate him. Bunche complied, commenting later in a letter to Hammarskjöld that "Job had nothing on me. Really."[39]

Lumumba's threat to invite Soviet intervention had the effect of speeding up the departure of Belgian troops from Leopoldville and gaining additional Security Council support for the territorial integrity of the Congo. However, the ultimatum had a number of negative consequences as well. First, it helped to alienate Bunche and other UN officials, who had been making heroic efforts to remove the Belgians and restore order. At one point during the army mutiny, Hammarskjöld had indirectly suggested that Bunche might want to escape to Brazzaville for his own safety. Bunche had declined, saying it would contribute to the panic. Moreover, Lumumba's criticism of the UN fueled attacks against UN personnel. These incidents and Bunche's reports left UN officials questioning the mental stability of the prime minister. Second, Khrushchev, who had offered only rhetorical support to the Congolese, was now placed in a position that forced him to back Lumumba or lose credibility among radical Afro-Asians and within the Communist bloc. After all, the Soviets could have vetoed rather than voted for the initial resolution creating the UN force. Third, Lumumba's threat shattered the unity of the newly independent African nations. Kwame Nkrumah, leader of the Pan African movement, stressed that what was at stake was the most vital region of Africa: "Military control of the Congo by any foreign power would give it easy access to most of the continent south of the Sahara."[40]

A fourth negative consequence was the threat confirmed the suspicions of officials in Washington that the prime minister was a Communist and not to be trusted. Up until the day before the ultimatum, the U.S. embassy had attempted to maintain cordial contacts with Lumumba and had deflected the concerns of those who accepted Belgian characterizations of him. Following the ultimatum, CIA Director Allen Dulles labeled Lumumba "a person who was a Castro or worse," and the U.S. ambassador in Brussels advocated the removal of the Lumumba government.[41]

Kanza, who was presenting the Congo's case to the UN in New York, recognized that the stakes had increased.

> I was as well aware as anyone among all our friends that Lumumba was involved in a dangerous, perhaps mortal, struggle; for though the West wanted to save the Congo, it had had enough of him. I knew that basically my job was to defend the Congo *and* save Lumumba.[42]

Of his statement, a response from the Soviets, and another from Henry Cabot Lodge of the United States, Kanza said, "Listening to the speech of Kuznetzov we realized that from then on all the debates would centre upon the cold war between East and West."[43]

Kanza's words proved prophetic, and the situation of which he spoke made Bunche's job impossible. July 24–26 found Lumumba in New York, where he met with Hammarskjöld, received African and Asian ambassadors, held a press conference, and even visited Harlem. The meetings with the secretary-general did not go well; Kanza, who was present, characterized the conflict as a clash of personalities in which Lumumba was extremely demanding and impatient, and Hammarskjöld cool and diplomatic. Their joint communique did little to clarify the misunderstandings between the two men. In fact, after becoming acquainted with Lumumba, Hammarskjöld decided that to establish a collaborative relationship was impossible.[44]

Things did not go any better for Lumumba in Washington. After initially holding out the prospect of a meeting with President Eisenhower, American officials said the president would be out of town, possibly an expression of their unhappiness with Lumumba's having met with Kuznetzov, the Soviet UN ambassador, in New York. Annoyed, Lumumba was persuaded by his advisers to make the trip to Washington anyway, and he spent a frustrating half hour there with Secretary of State Christian Herter. To every request for aid made by Lumumba, Herter responded that assistance would be channeled through the UN. Lumumba was not convinced that all aid should flow through the UN, and the American officials came away from the meeting convinced that the prime minister was "just not a rational being." It was soon after Lumumba's Washington trip that the possibility of an assassination attempt was raised for the first time at a Pentagon meeting. By contrast, Lumumba painted such a positive picture of U.S. support, that the State Department was afraid the Belgians would be offended and hence issued a statement commending Belgian cooperation with the UN.[45]

While Lumumba was traveling, Bunche was left to deal with Vice Prime Minister Antoine Gizenga and to prepare for Hammarskjöld's visit to the

Congo July 28. Gizenga was even more troublesome and unpredictable than Lumumba and immediately proceeded to reaffirm his reputation at a welcoming reception for Hammarskjöld, during which he launched a long and bitter attack on the UN.[46] Increasing pressure for UN action on Katanga came from the Congolese and was amplified by the Soviet and Ghanaian embassies.

Hammarskjöld responded by increasing his pressure on the Belgians to withdraw from Katanga. In the face of Belgian intransigence and threats from Lumumba that he might fire Foreign Minister Justin Bomboko and Kanza (who the UN believed were the most reasonable Congolese leaders), the secretary-general sent Bunche to Elisabethville to pave the way for the arrival of UN troops. It was planned that Bunche's initial talks with Tshombe and the Belgians would be followed by the landing of UN troops within twenty-four hours.

This pivotal trip was almost scuttled when Gizenga insisted that Bunche be accompanied by three Congolese representatives and twenty armed Ghanaian soldiers. Bunche took only two UN colleagues with him and arranged a complicated set of codes with Hammarskjöld to guide the deployment of UN troops. On the five-hour flight to Elisabethville, he wrote the following to Ruth:

> What awaits us we do not know. There may be hostility, of course. . . . I'm dreadfully tired and sleepy as I got less than three hours sleep last night and even that was more than the night before. I cannot begin to tell you how complicated and maddeningly frustrating our operation out here is. . . . It is like trying to give first aid to a wounded rattlesnake. How much longer we can hang on here is anybody's guess. How long I can stand this physically is still another question.[47]

Given Bunche's pessimism, the airport reception was a pleasant surprise. The Belgians—Robert de Rothschild and Count Harold d'Aspremont-Lynden—received him generously, and a military band played.

The meetings with Tshombe, his interior minister Godefroid Munongo, and the Belgian officials were another matter. Try as he might to explain the need for UN intervention, the stock response was that there would be European flight, economic collapse, and tribal warfare if the UN took over. After the meeting with Tshombe, Tshombe announced that the decision to send UN troops to Katanga had been canceled, forcing Bunche to issue a counterstatement that no decision had been made. Bunche did not have a high opinion of Tshombe and several years later would write that Tshombe's decision to secede was influenced by European mining interests. "Mr. Tshombe has been receiving approximately $40,000,000 per year from Union Minière, much of which has been expended in the hiring of mercenaries and equipping them with arms."[48] Bunche was also aware that Tshombe had a "quite formidable propaganda apparatus which was very active in the Western world and had especially strong impact in the United States."[49]

Bunche met with Tshombe again the following day in an effort to ascertain whether it was safe for the lightly armed UN troops to land. Just as he felt some progress was being made, de Rothschild and d'Aspremont-Lynden, highly agitated, interrupted to announce that Katangese soldiers were about to shoot down the UN plane being sent to pick up Bunche. Rushing to the airport, Bunche found Munongo ordering Katangese soldiers and Belgian officers to fire on the plane if it landed. Bunche eventually calmed Munongo by assuring him that the plane contained no soldiers or weapons and allowing him to talk to the pilot from the control tower. The plane was allowed to land, Munongo inspected it, and Bunche boarded and took off. To his consternation, he found that "despite my explicit instructions, some fool in Leopoldville had permitted arms to be stored on the plane and had also permitted a Ghanaian to come aboard."[50] Had Munongo been more thorough in his inspection, disaster could have been the result. Nonetheless, the narrow brush convinced Bunche that it would be foolish to send unprotected UN troops into such a situation.

Despite the evident risk, Bunche's decision to advise Hammarskjöld against the use of UN troops in Katanga was met with near-universal condemnation. The Soviets demanded that the Security Council replace the ONUC forces if they were not prepared to enter Katanga. Gizenga broadcast a statement linking Bunche to Tshombe's action. And even the Belgian officials in Katanga tried to blame Bunche for creating a crisis at the Elisabethville airport.

Hammarskjöld quickly returned to New York to urge further Security Council action on Katanga. Congolese mistrust of the UN was growing, and the Soviets were insisting that UN troops use force. For the first time the Security Council voted to demand the immediate withdrawal of the Belgian forces and declared the intervention of UN troops "necessary" but also declared that they would not "influence the outcome of any internal conflict, constitutional or otherwise."[51]

With his new UN mandate, Hammarskjöld informed Tshombe that he would be leading UN troops to Elisabethville himself on August 12 and would accept no conditions. He let Bunche in Leopoldville explain the meaning of the Security Council resolution to Lumumba, who was incensed that Hammarskjöld had not consulted with him personally. Hammarskjöld had more success in Elisabethville than Bunche had in Leopoldville. Lumumba refused to accept Bunche's claim that once the Belgians were gone, the UN forces could not be used to suppress a domestic conflict—namely, with Tshombe. Furthermore, Lumumba wanted the ANC to take control of Leopoldville's Ndjili Airport. Bunche urged him to take these matters up with the UN secretary-general.

When Hammarskjöld returned to Leopoldville on August 14, Lumumba canceled a scheduled meeting with him and then sent him a series of hostile letters. On August 17, when two of Bunche's security men tried to deliver a letter to Lumumba, they were arrested and threatened with death. These events removed any hope Bunche and Hammarskjöld had of working with Lumumba. Bunche wrote to Ruth:

> That madman Lumumba is recklessly on the attack now—and most viciously—against Dag and the UN—and we will probably be in for a rough time since the public will be stirred up by the radio broadcasts. It is a tragedy, but it looks as though this greatest of international efforts will be destroyed by the insane fulminations of one reckless man. We may be washed up here in a few days.[52]

Bunche's words were prophetic. The final events involving Lumumba and Bunche played themselves out around the airport. On August 16, sixteen Norwegian soldiers who arrived on a UN transport plane were arrested and beaten by Congolese soldiers. Bunche attempted to see Lumumba personally about the crisis but was rudely shunted to a Belgian deputy of Lumumba's, with whom he refused to speak. On August 24, Lumumba announced that the ANC would seize control of the airport, and Bunche asked Hammarskjöld for instructions as to whether the UN should fight to hold it. Lumumba took no further action, given that the Conference of the African Countries (Algeria, Congo, Ethiopia, Ghana, Guinea, Lybia, Liberia, Morocco, Sudan, Togo, Tanganyika, Tunisia, and the UAR) called by Lumumba was to start the next day in Leopoldville.

With Bunche scheduled to depart the Congo at the end of August, the African conferees provided a boost to his spirits. The delegates, who had to be carried from Brazzaville to Leopoldville in UN planes, agreed on a policy of support for the UN in the Congo, with only Guinea dissenting. They condemned the secession of Katanga but did not settle on how to deal with

Tshombe. Moreover, in a strong rebuke to Lumumba, they praised the work of the UN and sent a unanimous message of appreciation to Bunche.[53]

Bunche's participation in the Congo crisis had come at a high price. When he briefed his successor, Rajeshwar Dayal, in New York on his future duties, Dayal was dismayed by what he saw:

> My first shock was Ralph Bunche's physical appearance: he was obviously very tired and he looked much older. He spoke of the great strain under which the Operation was being conducted, and the complex nature of its functions.[54]

Bunche had little appetite, a varicose ulcer on his leg was dangerously aggravated, and worst of all, he had lost much of his optimism.

If Bunche anticipated any rest and relaxation in New York, he was mistaken. The General Assembly's 1960 session was just beginning and the Congo crisis was the major event. Along with such established figures as Eisenhower, Khrushchev, Jawaharlal Nehru, Harold Macmillan, and Marshal Tito, there were young new leaders like Gamal Nasser, Sékou Touré, Fidel Castro, and Nkrumah. Bunche and Hammarskjöld were particularly distressed at Nkrumah's performance; Bunche privately called him "an out and out racialist and an unprincipled demagogue."[55] His views had apparently changed from earlier in the year, when he had included Nkrumah and Touré in a group of outstanding young leaders he enumerated in a speech at Colby College.[56] Bunche also publicly criticized the Belgians for their failure to prepare the Congo for independence, drawing a strong official protest from Belgium.

The Soviets replaced the moderate Kuznetsov as their UN ambassador with the more aggressive Valerian Zorin. When Khrushchev himself arrived in New York, the attack on Hammarskjöld and his staff reached a peak. Deploring the actions of the UN in the Congo, the Soviet leader suggested a "troika" arrangement to replace the office of secretary-general that would give representation to Western nations, the socialist states, and the nonaligned countries. Bunche deemed the proposal the negation of the very concept of an international career service as objective, neutral, and nonpolitical. He saw the attacks on the UN as not related to the Congo except for their timing: "They are fundamental expressions of rejection of the notion of the UN and that in addition to its function as a world forum and its executive power, the authority needs to act, to intervene in threatening situations on the spot, in Kashmir, Palestine, Suez, and the Congo."[57]

Khrushchev pressed his attack in an October speech calling for Hammarskjöld's resignation. This action drew a rare public and personal response by Hammarskjöld, who then wrote a note to Bunche asking, "[D]id I read it all right?" However, the secretary-general's defense of the neutrality of his office was not helped by events unfolding in the Congo. Rajeshwar Dayal, Bunche's replacement, had arrived in the country just as Kasabuvu and Lumumba had split the government. With the help of ten Soviet transport planes, Lumumba had launched an attack on rebel forces in Kasai province with the intention of moving on the Katanga border. However, the campaign was not going well and the use of Soviet military aid prompted action by the ever-cautious President Kasavubu. On the evening of September 5, 1960, he interrupted the broadcast of the Leopoldville radio station to announce that he was dismissing Prime Minister Lumumba for betraying his trust, depriving numerous citizens of their fundamental liberties, and involving the country in an "atrocious civil war." He called on the army to lay down its weapons, called on the UN to maintain order, and asked Senate president Joseph Ileo to form a new government.[58]

Kasavubu had carefully plotted his move. He had popular support in the Leopoldville area, had seen the negative impact of Lumumba's Soviet ties on the Western powers, and felt certain of UN support. And, in reality, UN action played a crucial role in the immediate aftermath of the announcement. Although Lumumba was a skilled politician and charismatic speaker, held a majority in parliament, and controlled at least some of the armed forces, the UN denied him and all other political leaders the use of the radio station and the airports. Andrew Cordier, Hammarskjöld's executive assistant, who had taken over for the transition from Bunche to Dayal, was still in charge of the UN operation because Dayal had arrived only that day. Kasavubu had conferred with Cordier two days before his announcement, and all the top UN officials had been alerted. Cordier justified his actions as strictly neutral because the UN denied access to either side. However, the real effect was to give Kasavubu access to his supporters through Radio Brazzaville, which his friend President Fulbert Youlou had made available; Lumumba had no way to reach his followers, and his troops in Stanleyville and Luluaborg were denied use of the airports by the UN. Even the Soviet plane carrying General Victor Lundula, commander of the ANC, was denied permission to land in Leopoldville.

Incensed, Lumumba sent army chief of staff and second in command, Colonel Mobutu, to meet with Cordier. Cordier refused to see Mobutu. In the meantime, Lumumba had picked up valuable support in both houses of Parliament, which voted to annul Kasavubu's dismissal of him. Washington was worried that Kasavubu was not capable of taking charge and began to court Mobutu. Mobutu, a former journalist, was insisting that the army stay out of the political struggle and becoming increasingly depressed. He would carry out Lumumba's orders to arrest his opponents but give them advance warning of his action. UN representative Dayal pressed for the reopening of the radio station and a number of African states swung behind Lumumba.

On September 13, Kasavubu dismissed General Lundula as commander in chief of the army and replaced him with Mobutu. Mobutu, whom Hammarskjöld had dismissed as a figure with no influence, had been carefully weighing the forces engaged in the conflict. The next day at Camp Leopold II, hundreds of army officers who were frustrated by the governmental stalemate urged Mobutu to seize control. On September 10, Mobutu had gained prestige in the eyes of the soldiers when he helped distribute $1 million in back pay to the five thousand troops in the Leopoldville garrison. The UN, on the advice of General Kettani—the Moroccan UN officer who had been asked by Lumumba to reorganize the Congolese army—had supplied the money.[59] Thus, on September 14, 1960, the twenty-nine-year-old Mobutu announced he was taking power in the name of the "Council of Technicians" (read: army) and ordered the Soviet and Czechoslovak embassies to leave the Congo within forty-eight hours. He still retained power in the Congo until 1997.

Mobutu had taken over but Hammarskjöld refused to recognize Mobutu's government formally. Finally, in November, after heavy U.S. pressure, the General Assembly narrowly voted to give the Congolese seat in the UN to Kasavubu and Mobutu.[60] This led Lumumba to leave his house in Leopoldville, where he was protected by ONUC forces, to generate grassroots support in other regions. On his way to Stanleyville, Lumumba was arrested by Mobutu's troops shortly after delivering a speech at Mweka in Kasai province on December 2.

Just before Kennedy's inauguration in January 1961, it was reported that Lumumba had been taken to Katanga, which fueled speculation that powerful Western interests wanted to see Lumumba eliminated before the new administration took office. Kennedy's election in November 1960 had given hope to Lumumba supporters that there would be a change in U.S. policy. During the campaign Kennedy had been sharply critical of Eisenhower's policy in Cuba and in the Congo. The Democratic candidate had made it clear that winning the favor of the newly emergent Afro-Asian bloc would become a priority for his administration.[61]

The CIA had responded to the Soviet challenge in the "third world" by conceiving of parallel assassination plots directed against Castro and Lumumba. When the CIA operatives failed to find a secure enough agent with the right access to Lumumba, the plan was put on hold. After Mobutu's coup, it was believed that the opposition to Lumumba might be convinced to eliminate him with the proper clandestine support from the United States. But local operatives were again overruled by the latest CIA plans from Washington, which called for a "commando type group" to abduct Lumumba.[62]

CIA station chief Devlin remained convinced that the simplest solution was to have Lumumba arrested, and Ambassador Timberlake agreed. The UN did not see things that way. Neither Hammarskjöld nor Dayal could be persuaded that the new Congolese government had the right to arrest Lumumba. They believed he should be protected, more or less under house arrest, by UN forces, until the politicians resolved their differences. In addition, it was not at all certain that the Ghanaian UN soldiers guarding Lumumba would accept an order to withdraw from Dayal. Dayal, in fact, told Timberlake that he felt any effort to arrest Lumumba was really a "trick" to assassinate him.[63] Hammarskjöld supported Dayal's refusal to cave in to American pressure to permit Lumumba's arrest.

Lumumba refused several conciliatory gestures that would have made him a part of the new regime and—against the advice of his closest supporters—made his fateful start to Stanleyville.[64] The Americans were pleased that Lumumba had finally been arrested. The UN was more ambivalent: General von Horn believed Lumumba's capture reduced the chances of further civil war; Hammarskjöld thought it would probably make things worse. Political assassination was not an immediate concern, given that no leaders had been killed in five months of almost constant turmoil. Ironically, the first official instructions of the Kennedy administration seemed to follow the Eisenhower line of not intervening with Tshombe concerning Lumumba's treatment. Lumumba was probably killed the day of Kennedy's inauguration, on January 20, 1961.[65]

News of Lumumba's death, allegedly at the hands of unnamed villagers, intensified the attack on the UN. A riot broke out in the public gallery of the Security Council, where demonstrators verbally castigated Hammarskjöld and U.S. representative Adlai Stevenson. When Bunche issued a formal apology to senior UN officials for the scandalous conduct of the demonstrators, he was buried in an avalanche of angry letters from African Americans. One writer asked why a Black American would apologize for the grief expressed over the death of a fellow Black. Another writer accused him of remaining silent in the face of injustices until they touched him personally.[66] When protesters gathered outside the UN building, Bunche approached one carrying a sign reading "Kill Bunche." He asked the protester who this Bunche was and was told "I guess he's some joker in the UN."[67] Despite his ability to laugh about it, the rebuke from his own people had to have hurt Bunche.

Increasing charges of U.S. influence in the UN Secretariat concerned Bunche. Hammarskjöld met each evening with his senior advisers in what came to be known as the "Congo Club." The Soviets and others were aware that its three principal members were Americans: Bunche, Cordier, and Harry Labouisse. Possibly because of the personal attacks and the shadow cast on the UN's impartiality, Bunche submitted a formal letter of resignation on June 27, 1961. Of course, Hammarskjöld immediately appealed to Bunche not to abandon him, and the matter was dropped.[68]

In August, the Congolese Parliament, meeting under UN protection, approved a new government of national unity with Cyrille Adoula as prime minister and Antoine Gizenga as vice–prime minister. The new government passed an ordinance expelling foreign mercenaries and asked for ONUC help in enforcing it against Tshombe's army. Hammarskjöld decided that the best way to prevent the Congo from splitting the UN's forthcoming General Assembly session as it had in 1960, was to travel to the Congo to bring Adoula and Tshombe together.

The Bunches were on their way to Colby College, where Ralph, Jr., was returning for the fall semester, and his parents were anticipating a brief vacation in Quebec when Bunche received a message from Hammarskjöld. The secretary-general had decided to go to the Congo and wanted Bunche to go with him. Upon returning to New York, Bunche found that Hammarskjöld had changed his mind and asked Heinz Wieschhoff to go so that Bunche could "hold the fort" in New York. At Idlewild Airport, where Bunche went to see them off on September 12, Wieschhoff's wife, Virginia, told Bunche that her husband was sick with a high fever. Bunche immediately volunteered to go, but both Wieschhoff and Hammarskjöld begged him to stay in New York.[69] Once again fate would place Bunche out of harm's way.

Washington was not pleased with the UN action to round up mercenaries and urged Hammarskjöld to work toward some kind of federation with Katanga. Hammarskjöld in turn was not pleased with what he saw as U.S. support for the mercenaries and urged instead application of some pressure on Tshombe. On September 17, the secretary-general decided, against Adoula's advice, to go to Northern Rhodesia personally and attempt to bring Tshombe back to Leopoldville for talks with Adoula. Early the next morning, his UN DC-6 aircraft was reported missing; later that day the crash site was discovered less than ten miles from the Ndola airport in Northern Rhodesia. Hammarskjöld, Wieschhoff, and all others aboard were dead.

Hammarskjöld's death was a crushing blow for all of those who knew and worked with him. He considered Bunche one of his few close friends and confidants, and Bunche regarded Hammarskjöld as "the most remarkable man I have ever seen or worked with. . . . I learned more from him than from any other man."[70] When Bunche went to Sweden for Hammarskjöld's funeral, he stopped to pay his respects to Estelle Bernadotte and to visit Folke Bernadotte's grave. Ironically, Bunche had narrowly escaped death with each of his Swedish friends, both of whom had died, years apart, on September 17.

There was little time to mourn. Bunche was in charge until a new secretary-general could be named and the circumstances surrounding Hammarskjöld's death only added to the tension. He suspected that Tshombe would use the temporary cease-fire that followed the crash to build up his own forces for an attack on the UN troops. Perhaps the only positive effect of the tragedy was a new American attitude toward finding a solution to the crisis.

U Thant, the Burmese representative to the UN, was chosen to fill out Hammarskjöld's term. No two men could have been more different in their personal characteristics. Thant was a devout Buddhist who seldom spoke and always remained calm. Hammarskjöld was not religious in the conventional sense and, although very articulate, often seemed aloof and intellectual. Both had courage and integrity, and both had complete confidence in Ralph Bunche. The Soviets eventually succumbed to Thant's refusal to change his advisers, and Bunche soon became Thant's "right-hand man" and was left in complete charge of the Congo operation.

By November 24, 1961, the Security Council was frustrated enough by Tshombe's intransigence to adopt a resolution denouncing the secession and authorizing the ONUC to use force to eliminate the foreign mercenaries. Tshombe's response was to harass UN troops. Bunche attributed this action to the misguided influence of Europeans.

> In December 1961 a large part of the European population of Elisabethville had made the mistake of becoming involved with a clique of OAS French officers who had been expelled from Algeria. Many of the Europeans had connived with this small and fanatical group in a planned attack on the UN in Elisabethville, which was—overoptimistically—designed to annihilate the UN force in that city.[71]

During the battle, twenty-one UN soldiers were killed and eighty-four wounded.

The renewed fighting in Katanga prompted conservatives in Washington and London to attack the UN and call for a cease-fire. President Kennedy personally intervened with his ambassador in Leopoldville, Edmund Gullion, to encourage Adoula to enter negotiations. He then asked the French to pressure Tshombe to meet with Adoula. Bunche and Gullion were given the joint task of bringing the parties to the negotiating table. The meeting took place in a hospital building at the Kitona base guarded by UN Nigerian soldiers, and after two days broke up with no agreement. Fortunately, the plane that was to take Adoula back to Leopoldville was delayed, giving Bunche and Gullion another chance to draft a proposal. Adoula finally agreed to an eight-point declaration that Tshombe would make unilaterally in which he recognized the indissolubility of the Congo under President Kasavubu and agreed to have Katangese representatives take seats on the constitutional commission and in the Congolese Parliament. He also agreed to integrate his military forces with the Congolese army.

Both the far right and the Soviets contended that Bunche and the U.S. ambassador were the principal authors of the Kitona agreement. Bunche responded with the African proverb "Corn cannot expect justice in a court whose judge is a chicken." He also fired back at the members of the John Birch Society, William Buckley and his *National Review*, Soldiers of the Cross, and "those muddled and addlepated ladies of the D.A.R."[72]

For more than a year Tshombe maneuvered to delay implementation of the Kitona agreement. The usually unflappable Thant became so exasperated that he called Tshombe and his colleagues "a bunch of clowns."[73] In August 1962, Thant proposed the comprehensive Plan of National Reconciliation that he said was nonnegotiable. During the entire week of the Cuban missile crisis, Bunche was in Leopoldville trying to gain Adoula's and Tshombe's acceptance of the plan. Failing, Bunche and Thant ordered UN troops to begin to remove Katangese soldiers from the Elisabethville area on December 28. Under two new UN Indian generals, the UN troops quickly routed the Katangese soldiers, but to the dismay of Thant and Bunche, the UN soldiers advanced so rapidly that they outran their orders and created a diplomatic embarrassment. Bunche put the proper diplomatic spin on the incident but was secretly delighted that the UN forces had gained the upper hand.

Belgium and France then began to pressure Tshombe to accept the Plan of National Reconciliation. Despite being urged by the United States pressure to bargain with Tshombe, Bunche maintained a hard line. On January 14, Tshombe announced his acceptance of the plan, and Bunche noted that "I've done something for Dag now."[74]

The two-and-a-half-year operation in the Congo was the largest and most-expensive UN operation up to that point.[75] Whether the effort, which cost Hammarskjöld and Lumumba their lives, was worth it was widely debated. Initially, there was almost universal support and enthusiasm for UN intervention. Bunche said the UN had no reasonable alternative to its favorable response to the weak government of a new state.

> In so doing, the United Nations strengthened itself morally and won new prestige. And it also gave to itself, no doubt unknowingly at the time, a far wider role and meaning in world affairs than it had ever had, and made indispensable a much stronger position for the Secretary-General as the executive arm. An unfettered executive with authority to act is imperative to the effective conduct of a peacekeeping field operation.[76]

Not everyone was as pleased as Bunche about the growing strength of the UN executive arm.

The Congo expert Washington Okumu's views reflected those of a number of Africans who initially supported UN intervention. Okumu wrote that the UN put Lumumba in the situation of having no option but to accept Soviet aid: "The United Nations refused not only to cooperate in his attempts to bring back Katanga into the central government but also thwarted Lumumba's action by seizing the radio station and the airports."[77] Of course, it was naive to believe, added Okumu, that the UN could operate neutrally in an operation as important as the Congo: it represented the real world and mirrors the conflicting interests of the imperialist states and the newly independent African and Asian countries as well as the socialist and communist camps.

Certainly the events in the Congo had the effect of splitting the newly emerging African bloc. African nations enjoyed their finest hour as the vanguard of the UN forces sent in to prevent the spread of the Cold War into the Congo, as later happened in Angola and Mozambique. Although the division that developed had the appearance of the French-speaking Africans against the rest, it was more fundamental than that. In the end, one group of African states recognized the Gizenga government in Stanleyville and eventually became the Casablanca Powers. These countries took a clear Lumumbist line in the Congo and became a minority group within the

African group at the United Nations. Another group of African states recognized the Kasavubu government in Leopoldville and established themselves as the Monrovia States. Both groups tended to speak out strongly on
questions involving colonialism but divided on other issues.[78]

Soviet charges that the "Blue helmets are turned in the Congo into a
screen behind which the imperialist plunderers are acting"[79] also deserve
examination. It is true that the Soviets were interested in establishing a
beachhead in the Congo and winning the favor of the Afro-Asian bloc in
general, but the allegation of Western bias in the UN operation has some
merit. According to one account, the operation had 45 military staff officers
from the United States and its allies, none from the socialist countries; 546
representatives in police and liaison units from Western powers, 24 from
Africa, and none from the socialist countries who refused to send troops; and
220 nonmilitary staff from the Western powers, none from the socialist
countries.[80] These numbers do not necessarily mean that all the Western
powers agreed on Congo policy—they surely did not—but they do suggest
that the socialists and communists had good reasons to be suspicious. The
Soviet Union refused to pay any costs, hence the entire operation was largely
financed by the United States.

The Americans in Hammarskjöld's "Congo Club" drew the most fire,
and the situation was exacerbated by the secretary-general's refusal to share
the Congo file with high-ranking Soviets in the Secretariat. It was clear
that Hammarskjöld and his senior advisers, including Bunche, had a view
in common with the Western nations: the Soviets should be kept out of
the Congo at all costs. Bunche admitted that Hammarskjöld's strategy was
to rely on the Afro-Asians as a check on the USSR.[81] After initial attempts
to work with Lumumba, it became clear that the UN administrators believed Lumumba was unstable and could not be worked with (there is no
evidence to support any UN involvement in his death). For example, Kalb
quotes Hammarskjöld to the effect that his "primary objective" was to
"explode" the Soviet effort in the Congo, and that the secretary-general
was "still convinced he must break Lumumba "despite the poor alternatives."[82]

Perhaps the most objective observer/participant in the whole affair was
Bunche's replacement, Rajeshwar Dayal. Representing neither the East nor
West and highly regarded by Hammarskjöld and Bunche as well as Nehru,
Dayal believed strongly in the role of the UN as an impartial arbiter. Even
as a strong anticolonialist who was often critical of the U.S. and British rep-

resentatives in the Congo, he was equally critical of Lumumba, Mobutu, and Kasabuvu. It was perhaps a sign of the impossibility of the role that it was not until Dayal temporarily left the Congo for New York that the formation of a coalition government took place. Bunche had been right: Job had nothing on him. Really!

12

The Cultural Politics of Civil Rights

I abhor racism as a dangerous virus, whether it is spread by white or black peoples. I seek total integration, which to me means the Negro taking his place in the very mainstream of American life. . . . My ancestors have contributed very much to the development of this country and therefore I have a vested interest in it that I intend to realize and protect.   —Ralph Bunche, "Upheavals in the Ghettos,"
in *Ralph J. Bunche: Selected Speeches and
Writings*, edited by Charles P. Henry

What also distinguishes Bunche from his country is the contrast between their notions of public service and responsibility, indeed their very notions of the nature of man. Bunche was a moral stranger in this immoral land, a prophet without honor, a man whose principles were rejected as a way of life by the land he so diligently tried to serve, but with which he could find no real common ground. So America exported Bunche to other pastures where his ideals would not prove a constant embarrassment to it, an obstacle to its running of the world.
—Vincent Harding, "Ralph Bunche: The Man without a
Country," Institute of the Black World Monthly Report

Ralph Bunche, whose accomplishments often led the press and public to describe him as the "first Negro to achieve *x*" or "a Black man who has overcome extreme poverty and his slave ancestry," regularly rejected such portrayals. He and other members of the Johnson family were especially upset when he was labeled the "grandson of slaves"—although he *was* the great grandson of slaves.[1] Moreover, Bunche tended to downplay the poverty his family faced and the absence of his father from the home during his teenage years. All in all, Bunche recalls his childhood as a happy one full of picnics, ball games, and music.

As a self-made man eager to demonstrate the abilities of his race, Bunche, it seems, should have acknowledged the obstacles he had overcome or even embellished them—as many of his contemporaries had done. Yet Bunche's project to redefine the American "other" operated within limited parameters. Slavery and extreme poverty were experiences outside the realm of White Americans, and their inclusion in the Bunche story of success was difficult to assimilate. After all, slavery itself ran counter to the very Enlightenment values that Bunche embraced as the defining qualities of not just American politics but of American culture.[2]

In his writings and speeches, Bunche revealed a deep faith in the democratic potential of modernity. If modernity is understood as a distinct configuration with its own spatial and temporal characteristics, including the emergence of civil society, the modern state, and industrial capitalism, then the institution of slavery was problematic for Bunche and best ignored or treated as a premodern residue. According to Paul Gilroy, there is scant sense that the universality and rationality of enlightened Europe and America were used to sustain and relocate rather than eradicate an order of racial difference inherited from the premodern era. John Locke's colonial interests and the effect of conquest of the Americas on Descartes and Rousseau are simply nonissues for White Western scholars.[3] Bunche confronted colonialism head-on but sidestepped the legacy of slavery.

Rather than viewing modernity and slavery as intimately associated, Bunche chose to see slavery as a premodern aberration. To identify himself as the grandson of slaves would simply have emphasized the tradition of ascriptive attributes that modern society transcended. Colonial Africa, on the other hand, was neither traditional or modern. Black Africans were in a state of transition that Negroes—Bunche rejected the term *Afro-Americans*—had already passed through. Thus Bunche rejected the notion of African survivals in the United States and downplayed the significance of slavery in order to rearrange and reconstruct the key words and symbols that define an "American."

The rejection of the slave legacy as at best dysfunctional runs counter to most of the recent scholarship on American slavery. Beginning most prominently with John Blassingame's *The Slave Community* (1970), the revisionist view of slavery contended that much of what we value in Black American culture was produced by the horrors of an institution that never fully succeeded in dehumanizing its victims. This school of thought argued that the slaves managed—more or less—to establish families, worship a just and liberating God, to create an influential and sustaining culture, and to resist their oppression in both sublime and dramatic ways.[4]

This post-1960s school of thought contradicted the revisionist thinking of Bunche's peers who saw slavery as unremittingly traumatic, degrading, and brutalizing. Writing in the 1940s and 1950s, Kenneth Stampp and Stanley Elkins emphasized the psychological effects of a system that brainwashed its victims, making them dependent and childlike.[5] The Sambo-like personality produced by the "peculiar" institution was seen as a result of oppressive conditions rather than a natural characteristic of the African personality. This interpretation was a liberal advance over the biological determinism of early scholars writing on slavery and complemented nicely the psychological aberrations Myrdal found in the Black community.

E. Franklin Frazier, Bunche's friend and Howard colleague, saw Elkins's work as supporting his own, which argued that many pathological aspects of Black American institutional life could be traced to the trauma of slavery. What Frazier saw as deviance, the result of imperfect assimilation of American social norms, Melville Herskovits viewed as legitimate cultural difference reflecting African survivals in Black American culture.

Bunche, who, as we have seen, was intimately associated with both Frazier and Herskovits, adopted the former's line of reasoning and rejected the latter's. In so doing, he joined a long list of Black leaders from the antebellum period and after who were hostile to the mass culture and failed to view it as a means of creating a true cultural nationalism. Nineteenth-century Black nationalists preferred a theory of civilization that would trickle down from the top and eventually penetrate to the lower levels of society. Many Black and White abolitionists, on the other hand, were never tempted to romanticize slave culture. The worse they could portray the effects of slavery, the better their chances of reaching the conscience of Whites. This led to some extremely degrading images of Black slaves.[6]

Although Bunche could accept the Stampp, Elkins, and Frazier view of slavery as a degrading experience, he could not totally embrace it. He rejected the "grandparents as slaves," "extreme poverty" image because he rejected victim status. Victim status is a metaphor that describes an ideological discourse that mediates the conflict for mutual recognition that lies at the heart of the oppressed–oppressor interrelationship.[7] If the victim succeeds in getting the victimizer to accept the condition or indeed the creation of the victimized as a product of the victimizer, then the victim has succeeded in being recognized and even in having his or her humanity confirmed. It does not necessarily, however, challenge the superiority of the victimizer. In fact, by appealing to the morality and rationality of the victimizer, the victim confirms the humanity and goodness of the victimizer. Much of the discourse on race relations in this country from the abolitionists to Shelby Steele revolves around this concept.

Recognizing that the simple acknowledgment of the horrors created by the institution of slavery did nothing to resolve the dilemma of the "other," Bunche rejected any victim-status syndrome. Thus he could not fully accept the pathological character of the Black community that emerged from the work of E. Franklin Frazier. Neither could he accept alternative Black nationalist or cultural pluralist notions of the world, which he labeled as escapist. He might agree with Kimberle Williams Crenshaw's position that what is the most significant aspect of Black oppression seems to be what is believed *about* Black Americans, not what Black Americans believe. That is, if ideology convinces one group that the coercive dominance of another is legitimate, it matters little whether the coerced group rejects the dominant ideology and can offer a competing conception of the world. If it has been labeled "other" by the dominant ideology, it is not heard.[8]

Early in his career, Bunche stepped outside the victim-status syndrome by adopting Marxism (or some version of it), which redefined the relationship between the oppressed in such a way that the dependency of the oppressed was no longer an issue. The syndrome is further rejected when he states that Gandhian nonviolence would not work in the United States because Black Americans lacked the Hindu tradition of "passive" resistance. However, a class-based approach to oppression made such passive techniques irrelevant.

The rise of Nazism at home and abroad and the influence of Myrdal turned Bunche into a mainstream social democrat. It also led him to give Black Americans a new symbolic role as the vanguard of American democracy. The postwar environment combined with Bunche's unprecedented status as a Nobel laureate presented new cultural opportunities to define what an American is. The new strategy Bunche adopted was not, however, group-based; it was a type of heroic individualism.[9] During the 1950s, this heroic individualism fit nicely with a tradition established by Frederick Douglass and manifested in the twentieth century most prominently by such sports figures as Jack Johnson, Joe Louis, and Jackie Robinson.[10] Yet as the mass action of the civil rights movement unfolded, such heroic individualism seemed increasingly isolated and distant from the struggles of common people.

In April 1959, Ralph, Jr., who was a junior at Manhattan's Trinity School, began lessons with George Agutter, the tennis professional at the West Side Tennis Club. The club courts were within walking distance, and Agutter and his staff were permitted to give lessons to outsiders. After the fifth of the weekly lessons, Agutter suggested that Ralph, Jr., become a junior member of the club, which would entitle him to play on the courts at any time. Although the tennis pro knew who the elder Bunche was and had arranged the lessons by telephone with him, he did not know the Bunches were African Americans.

Ralph, Jr., asked his father about joining the club. Bunche called some of his White friends who were prominent in the tennis world and they reported the situation was unpromising. Subsequently, he had two telephone conversations with Wilfred Burgland, a public relations executive who was president of the club, in early June and again on July 6. He had Burgland's July comments taken down verbatim. Among the questions Bunche asked was the following: "From your position as president of the Club, do you think it likely that this exclusive policy relating to Negroes and Jews would be in prospect of change anytime soon?" Burgland replied: "I would not think so. Of course, this is only a personal opinion. However, there is a question whether the Century club up here in Westchester, which is an exclusively Jewish Club, would take me in if I make an application to get into that club...." When Bunche said the policy was rather archaic, Burgland asserted there would be "two or three hundred resignations from the club within a week" if it accepted a Negro. Bunche said he doubted that, and would put in an application "just for the hell of it" if he were younger. Burgland implied that such an application would not be welcome.[11]

It seems clear from the fact that Bunche chose secretly to have Burgland's statements taken down that he planned to challenge the club's policy. When the story broke in the *New York Post* on July 8, 1959, it created an uproar. For three days, the New York papers carried stories on the incident.[12] The city's Commission on Intergroup Relations called for a July 21 hearing with club officials. Some city, state, and federal officials, as well as private groups, assailed the West Side Tennis Club and asked that the Davis Cup challenge-round matches, scheduled for August at the club, be moved. The acting mayor of New York wired the United States Lawn Tennis Association (USLTA) urging it to stop sponsoring matches "played at any club which adheres to such a membership policy."[13] In Washington, Senator Jacob Javits of New York, addressed the issue on the Senate floor, and along with four other senators wired the USLTA. Senator John F. Kennedy also agreed that the national tournament should be moved. The president of the Borough of Queens, the NAACP, the American Jewish Congress, the Anti-Defamation League of B'nai B'rith; the Jewish Labor Committee, the New York Board of Rabbis, the New York Civil Liberties Union, and Black tennis star Althea

Gibson all joined Bunche in denouncing the club's policy. Bunche received many calls at home expressing disgust with the club's discrimination. And he reported that the police had given him an extremely friendly reception at the Midtown Tunnel the day after the story broke. On that same day, as Joan and he were walking down Eighth Avenue, a man suddenly said, "Mr. Bunche I hope they close the damn play [*sic*]." Bunche and his son had an offer from Sidney Wood, president of the Town Tennis Club, to join him at any time as guests (no mention of membership). Bunche noted, too, that David Sarnoff of NBC had responded favorably to a suggestion from Tex McCreary that NBC ought to refuse to telecast matches at the West Side Tennis Club.[14]

On July 15, the Board of Governors of the West Side Tennis Club issued a statement that read, in part:

> Recent questions concerning possible racial bars to membership in the club are a matter of deep regret and embarrassment to the board of governors. They have come about as the result of misunderstanding. So that the facts will be unequivocally clear, the Board of Governors of the West Side Tennis Club wishes to state that it is the policy of the club to consider and accept members without regard to race, creed, or color.[15]

The club stated it would be willing to entertain an application from Dr. Bunche or his son. Burgland resigned as president. Neither Bunche nor his son joined the West Side Tennis Club.

One wonders what the reaction to the West Side Tennis Club incident was in Harlem—not of the Black elites but of the ordinary folk. Did they vicariously enjoy Bunche's confrontation with the White elites of Forest Hills or did they see it as a distant, isolated event? And what about the Mississippi sharecropper—did he or she know or care that young Bunche had been denied a junior membership? And what of the reaction? Would the lynching of a Black Delta youngster of the same age have brought about as strong a response?

Bunche was not unaware of the scale of the incident in relation to the historic struggles of African Americans. Nonetheless, he felt it was an important lesson in racial solidarity for his son:

> I deliberately revealed this experience only because I find it to be rather shocking in New York City and think citizens of the city and of the country generally are entitled to know about it. But I keep the story in proper perspective. Neither I nor my son regard it as a hardship or a humiliation. Rather, it is a discredit to the Club itself. It is not, of course, in the category of the dis-

franchisement, deprival of other rights, segregation, and acts of intimidation suffered by many Negroes in the South and of discrimination in employment and housing suffered by most Negroes in the North as well as the South. But it flows from the same wells of racial and religious bigotry. It confirms what I have often stated, namely that *no* Negro American can be free from the disabilities of race in this country until the lowliest Negro in Mississippi is no longer disadvantaged solely because of race; in short, until racial prejudice has been everywhere eliminated. I am, in fact, glad to have this unpleasant but necessary lesson made real in this way to my son.[16]

The incident may have underscored the racial identity of Ralph, Jr., but it is unclear whether discrimination at an exclusive tennis club helped the masses of Blacks see Bunche as a hero involved in their struggle or removed from it. A number of other incidents during the civil rights era reinforce this ambiguity.

When Congressman Adam Clayton Powell proclaimed that Black Americans should boycott the NAACP because it had White people in high positions, it drew a strong response from NAACP board member Bunche: "I think such a statement is absurd and deplorable. It is basically a racist statement and I'm against racism whatever its source." Bunche added that he applauded White involvement in the civil rights struggle: "The fact that the Negro wins, increasingly, white suppport for his struggle for equality is to me a most encouraging and reassuring social fact, and I would wish to encourage it . . . not reject it."[17]

Powell replied in the *New York Amsterdam News*, saying that Black Americans "had not heard from Ralph Bunche since we helped fight to get his son into the Forest Hills Tennis Club." Bunche shot back that Powell had not heard from him because he "does not speak in the deep south as I do and seems to avoid NAACP meetings."[18] He went on to list fifteen speeches he had given in the South on race relations and integration:

Montgomery, Alabama (in the midst of the bus boycott), 1956

Huntsville, Alabama, 1956

Chapel Hill, North Carolina, 1956

Durham, North Carolina, 1959

Charlottesville, Virginia, 1961

Richmond, Virginia, 1963

Medgar Evers Funeral, Jackson, Mississippi, June 1963

Jackson, Mississippi, October, 1963

Major speeches at NAACP National Conventions: Atlanta, Georgia, July 1951

Dallas, Texas, July 1954

Atlanta, Georgia, July 1962

NAACP Legal Defense & Education Fund—Second Anniversary Supreme Court Decision, May 1956.[19]

For good measure, Bunche added that he and Mrs. Bunche saw little of Powell, and Malcolm X not at all when he addressed the March on Washington in 1963.

Bunche had been an early and strong supporter of the first march on Washington movement led by A. Philip Randolph in 1941. Randolph praised "the totally committed young people like Ralph Bunche whose spirit and resilience, in the face of overwhelming odds, gave strength to the rest of us."[20] As early as 1935, Bunche noted that minorities cannot successfully use violence. Even strikes were not a dependable tactic because the government broke them. Complete noncooperation, said Bunche, was a new but unworkable tactic.[21] A year later at the City-Wide Young People's Forum in Philadelphia, he dismissed such tactics as violence, emigration, passive resistance, self-segregation, civil libertarianism, and goodwill. First, he said, one must fight *war* and *fascism*. Second, one must actively and energetically participate in developing a militant American labor movement.[22]

By 1950, as we have seen, his radicalism had mellowed; however, his view of rights remained broad. In a letter to Alma Booker, he wrote, "I believe firmly in women's rights. I have often in my speeches emphasized that the status of women in most parts of the world is similar to that of an underprivileged minority group."[23] Unlike many of his contemporaries in the civil liberties and human rights movement in the United States, Bunche was convinced that economic rights were just as important as political and civil rights. In the prestigious Walgreen Lectures at the University of Chicago, he said there was "no necessary conflict between the notion of individual liberty on the one hand, and the right to economic security on the other." Neither did he think the state was the only threat to individual rights: "The threats to the rights of the individual may come as well from organized groups within the society as from the exercise of excessive authority by the state." However, he did not see rights as a license: "They carry reciprocal obligations and should be enjoyed only with a deep sense of responsibility."[24]

Evidence of Bunche's newfound fame came in the form of an invitation to address the 42nd annual convention of the NAACP in Atlanta in 1951. There he stated that "no Negro however high he may think he has risen, no matter how much wealth he has amassed is worth very much if he forgets his own people and holds himself aloof from the unrelenting struggle for full Negro emancipation." He went on to argue that segregation by law "demeans the white southerner as well as the Negro"; the former really did not know the "good Nigras" of the South. The pace of progress had to be greatly accelerated: "It is not time that will solve the Negro problem; there is not time to wait, in any event."[25] That acceleration was to come faster than perhaps even Bunche anticipated.

Three years after his Atlanta speech, Bunche addressed the annual meeting of the NAACP in Dallas. Commenting on the momentous *Brown* decision by the Supreme Court, Bunche was unduly optimistic. He believed it would be implemented because Americans are law-abiding. In contrast to the views he had expressed while working on the Carnegie study, he now declared: "I am quite convinced that there are great many citizens of the South who are restrained only by the laws from giving expression to their instinctive democratic impulses as regards relations with their darker fellowmen." He added, "[T]he problem of race is now less than it used to be a problem of economics and politics and more a problem of our minds, our thinking and concepts."[26]

Both Martin Luther King, Jr., and Ralph Bunche were overly optimistic about the role "good" Southern Whites would play in the coming struggle.[27] However, neither withdrew from combat when White support failed to materialize. Shortly after the Montgomery bus boycott began, Bunche sent King a telegram that read, in part, "I greatly admire and warmly congratulate you all. I know that you will continue strong in spirit and that you will stand firm and united in the face of threats and resorts to police-state methods of intimidation. Right is on your side and all the world knows it."[28] Bunche met King three months later when he introduced him as the main speaker at the NAACP Legal Defense and Education Fund's second-anniversary celebration of the *Brown* decision. In his remarks, Bunche stressed the youth of King and the spontaneity of the movement, which consisted of ordinary people. He also compared King's bold leadership in social action to the traditional lack of such church leadership among Negroes in the South.[29]

Despite Bunche's public support for the Montgomery movement, he still had the same doubts about nonviolent direct action that he had expressed some twenty years earlier. A. J. Muste, secretary of the Committee on Nonviolent Integration, was supporting King in Montgomery and asked Eleanor Roosevelt for her support. Mrs. Roosevelt turned to Bunche for advice on what she should do. On April 20, 1956, he sent her the following reply: "1. I wonder if it is really necessary or advisable to set up an entirely new and separate organization," and "2. The use of the Gandhian 'non-violent' slogan seems to me somewhat misleading and inappropriate in the context of the effort of the American Negro. In India it had application and there were those who advocated it. In India, therefore, there was a non-violent alternative. There is none here, although the use of 'non-violent' would seem to imply that there is."[30] Although Bunche was technically right, that the threat of a violent alternative was much less realistic in the United States than in India, the symbolic importance of nonviolence in attracting White support could not be denied and Bunche's objection probably had more to do with protecting the organizational turf of the NAACP.

A year later Bunche called the 1957 Civil Rights Act "disappointingly weak." By 1960, he was supporting the student sit-ins sweeping the South. The crisis in the Congo kept him occupied for much of the next two years; however, he emerged in the public spotlight on civil rights again in a February 23, 1963, speech delivered to the Virginia Council on Human Relations in Richmond. The speech was picketed by ten boys who belonged to the Order of Demolay (a junior Masonic group) and who carried signs that read "Bunche for Communism" and "Free America."

The incident was significant for a number of reasons. First, it reminded the general public of Bunche's national and international stature at a time when younger Black leaders had been the focus of national attention. Second, the signs, in their recalling of Bunche's radical past attracted the attention of the FBI and also followed the pattern of red-baiting all Blacks who challenged the status quo in the South. The picketing and the newspaper editorial that sparked it drew an uncharacteristically emotional response from Bunche.

The day before Bunche's speech, the editor of the *Richmond News Leader*, segregationist James J. Kilpatrick, had accused him of bias toward internationalism and socialism in an editorial. In supporting his charges, he dragged up "Dr. Bunche's pro-Communist record in the years previous to 1940."[31] This record, said Kilpatrick, included his Marxist-oriented articles in the *Journal of Negro Education* and his booklet *A World View of Race*, which had been praised by Black Communist Abner Berry. Also mentioned was his role in founding the National Negro Congress (NNC) and his association with the Marxist journal *Science and Society*, the Institute for Pacific Relations, and Alger Hiss.

Denying that he had ever been a Communist or a supporter of communism, Bunche attacked Kilpatrick's well-known belief in Black inferiority. He went on to challenge the Whites who would say he was isolated from racial discrimination because of his preeminence:

> They are surprised when I tell them that I am more directly and more emotionally involved with the problem of the status of the Negro now than I have ever Been. Why? What they say about my daily contacts with the rougher impacts of segregation and discrimination is true, of course. Even so, when I go to Birmingham to speak, or to Atlanta, as I did for the NAACP last June, I can't get a hotel room [at the Dinkler-Tutweiler Hotel]. . . . Gromyko would be welcome, but I wouldn't.[32]

He recalled many humiliating and degrading experiences, and said he wouldn't speak at the centennial celebrations of the Emancipation Proclamation because there was nothing to celebrate. He concluded with an imaginary dialogue between himself and a White listener, ending with the following lines: "And then, invariably, I stop and say, what the devil [hell is crossed out], it's all so utterly absurd. There's no place for reason here because it's all too irrational and emotional and nonsensical. . . . Anyone who exposes his prejudices to thought and reason, however, will soon see them dissolve."[33]

Perhaps the fullest expression of Bunche's views on the civil rights movement appeared in an Associated Press interview during the Birmingham campaign that appeared in newspapers across the country. He called Eugene "Bull" Connor a fascist and said that the local, state, and federal governments had not done enough. Stating that the Negro's struggle was in its climactic phase, he defended the use of children in the demonstrations. Blame for the violence rested on the police, not the protesters or the general White population. He added that there was always the potential for pent-up violence on the part of impatient Negroes, and it could erupt in the North as well as the South. Answering other questions, Bunche said the appointment of a Negro to the cabinet or Supreme Court (he suggested his friend William Hastie) was long overdue. He also again condemned Adam Clayton Powell's proposed boycott of the NAACP and the program of the Black Muslims.[34]

Even more interesting than the released interview were parts of the transcript that were not printed. When asked if race had impeded his academic career, Bunche responded that few, if any, White institutions would have hired him when he left graduate school. He told again of having declined President Truman's offer to appoint him assistant secretary of state for Near

Eastern and African Affairs in 1949 because of the pervasive segregation in the national capital. He concluded that now there was much more understanding, sympathy, and active support from White people than ever before—running counter to his Richmond speech and perhaps reflecting the outpouring of White support surrounding events in Birmingham.[35]

In a July 8, 1963, press statement "Why I Went to Jackson," Bunche explained his "pilgrimage" to the Medgar Evers funeral: "I went to Jackson to thank a dedicated and courageous man who died for a cause as righteous as any cause can be, and who was a hero and is a martyr in the truest and noblest sense."[36] During that same trip, Bunche attempted to visit seven female students from Tougaloo Southern Christian College who had been jailed for trying to worship in White churches in Jackson, Mississippi. Although he was unsuccessful in reaching them, he delivered a blistering speech at the college in which former president Truman was criticized for his comments about "Northern busybodies" and Mississippi was described as more in need of the UN than South Africa.[37] The speech drew a tremendous press reaction when Governor Ross Barnett accused Bunche of slandering Mississippi.[38] One local newspaper ran a story featuring all of the old Communist charges against Bunche.

At the 1963 March on Washington, Bunche addressed the enormous crowd just before King's memorable speech. On the tenth anniversary of the *Brown* decision, he spoke at the NAACP Legal Defense Fund celebration, and in introducing King said that the most significant development since World War II had been the Negro's loss of fear. Bunche by then had fully embraced the tactics of direct mass action and described King as a person who "understood the nature of the weapon of direct, mass non-violent action" and how to use it. "These are tactics and not ends; and they must be planned well, timed well, and used judiciously; their reason and objectives clear; their targets unmistakable." As an example of misuse, he cited the "so-called stall-in last month on [the] opening of [the] World's Fair."[39] On his way to receive the Nobel Peace Prize in 1964, King, accompanied by Andrew Young, had dinner with Bunche.

Bunche joined King in the front line of the march on Montgomery from Selma. An FBI report to the secretary of state and the president on his activity indicated that he could not walk more than one and a half hours and that he needed a private room because "he lives on the needle."[40] No mention was made of Bunche's diabetes and phlebitis. On aching legs, he addressed the crowd from the steps of the state Capitol:

Governor [George C.] Wallace and some others denounce many of us who are not Alabamians of being "outsiders" and "meddlers," and that includes me. I stoutly deny this. I am here as an American; an American with a conscience, a sense of justice, and a deep concern for all of the people and problems of our country. I came here to identify with the just cause of the right of Alabama Negroes to vote as our President himself has said every good American should. I say to Governor Wallace that no American can ever be an "outsider" anywhere in this country.[41]

The speech brought Bunche considerable hate mail; it also moved him to the inside of the civil rights movement. Not since his efforts with the National Negro Congress in the thirties had he been involved in mass action. Now he was no longer Ralph Bunche the radical outsider criticizing the NAACP, nor was he Ralph Bunche the world diplomat above the race struggle. He was now Ralph Bunche the "civil rights leader."

Just as the civil rights movement drew to a close with its last great march and the violence that would erupt in Watts, Bunche was assuming a more public role in its leadership. Early in 1965, a slightly indignant Bunche responded to a letter asking why he had not been more involved in the civil rights struggle: "For your information, I have been involved in the civil rights struggle all my adult life, and I believe that there are only a few Negroes—and these were the leaders such as Du Bois, James Weldon Johnson, Walter White, A. Philip Randolph, Roy Wilkins, Martin Luther King and James Farmer—whose voices were heard on the issue more than mine."[42] The historical record confirms Bunche's claim, yet he received little credit for his efforts and later generations would forget his contributions entirely. Perhaps the answer to this amnesia lies in Bunche's unique status. Unlike the leaders he cites, for many Blacks and Whites he was perceived as transcending race. A few remarkable incidents underscore his singular role.

In 1954, Bunche told a Michigan audience the following story:

Not so long ago I was at a dinner in New York given by the former secretary-general of the United Nations, Mr. Trygve Lie. I was sitting next to a lady, an American lady married to a European industrialist. She was on my left. At the beginning of the dinner we had some chit chat and then a standing toast was offered to the President of the United States, who happened at that time to be Harry Truman. And after we drank the toast and we went to sit down this lady on my left hissed, "I hope he chokes!" Now I said to her, "Who? Mr. Lie?" And she said, "No. The President!" And I said, "Why? You don't like his politics?" She said, "That has nothing to do with it. I don't like him." And then she went on to explain why she didn't like him—because of his origins, because he failed as a haberdasher, because he came from nothing, and so on. "Well," I parried without any partisanship that after all this was sort of in the American tradition, log cabins and the like, Horatio Alger tradition—all the rest, what was wrong about that? And when I said this, this seemed to set her off and she said, she looked me straight in the eye, and she said, "You talk like some of these people who believe that Negroes ought to be equal." Well, it never occurred to me that this lady had not identified me, but then it occurred to me that probably the reason she had not identified me was because this was a very formal affair, white tie, and so on, and she just assumed in her sort of unconscious prejudice a Negro just couldn't be there, and therefore I must be something else—Egyptian, or South American, Gypsy, or something, you see. And so instead of getting angry I led her on, which wasn't very gallant I must admit. And we got into a discussion of race. And in the course of it I threw the book at her, all the books, biology, psychology, anthropology— I gave her the works, you see. She listened rather bored. She wasn't offensive at all. She—well, she was just unique in my experience and when after I talked at some length, she said, "You know, Mr. Bunche, I've heard all that before. That's old stuff." She said, "I don't believe it and neither do you." I've been working in the field of racial relations most of my life and this lady sort of stopped me every once in a while. And then after a few more words she said, "Oh, let's get at the heart of this." She said, "A while ago you said you had two daughters. Now tell me, Mr. Bunche, would you wish your two daughters to marry Negroes?" Well, after I got my breath and my words back I said, "My dear lady, I don't know what you've taken me for, but it happens that I couldn't possibly object to my daughters marrying Negroes, because *I* am a Negro and by all standards, therefore, my daughters would have to be, and you would understand there could be no objection. She said (didn't phase her a bit), she said, "Yes, but you're different."[43]

Bunche protested that it would be difficult for her to know if he was different from any of the other fifteen million American Negroes if she didn't know any. She admitted that the only Negroes she had ever spoken to were porters or domestics, and that she had never really thought about the race problem. When she asked Bunche for suggestions, he told her to join the NAACP.

Another incident involved a speaking engagement at the University of Arkansas, which Bunche had agreed to only on the condition that the audience would not be segregated. After he spent two pleasant, integrated days in Fayetteville, one of his hosts told him how much trouble he had caused. He said that after they had agreed to Bunche's condition, they realized that there were "only a couple of hundred Negroes in the whole county" and "they're sharecroppers and tenant farmers and they wouldn't come to hear Booker T. Washington much less you, lecture."[44] To avoid the embarrassment of having Bunche think he had been tricked into speaking before an all-White audience, the faculty sent emissaries some 250 miles to Pine Bluff and Little Rock to round up Negroes to attend Bunche's lecture. The amused Bunche concluded that "those Negroes who had to travel over those hard Ozark mountain roads 250 miles each way to hear me lecture would probably be hating me for the rest of their lives."[45]

Recalling that Martin Luther King, Jr., said that Birmingham was the most segregated city in the South, one final example of Bunche's status is appropriate. On February 13, 1959, Bunche was to address the Periclean Club of that city. Bad weather forced his plane to land in Macon, Georgia, some 180 miles from his destination. At three in the afternoon, Bunche phoned his hostess to say that it would be impossible for him to make his eight o'clock engagement. The hostess responded that the club would hire a limousine to rush him to Birmingham and the audience would wait for him until midnight if necessary. The limousine made the first hundred miles without incident but broke down just inside the Alabama state line. Bunche called his hostess to say it now looked hopeless. She thought for a minute and then told him to sit tight. Fifteen minutes later the local White sheriff pulled up, sirens screaming, and asked for Dr. Bunche. "I'm he," said Bunche, with justifiable trepidation. Sheriff: "By God, git in the car." Then, in a driving rain, the sheriff raced to the county line, where Bunche was transferred to another local sheriff who took off, sirens screaming and lights flashing. Sheriffs relayed Bunche across four counties—some eighty miles—in this fashion in less than an hour while news of his progress was sent over shortwave radio to the Birmingham police who passed it on to the waiting audience. Each update was greeted with shouted "Amens" and "Hallelujahs." Upon their arrival, the White sheriff accompanied Bunche into the church and sat nearby while from the pulpit his distinguished passenger proceeded to give segregation hell.[46] Bunche recalled racial incidents from his youth and urged his listeners never to run from a fight for principles. There was, he said, no better place than Birmingham to point out that this is not a White man's world; only one-third of it is White. The country cannot afford any more Little Rocks; the Negro has waited long enough. Negroes are winning against the odds "because we are *right*," Bunche declared, and he criticized television newscaster Chet Huntley for urging Negroes to stop their pressuring and court appeals. He ended by reaffirming his unity with all Negroes and their proud ancestry.[47]

Bunche was refused a room at Birmingham's Dinkler-Tutweiler Hotel during that visit. Ironically, the mayor had given Bunche the key to the city. Apparently, it did not open hotel-room doors.[48]

More mundane battles against discrimination had been fought and would continue to be fought. From refusing to identify his race on visa applications, to fighting for fair employment practices at the UN, to closing his credit account at Hecht's department store, to refusing to deal with racist insurance agents at Metropolitan Life, Bunche fought many of the same battles that daily assault the dignity of African Americans. Privately and publicly, he attacked Black self-segregation, as he did in a 1953 Phi Beta Kappa speech at Howard University reported in *Jet* magazine: "Unless radical changes are made in the policies of many of these [Black] institutions, they may find themselves in the unenviable position of obstructing the elimination of segregation in higher education."[49]

Still an academic at heart, Bunche was a Black intellectual without a home. "Successful" Black intellectuals by definition tended to be on predominantly White campuses and therefore distant from the Black community. Bunche himself had accepted an appointment at Harvard before finally being persuaded to remain at the UN. "Unsuccessful" Black intellectuals were disdainful of the White intellectual world but removed from the great academic debates of the time. Two organic intellectual traditions sustained some Black intellectuals. Dr. Martin Luther King, Jr., was rooted in the Black Christian tradition of preaching, which gave him not only an identity but also a mass base. A Black intellectual without an institutional base, like Ralph Ellison, could find a home in the Black musical tradition of performance. Indeed, Ellison came to accept the blues as a metaphor for human existence—an indigenous American form of existentialism.[50]

As a secular humanist who rejected any single form of organized religion,[51] Bunche relied on reason rather than faith in his struggle for equality. Reason and science led him to reject any essentialist notions of race, as we have seen from his attacks on Garvey through to the Nation of Islam. The other major intellectual standpoint from which to view race was cultural pluralism. Although this alternative was attractive and Bunche taught on the same campus as one of its major proponents—Alain Locke—he never invoked the immigrant analogue. Initially, his strong class views worked against ethnic or racial pluralism, but as they moderated and race relations improved, Bunche was optimistic that such artificial constructions as race would soon disappear.

For Bunche, integration meant the affirmation and encouragement of difference rather than simple passive permission or allowance of difference. He recognized that the absence of such recognition is a strategy that facilitates making those who do not conform into the "other." Yet like Ellison and Frazier, having denied any African survivals or dynamic folk culture, he lacked any non-Western perspective from which he could critique Western cultural hegemony.

By 1965, it was becoming increasingly obvious that institutionalized racism was a more difficult and more complex phenomenon than the individual prejudice featured in the Myrdal study.[52] Bunche had made it clear that he was asking for equality on his own terms, as in a 1962 "Youth Night" speech at the NAACP convention:

> I want to be a man on the same basis and level as any white citizen. I want to be as free as the whitest citizen. I want to exercise, and in full, the same rights as the white American. I want to be eligible for employment exclusively on the basis of my skills and employability, and for housing solely on my capacity to pay. I want to have the same privileges, the same treatment in public places as every other person. But this should not be read by anyone to mean that I want to be white—I am as proud of my origin, ancestors and race as anyone could be. I want to go and do only where and what all Americans are entitled to go and do.[53]

Despite his desire not to be "White," Bunche was fundamentally defined as White by the dominant culture. In many instances it was willing to make an exception for Bunche and treat him as an equal, as an "honorary" White. Liberals, in particular, tended to reflect the Aristotelian principle of equality as *sameness*. Individuals with the same attributes, status, or condition were treated equally; those who were different were treated unequally.[54]

More perniciously, however, the dominant culture designated Bunche as a "model Negro." To do so was to create, isolate, and reify specific but ultimately arbitrary qualities that supposedly constituted the meaningful core of potentially shared group traits. Moreover, it was to employ these traits as the most significant indicators of the individual group member's human essence. At first Bunche participated in the creation of the "model" Negro, but in the sixties he began to see himself as a token and rebelled at the model label.

13

Black Power and "Blackism"

But there is very little knowledge or understanding of the comparatively recent phenomena of the "black man," of "black people" and the black people's revolution. This is the country's greatest domestic problem. No other is so difficult, so stubborn, so challenging or so fraught with danger.

—Ralph Bunche, "The Black Revolution,"
in *Ralph Bunche*, edited by Charles P. Henry

The problem of race and color prejudice remains America's greatest moral dilemma. When one considers the impact it has upon our nation, its resolution might well determine our destiny. . . . How we deal with this crucial situation will determine our moral health as individuals, our cultural health as a region, our political health as a nation, and our prestige as a leader of the free world.

—Martin Luther King, Jr.,
in Charles P. Henry, *Jesse Jackson*

Racism is a disease of the soul. Racism has blinded Europe, North America, and most of the "white Western world," and has left moral cataracts and scar tissue on our world eyes. Racism is fundamentally a moral problem, a problem of human values, running from our minds to our local communities and to our international community.

—Jesse Jackson, in Charles P. Henry, *Jesse Jackson*

How do you fight racism—the belief that one racial group is superior to another? Do you try to prove that all racial groups are equal in their innate capacities? If so, do you concede the validity of racial groupings in the process? Do you deny the existence of racial groups? If so, how do you explain the obvious differences in status and behavior among them? If the causes of the differences are environmental, how do you gain the status and power to change the environment? The sixties brought all of these questions to the front of the nation's domestic agenda.

Watts ended the civil rights movement. When south central Los Angeles went up in flames in August 1965, traditional explanations of race relations in the United States lost their credibility. Not that they weren't put forth; they were just unconvincing. Blacks in Los Angeles were not seen to be as poor as Blacks in the rural South or as packed and squeezed as Blacks in the urban North. In fact, in terms of socioeconomic indicators, they were relatively well off—for African Americans. Yet rumors of police brutality sparked a rage that would be felt in quick succession in Black communities across the country.

The urban violence that left 34 dead, 1,032 injured, 3,952 arrested, and property damage estimated at $40 million had no overall direction or goals, but it made some things perfectly clear. First, traditional Black leadership was rejected. Martin Luther King, Jr., was booed when he called for an end to the violence, and comedian-activist Dick Gregory was shot in the leg as he walked the streets of South Central. Assemblyman Mervyn Dymally was told to go back to Baldwin Hills—a middle-class enclave in Los Angeles. Second, shouts of "Burn, Baby, Burn!" and "Get Whitey!" as well as the pattern of destruction of White businesses signaled a new level of anti-White hatred and bitterness only glimpsed in public before. Third, in terms of urban violence, it marked a turning point in the history of rioting in the United States. Although Blacks had often been the victims of enormous urban violence, they had seldom been its practitioners. Now they were the aggressors. Public officials cited the violence as the acts of a small, criminal element; others proclaimed the events as an escalation of tactics in the civil rights movement.[1]

The impact of Watts was swift and dramatic. Martin Luther King, Jr., made plans to shift his attention from the South to Chicago and a campaign for fair housing. SNCC, CORE, and the young activists who had provided the shock troops for the Southern civil rights movement began to look inward and gave birth to Black Power. A young minister's son named Ronald Barnes in Los Angeles changed his name to Maulana Karenga and formed a cultural nationalist organization called United Slaves (US). Two young men in Oakland, California, named Huey Newton and Bobby Seale, began to think of forming an organization to defend the Black community against the police.

Ralph Bunche began to look inward as well. Shaken by the events in his adopted hometown, he released a public statement on August 17 that read in part:

There can be no doubt about this: Negroes throughout the country will have to pay for what has happened there....

There was no "insurrection" in Los Angeles; the rioting had no politically motivated leadership or organization and no rational purpose. It was sheer lawlessness in the mass to the dimension of madness. It is no apology for the crime to say that many heretofore innocent and decent people were apparently caught up in the tidal wave of emotion. The victims, black and white alike, and far more black than white, have suffered enormously.... There is but one remedy: city, state and national authorities must quickly show the vision, the determination and the courage to take those bold—and costly—steps necessary to begin the dispersal of every black ghetto in this land.[2]

For Bunche and for King, Watts was a sharp reminder that their earlier predictions of the eminent death of segregation and the birth of equality had been overly optimistic. Like King, Bunche grew more introspective, more pessimistic, and more radical in the steps advocated to bring about change.

A year before Watts, Bunche cited the two greatest dangers to the world as the ever-widening gap in income between developed and developing nations and "the population ogre."[3] Although Bunche was absolutely accurate in focusing on these issues as crucial, Watts brought him back to racism as a fundamental cause of domestic and international inequality, as well as a reason for the resistance to population planning in developing countries.

Over the next four years, Bunche would offer a remarkably astute analysis of the causes of urban violence. He would begin by denouncing the advent of Black Power but ultimately embrace it. And finally, he would give up the quest for "brotherhood" in exchange for a "little justice" and did not rule out violence as a means of revolutionary change.

His Watts statement, which was sent to California governor Edmund Brown at his request, assumed the tone of a dire warning. Those warnings took the form of reality in more urban violence in 1966 and the call for Black Power. As Bunche witnessed the end of his peacekeeping efforts in the Six-Day War in the summer of 1967, he seemed more disturbed by events in Newark and Detroit during the same summer. Having been born in Detroit and then lived in the New York area, Bunche felt these eruptions as strongly as he had Watts. For the first time since his academic days at Howard, he wrote a long critical assessment of race relations in the United States and submitted it for publication to *Look* magazine. "Upheavals in the Ghettos" was too long for one issue, and *Look* suggested a syndicated six-part series. Bunche rejected the idea, and the paper was circulated to a few friends only.

Starting out with a psychological discussion of the shame and bitterness that ghetto residents feel, Bunche said that because the violence in Newark and then Detroit "struck me so hard" he had to analyze what happened. Fearing that American racial violence could broaden into Cyprus-type communal warfare, Bunche attempted to get at the root causes of the conflict. "Upheavals in the Ghetto" criticizes the superficial responses of state and local officials to urban violence. Blaming "outsiders" and "agitators" is fallacious and misleading, says Bunche. Violence can be sparked only because the conditions in scores of cities are ripe for a conflagration. City officials exacerbate the situation by sending large numbers of police into the area. Then once the violence has subsided, "the concentration is on placing blame and establishing guilt rather than seeking out and attacking causes."[4]

Stressing that his analysis was purely personal and no way involved the UN, he criticized the performance of Governor Richard Hughes of New Jersey and Mayor Hugh Addonizio of Newark, calling some of their statements inflammatory and even racist. Not only did the governor dismiss allegations of police brutality but "he seemed to assume that there are no valid Negro grievances as such."[5] Governor George Romney of Michigan, at least avoided the traps into which Hughes literally leaped, said Bunche.

The social scientist's trained eye did not miss the feeling of liberation that swept through riot areas as police were put on the run:

> At the moment of participation, the riots are, to the participants and no doubt to the onlookers as well, triumphs of liberation, of throwing off shackles, of getting out from under white domination, of saying to the white bosses and the power structure and to white people generally: you do not want us or like us, and you mistreat us, but for once you are going to know who the hell we are, where we are and what we are going to have—or else.[6]

Among established Black leaders, Bunche was almost alone in understanding—or at least putting on paper—the fleeting moment of liberation these urban uprisings produced.[7]

Bunche understood that ghetto residents outside the South had seen little change in their political and economic status as a result of the civil rights movement. "All of the relatively easy steps have been taken," he said, "any significant new advances require an all-out white *acceptance* of the Negro as a person—in residential areas, in the schools, the churches, in organizations, in the power structure, in every aspect of life."[8] It was the refusal of Whites to accept Blacks that is the root cause of ghetto violence, and Bunche explicitly identified with the dissatisfaction and bitterness it produced: "I am no exception" (18).

Yet the revolution in attitudes that is needed lacked leaders. The Black Power advocates who rode to prominence on the wave of racial violence came in for harsh criticism by Bunche. He called Black Power an "extreme and racist doctrine"; however, "its advocates are symptomatic of the condition and not the cause, not even a contributing cause of it." Criticizing the fondness of Black Power leadership for maximum exposure and sensational slogans, he asserted that none of the leading figures were found in the front ranks of the mobs confronting police and troops in Newark or Detroit: "There is no great risk in threatening from Havana, Cuba, to 'burn America down' or to 'wage guerrilla war in American cities'" (20).

Bunche admitted that the civil rights organizations denounced by Black Power leadership were also very short on tactics and tacticians, but he could not personally "accept the Black Power thesis or any separatist movement because I see them as racist and escapist" (20). Comparing Black Power to the Black chauvinism of the Garvey movement he had analyzed in the 1930s, Bunche said that in seeking Negro unity, it had the same goal as the National Negro Congress he had cofounded in the 1930s. However, in its separatist doctrine, it followed a course similar to that of such earlier movements as Garvey's, the National Movement for the Establishment of the 49th State, the Peace Movement of Ethiopia, and the National Union for People of African Descent. Bunche added that both Du Bois and the Communist Party in the United States had sought to build Black separatist communities during that period but all of these efforts failed because they were escapist.

The reaction to Black Power was backlash. Bunche was not cheered or reassured by the announcement that J. Edgar Hoover and the FBI would have an active role in investigating urban violence. Nor did he see the new efforts in riot control as the ultimate solution to riot prevention. Most dangerous, he thought, were liberal efforts to pump more resources into, or "gild," the ghetto. It would simply create a uniquely American form of apartheid.

> Anti-poverty projects, more employment, better teachers and better schools, slum clearance, Head-start and all such efforts are immediate necessities, but everyone knows that the ghettos will still be there. The danger will be there as long as the ghettos are. I must repeat that people forced to live in these racial concentrations develop a characteristic ghetto psychology of feeling "different," unwanted and despised and this makes for a volatile atmosphere. That is to say that the menace of the ghetto stems from a state of mind as well as body. Thus, expanded assistance may help to relieve some tensions but at best can only put off the evil day of ghetto reckoning. That is the rub. (25)

In short, Bunche was saying that one cannot expect Blacks in the ghetto to "be generally upstanding, self-respecting, law-abiding, love-your-country-citizens" when they are treated as the *other,* as *non-Americans* (25). The inescapable conclusion was a massive and "staggeringly expensive" program to eliminate the ghettos, yet the cost "would be far less than the cost for even a short period of the war in Viet Nam or the cost of placing a man on the moon, and it would be small compared to the cost of some more billion dollar riots; moreover, lives would be saved rather than taken" (27).

By 1968, President Johnson's National Advisory Commission on Civil Disorders (the Kerner Commission) had reached many of the same conclusions as Bunche. Even so, the momentous events of that year, including the success of George Wallace's American Independence Party, the assassinations of King and Robert Kennedy, the violence at the Democratic National Convention, and worldwide student unrest, would serve to make more difficult Bunche's and the Kerner Commission's goal of one society.

On August 20, Bunche began to write "Notes on the Black Revolution" in order to "try to put down some of my thought on the crisis of race in America." The unfinished manuscript was characterized by the "monumental sadness" Southern writer Harry S. Ashmore found in Bunche in the sixties.[9] Most remarkable was Bunche's embrace of Black Power or "Blackism."

"Notes on the Black Revolution" moves from the level of factual analysis that characterized "Upheavals in the Ghettos" to conceptual analysis of "Blackism"—"the darker side of the coin of Americanism."[10] Like Frederick Douglass after the *Dred Scott* decision by the U.S. Supreme Court, Bunche says, "[E]ven true believers of integration like myself, all of the firm advocates of it in the black segment, are assailed by unavoidable doubts these days."[11] Contending that it's tougher to be Black in America than at any time since abolition, Bunche accepts the need for Black Power.

> Black power is not a new concept. The need for unity of aim and effort by black Americans is as old as the black man's struggle. The national Negro Congress of the thirties was, in this sense, a "black power" movement. Today's black power demand however, is stronger, more insistent and more widely based, and therefore gives new strength to the development of black unity.[12]

Of course, the young Bunche of the thirties would have rejected any such characterization of the National Negro Congress.

Yet Bunche sees differences that he had not acknowledged the year before between the Black Power advocates and the racial chauvinists of the Garvey movement. For the latter, race was defined in physical terms; for the former being black "is less a matter of actual skin color than a state of mind. Being black is thinking black."[13] Contending that no White man can ever think Black, Bunche declares that every Negro has the potential to think Black. Anticipating the charge of racism, he concedes that "Blackism can be racist"; however, "it is not by any means synonymous with racism."[14] Citing the need for pride in ethnic identity, Bunche recalls the work of the Association for the Study of Negro Life and History in reclaiming the past achievement, culture, and civilization of Black people. He could have cited his own framework for a course on Negro history outlined in a 1940 speech to the Toussaint L'Ouverture Society at Hunter College. In it, Bunche makes a conscious attempt to avoid racial chauvinism by emphasizing the impact of American movements and forces on the Negro rather than isolated examples of Negro achievement, heroism, and distinction. By 1968, Bunche seemed more willing to risk the charge of racial chauvinism.[15]

Having been born and raised in an integrated environment, Bunche had adopted a liberal optimism that accepted no barriers to domestic or even world integration. Comfortable with his own identity, he could think Black "but not exclusively Black." The failure of the civil rights movement to bring about full integration pierced his liberal optimism. It also led him to question his own role vis-à-vis the Black community and in the end fully embrace that community.

> I am, admittedly, in a privileged position. At my age and in my line of work, I do not experience the discriminations, humiliations and the degradations which are so intolerably a part of the daily life of most black people, and constitute so formidable a handicap. My dignity as a man is seldom assaulted. I harbor no ambitions which would be thwarted because of race. I do not live in the ghetto. I have free and wide contact with all people, white as well as black. In effect, I do not any longer feel the color bar, personally, in a tangible sense. But I feel it strongly, nonetheless, because I know it is there, because I see its brutalizing impact on most members of my group, because I have always had sense enough to know that as long as black people anywhere in this country are discriminated against, deprived of opportunity, rights and dignity solely because of race, there is no escape from the stigma of race for any member of the group, no matter how well off he may seem to be or think himself to be. When any black men are rejected by the dominant white society, all are rejected. No black man should have any illusions about that. There is a decisive difference between being accepted genuinely, as an equal, and being tolerated for some reason, such as recognition of ability and need for it, a minimal bow to a pricking conscience or a missionary-spirit.[16]

Bunche could embrace Black Power because he saw it reaching the masses of ghetto residents in a way that the NAACP and Urban League did not, and he fully identified with the Black masses.

In his last major public address, at the Fifth East-West Philosophers Conference in Honolulu, Bunche gave a speech that in a sense represented a closing of the circle. Back in the multicultural West, he was again talking about his first love: philosophy. As he had as a young UCLA student, he saw race as a fundamental and all-pervasive problem. Race, not class, is the decisive element in the conflict between White and non-White peoples. "Racism," said Bunche, "is the foremost obstacle to harmonization of peoples; it is the antithesis of harmony, being alienation at its emotional worst."[17] He attributed the most pressing problems of the day to an undercurrent of racism. In the United States, the growing estrangement of Black citizens was due to racism. The failure of the United States or the United Kingdom (which had intervened in Kenya, Tanzania, and Anguilla) to intervene on behalf of the oppressed Black majority in southern Rhodesia was attributed to racism. In the United Nations, race was "all-pervasive and often decisive." The failure of the United Nations to admit China was due to racism, not ideology, according to Bunche. The refusal of developing peoples to accept efforts at birth control was motivated by their suspicions of affluent White societies. The increasing gap between the poorest countries in the world and the wealthiest countries was also a gap between the non-White and White.

In a stunning reversal of his analysis in *A World View of Race*, Bunche cited racism as the underlying cause of colonialism:

> In the international sphere, colonialism in its various manifestations has been the major cause of alienation and of estrangement between white and non-white peoples. The colonial system in its modern version, implicitly arrogant and self-serving, was instituted and perpetuated chiefly by self-righteous and superior-minded Europeans. Its positive achievements notwithstanding, colonialism's evil legacies will bedevil the world for years to come. It has been the cause of many wars since it was instituted and is the direct source of the major conflict situations, all of them having racial aspects, now confronting the world: Vietnam, the Middle East, Nigeria, southern Rhodesia, and Kashmir.[18]

Of these wars, the most surprising was Bunche's analysis of Vietnam.

In early 1964, Bunche had cited Vietnam as the number-one immediate crisis. He saw it as a war that the United States did not want and in which had no clear objectives. He seemed to put the burden on Hanoi for producing "some encouraging sign." Later, in the spring, he had stated the

United States was "alone in its commitment to protect the independence of South Vietnam."[19] However, he stressed, negotiation and not military victory was the only sensible goal. In fact, Bunche had worked tirelessly with U Thant to negotiate a settlement.[20]

When Martin Luther King, Jr., began to publicly criticize the Vietnam War and urge Blacks and Whites to become conscientious objectors, Bunche attacked him for mixing up the civil rights movement with the antiwar movement. Other civil rights leaders, including Roy Wilkins, Whitney Young, and A. Philip Randolph, also denounced King for weakening the support for civil rights. Neither Bunche nor his peers saw any link between the war in Vietnam and the struggle for human rights in the United States.[21]

King was especially hurt by the criticism of Bunche. He called Bunche from Los Angeles on April 13, 1967, and denied emphatically that he was for a fusion of the civil rights and anti–Vietnam War efforts. His actions were a consequence of his clergyman's conscience. He and Bunche made up. Three days later, Bunche received King, Benjamin Spock, David Dellinger, and several others in his office during a huge anti–Vietnam War demonstration outside the UN and told them of U Thant's unsuccessful efforts to stop the bombing and bring about U.S. action to end the war.[22]

A new twist was added to Bunche's preoccupation with Vietnam when his son, Ralph, Jr., was drafted. Ruth felt that his father should have tried to prevent the call-up, but the two men thought to have done so would have been improper. Nonetheless, when Ralph, Jr., left for Vietnam on November 3, 1969, his father could not suppress his emotions:

> As I began to think about the boy's departure, I became furious and outraged. . . . Our one son . . . was being taken off to an utterly senseless, useless war, a war that could bring no good to anyone, that no one could possibly win. That our country had never intended to get into, but had got into simply by stages and accidents and now lacked the courage to get out of. I would not like my son to have to go to any war, but if he had to go in defense of his country, he would have my blessing. But to go to war and risk his life when there was really no question of the country's defense or even its interest at stake was just too damned much. I felt like going out into the street and denouncing in the strongest terms at my command the war, all of those who got us into it and those who keep us in it and the establishment in general.[23]

In October 1970, Ralph, Jr., returned home without incident.

It was in his Hawaii speech that Bunche examined the racial roots of the war.

The Viet Nam war has very deep racial implications. There, the United States is fighting "yellow" men who are also considered communists. This makes it rather easy for Americans to rationalize their involvement and to broadcast daily the number of those despised little yellow men that the American and South Vietnamese forces have killed. The derogatory name Americans give to their South Vietnamese opponents is "Viet Cong," which literally means, I understand, "yellow bandits." Would the United States be engaged in that war if the North Vietnamese and the National Liberation Front were white?[24]

Taking King's line, Bunche made a direct link between the Black Americans who were asked to fight in Vietnam but were given little opportunity to fight for their rights in this country.

Bunche went further than King in his refusal to rule out violence as a legitimate means of struggle for Blacks in this country:

I am not against violence in principle because I think we are in a revolutionary situation here. The struggle of the black man is a revolution. It means a revolutionary change in the mores and the status of a tenth or more of the population and, of course, in revolution any means are justifiable in my view, but I think violence for the Negro is not a practical step forward.[25]

This statement, coming on a major television news program, marks a distinct break with the traditional civil rights establishment. Yet Bunche had always argued that nonviolent direct action was really a misnomer because Blacks did not really possess the option of violence. Ironically, he had also contended in the thirties and forties that Gandhi-like nonviolent demonstrations would not work with African Americans because they lacked the Hindu tradition of passive resistance.

Rational or logical analysis had brought Bunche to these positions, he said, not emotion or bitterness. However, pessimism, if not bitterness, characterize a number of his statements during this period. In a *Today Show* interview, he remarked that he had given up on brotherhood: "I used to use the term . . . brotherhood and brotherly love. . . . [A]ll that is needed in my view [now] is for people to have mutual respect for each other."[26] Later in the interview, he rejected the notion that his life could serve as a model for others: "[I]t is humbug to talk about me as an example, in that in this society, no black boy, or no boy, ought to have his future depend upon . . . the accident of having a grandmother such as my grandmother, Nana, because they're not . . . going to have it."[27] Further evidence of Bunche's new recognition of the exceptional course his life had followed came in an interview with *Psychology Today:* "I've been the token Negro at too many parties for too many years."[28]

Not content merely to express his frustration in words, Bunche used his influence to direct resources into radical new social programs. At a trustees meeting of the Rockefeller Foundation in December 1967, he voiced an emotional appeal that the Foundation make eliminating the Black ghetto its highest priority. Stunned by the depth of Bunche's feeling, the trustees agreed to formulate a program. After much outside advice and many program proposals, the trustees—led by IBM chair Tom Watson—announced the ghetto project was dead. Bunche persisted and convinced John Rockefeller to go ahead with the project.[29]

Eventually, Bunche's former student Kenneth Clark was appointed director of the Metropolitan Applied Research Center (MARC). During its existence from 1968 to 1976, MARC was the foremost urban think tank on problems of the poor. Its focus was applied research, and ironically one of its first initiatives involved the creation of community-controlled schools in the Oceanhill–Brownsville area of New York City.[30]

The remarkable changes in Bunche's views went largely unnoticed by the public. His friends in the civil rights leadership did not criticize his increasing radicalism, as they did King's. His former adversaries among the Black Power advocates did not acknowledge his acceptance of Black Power or embrace his radical views, as they did King's after his death. In part, the absence of a reaction is due to the behind-the-scenes nature of much of Bunche's activity. His constant criticism of Black Power advocates as long on rhetoric and short on action probably hit too close to home for many. In fact, some of Bunche's criticism bordered on being unfair. He asked why such militants had not been more active in pressuring the U.S. government to act on behalf of Blacks in South Africa, Southern Rhodesia, Angola, and Mozambique. Similar criticism was not directed at the NAACP and Urban League, and groups like the Student Nonviolent Coordinating Committee (SNCC), the Congress of Racial Equality (CORE), the Revolutionary Actions Movement (RAM), and the Black Panther Party in reality had definite internationalist tendencies. Borrowing from Malcolm X, they decided to internationalize the struggle for human rights, and the United Nations became a focal point for action. They could have learned much from an African American who had been pursuing the same path for twenty-five years: Ralph Bunche.

Perhaps one reason Bunche became more blunt in his criticism of the lack of progress in the United States was his knowledge that the end was near. One ailment or another since his early student days at UCLA, the long hours of stressful work, the years of chain-smoking, constant travel, and a poor diet were taking their toll. Although his extraordinary mind still functioned, by the late sixties he was nearly blind. Added to the ailments he had put up with for years, were pinched nerves in his neck that forced him to wear a brace. He also had fits of hiccuping that lasted for days at a time—these became extremely painful when he fell and broke a rib in August 1970.[31]

U Thant, too, was not fully well and was frequently hospitalized. The other undersecretary for political affairs, José Rolz-Bennett, was dying from a brain tumor. Bunche continued to work with his small staff, frequently from home and on occasion from a New York hospital. In June 1971, he fell into a coma for several days after breaking his right arm in a fall at home. Only then did U Thant agree to relieve him formally of his post in the Secretariat in order to ensure that his family would receive a third of his pension as a lump sum. His condition improved when he went on kidney dialysis in July, and some of his old humor returned. He died on the eve of International Human Rights Day, December 9, 1971.

Epilogue

I thought of white men arriving for the first time in an African village, strangers there, as I am a stranger here, and tried to imagine the astounded populace touching their hair and marveling at the color of their skin. But there is a great difference between being the first white man to be seen by Africans and being the first black man to be seen by whites. The white man takes the astonishment as tribute, for he arrives to conquer and to convert the natives, whose inferiority in relation to himself is not even to be questioned, whereas I, without a thought of conquest, find myself among a people whose culture controls me, has even, in a sense, created me, people who have cost me more in anguish and rage than they will ever know, who yet do not even know of my existence. The astonishment with which I might have greeted them, should they have stumbled into my African village a few hundred years ago, might have rejoiced their hearts. But the astonishment with which they greet me today can only poison mine.

—James Baldwin, in bell hooks, *Black Looks*

When Ralph Johnson Bunche died on December 9, 1971, the *New York Times* noted his passing on its editorial page, and the NAACP's main publication, *The Crisis*, devoted an entire issue to his accomplishments. Yet a generation later Bunche has been virtually forgotten. Several years ago a prominent Black-oriented magazine, which had featured Bunche on its cover several times in the past, ran a photograph commemorating the march from Selma, Alabama. Everyone on the front line of the march was identified with the exception of the frail-looking man linked arm in arm with King. The unidentified man was Ralph Bunche.

Dozens of schools throughout the country are named for Bunche, as is the largest building on the campus at UCLA. Ask any of the students using these buildings who Bunche was, and you are likely to get a blank stare. The same response would be forthcoming from the thousands of students who tour the impressive meeting rooms of the UN that the Detroit native dominated for two decades. What accounts for this absence of memory? Why is Bunche and his legacy missing in action?

Bunche's fame derived from his skill as a troubleshooter. By its nature, troubleshooting is most successful when the conflict that is its target is prevented or minimized. Therefore, Bunche's most successful actions were those the public was likely to hear the least about. In the dramatic cases where conflict did break out, as in Palestine and the Congo, Bunche was indeed a daily subject of the news. However, prominence in the news—as Bunche recognized—is as fleeting as yesterday's headlines. The recent direct negotiations between the Israelis and Palestinians were the first since Bunche's Rhodes agreement in 1949, but none of the stories in the media noted this fact. Moreover, Bunche did nothing to publicize his role in historic agreements. In part, he was protecting the sensitive nature of events he had participated in that still had the potential to cause concern, like those in the Middle East. In part, he was too busy troubleshooting almost to the very end to relive events of the past. Finally, he was a genuinely humble individual who enjoyed his role in international affairs but sought no profit or glory from it. He was an international public servant.

The dramatic increase in UN peacekeeping has been a subject of much attention and debate, yet nowhere in the discussion is there a reference to the creator of the UN peacekeeping forces: Ralph Bunche. More important, nowhere is there reference to the principles of peacekeeping laid down by Bunche. Had those principles been followed, the debacle in Somalia might have been averted. By the same token, Bunche's work on atomic energy, population control, and closing the gap between the rich nations of the North and the poorer nations of the South would seem to have relevance today.

Bunche's disappearance from the world's memory is not as surprising as his disappearance from that of the African American community. Granted those who toil in the fields of foreign affairs seem far removed from domestic politics and especially from the day-to-day survival of rank-and-file Black folk. Ironically, the African American community of today seems less interested in Africa, the Caribbean, and South America than it was fifty or even twenty-five years ago. Still, such international figures as Marcus Garvey, W. E. B. Du Bois, and Paul Robeson have enjoyed a new popularity since their deaths. Bunche knew and wrote more about African politics than either Garvey or Robeson and was at least as familiar with domestic politics as Du Bois. Yet none of Bunche's scholarly work is readily available.

Was it because Bunche was not a nationalist? Neither was King nor Robeson nor—to a lesser extent—Du Bois. Was it because Bunche was not an activist? Bunche *was* an activist, marching through Southern streets, sitting on a host of civil rights and foundation boards, giving hundreds of speeches promoting civil rights, and even—in the end—defending Black Power.

Bunche is absent from our memories today not for what he did, for there can be no disputing that, but for what he came to represent. Bunche's identity does not fit into any of the neat categories we use to store legacies. He grew up poor and without a father's guidance but was successful. He was an integrationist but comfortable with and proud of his racial identity. He was a liberal who believed in the old-fashioned values of individualism and hard work. He was an internationalist who was proud to be an American. He was a scholar who spent his most productive years in the bureaucratic politics of the United Nations.

Racial identity suppresses individual difference. No Black people on the planet are more identity conscious than African Americans.[1] Identity and difference are interdependent. There was no such thing as Africa until there was a Europe. There were no Black Americans until European ethnics in the United States submerged their European differences and became White Americans. Writers like Frantz Fanon and the older Du Bois recognized that race is not biological or cultural but social and historical. They took over the race-construction process, turning it to their own ends in their written work. Bunche too recognized the contingent nature of race construction. In his early written work, he simply chooses to transcend it by calling for working-class unity. However, as World War II approached and as a result of his work on fundamental American values with Myrdal, Bunche saw that he must change the dominant paradigm from within.

The dominant paradigm operated on at least two fundamental levels in the area of racial representation. On one level, through stereotype and symbol, it constructed the image of the "other." Thus, as Du Bois reports, immigrants to this country quickly learn they can become American by treating Blacks as the "other," as inferior. On another level, the paradigm works to shape the very perceptions of the "other" to conform to the paradigm. Thus today's youths criticize their peers who succeed in speaking non-Black English or getting good grades for selling out or joining the system. In short, a role reversal has taken place. The negative has become positive, but only in the Black community. However, mere role reversal still accepts the representation of the "other." It does not change the paradigm. How do the portrayals of Blacks in "gangsta rap" serve to change the reality of crime in the Black community?

> The ways in which black people, black experiences, were positioned and subjected in the dominant regimes of representation were the effects of a critical exercise of cultural power and normalization. Not only, in Said's "orientalist" sense, were we constructed as different and other within the categories of knowledge of the West by those regimes. They had the power to make us see and experience *ourselves* as "Other." . . . It is one thing to position a subject or set of peoples as the Other of a dominant discourse. It is quite another thing to subject them to that "knowledge," not only as a matter of imposed will and domination, but by the power of inner compulsion and subjective conformation to the norm.[2]

Bunche attempted to destroy the "other." He attempted to redefine the concept of American to include the "other." He succeeded only partially in this task. The general public was forced to accept him as American but redefined him as non-Black. At the same time, he was put forth as a model of Black success.

Were Bunche's colleague E. Franklin Frazier or any of his latter-day disciples to write about Bunche's childhood, they might say that he came from a dysfunctional family. In his early years, the family moved several times, and when he was thirteen his mother died. His father abandoned the family shortly afterward. In the same year, his favorite uncle committed suicide and the family moved again. Despite these hardships, Ralph and especially his aunt Ethel downplayed the family's difficulties.[3] Bunche contended that his childhood was a happy one and that his maternal grandmother, Lucy "Nana" Johnson, kept the family together. Indeed, Nana succeeded in instilling in Ralph a sense of optimism, a belief in hard work, and a feeling of racial pride. Bunche often repeated stories that demonstrated his grandmother's racial pride. He says of her:

> She had "soul" long before it became a racial byword. . . . Strong in character and spirit and deeply religious, she was fiercely proud of her origin and race, and everyone in our clan got the race-pride message early.[4]

Despite this strong sense of racial pride instilled by his grandmother—who had refused to pass for White, unlike her twin brother—Bunche subconsciously also absorbed the dominant racial representations of the day (most notably in his appearance as the interlocutor of a school minstrel show). Somehow he did not feel as Black as his schoolmates. At the peak of the Garvey movement and the Harlem Renaissance, Bunche entered UCLA, rejecting separate Black fraternities and sororities as counterproductive and challenging the old-time community leaders on issues like swimming-pool segregation.

His discriminatory exclusion from the UCLA debating team notwith-standing, Bunche flourished in college. Attracted to philosophy, he em-braced a kind of youthful idealism and internationalism. In his commence-ment address he states "that human nature is already biased toward fellow-ship and service."[5] At the same time, he was driven to compete because of his race: "I must confess," he once said, "success had a sweeter taste because of color." Thus dual phenomena are at work. On the one hand, he attempts to transcend racial difference through universal fellowship, but on the other hand, his identity and worth are measured through overcoming the stereo-types and low expectations of Whites by defeating them in fair competition.

At Harvard and Howard, Bunche joined a group of young Black schol-ars who rejected the stereotypes and the representations of race in the dom-inant society and the religiosity of older scholars and family in their own community as well.[6] The salvation of the race rested in knowledge and sci-ence, not in spirituality. But the new generation of Black scholars refused to think in racial terms alone. They criticized older scholars like Du Bois, Carter Woodson, and Kelly Miller, who tended to look at all problems and possible solutions from the perspective of race.

Bunche's earliest published work, written while a graduate student at Harvard, viewed the city as a laboratory for Negro politics. Modern social science can be used in an objective and rational way to improve the status of Negroes. Young Black intellectuals like Bunche, E. Franklin Frazier, and Abram Harris joined Black activists such as A. Philip Randolph and Chan-dler Owen in their belief that Black Americans would enter the urban pro-letariat and that Africa would undergo a secular revival. They saw no virtue in retaining traditional Black culture, which only slowed the modernization process.

At the Amenia conference and elsewhere, Bunche and his colleagues clashed with Du Bois, who had already passed through the rational, objec-tive, scientific phase of his career with the *Philadelphia Negro* and the Atlanta University publications. Like the postmodern discourse of today, Du Bois held that conventional culture and discourses of the Left emphasizing "ob-jective contradictions," "impersonal structures," and processes that work "be-hind men's backs" have disabled us from confronting the subjective dimen-sion in politics in any very coherent way.[7] In the lynching of Sam Hose, Du Bois saw an irrational urge and unconscious habit at work that escaped the rational, objective solutions of scientific analysis. In the late thirties, Bunche too rejected the deterministic thinking of the Left but chose not to follow Du Bois in adopting a race-conscious strategy of liberation.

The failure of the National Negro Congress, the possibility of a domestic fascism, and his work with Myrdal convinced Bunche that he must shift from radical critic to internal reformer. That is, he must participate in the dominant discourse to change beliefs held about Blacks. As Kimberle Williams Crenshaw states:

> The most significant aspect of Black oppression seems to be what is believed about Black Americans, not what Black Americans believe. . . . Ideology convinces one group that the coercive dominance of another is legitimate. It matters little whether the coerced group rejects the dominant ideology and can offer a competing conception of the world; if they have been labeled "other" by the dominant ideology, they are not heard.[8]

By the time he went to work for the State Department, Bunche had fully accepted Myrdal's position of working within the dominant paradigm to close the gap between the rhetoric of the American creed and the reality of American practice.

Only by having Blacks accepted as Americans rather than rejected as the "other" could Bunche hope to close the gap. To the extent he succeeded in accomplishing legitimacy, he foreclosed greater possibilities. Liberal reform both transforms and legitimates—Bunche's very success proscribed more radical systemic change.

Myrdal's moral-dilemma approach to race relations and Bunche's contribution to it did have an impact on how we think about race. For twenty years Myrdal's paradigm dominated the scholarly writing on race relations and also began to reach the general public. However, World War II was the catalyst in changing American race relations. How could Black Americans who fought and died to save democracy from Aryan supremacy be denied equality in their own country? *Integration* was a new term that began to be widely used, and Bunche seized the opportunity the new environment presented to move to a different stage. The "one-world" internationalism of Wendell Willkie and the unquestioned superiority of U.S. military might gave new importance to U.S. foreign policy. Bunche saw and looked for opportunities to shape that policy, especially in regard to colonialism.

Beginning at San Francisco in 1945, Bunche sought to end colonialism by moving colonies away from the control of European powers to some form of international supervision. The principle of trusteeship provided both a normatively defensible and a practical answer to the progressive demise of the colonial state. Bunche worked to make the Trusteeship Council a coequal branch of the UN machinery rather than an afterthought. Moreover, he succeeded in installing himself as the chief staff person responsible for that machinery. Yet, as with Myrdal's moral dilemma, the acceptance of trusteeship implied the acceptance of the dominant ideology.

Why does a society need to be prepared for self-government when it was self-governing before it was conquered? It was colonial tutelage that created the native elites Bunche criticized for lacking the cultural self-respect and self-confidence to develop independently. In fact, Bunche like other African American intellectuals and the African elites themselves saw the African as backward. The African was not the "other" in the sense of any biological or genetic inferiority, however; Africans were backward as a result of environmental factors (see Frazier's analysis of African Americans). Thus, says Bunche, Africans "are culturally in a transitional stage, in reality, they were neither primitive nor civilized in their present mode of living."[9] In short, they were in a state of "becoming."

It has been suggested that Bunche refused suggestions that he publish his dissertation because it lacked sufficient attention to the African view of colonialism. Indeed, had the dissertation given more attention to representations of Whiteness in the Black imagination rather than the reverse, Bunche might have sought different solutions. However, Bunche was a political scientist and practical policy maker. He saw the United Nations program of decolonization as the most feasible solution to imperialist domination. Once Bunche conceded the backwardness of African society, for whatever reasons, it was difficult to repudiate the imperial ideology of the civilizing mission. As W. Ofuatey-Kodjoe states, "The principle of 'trusteeship,' 'guardianship,' or 'wardship' that Bunche subscribed to represents an affirmation of the civilizing mission, even if it is a more humane and temporary version."[10] Once again, Bunche had chosen to push the dominant paradigm to its limits and gradually work to eliminate the "other" by expanding the definition of the civilized to include the African.

When fame catapulted Bunche to the status of icon in 1950, he seized a new opportunity to reform or reshape the dominant paradigm. He did not seek to change the paradigm or the basic values underlying it because they were ones he firmly believed in: equality, individualism, due process, and hard work. However, he did seek to destroy the Black "other" by inclusion of the Black experience into the American experience. He sought to downplay his childhood poverty and slave roots. Instances of discrimination against him became parables of interracial brotherhood or obstacles that could be overcome through hard work. And like the characters in the popular Horatio Alger children's books, Bunche's good fortune was not planned or calculated but the result of luck.

To an amazing extent, Bunche succeeded. Americans of all races took pride in his accomplishments, and he became as popular as the Black sports figures and entertainers he became friends with. His status was such that White Alabama sheriffs escorted him to a gathering where he advocated civil rights in the early fifties. University of Arkansas officials bused Blacks for more than a hundred miles to fulfill his condition that the audience be integrated. And, in fact, spurred by World War II, the Cold War, and activists across the country including Bunche, American race relations began to change. The success of the civil rights movement in ending the segregation of public facilities, transportation, and education, led Bunche, King, and others to predict the imminent arrival of full and complete integration.

Yet unlike the professions where Jackie Robinson and Sidney Poitier were soon followed by other Blacks, Black representation in the world inhabited by Bunche did not increase, leading Bunche to bemoan that he had been "the token at too many parties" and was "not worth a damn as an example." The dominant paradigm had reached its limits. It could not absorb the demand for equality from those who rejected its emphasis on sameness or cultural homogeneity. King joined Black Power advocates in criticizing liberals and liberal reform as the main obstacle to full equality; it is a final rejection of the civilizing mission both at home and abroad: "The Western arrogance of feeling that it has everything to teach others and nothing to learn from them is not just."[11]

Bunche's rejection of himself as a "model Negro" implied a recognition that his experience was not typical or atypical of the Black community. Some of his boyhood buddies had gone on to successful careers and others had not. What makes Bunche a poor model was the success of the dominant ideology in defining him as non-Black. His achievements were so spectacular they could not be ignored. Like his high school principal, however, the larger society chose to see him as non-Black—if not White, then somehow above race.[12] During the Cold War, however, Bunche's race became an important ideological weapon in fending off Communist attacks on the hypocrisy of American democracy. Even as his success was used as an instrument of ideological warfare, he had to defend himself against charges of disloyalty.

The failure of the civil rights movement to bring about full integration led to urban violence in the North and a fundamental and final rethinking by Bunche. In a sense, he returned full circle to the kind of racial pride exhibited by his grandmother. In college, this pride was submerged by a philosophical idealism and internationalism that saw all people as brothers and sisters and racism as a product of bad thought. By the midthirties, Bunche's idealism had been replaced by an economist or materialist notion that saw racism as a function of economic exploitation or competition. His work with Myrdal led him to a more psychological explanation for racism as arising from pathologies in the unconscious and/or conscious minds of individuals. Starting with Watts in 1965, Bunche first rejected and then finally embraced Black Power. Acknowledging that it could easily become antiracism racism, he argued that "no one can deny that it is good for any people to look back with pride and gratitude on their origins and ancestry." He seemed to adopt a more cultural definition of *race* when he stated that "being a black man in the U.S. today is less a matter of actual color than of a state of mind. Being black is thinking black."[13] Yet radical Whites who simply chose to identify with Black culture were not Black because Whites lacked the racial background experience to do so. Bunche called himself a partisan of the new Black revolution but still maintained that separatism would lead to American-style apartheid.

The final stage in the evolution of Bunche's racial thinking left him the most pessimistic. As a young idealist he saw education as a solution for racism. As a young class-oriented scholar, revolution seemed the only possible answer. The middle-aged Bunche sought by personal example to remove the pathology of racism from individuals who believed Blacks inferior. Yet Black Power was viewed by the aging Bunche as an essential defensive reaction necessary for survival. Defense was not a natural or desirable position for Bunche.

All of his life Bunche had worked to be treated equally. His thinking reflected the Aristotelian principle of equality as *sameness*. Those with the same attributes, status, or condition were treated equally. This reflected the liberal tendency to treat the "other" as equal only after the "other" had been redescribed as oneself. Only with the rise of Black Power did Bunche come to understand—as his grandmother must have instinctively understood—that the act of redescription is still an attempt to appropriate others. Race in the United States still rested on physical traits despite his best efforts at social reconstruction.

Bunche the human being and his legacy had been appropriated by the dominant ideology. He was redefined to make him an acceptable "other." When the larger society no longer needed his legacy for its purposes, he was forgotten. For the Black community, Bunche became invisible—his identity lost. That is why Ralph Johnson Bunche is unknown today and that is why his story must be told.

Notes

NOTES TO THE PROLOGUE

1. Ralph Bunche, in Benjamin Rivlin, ed., *Ralph Bunche: The Man and His Times* (New York: Holmes & Meier, 1990), 218.

2. Booker T. Washington, William E. B. Du Bois, and James Weldon Johnson, *Three Negro Classics* (New York: Avon Books, 1965), 214–15.

3. Ibid., 215.

4. The term *public intellectual* emerged in 1987 when Russell Jacoby published *The Last Intellectuals*. It originally referred to White writers whose marginal ties to the academy gave them the freedom to view American society in an autonomous, macroscopic way. According to Adolph Reed, Jr., the notion of Black public intellectuals was created by young professors on the academic left who used it to refer to themselves, but it has now been expanded to cover those on the right as well. Reed cites Cornel West, Henry Louis Gates, Jr., bell hooks, Michael Dyson, and Robin Kelley as examples of the former, and Stanley Crouch, Stephen Carter, and Shelby Steele as examples of the latter. Both sides would agree, I believe, that the primary role of the Black public intellectual is to interpret Black behavior for a predominantly White audience. Afro-centrists, on the other hand, speak primarily to a Black audience. For a discussion of the role of Black public intellectuals, see the following: Adolph Reed, "The Current Crisis of the Black Intellectual," *Village Voice*, April 11, 1995; Michael Eric Dyson, *Race Rules* (New York: Vintage, 1997); David Steigerwald, "Cornel West and the Predicament of Black Intellectuals," *Civic Arts Review* 8, nos. 3–4 (summer–fall, 1995); and Cornel West, "The Dilemma of the Black Intellectual" in Cornel West and bell hooks, *Breaking Bread* (Boston: South End Press, 1992).

5. Thomas Byrne Edsall and Mary D. Edsall, *Chain Reaction* (New York: Norton, 1992); Edward G. Carmines and James A. Stimson, *Issue Evolution*, (Princeton: Princeton University Press, 1989).

6. Andrew Hacker, *Two Nations* (New York: Ballantine, 1992).

7. Stanley Greenberg, quoted in John Brenkman, "Race Publics," *Transition* 66 (summer, 1995): 17.

8. Harold Cruse, *The Crisis of the Negro Intellectual* (New York: William Morrow, 1967), 13.

9. Troy Duster, quoted in William M. Banks, *Black Intellectuals* (New York: Norton, 1996), 226–27.

10. See Lorenzo Morris and Charles Henry, *The Chitlin' Controversy: Race and Public Policy in America* (Lanham, Md.: University Press of America, 1978), ch. 1, for a discussion of Du Bois's strategic use of these concepts.

11. James MacGregor Burns distinguishes between transactional leadership and transforming leadership. Transactional leadership is the routine exchange of one thing for another: jobs for votes, or subsidies for campaign contributions. Transforming leadership, however, is a mutually stimulating and elevating relationship that converts followers into leaders and may convert leaders into moral agents. See Burns, *Leadership* (New York: Harper & Row, 1978), 4.

NOTES TO CHAPTER 1

1. David M. Katzman, *Before the Ghetto: Black Detroit in the Nineteenth Century* (Urbana: University of Illinois Press, 1973), 3–50.

2. Ibid., 164.

3. Melvin G. Holli, ed., *Detroit* (New York: New Viewpoints, 1976), 116–17.

4. Robert Conot, *American Odyssey* (New York: Morrow, 1974), 129.

5. Holli, *Detroit*, 115–23.

6. Katzman, *Before the Ghetto*, 210–11.

7. Bunche's grandmother, Lucy Johnson, added the "e" to the surname when the family left Albuquerque for Los Angeles in 1917. To avoid confusion, I will use Bunche throughout this work. There has also been some confusion surrounding Bunche's birth date. Many sources cite 1904 rather than 1903 as the date, some relying on the Kugelmass biography, which has numerous errors. In fact, Bunche himself was confused about the date (because of the absence of a birth certificate) and was told by his aunt Ethel that it was 1904. However, early school and college records give the date as 1903. See Brian Urquhart, *Ralph Bunche: An American Life* (New York: Norton, 1993), 25.

8. Bunche listed Columbus, Ohio, as the birthplace of his father on several occasions. Most of the details concerning Bunche's family come from his late cousin Jane Johnson Taylor, who was considered the family historian. Audiotaped interview with Jane Taylor by William Greaves (New York: William Greaves Productions, September 7, 1992). Also Bunche to Master Dwight Fuller, January 24, 1964, box 126, Ralph Bunche Papers, University of California, Los Angeles. Cited hereafter as Bunche Papers.

9. Taylor interview, (see n. 8, above).

10. Katzman, *Before the Ghetto*, 219–21.

11. Ralph Bunche, "Prejudice in World Prospective" (address, Fountain Street Church, Grand Rapids, Mich., April 24, 1954), 10, box 50, Bunche Papers.

12. Ibid., 11.

13. On several occasions, Bunche said he was born on Macomb Street in "Black Bottom." See, for example, Bunche to Judy Skillman, November 3, 1961, box 156, Bunche Papers. See Katzman, *Before the Ghetto*, 69, on areas of Black concentration.

14. Du Bois noted this tendency in his own proud but poor family, the Burghardts in Great Barrington, Mass.

15. Urquhart, *Ralph Bunche*, 27.

16. Bunche to Elizabeth Riley, January 25, 1956, box 126, folder 57, Bunche Papers.

17. The incident is recalled in a speech to the American Baptist Convention, May 18, 1963, 1, box 55, Bunche Papers. In a letter to Mary Eleanor Jones, August 15, 1951, Bunche says he was raised as a Baptist but is now nondenominational, box 126, folder 43, Bunche Papers.

18. Bunche, "Prejudice," 11.

19. Urquhart, *Ralph Bunche*, 28.

20. See Kenneth C. Balcomb, *A Boy's Albuquerque, 1898–1912* (Albuquerque: University of New Mexico Press, 1980), and Balcomb, *New Mexico* (New York: Hastings House, 1940).

21. Bunche, "Prejudice," 12.

22. Urquhart, *Ralph Bunche*, 29.

23. Ralph Bunche, "Gold Key Award Speech" (American Association of School Administrators, Atlantic City, N.J., February 17, 1962), Bunche Papers.

24. Several accounts of Bunche's life indicate that his father died around the same time as his mother; perhaps the accounts mistake Uncle Charlie for Fred. Fred Bunche married again after Olive's death. One report has him working as a barber in Granville, Ohio, for about a year in 1920. From there he went to Puerto Rico. In 1928, he made contact with Aunt Ethel in Los Angeles in an attempt to reach his daughter, Grace. Ralph never saw him again but made an unsuccessful attempt to contact him through his second wife, Helen. Included in a box that held Ralph's most valued possessions was a tiepin his father had given him when he left Albuquerque. See Bunche to Edgar A. Roberts, Granville, Ohio, September 10, 1962, box 142, Bunche Papers; Urquhart, *Ralph Bunche*, 30–31.

25. Ibid., 29.

26. *Black Angelenos: The Afro-American in Los Angeles, 1850–1950* (Los Angeles: California Afro-American Museum, 1989), 9.

27. J. Max Bond, *The Negro in Los Angeles* (1936; San Francisco: R and E Research Associates, 1972), 14.

28. Emery J. Tolbert, *The UNIA and Black Los Angeles* (Los Angeles: Center for African American Studies, University of California, Los Angeles, 1980), 25.

29. Ibid., 31.

30. Ibid., 35–36.

31. Ibid., 27–28.

32. Bunche interview by Edward R. Murrow, *Person to Person*, January 15, 1954, box 50, Bunche Papers.

33. Interview with Mrs. Ralph J. Bunche by Vincent Browne, April 20, 1984, Ralph J. Bunche Oral Documentation Project, Howard University, box 57, Bunche Papers. See also Taylor interview (see n. 8, above).

34. Bunche, "Prejudice," 12. Bunche later served as a "pig boy" in the paper's printing plant, bringing lead bricks to the linotype machines from 5:30 P.M. to 1:00 A.M. See Urquhart, *Ralph Bunche*, 35.

35. In an early version of the "model-minority thesis," Bond argues that a non-white minority group (the Japanese) has been able, through its superior organization, working agreements, and attitudes and values, to compete successfully as a unit in American life. However, unlike modern-day versions of this thesis, Bond's 1936 study does not argue that Blacks deviate from the White majority—in fact, he argues the opposite:

> We are aware of the fact that two different culture groups have been under discussion. The cultural background of the Japanese in Los Angeles is that of the East. . . . [T]he culture of the Negro appears to be that which is characteristic of America. As such, it contains predominant traits that represent individualism, mechanization, democracy, and Christianity; whereas, the Japanese are bearers of a culture that is dominated by the traits representing bureaucracy, paternalism, Shintoism, and an intense nationalistic patriotism, or 'we' feeling. It thus appears that an attempt to judge the Negro by Japanese standards would be as unfair to the Negro as it would be to judge the American white man by Japanese standards, since it is evident that the Negro has patterned his society after that of the majority group. Bond, *The Negro in Los Angeles*, 159.

Also see Ronald Takaki, ed., *From Distant Shores* (New York: Oxford University Press, 1987), for a contemporary account of the "model-minority thesis."

36. Ralph Bunche, "Remarks" (Thomas Jefferson High School Alumni Association Fiftieth Anniversary Banquet, Beverly Hills, Calif., May 13, 1966), box 58, Bunche Papers.

37. Ralph Bunche, *California Teachers Journal*, October 1955, box 143, Bunche Papers.

38. Urquhart, *Ralph Bunche*, 33.

39. Ralph Bunche, quoted in a letter from Sherman Hayden, September 23, 1943, box 126, Bunche Papers.

40. Urquhart, *Ralph Bunche*, 33.

41. Ibid., 35.

42. Bunche, "Prejudice," 13.

NOTES TO CHAPTER 2

1. Claude McKay, *Selected Poems* (San Diego: Harcourt, Brace, Jovanovich, 1969).

2. Paul Laurence Dunbar, *When Malindy Sings* (New York: Dodd, Mead, 1903).

3. See William Toll, *The Resurgence of Race* (Philadelphia: Temple University Press, 1979), 194.

4. Ralph Bunche, "Some Current Dangers and Hopes" (speech, University of California, Los Angeles, April 21, 1965), 2, box 57, Bunche Papers.

5. Ralph Bunche, "Jefferson High Alumni Remarks," 4, box 57, Bunche Papers.

6. Brian Urquhart, *Ralph Bunche: An American Life* (New York: Norton, 1993), 34.

7. Ralph Bunche, handwritten notes on the development of his racial consciousness in Los Angeles, Urquhart files.

8. Ralph Bunche, "Memories," notes, no date, Urquhart Files. In an interview, Jane Taylor noted that Bunche read Dunbar in dialect for a group of women convened by Dean C. H. Rieber's wife around 1923–1924, for which she paid him $50. Audiotaped interview by William Greaves (New York: William Greaves Productions, September 7, 1992).

9. See, for example, W. E. B. Du Bois's "Conservation of the Races" American Negro Academy Occasional Papers, no. 2 (Washington, D.C.: American Negro Academy, 1897), or Booker T. Washington's *The Future of the American Negro* (Boston: Small, Maynard and Company, 1899).

10. Urquhart, *Ralph Bunche*, 37.

11. Bunche to Montaque Cobb, September 22, 1949, Bunche Papers.

12. Notes from speaking tour, Reed College and Whitman College, February 12–15, 1966, Urquhart Files.

13. *California Teachers Journal*, October 1955, box 143, Bunche Papers.

14. Ralph Bunche, "Prejudice in World Perspective," April 6, 1954, 3, box 50, Bunche Papers.

15. Urquhart, *Ralph Bunche*, 39.

16. Ralph Bunche, "Across the Generation Gap," box 43, Bunche Papers.

17. Ralph Bunche, "That Man May Dwell in Peace," spring 1926, 3–7, box 43, Bunche Papers.

18. The story probably came from Nana and also reflected her nonpartisanship and emphasis on judging people on their merits. The speech combined elements of both Booker T. Washington and W. E. B. Du Bois. Nana was also an admirer of Teddy Roosevelt.

19. Bunche, "That Man May Dwell in Peace," 3–7.

20. Souad Halila, "The Intellectual Development and Diplomatic Career of Ralph J. Bunche: The Afro-American, Africanist, and Internationalist" (Ph.D. diss., University of Southern California, 1988), 25.

21. Urquhart, *Ralph Bunche*, 37.

22. Benjamin Rivlin, *Ralph Bunche: The Man and His Times* (New York: Holmes & Meier, 1990), 221–22; Urquhart, *Ralph Bunche*, 41.

23. Urquhart, *Ralph Bunche*, 42.

24. Rivlin, *Ralph Bunche*, 218.

25. Seymour Martin Lipset, *Rebellion in the University* (Boston: Little, Brown, 1972), 143.

26. John Trumpbour, ed., *How Harvard Rules: Reason in the Service of Empire* (Boston: South End Press, 1989), 304. In 1850, only eight of thirty-five faculty at Harvard were antislavery.

27. Rivlin, *Ralph Bunche*, 6.

28. Urquhart, *Ralph Bunche*, 44.

29. Bunche to Dean C. H. Rieber, October 26, 1927, Bunche Papers.

30. Ralph Bunche, "The Political Theory of Sir Robert Filmer," box 12, folder 3, Schomberg Collection, New York Public Library.

31. Ralph Bunche, "The Negro in Chicago Politics," *National Municipal Review* 17, no. 5 (May 1928): 264.

32. Ibid. See also Ralph Bunche, "The American City as a Negro Political Laboratory," *Proceedings* (Thirty-fourth Annual Meeting, National Municipal League, December 1928), 50.

33. Many years later Henry Lee Moon would make the same argument in *Balance of Power: The Negro Vote* (Garden City, 1948).

34. Robert Weaver said that he had joined the Young Socialist Club at Harvard; Bunche had not. Thus, Bunche's real radicalization occurred at Howard. Interview with Robert Weaver by author, May 6, 1986.

35. Audiotaped interview with Jane Johnson Taylor by William Greaves (New York: William Greaves Productions, September 7, 1992).

NOTES TO CHAPTER 3

1. Kenneth R. Manning, *Black Apollo of Science* (New York: Oxford University Press, 1983), 116.

2. The Morrill Act of 1862 made no special provision for Negro colleges, and only three Southern states had designated Negro schools as recipients of federal funds under the land-grant program. In 1890, Congress enacted a second Morrill Act that forbade discrimination and required that land-grant monies be distributed among Black institutions as well as White. Egalitarians warned that this legislation would lead states to transform academically oriented Black colleges into vocational schools, which is what happened. See Raymond Wolters, *The New Negro on Campus* (Princeton: Princeton University Press, 1975), 10.

3. Manning, *Black Apollo of Science*, 116–17.

4. Ibid., 132.

5. Woodson, who had founded the Association for the Study of Negro Life and History in 1915 and published the first issue of the *Journal of Negro History* in 1916, was fired when he refused to apologize to President Durkee after a dispute in 1920. See Rayford W. Logan, *Howard University, 1867–1967* (New York: New York University Press, 1969), 208.

6. Wolters, *The New Negro on Campus*, 70–136.

7. Prior to the 1928 bill (Public Law 634) Congress simply voted annual "gratuities" to Howard. The bill gave Howard an annual appropriation amounting to about 60 percent of its operating costs, which has continued to the present. See Ben Gareth Keppel, "The Work of Democracy: Ralph Bunche, Kenneth B. Clark, Lorraine Hansberry and the Cultural Politics of Racial Equality" (Ph.D. diss., University of California, Los Angeles, 1992), 80–81.

8. In a letter dated June 26, 1928, Dean E. P. Davis of Howard offered Bunche the position of political science instructor at an annual salary of $1500. See box 135, Bunche Papers.

9. Interview with Mrs. Ralph J. Bunche by Vincent Browne, March 8, 1973, 3, Ralph J. Bunche Oral Documentation Project, Howard University.

10. Brian Urquhart, *Ralph Bunche: An American Life* (New York: Norton, 1993), 46.

11. In her interview with Vincent Browne (see n. 9, above), Mrs. Bunche says that thirty-two Whites worked under her father at the post office. See also Urquhart, *Ralph Bunche*, 46.

12. Bunche told Ruth that the pressures were so great that the brightest student at Harvard Medical School committed suicide. Mrs. Bunche interview (see n. 9, above).

13. Urquhart, *Ralph Bunche*, 47.

14. Ralph Bunche, "Notes from Harvard," box 133, folder 9, Bunche Papers.

15. E. P. Davis to Ralph Bunche, February 9, 1929; Ralph Bunche to Emmett Dorsey, October 16, 1931; Ralph Bunche to S. McKee Rosen, September 23, 1931; Paul Lewinson to Ralph Bunche, June 6, 1932; all in box 135, Bunche Papers.

16. Ralph Bunche, "Course Notes," boxes 133, 134, Bunche Papers.

17. Bunche told this story many times to indicate that he was too blunt to be a diplomat. See box 135, Bunche Papers.

18. Ralph Bunche to Dean Davis, May 18, 1936, box 135, Bunche Papers.

19. Various letters of recommendation, box 133, folder 4, Bunche Papers. John A. Davis reports that when he joined the Howard faculty on a temporary basis, he was amazed to find that Bunche seldom slept, preferring to keep his friends and colleagues up at all hours discussing issues of the day. He adds that Bunche's leg problems made it difficult for him to play basketball, but he did play tennis. Interview with John A. Davis by author, May 1995.

20. Emmett Scott to Ralph Bunche, September 9, 1931, box 137, Bunche Papers.

21. Interview with Kenneth Clark by author, New York, November 25, 1985.

22. See "Notes on the Thompson-Julian Affair," December 17, 1931, box 137, Bunche Papers.

23. Urquhart, *Ralph Bunche*, 45.

24. Ralph Bunche, "Some Observations of a Faculty Member on Universities, etc." (Howard Club of Philadelphia, Charter Day Dinner, March 2, 1935), box 43, Bunche Papers.

25. Bunche memorandum, May 23, 1939; and Kelly Miller to Ralph Bunche, December 21, 1938, box 3, Bunche Papers.

26. Ralph Bunche, "Gandhi and the Future of India," December 20, 1930, box 43, Bunche Papers. By the midthirties Bunche would conclude that passive resistance could not work in the United States because Blacks lacked the tradition (Hindu religion) that supported it. See "The Power of Non-Violence," Women's International League for Peace and Freedom, panel discussion, March 16, 1935. Still later he would embrace nonviolent direct action in the United States. See Gandhian Seminar speech, New Delhi, January, 1952, in Charles P. Henry, ed., *Ralph J. Bunche: Selected Speeches and Writings* (Ann Arbor: University of Michigan Press, 1995), 249–58.

27. Ralph Bunche, "Academic Freedom" (Capitol City Forum, October 22, 1935), 3, box 43, Bunche Papers.

28. Remarks at Scottsboro Defense Committee mass meeting, Washington, D.C., February 10, 1936, box 43, Bunche Papers. In 1931, nine Black youths were convicted of raping two White women in a railroad boxcar near Scottsboro, Alabama, by an all-White jury from which Blacks had been excluded. They were sentenced to death, and only after international protests were the sentences commuted to life in prison. Although one of the women later admitted that she and her companion had not been raped, the youths served long prison terms before their release.

29. Todd Duncan to Ralph Bunche, February 26, 1936, box 136, Bunche Papers.

30. H. Naylor Fitzhugh, quoted in Gilbert Ware, *William Hastie: Grace Under Pressure* (New York: Oxford University Press, 1984), 68.

31. Ralph Bunche, "The Tragedy of Racial Introversion" (New Negro National Forum, Washington, D.C., March 17, 1935), box 43, Bunche Papers.

32. Ware, *William Hastie*, 68.

33. Nancy J. Weiss, *Farewell to the Party of Lincoln: Black Politics in the Age of FDR* (Princeton: Princeton University Press, 1983), 9–14.

34. Ibid., 20, 200.

35. Ibid., 55, 166; Raymond Wolters, *Negroes and the Great Depression* (Westport, Conn.: Greenwood Press, 1970), 110, 178.

36. Keith Griffler, "Let Us Build a National Negro Congress: John P. Davis' Program for the Advancement of Black Workers" (Ph.D. diss.), 10–12. Weaver and William Hastie went to work for the federal government: Weaver was appointed to the National Defense Advisory Commission to plan for Black employment in defense industries; Hastie was named civilian aide to the secretary of war.

37. Ibid., 35.

38. Ibid., 34.

39. Ralph Bunche, "A Critique of New Deal Social Planning as It Affects Negroes," in Charles P. Henry, ed., *Ralph J. Bunche* (Ann Arbor: University of Michigan Press, 1995), 70.

40. Letter from the Office of the Solicitor of the Secretary of the Interior on

whether free speech could be regulated at Howard. Miller had suggested that both Theodore Roosevelt and Shelburne resign. Shelburne did resign but asserted it was not due to this incident. See Office of the Solicitor of the Secretary of the Interior to Bunche, October 17, 1935, box 3, Bunche Papers.

41. Loyalty Hearings, 28–29, box 3, Bunche Papers.

42. Albert Bushnell Hart to Colonel Theodore Roosevelt, January 2, 1935, box 135, Bunche Papers.

43. More than 50,000 copies of the pamphlet were printed and distributed. See Griffler, "Let Us Build a National Negro Conference," 49.

44. Official Proceedings of the National Negro Congress, Chicago, February 14–16, 1936.

45. Ralph Bunche, "Triumph? Or Fiasco?" *Race* 1, no. 2 (1935–1937).

46. Bunche was traveling in Africa on a Social Science Research Council grant when the second national meeting of the NNC was held in Philadelphia in 1937. Although the NNC established more than seventy local councils, it did not hold national conferences in 1938 or 1939.

47. Ralph Bunche, "Programs, Ideologies, Tactics, and Achievements of Negro Betterment and Interracial Organizations," memorandum prepared for the Carnegie-Myrdal study, New York, 1940, 71–72.

48. Ibid., 75. The phrase "peace, sister" is a reference to the then very popular peace movement led by Father Divine.

49. Ibid., 84. Robert Weaver was even more critical of Davis, calling him an opportunist who joined the leftists only because he could get money from them. Interview with Weaver by author, New York, May 6, 1986. Bunche and Davis never worked together again, but they seem to have put this incident behind them in later years. Davis asked Bunche for a letter of recommendation on at least one occasion, and Davis later testified during the loyalty hearings that Bunche had had nothing to do with the Communist Party.

50. In addition to their national lobbying efforts on behalf of federal antilynching legislation and Negro voting rights, local NNC councils fought against discrimination in higher education (the Oakland council, for example, pushed for student integration of the University of California, Berkeley) and police brutality. They campaigned for racial equality in employment opportunity, recreational facilities, and union membership. Some councils remained active into the 1950s. See Harvard Sitkoff, *A New Deal for Blacks* (New York: Oxford University Press, 1978), 259–60.

NOTES TO CHAPTER 4

1. Cornel West argues that Black intellectuals today are even more isolated from the Black community than were those of Bunche's generation. Those on predominantly White campuses may be closer to mainstream debates (although many are separated by their association with African American studies programs) but are even

further removed from the Black community. See West, "The Dilemma of the Black Intellectual," in Cornel West and bell hooks, *Breaking Bread* (Boston: South End Press, 1992). Adolph Reed contends that Black intellectuals like West who presume to interpret the Black community to a White audience are the most removed from the community they seek to interpret. See Reed, "The Current Crisis of the Black Intellectual," *Village Voice*, April 11, 1995.

2. Jerry Gafio Watts, *Heroism and the Black Intellectual* (Chapel Hill: University of North Carolina Press, 1994), 16.

3. Ibid., 20.

4. Ralph Bunche, "Conversation," March 7, 1932, box 135, Bunche Papers.

5. James O. Young, *Black Writers of the Thirties* (Baton Rouge: Louisiana State University Press, 1973), 3–5; Raymond Wolters, *Negroes and the Great Depression* (Westport, Conn.: Greenwood Press, 1970), 219–23.

6. William Toll, *The Resurgence of Race* (Philadelphia, Temple University Press, 1979), 105.

7. Young, *Black Writers of the Thirties*, 9–16.

8. The biological/genetic paradigm is not dead yet and surfaces periodically, as in the debates over IQ testing. See Elaine Mensh and Harry Mensh, *The IQ Mythology* (Carbondale: Southern Illinois University Press, 1991), and Russell Jacoby and Naomi Glauberman, eds., *The Bell Curve Debate* (New York: Random House, 1995).

9. Herbert Aptheker, ed., *Against Racism* (Amherst: University of Massachusetts Press, 1985), 144.

10. William Darity, Jr., ed., *Race, Radicalism, and Reform* (New Brunswick, N.J.: Transaction Books, 1989), 204.

11. Ibid.

12. Ibid., 41–42.

13. Ibid., 169–70.

14. Ibid., 209.

15. Ibid., 211.

16. Young, *Black Writers of the Thirties*, 43–44; Darity, *Race, Radicalism and Reform*, 204.

17. Darity, *Race, Radicalism and Reform*, 18.

18. See Cedric J. Robinson, *Black Marxism* (London: Zed, 1983), for a discussion of the origins of the national-minority thesis.

19. Ralph Bunche, "Marxism and the Negro Question," in Charles P. Henry, ed., *Ralph Bunche* (Ann Arbor: University of Michigan Press, 1995), 36.

20. Ibid.

21. Ralph Bunche, "The American Negro and His Achievements," lecture notes, box 134, Governments of Europe folder, Bunche Papers.

22. Ralph Bunche, "A Critical Analysis of the Tactics and Programs of Minority Groups," in Henry, *Ralph Bunche*, 62.

23. Ralph Bunche, *A World View of Race* (Washington, D.C.: Associates in Negro Folk Education, 1936), 3–14.

24. Ibid., 36.

25. Ibid., 41–57.

26. Ibid., 60.

27. Ralph Bunche, "Lecture notes on *The Souls of Black Folk*," box 133, folder 4, Bunche Papers.

28. Ibid., 90.

29. Ralph Bunche, "A Critique of New Deal Social Planning as It Affects Negroes," *Journal of Negro Education*, 5, no. 1 (January 1936): 60.

30. Ibid., 63–64.

31. Ralph Bunche, "Education in Black and White," *Journal of Negro Education* 5, no. 3 (July 1936): 355.

32. Ibid., 358.

33. Young, *Black Writers of the Thirties*, 47.

34. Frazier and Du Bois established a better relationship in later years, with Frazier chairing a controversial dinner honoring Du Bois during the McCarthy era. See Anthony M. Platt, *E. Franklin Frazier Reconsidered* (New Brunswick: Rutgers University Press, 1991), 18, 133.

35. James E. Blackwell and Morris Janowitz, eds., *Black Sociologists* (Chicago: University of Chicago Press, 1974), 89–90.

36. Ibid., 92.

37. G. Franklin Edwards, ed., *E. Franklin Frazier on Race Relations* (Chicago: University of Chicago Press, 1968), xi.

38. Ibid.

39. Vernon J. Williams, Jr., *From a Caste to a Minority* (Westport, Conn.: Greenwood Press, 1989), 152.

40. Young, *Black Writers of the Thirties*, 53.

41. E. Franklin Frazier, "The Failure of the Negro Intellectual," in Joyce A. Ladner, ed., *The Death of White Sociology* (New York: Vintage, 1973), 54.

42. Johnny Washington, *Alain Locke and Philosophy* (Westport, Conn.: Greenwood Press, 1986), 45.

43. Russell J. Linnemann, ed., *Alain Locke* (Baton Rouge: Louisiana State University Press, 1982), 69.

44. Ben Gareth Keppel, "The Work of Democracy" (Ph.D. diss., University of California, Los Angeles, 1992), 100.

45. Washington, *Alain Locke*, 41.

46. According to Johnny Washington, Du Bois and Locke differ in four ways. First, Du Bois insisted that cultural values pertained primarily to the genteel tradition, and he encouraged the elite to draw from that tradition rather than a folk tradition. Second, Du Bois insisted that Black art should be conscious propaganda; Locke promoted art for art's sake. Third, Du Bois tended to stress the role of politi-

cal and civil equality in liberating Blacks, but Locke believed cultural equality was just as important. Fourth, Du Bois was more politically active than Locke, who acted mainly through his scholarship. Washington, *Alain Locke*, 15–16.

47. Bunche's favorite professors at UCLA and at Harvard were both philosophers. See Bunche to Dean Rieber, June 10, 1947, box 126, Bunche Papers; also Linnemann, *Alain Locke*.

48. Robinson, *Black Marxism*, 293.

49. Donald Matthews, quoted in Irwin Katz and Patricia Gurin, eds., *Race and the Social Sciences* (New York: Basic Books, 1969), 113.

50. Matthews states that "the study of Negro politics is most likely to enter into the mainstream of American political science *if it can be shown that the subject can be analyzed in systems terms* (emphasis added). Mack Jones has argued that the establishment of academic disciplines and the determination of their substantive content is a normative exercise that is necessarily parochial because a people's need to know is a function of their anticipation and control needs. This means, says Jones, that a dominant paradigm leads the practitioner to study the adversary community only to the extent that the adversary constitutes a problem and that the problem does not itself challenge the pluralist (or systems) paradigm. See Mack Jones, "Ethnic Politics and Civil Liberties," in Lucius J. Barker, ed., *National Political Review*, vol. 3 (New Brunswick, N.J.: Transaction Books, 1992), 30–32. Michael Dawson and Ernest Wilson III have also documented the marginality of Black politics compared to the sister disciplines in history and sociology. They also reveal significant differences in approaches to the subject between Black and White political scientists. See Michael C. Dawson and Ernest J. Wilson III, "Paradigms and Paradoxes: Political Science and African American Politics," in William Crotty, ed., *Political Science* (Evanston: Northwestern University Press, 1991), 223–24.

51. Robert R. Edgar, ed., *An African American in South Africa* (Athens: Ohio University Press, 1992), 11.

52. Young, *Black Writers of the Thirties*, 76.

53. Ibid., 53.

NOTES TO CHAPTER 5

1. Souad Halila, "The Intellectual Development and Diplomatic Career of Ralph J. Bunche: The Afro-American, Africanist, and Internationalist" (Ph.D. diss., University of Southern California, 1988), 54.

2. Harvard Sitkoff, *A New Deal for Blacks* (New York: Oxford University Press, 1978), 35.

3. Ralph Bunche to Dean Davis, Howard University, December 22, 1930, box 65, folder 4, Bunche Papers. W. E. B. Du Bois had completed a dissertation at Harvard, "The Suppression of the African Slave Trade" (Harvard Historical Studies, 1896).

4. Ralph Bunche to John Sly, University of West Virginia, February 28, 1931, box 65, folder 4, Bunche Papers.

5. Ralph Bunche to Arthur Holcombe, Harvard University, February 28, 1931, box 65, folder 4, Bunche Papers.

6. Arthur Holcombe to Ralph Bunche, February 17, 1931, box 65, folder 4, Bunche Papers.

7. Halila, "The Intellectual Development . . . Bunche," 49–50. Some years later, Bunche's colleague E. Franklin Frazier completed a comparative study of Blacks in Brazil and the United States, arguing that Brazil was much more advanced in race relations. See Anthony M. Platt, *E. Franklin Frazier Reconsidered* (New Brunswick: Rutgers University Press, 1991).

8. Edwin Embree to W. C. Haygood, May 21, 1941, box 65, folder 4, Bunche Papers. Speech by Ralph Bunche (Dillard University, May 9, 1954), box 50, Bunche Papers.

9. Halila, "The Intellectual Development . . . Bunche," 50.

10. Ibid., 51.

11. Ibid., 53.

12. Brian Urquhart, *Ralph Bunche: An American Life* (New York: Norton, 1993), 52.

13. Ibid.

14. Ibid., 53.

15. Ralph J. Bunche, "French Administration in Togoland and Dahomey" (Ph.D. diss., Harvard University, 1934), ii.

16. Only ninety-seven natives of Dahomey were accepted as French citizens from 1912 to 1932.

17. Nathan Irvin Huggins, "Ralph Bunche the Africanist," in Benjamin Rivlin, ed., *Ralph Bunche: The Man and His Times* (New York: Holmes & Meier, 1990), 78.

18. Ralph Bunche, "French Educational Policy in Togoland and Dahomey," *Journal of Negro Education* 3, no. 1 (January 1934).

19. Ralph Bunche, "Modern Policies of Imperialistic Administration of Subject Peoples" (paper delivered at Howard University, April 5, 1935), box 43, Bunche Papers.

20. Ralph Bunche, "Imperialism in West Africa" (speech, Capital Pleasure Club, Washington, D.C., December 14, 1935), box 43, Bunche Papers.

21. Herbert Aptheker, ed., *Against Racism* (Amherst: University of Massachusetts Press, 1985), 103.

22. Martin Kilson calls Bunche a progressive pragmatist. See Martin Kilson, "Ralph Bunche's Analytical Perspective on African Development" in Rivlin, *Ralph Bunche*, 84.

23. Ralph Bunche, *A World View of Race* (Washington, D.C.: Associates in Negro Folk Education, 1936; reprint, Port Washington, N.Y.: Kennikat Press, 1968), 44.

24. Although Bunche attended the independence day ceremonies of Trinidad

and Tobago as an honored guest, he seems not to have been an admirer of Williams. When Williams was hired to teach some of Bunche's courses during one of his frequent absences, Bunche was critical of the work Williams did.

25. Melville Herskovits quoted in Robert R. Edgar, ed., *An African American in South Africa* (Athens: Ohio University Press, 1992), 12.

26. Urquhart, *Ralph Bunche*, 63.

27. Ralph Bunche, "Psychological Types in Cultures" (paper written at Northwestern University, fall 1936), box 43, Bunche Papers.

28. Ralph Bunche, diary, January 6, 1937, Urquhart family private collection. Bunche kept a daily diary separate from his research notes from the fall of 1936 through his travels to London, Paris, and Africa. It and his letters to Ruth are the most candid expressions of Bunche's thought available.

29. Radcliffe-Brown and Malinowski are the bridge between Durkheim and modern sociological functionalism. Although both were heavily influenced by Durkheim, each developed his own interpretation of functional anthropology. For Radcliffe-Brown, almost all institutions of primitive society, from dancing to subsistence-getting, were useful for social solidarity. However, Malinowski moves away from this more Durkheimian emphasis on social order to a more Marxist rooting of social institutions in the universal needs of the individual and his or her species characteristics. Yet both agree on an antievolutionary view of human development. A practice, custom, or belief was to be interpreted in terms of its present and ongoing functions in the surrounding society—there was no such thing as an archaic survival. This functionalist view dealt a death blow to the positivist theory of cultural lag, as well as provided an intellectual underpinning for the British colonial policy of indirect rule. See Alvin W. Gouldner, *The Coming Crisis of Western Sociology* (New York: Avon, 1970), 128–29.

30. Urquhart, *Ralph Bunche*, 64.

31. Ralph Bunche, diary, April 21, 1937.

32. Urquhart, *Ralph Bunche*, 67. Note that Martin Duberman's biography of Paul Robeson includes only a brief and critical comment from Robeson concerning this contact with Bunche. See Duberman, *Paul Robeson* (New York: Knopf, 1988).

33. Ralph Bunche, "Race," in Ralph Bunche, diary, April 7, 1937.

34. Ibid., April 1937.

35. Ibid., April 5–6, 1937.

36. Ibid., July 6, 1937.

37. Ibid., March 24, 1937.

38. Urquhart, *Ralph Bunche*, 67–68.

39. Edgar, *African American*, 16.

40. Urquhart, *Ralph Bunche*, 71.

41. Ralph Bunche, "Race," in Ralph Bunche, diary, September 1937.

42. Bunche continued to use the term *native* even though he was told it was politically incorrect. South African notes, box 65, Bunche Papers.

43. Of the three anthropologists he studied with, Bunche seemed most comfortable with Schapera. On his experience with Malinowski, Bunche commented, "There's never been a primitive religion so demanding as 'Malinowskism' is here. But I ain't converted. The Baptists dipped me in a tank and couldn't convert me, and I know damn well I can't get no kind of religion in a classroom." Quoted in Edgar, *An African American in South Africa*, 13.

44. Ibid., 280.

45. Ibid., 231.

46. Ralph Bunche, "Race," in Ralph Bunche, diary, January 4, 1938.

47. Urquhart, *Ralph Bunche*, 75.

48. Halila, "The Intellectual Development . . . Bunche," 61.

49. Ralph Bunche, "The Irua Ceremony among the Kikuyu of Kiambu District, Kenya," *Journal of Negro Education* 26, no. 1 (January 1941).

50. Urquhart, *Ralph Bunche*, 77.

51. Ibid.

52. Halila, "The Intellectual Development . . . Bunche," 63.

53. Ralph Bunche, Notes on Uganda, box 65, Bunche Papers.

54. Halila, "The Intellectual Development . . . Bunche," 63.

55. Ralph Bunche, Notes on Tanganyika, box 65, Bunche Papers.

56. Ibid.

57. Urquhart, *Ralph Bunche*, 79–80.

58. W. Ofuatey-Kodjoe, "Ralph Bunche: An African Perspective," in Rivlin, *Ralph Bunche*, 100.

59. Ndabaningi Sithole, *African Nationalism* (London: Oxford University Press 1968), 97.

60. Rupert Emerson and Martin Kilson, eds., *The Political Awakening of Africa* (Englewood Cliffs, N.J.: Prentice-Hall, 1965).

61. Lawrence S. Finkelstein, "Bunche and the Colonial World: From Trusteeship to Decolonization," in Rivlin, *Ralph Bunche*, 112.

62. Colin Legum, *Pan-Africanism* (London: Pall Mall Press, 1962), 44, 104.

63. See Adda B. Bozeman, *Conflict in Africa* (Princeton: Princeton University Press, 1976), for a more anthropological approach to the political problems of Africa.

NOTES TO CHAPTER 6

1. Stephen Steinberg, *Turning Back* (Boston: Beacon Press, 1995), 25.

2. Walter Jackson, *Gunnar Myrdal and America's Conscience* (Chapel Hill: University of North Carolina Press, 1990), 21.

3. Ibid., 13.

4. Ibid., 25. Also, Robert L. Harris, "Segregation and Scholarship: The American Council of Learned Societies Committee on Negro Studies, 1941–50," *Journal of Black Studies* 12, no. 3 (March 1982): 317–21. Herskovits was initially recommended

to Keppel, by psychologist Edward L. Thorndike of Columbia, as the best person in the country to undertake the study. When Keppel checked with several other experts, they raised objections to Herskovits. Had he been chosen, the study would have focused on the process of cultural diffusion from West Africa to the United States rather than limiting itself to the values of mainstream American society, as it did under Myrdal. In 1939, Herskovits obtained Bunche's help in arranging a conference of scholars working in Negro studies on Howard's campus. However, Herskovits did not invite Bunche to join the Committee on Negro Studies, saying, "Bunche has not produced for many years as we have hoped he would, and I do not think that he ought to be included" (319).

5. Steinberg, *Turning Back*, 29.

6. James Bryce was the English author of the classic study *The American Commonwealth*, published in 1893.

7. Jackson, *Gunnar Myrdal*, reports that Herskovits had strongly recommended Abram Harris to Myrdal (108). Mrs. Bunche recalled that her husband met Myrdal for the first time at Harvard. Interview with Mrs. Ralph J. Bunche by Vincent Browne, March 8, 1973, 6, Ralph J. Bunche Oral Documentation Project, Howard University.

8. Jackson, *Gunnar Myrdal*, 111.

9. Gunnar Myrdal to Ralph Bunche, May 5, 1942, box 81, Bunche Papers.

10. Jackson, *Gunnar Myrdal*, 111.

11. Telephone interview with Hal Baron by author, June 5, 1985.

12. The Bunches and the Myrdals would visit socially whenever the opportunity presented itself. The Myrdals were the only couple ever to win Nobel prizes: Gunnar, the Nobel Prize for Economics (1974); Alva, the Nobel Peace Prize (1982). Ironically, Gunnar was a primary candidate for the position of UN secretary-general that eventually went to his Swedish rival, Dag Hammarskjöld.

13. Brian Urquhart, *Ralph Bunche: An American Life* (New York: Norton, 1993), 85.

14. Bunche and Myrdal stayed in separate hotels (or often homes, in Bunche's case); Bunche interviewed Blacks and Myrdal interviewed Whites. Ibid.

15. Ibid., 87. Bunche's legs gave him constant problems during this time; he often worked while in bed. He wrote to Walter White that "my legs are still in bad shape and it seems definite that I am going to have to be laid up for sometime either in New York or at the Mayo Clinic with an operation in which the troublesome veins are to be extracted." He later did go to the Mayo Clinic. Bunche to Walter White, January 23, 1940, box 166, Bunche Papers.

16. Interview with William Bryant by author, February 14, 1986.

17. Ralph J. Bunche, *The Political Status of the Negro in the Age of FDR*, ed. Dewey W. Grantham (Chicago: University of Chicago Press, 1973), viii–ix.

18. Ibid., xvi.

19. Ibid., 79.

20. Ralph Bunche interview with Justice Hugo Black, February 13, 1940, box 85, Bunche Papers.

21. Bunche, *The Political Status of the Negro*, 79.

22. James Jackson to Ralph Bunche, November 29, 1939, Bunche Papers.

23. Bunche to Rowena Hadsell, December 8, 1939, Bunche Papers.

24. Ralph Bunche, "An Analysis of the Dynamics and Mechanisms of Negro Disfranchisement" (paper presented at the annual meeting of the American Political Science Association, Chicago, Ill., December 27, 1940), 4–5, box 43, Bunche Papers.

25. Gunnar Myrdal, *An American Dilemma* (New York: McGraw-Hill, 1964), 518.

26. See interview with Hugo Black (see n. 20, above), 2–5.

27. Bunche, *Political Status of the Negro*, 4.

28. Ibid., 14.

29. Hanes Walton, Jr., ed., *Black Politics and Black Political Behavior* (Westport, Conn.: Praeger, 1994), 30.

30. Bunche, *Political Status of the Negro*, 87.

31. Ibid., 93.

32. Myrdal, *An American Dilemma*, 506.

33. Ibid., 493.

34. Ibid., 507.

35. See, for example, Charles P. Henry, *Jesse Jackson: The Search for Common Ground* (Oakland: Black Scholar Press, 1991).

36. Bunche to James Jackson, November 30, 1939, and Bunche to Walter White, January 17, 1940, Bunche Papers.

37. Myrdal, *An American Dilemma*, 490.

38. Harold Gosnell to Donald Young, February 18, 1941, box 81, Bunche Papers.

39. Bunche, *Political Status of the Negro*, xxvii.

40. Ralph Bunche, "Memorandum on the Conceptions and Ideologies of the Negro Problem" (unpublished research manuscript prepared for the Carnegie-Myrdal study, 1940), 16, boxes 80–90, Bunche Papers.

41. Ralph Bunche, "Conceptions and Ideologies of the Negro Problem," *Contributions in Black Studies* 9/10 (1990–92): 76.

42. Bunche, "Memorandum on the Conceptions," 37.

43. James Weldon Johnson, quoted, ibid., 169.

44. Bunche, "Conceptions," 73–74.

45. Stanford Lyman, "Race Relations as Social Process," in Herbert Hill and James E. Jones, Jr., eds., *Race in America* (Madison: University of Wisconsin Press, 1993), 391.

46. Ibid., 88.

47. Louis Wirth to Samuel Stouffer, August 31, 1940, 36, box 81, Bunche Papers.

48. Bunche, "Memorandum on the Conceptions," 37.

49. Bunche, "Conceptions," 104.

50. Bunche had been a cofounder of the NNC with Davis but by 1940 was very critical of the pro-Communist line being taken by Davis.

51. Ralph Bunche, "Programs, Ideologies, Tactics, and Achievements of Negro Betterment and Interracial Organizations" (unpublished research manuscript prepared for the Carnegie-Myrdal study, 1940), 4–5, boxes 80–90, Bunche Papers.

52. In a section of *An American Dilemma*, "Negro Achievements," Myrdal notes that the Negro's opportunities have been limited; therefore "his achievements are also small." He states there have been perhaps a half dozen outstanding Negro natural scientists and a dozen or so outstanding social scientists, with sociologists leading the way. Contrary to Bunche, Myrdal adds that a number of Black race leaders would have been national leaders if color had not been an obstacle. See Myrdal, *An American Dilemma*, 986–87.

53. Gunnar Myrdal to Walter White, June 30, 1942, Bunche Papers.

54. Walter White to Guy Johnson, March 15, 1941, Bunche Papers.

55. Ibid.

56. Roy Wilkins to Walter White, March 12, 1941, 1, Bunche Papers.

57. Walter White to Gunnar Myrdal, August 4, 1942, Bunche Papers.

58. Wilkins to White, 16.

59. Roy Wilkins to Gunnar Myrdal, August 11, 1942, 9, Bunche Papers.

60. Myrdal, *An American Dilemma*, 831.

61. Ibid., 833–34 n.

62. Eugene Kinckle Jones to Guy Johnson, August 8, 1940, Bunche Papers.

63. Eugene Kinckle Jones to Gunnar Myrdal, June 6, 1941, Bunche Papers.

64. Ralph Bunche to Gunnar Myrdal, September 26, 1941, box 81, Bunche Papers.

65. Myrdal, *An American Dilemma*, 841.

66. Ibid.

67. Bunche, "Programs," 537.

68. Myrdal, *An American Dilemma*, 68.

69. Bunche, "Programs," 699.

70. Ibid., 788.

71. Ibid., 754–55.

72. Ibid., 772.

73. Ibid., 488.

74. Myrdal, *An American Dilemma*, 1075.

75. Ibid., 1078.

76. Bunche, "Programs," 411–12.

77. Ibid., 412. When Myrdal interviewed the notorious racist Senator Theodore G. Bilbo, he found the Mississippian had a much higher view of Garvey. In fact, Bilbo said the secret behind his immigration bill that would send Blacks back to Africa was that groups like Garvey's and the Peace Movement of Ethiopia, and organizers like Carlos Cooks and James H. Thornhill in New York were for it. Myrdal interview with Theodore Bilbo, April 8, 1940, box 85, Bunche Papers.

78. Myrdal, *An American Dilemma*, 748.

79. Ibid., 746.

80. Ibid., 749.

81. At the end of "Programs," Bunche lists sixteen principles for effective Negro organization, which essentially call for a primary emphasis on economics with a strong program of political education and coalition building with White workers. Not surprisingly, Myrdal did not include any of the recommendations in *An American Dilemma*, 774–77.

82. Ralph Bunche, "A Brief and Tentative Analysis of Negro Leadership" (unpublished research memorandum prepared for the Carnegie-Myrdal study, 1940), 2, boxes 80–90, Bunche Papers.

83. Bunche draws on his own personal experience in providing an example of this phenomenon:

> Patronization remains a very real force in the world of Negro-white relationship and, it might be said, especially in the relations between black and white intelligentsia. To cite a specific example, when the Spingarns decided to hold a conference of young Negroes under the direction of Dr. Du Bois several years ago, and invited some thirty younger Negroes to the Spingarn estate at Amenia, New York, to discuss the young Negro's attitude toward the problems of the Negro, it soon became very evident that many of these young people, who were, by and large, just young Negroes and quite undistinguished, talked and spoke of themselves in terms of Negro "leaders." They had been chosen from the masses and this patronization and condescension, though most certainly not deliberately or consciously offered by the Spingarns, had almost magical effect upon the thinking of these young Negroes. Ibid., 30.

84. Ibid., 4, 50.

85. Myrdal, *An American Dilemma*, 739.

86. Ibid., 741.

87. Bunche, "Analysis of Negro Leadership," 20.

88. Myrdal, *An American Dilemma*, 69.

89. Bunche, "Programs," 791.

90. Myrdal, *An American Dilemma*, lxx.

91. This legalistic formalism, which was temporarily overcome during the civil rights movement, has often hidden the moral and political bases of public policy, thus causing the demand for racial justice and equality to be labeled a special interest. For a good discussion of this phenomenon, see Patricia Williams, *The Alchemy of Race and Rights* (Cambridge: Harvard University Press, 1991).

92. Jackson, *Gunnar Myrdal*, 246–49.

93. Myrdal had hoped the study would stimulate additional support, but Donald Young argued against further theoretical studies of race relations and for programs of reducing "inter-group" tensions within existing institutions. Young's view sees to have been the more popular among major foundations. Ibid., 264.

94. Telephone interview with St. Clair Drake by author, January 10, 1986; David W. Southern, *Gunnar Myrdal and Black-White Relations* (Baton Rouge: Louisiana State University Press, 1987).

95. Jackson, *Gunnar Myrdal*, 248. Jackson suggests that had Myrdal not depended on the White Southern historian Guion Johnson for his account of Black history, African Americans as historical actors rather than the objects of White action might have emerged (112).

96. Ralph Ellison, *Shadow and Act* (New York: Signet, 1966), 302.

97. Oliver C. Cox, *Caste, Class and Race: A Study in Social Dynamics* (New York: Modern Reader, 1948), 509–38.

98. See Robin Williams and Gerald David Jaynes, *A Common Destiny* (Washington, D.C.: National Academy Press, 1989); R. J. Herrnstein, "Still an American Dilemma," *Public Interest*, no. 98 (winter 1990): 3–17.

99. Samuel P. Huntington, *American Politics: The Promise of Disharmony* (Cambridge: Harvard University Press, 1981).

100. Charles V. Hamilton, *Adam Clayton Powell, Jr.* (New York: Atheneum, 1991).

101. Jennifer L. Hochschild, *The New American Dilemma: Liberal Democracy and School Desegregation* (New Haven: Yale University Press, 1984).

102. Rodgers M. Smith, "Beyond Tocqueville, Myrdal, and Hartz: The Multiple Traditions in America," *American Political Science Review* 87, no. 3 (September 1993): 549–66.

103. Myrdal's work was one of the principal references cited by the Supreme Court in its decision to reverse the "separate but equal" doctrine of *Plessy* in the *Brown* decision of 1954.

104. Martin Luther King, Jr., *Stride Toward Freedom* (New York: Harper & Row, 1958), 205.

105. Stanford Lyman, *The Black American in Sociological Thought* (New York: Putnam's Sons, 1972), 389.

106. See, for example, Winthrop Jordan, *White Over Black* (Baltimore: Pelican, 1968); Derrick Bell, *Faces at the Bottom of the Well* (New York: Basic Books, 1992).

107. Lyman, *The Black American*, 388.

NOTES TO CHAPTER 7

1. Ralph Bunche, "Problems, Programs and Philosophies of Minority Groups," Howard University, April 5, 1935, 18, box 43, Bunche Papers.

2. Ralph Bunche, "Fascism and Minority Groups" (paper presented at the 27th annual meeting of the NAACP, New York, July 2, 1936), 7, box 43, Bunche Papers.

3. Mary Frances Berry and John W. Blassingame, *Long Memory* (New York: Oxford University Press, 1982), 416.

4. Michael Barone, *Our Country* (New York: Free Press, 1990), 129.

5. Brian Urquhart, *Ralph Bunche: An American Life* (New York: Norton, 1993), 94.

6. Ralph Bunche, "Africa and the Current World Conflict," *Negro History Bulletin* 4, no. 4 (October 1940): 14.

7. Ralph Bunche, "The Role of the University in the Political Orientation of Negro Youth," *Journal of Negro Education* 9, no. 4 (October 1940): 572.

8. Ralph Bunche, "The Negro's Stake in the World Crisis" (speech, Association of Colleges and Secondary Schools for Negroes, Montgomery, Ala., December 6, 1940), 17–18, box 43, Bunche Papers.

9. In May 1941, Bunche had requested an interview with Mrs. Roosevelt concerning Blacks and the war effort. To his surprise, Mrs. Roosevelt invited him to the White House for lunch, admitting later that she had not known he was Black but saying it would not have mattered if she had known. Bunche's motivation for seeking out Mrs. Roosevelt is not clear; however, the interview did lead to her request for a memo on the Black worker from Bunche in September. See Urquhart, *Ralph Bunche*, 95–96.

10. Michael D. Davis and Hunter R. Clark, *Thurgood Marshall* (New York: Birch Lane Press, 1992), 60.

11. Ralph J. Bunche, "What America Means to Me," *American Magazine*, February 1950. In an interview, Mrs. Bunche indicated that the call from Read came on December 7, 1941 (Pearl Harbor Day). See interview with Mrs. Ralph J. Bunche by Vincent Browne, March 8, 1973, 19, Ralph J. Bunche Oral Documentation Project, Howard University.

12. Ibid., 101–2.

13. Bunche wrote to the Mayo Clinic for an appointment in February 1941: "My trouble with varicosity and a chronic condition in one ear has not improved and I now find it possible to come to the Clinic for a thorough diagnosis." See Bunche to Mayo Clinic, February 7, 1941, box 2, Bunche Papers. A later letter from the draft board extending Bunche's deferment for six months to work at the State Department confuses the issue of Bunche draft status. See James B. Opsata to Dr. James P. Baxter, 3rd, June 15, 1942, Bunche Papers.

14. Souad Halila, "The Intellectual Development and Diplomatic Career of Ralph J. Bunche" (Ph.D. diss., University of Southern California, 1988), 106.

15. Ibid., 107.

16. Ralph Bunche interview with William George, September 15, 1941, OSS Working Papers, box 73, folder 1, Bunche Papers. In a later letter to Walter White, Bunche was much more complimentary toward the Liberian government, box 73, Bunche Papers.

17. Ralph Bunche, "The Pan African Movement," OSS Report, December 15, 1943, box 73, Bunche Papers.

18. William Hastie to Walter White, on the Pan-African Conference, July 17, 1945, 2, box 114, Bunche Papers.

19. When Bunche suggested that experienced Black Americans be used as military commanders of African troops, Perry Jester, U.S. consul in Lagos, Nigeria, dur-

ing the war, stated that "although West African natives are 500 years behind the American Negro . . . the British would probably be somewhat reluctant to accept African troops led by Negro officers." See Halila, "The Intellectual Development . . . Bunche," 109–10, 114.

20. Ibid., 111.

21. U.S. Civil Service Commission, Investigations Division, "Ralph Johnson Bunche: Report on Special Hearing," May 5, 1943, 8, Bunche Papers.

22. Rayford Logan diary, February 11, 1943, Rayford Logan Papers, Library of Congress, Washington, D.C. Logan's papers indicate that Bunche stayed active in Howard University politics during this period, including attending academic council meetings.

23. Ibid., entry for September 8, 1941.

24. Halila, "The Intellectual Development . . . Bunche," 112.

25. Conyers Read to William Langer, October 29, 1942, Bunche Papers.

26. Urquhart, *Ralph Bunche*, 106.

27. Ibid.

28. Ibid., 107.

29. Ibid., 109.

30. Bunche, "What America Means to Me."

31. Robert Harris, "Ralph Bunche and Afro-American Participation in Decolonization," in Robert A. Hill, ed., *Pan-African Biography* (Los Angeles: University of California, Los Angeles, and Crossroads Press/African Studies Association, 1987), 128.

32. Harvard Sitkoff, *A New Deal for Blacks* (New York: Oxford University Press, 1978), 78–79.

33. One of the critics King was most distressed to hear from was Ralph Bunche. See Stephen B. Oates, *Let the Trumpet Sound* (New York: Harper & Row, 1982), 437–38.

34. In a famous case, President Jimmy Carter sent Muhammad Ali to represent the United States at meeting of African political leaders in Tanzania. President Nyerere of Tanzania refused to accept a boxer as qualified to participate in the political discussions.

35. Elliott P. Skinner, *African Americans and U.S. Policy Toward Africa, 1850–1924* (Washington, D.C.: Howard University Press, 1992), 4.

36. Ibid., 5.

37. Robert Dallek, *Franklin D. Roosevelt and American Foreign Policy, 1932–1945* (New York: Oxford University Press, 1979), 536–37.

38. Robert Dallek, *The American Style of Foreign Policy* (New York: Knopf, 1983), 139–41.

39. Ibid., 133.

40. Ralph J. Bunche, "The Issue of Colonialism" (lecture, National War College, Washington, D.C., February 21, 1956), 26, Bunche Papers.

41. William Rodger Louis, *Imperialism at Bay, 1941–45* (Oxford: Oxford University Press, 1977), 226.

42. Ibid., 46.

43. Welles, quoted, ibid., 155.

44. Bunche, "The Issue of Colonialism," 26–27.

45. Urquhart, *Ralph Bunche*, 113.

46. R. J. Bunche to Mr. Gerig, January 7, 1945, Bunche Papers.

47. Ibid.

48. Urquhart, *Ralph Bunche*, 115.

49. There was to have been a five-power consultation on the trusteeship question before the opening of the San Francisco conference. The meeting proved impossible to arrange, however, and the five powers (the United States, the Soviet Union, the United Kingdom, China, and France) met immediately after the conference convened. See Ralph Bunche, "Trusteeship and Non-Self-Governing Territories in the Charter of the United Nations," *Department of State Bulletin* 13, no. 34 (1945): 1038.

50. Bunche's colleague Lawrence Finkelstein has criticized U.S. insistence on some type of trusteeship at all costs on two grounds. First, the resulting victory was hollow, given the two types of trusteeship. Second, greater flexibility might have led to better solutions. At the same time that trusteeship partisans were concentrating on establishing the norm of trusteeship for some colonies, they were rejecting a British suggestion that might have led to some international surveillance of all colonies. See Finkelstein, "Bunche and the Colonial World: From Trusteeship to Decolonization," in Benjamin Rivlin, ed., *Ralph Bunche: The Man and His Times* (New York: Holmes & Meier, 1990), 123.

51. Mrs. Roosevelt had recommended Channing Tobias and Ira Reid for the delegation, but they were not included. W. E. B. Du Bois, Rayford Logan, and Max Yergan were there as observers. Bunche had resigned from Yergan's Council on African Affairs and avoided Yergan at the conference. Yergan suggested to friends that he possessed derogatory information on Bunche.

52. Urquhart, *Ralph Bunche*, 117.

53. Harris, "Ralph Bunche," 129.

54. Other members of the delegation included Secretary of State Edward Stettinius; Senators Tom Connally of Texas and Arthur Vandenberg of Michigan; Representative Sol Bloom of New York; and Dean Virginia Gildersleeve of Barnard College. Harold Stassen, who had resigned as governor of Minnesota to join the U.S. Navy, was a few years younger than Bunche; the two got along well, becoming lifelong friends. Bunche reported that Stassen made only one bad blunder: opposing inclusion of the word *independence* in the declaration on trusteeship.

55. Ralph Bunche, "Trusteeship," 1038.

56. Urquhart, *Ralph Bunche*, 121.

57. Harris, "Ralph Bunche," 131.

58. Urquhart, *Ralph Bunche*, 123.

59. See, for example, Bunche's remarks to the Pacific Forum Club, Pueblo Del Rio (Los Angeles), June 29, 1945, box 43, Bunche Papers.

60. When the new secretary of state James F. Byrnes asked the Dependent Areas staff to supply him with trusteeship agreements for the first Council of Foreign Ministers meeting in London over Labor Day weekend, Bunche and his colleagues were shocked to learn that Italy might be given responsibility for its former colonies Libya, Somaliland, and Eritrea. Bunche used the opportunity to draft a model trusteeship agreement because he believed the Italians would be in no position to bargain. Although the policy was changed and the drafts were not used, Finkelstein presents it as an example of Bunche's savy. See Finkelstein, "Bunche and the Colonial World," 125.

61. Urquhart, *Ralph Bunche*, 130.

62. Ibid., 134–35.

63. Ibid., 136.

NOTES TO CHAPTER 8

1. Benjamin Rivlin, ed., *Ralph Bunche: The Man and His Times* (New York: Holmes & Meier, 1990), 194.

2. Ralph Bunche, "Roundtable on Palestine" (Canadian Institute, August 17, 1946), box 44, Bunche Papers.

3. Rivlin, *Ralph Bunche*, 189.

4. Ibid., 191.

5. Bunche ignored their request for a meeting at the end of the negotiations.

6. Nathan A. Pelcovits, *The Long Armistice* (Boulder: Westview Press, 1993), 43.

7. The pacts were with Egypt, Syria, Jordan, and Lebanon, and created mixed armistice commissions.

8. Peggy Mann, *Ralph Bunche: UN Peacemaker* (New York: Coward, McCann & Geoghegan, 1975), 174.

9. Ibid., 196.

10. F. P. Henderson, "How to Write an Armistice," *Marine Corps Gazette*, April 1984, 67.

11. Brian Urquhart, *Ralph Bunche: An American Life* (New York: Norton, 1993), 234.

12. Ibid.

13. Andrew W. Cordier and Wilder Foote, eds., *The Quest for Peace* (New York: Columbia University Press, 1965), 100.

14. Ibid.

15. Ibid., 192.

16. Urquhart, *Ralph Bunche*, 367.

17. Egypt had placed seventeen obstacles in the canal to prevent passage.

18. Bunche sought the help of Baltimore entrepreneur Jacob Blaustein, who had extensive contacts in Israel. Blaustein helped persuade Ben-Gurion and members of the Israeli cabinet to cooperate or face Eisenhower's displeasure. He became an invaluable unofficial channel of communication to Ben-Gurion for Hammarskjöld and Bunche. Urquhart, *Ralph Bunche*, 275.

19. Ibid., 292.

20. Ibid., 294.

21. Ibid., 363.

22. Ibid., 364–66.

23. Quoted, in Brian Urquhart's contribution to *Dialogues on Conflict Resolution: Bridging Theory and Practice* (Washington, D.C.: U.S. Institute of Peace, 1993), 33.

24. By treaty rights Britain had maintained a force on Cyprus following the independence of Cyprus in 1960.

25. The downside of the Congo experience was that the Soviets forced through a resolution that made the funding of peacekeeping voluntary.

26. Bunche noted that Cyprus must be the only place in the world where men, women, and children needed an escort of armored cars, soldiers, and police to go to the beach. Urquhart, *Ralph Bunche*, 373.

27. Lasso's son, Ayala Lasso, was the first UN high commissioner for human rights.

28. Urquhart, *Ralph Bunche*, 373.

29. Bunche's failing eyesight led to an accident in Monaco that ruined a pleasure trip and led to a hospital stay in New York for an infected toe. Ibid.

30. Ibid.

31. Kofi Annan quoted in Dick Clark, *The United Nations, Peacekeeping, and U.S. Policy in the Post-Cold War World* (Queenstown, Md.: Aspen Institute, 1994), 18.

32. Rivlin, *Ralph Bunche*, 207.

NOTES TO CHAPTER 9

1. Bunche was nominated by Norman Angell.

2. Several years later when Bunche recounted this story for Hammarskjöld, the new secretary-general opined that the letter would have been sent had he been in office.

3. Bunche actually accepted the offer from Harvard, engineered by his former professor Rupert Emerson, and wrote a letter of resignation from the UN, which he carried in his pocket for six months before finally tearing it up.

4. Although he was an independent, Bunche seemed to lean toward the Democrats, having voted for Adlai Stevenson and later Hubert Humphrey for president.

5. Ben Keppel, "The Work of Democracy" (Ph.D. diss., University of California, Los Angeles, 1992), 150. (The dissertation was published by Harvard University Press

in 1995.) Bunche cited as an example of D.C. discrimination the burial of his children's pet dog in a segregated pet cemetery.

6. Mary McLeod Bethune to Ralph Bunche, June 28, 1949, box 2, folder B-1949, Bunche Papers. A number of other reasons have been offered to explain Bunche's refusal. Some observers have suggested that Bunche realized he could have more influence on the issues that concerned him by staying at the UN rather than returning to the State Department. One implied that Bunche preferred the higher salary and perks of the UN position, although evidence suggests that the United States was prepared to match his UN salary. At least one observer has stated that Truman made the offer only because he knew Bunche would decline.

7. *Ebony*, November 1955, 136.

8. C. L. R. James to Ralph Bunche, n.d., replying to a letter dated February 16, 1953, box 10, Bunche Papers.

9. Louis Lomax, *The Negro Revolt* (New York: Harper & Row, 1962).

10. Mary McLeod Bethune, quoted in Ben Keppel, *The Work of Democracy* (Cambridge: Harvard University Press, 1995), 61.

11. Martin Luther King, Jr., *Why We Can't Wait* (New York: Signet, 1964), 64.

12. Martin Luther King, Jr., "The American Dream" (Lincoln University commencement address), in James M. Washington, ed., *A Testament of Hope* (New York: Harper & Row, 1986), 212.

13. Richard Kluger, *Simple Justice* (New York: Knopf, 1975), 130.

14. Kenneth Clark, *Dark Ghetto* (New York: Harper, 1965), 193.

15. See, for example, Linda O. Murray, *George Washington Carver: Scientist and Symbol* (New York: Oxford University Press, 1981).

16. Ralph Bunche to Mrs. Michael Frank, September 13, 1969, Urquhart Files.

17. Interview with Edward R. Murrow, *Person to Person*, January 15, 1954, box 50, Bunche Papers.

18. Interview, *This I Believe*, May 26, 1953, box 49, Bunche Papers.

19. See Nancy J. Weiss, *Farewell to the Party of Lincoln: Black Politics in the Age of FDR* (Princeton: Princeton University Press, 1983); also references to luck in Ralph Bunche, "What America Means to Me," *American Magazine*, February 1950.

20. Ralph Bunche, speech (56th annual meeting, American Baptist Convention, Detroit, May 18, 1963), box 58, Bunche Papers.

21. Ibid.

22. *Vital Speeches*, July 1, 1949, 572–73.

23. Ibid., 573.

24. Ralph Bunche, "Nothing Is Impossible for the Negro," *Negro Digest*, 1949.

25. Roy Wilkins, *Standing Fast* (New York: Penguin, 1984), 207.

26. Ralph Bunche, speech (Freedom Fulfillment Conference, Washington, D.C., March 10, 1954), Bunche Papers.

27. Bunche, "What America Means to Me."

28. Nicholas Natanson, *The Black Image in the New Deal* (Knoxville: University of Tennessee Press, 1992), 17.

29. Donald Bogle, *Toms, Coons, Mulattoes, Mammies, and Bucks* (New York: Continuum, 1991).

30. Michael Barone, *Our Country* (New York: Free Press, 1990), ch. 21.

31. Thomas Cripps, *Making Movies Black* (New York: Oxford University Press, 1993), ch. 6.

32. Bogle, *Toms*, 178.

33. Ibid., 182.

34. Ibid., 217.

35. Keppel, "The Work of Democracy," 169–70.

36. Ibid., 173.

37. Ibid., 179.

38. Ibid., 168.

39. In two public speeches in 1953, one before the UN Association and the other before the All Pakistan Youth Movement, Bunche stressed that he was an American Negro who had been born in "the slums of Detroit" but had been able to secure his education and to achieve the measure of success he had under a democratic system of freedom where opportunities are ever increasing and progress is being made for his race. January 7, 1953, box 52, Bunche Papers.

40. In an August 21, 1951, letter to the publisher, Messner, Bunche asked that the book not be published. On December 17, he wrote to Kugelmass refusing to cooperate with the project. Almost a year later, November 21, 1952, Bunche threatens the publisher with a liability suit. In a January 25, 1956, letter to Elizabeth Riley of Crowell Publishing, Bunche expressed his distress over his depiction in Crowell's *Great American Negroes*, saying the information came from the Kugelmass biography, which was "90–95% fiction." Bunche points out a *few* corrections of the Crowell piece:

> his grandfather was Thomas not Ralph and was never a slave . . . Father's name was "Fred" Bunche . . . entire accounts of my grandmother's working, the poverty and my mother's working, are completely erroneous . . . my Detroit neighborhood was not a ghetto and was predominantly inhabited by Austrians and Germans who were recent immigrants . . . as a boy I was never "chunky" but was definitely scrawny, and shy and reticent rather than aggressive, so I am told . . . never thought of leaving school, never shined shoes, and my father never had a lung ailment . . . no "Jim Crow" cars in route to Albuquerque. . . in fact it was one of the most pleasant recollections of my youth . . . never a janitor in women's gym at UCLA . . . never had a room with bedbugs in Boston or cut my food budget—"even to get married." Played blackjack rather than poker—the story is badly distorted. Box 126, folders 53–57, Bunche Papers.

Bunche added that the Kugelmass book so distressed his aunt Edna that it permanently affected her health.

41. Bunche received a huge quantity of mail and apparently read it all and responded. Some wrote for jobs, money, personal advice or to give it, and prizes (some wanted to be nominated for the Nobel). Bunche's hate or "crackpot" mail tended to run in cycles, depending on news coverage. He received many such letters concerning Palestine in 1949, and again in 1959 about the Westside Tennis Club incident. Of course, his participation in civil rights marches or public comments about segregationists drew such responses. Bunche's typical reply was to say that the writer had every right to his or her opinion, but Bunche had an equal right to disagree. For examples of this correspondence, see boxes 42a, 42b, Bunche Papers.

NOTES TO CHAPTER 10

1. Brian Urquhart, *Ralph Bunche: An American Life* (New York: Norton, 1993), 48.

2. Ralph Bunche to Ruth Bunche, May 13, 1945, 192, Urquhart Files.

3. Ralph Bunche to Ruth Bunche, September 29, 1945 (details of trip with woman), 195, Urquhart Files.

4. Ralph Bunche to Ruth Bunche, April 24, 1947, 193, Urquhart Files.

5. Ralph Bunche to Ruth Bunche, August 5, 1947, 193, Urquhart Files.

6. Ralph Bunche to Ruth Bunche, July 27, 1948 (concerns Jane's suicide in 1966), 193, Urquhart Files.

7. Ruth Bunche to Ralph Bunche, March 15, 1952, 194, Urquhart Files.

8. Ruth Bunche to Ralph Bunche, January 14, 1960, 194, Urquhart Files.

9. Ruth Bunche to Ralph Bunche, March 7, 1949, 198, Urquhart Files.

10. Interview with William Mashler, n.d., 199, Urquhart Files. Mashler married Bunche's secretary, Doreen.

11. Urquhart, *Ralph Bunche*, 123.

12. Jane's relationship with her father was not ideal to say the least, but her relationship to her husband, Burton Pierce, was no better. Bunche felt that emotionally she was too young when she married Pierce, whom she idolized. Joan felt that her sister had married primarily to get away from home. See ibid., 393–94.

13. Ralph Bunche, "An Analysis of the Dynamics and Mechanisms of Disfranchisement" (paper presented at the annual meeting of the American Political Science Association, Chicago, December 27, 1940), and E. E. Schattschneider to Bunche, June 14, 1940, box 105, Bunche Papers.

14. Pittman Potter to Ralph Bunche, February 1, 1946, and Robert Carr to Ralph Bunche, February 5, 1946, box 105, Bunche Papers.

15. Telegram, Edward Litchfield to Ralph Bunche, December 19, 1950, box 105, Bunche Papers.

16. David Rockefeller to Ralph Bunche, January 31, 1955, box 106, Bunche Papers.

17. Urquhart, *Ralph Bunche*, 244.

18. Adlai Stevenson to Ralph Bunche, October 29, 1953, box 106, Bunche Papers.

19. Perhaps this best explains why Bunche chose to remain at the UN rather than return to university teaching and research. See Ralph J. Bunche, "Presidential Address," *American Political Science Review* 48, no. 4 (December 1954): 965.

20. Later investigations produced conflicting testimony. One interviewee said Bunche escorted students who used violence against the strikers to the dean's office; other interviewees said Bunche was not involved in the strike.

21. Bunche's position advocating mass action was that taken by the International Defense Fund, in contrast to the NAACP position calling for legal action only. The tactics in the Scottsboro case are discussed in Mark Naison, *Communists in Harlem During the Depression* (New York: Grove Press, 1983).

22. Max Yergan became a well-known Communist spokesman when he returned to the United States in 1936 after fifteen years as a director of YMCA work in South Africa. When Yergan assumed the leadership role in both the NNC and the International Committee on African Affairs in 1940, Bunche resigned. Yergan made an effort to keep Bunche from resigning from the latter but was hostile to Bunche at the 1940 NNC meeting, as we have seen. Bunche regarded the ICAA as a one-person operation—Yergan's—and did not withdraw his resignation from the group he had helped establish in 1936. As we have seen, Bunche was extremely critical of the Communist takeover of the NNC in his "Critique of the National Negro Congress" in the *Extended Memorandum on the Programs, Tactics and Achievements of Negro Betterment and Interracial Organizations* in the Myrdal study. On his split with the International Council on African Affairs, see a series of letters between Yergan, Bunche, and Mary van Kleeck in early 1941, and also Bunche to Clark M. Eichelberger, April 11, 1944, Bunche Papers.

23. FBI interview with Ralph Bunche, February 26, 1942, FBI files.

24. See FBI report on Bunche to Lawrence F. O'Brien, December 29, 1960, FBI files.

25. Michael Barone, *Our Country* (New York: Free Press, 1990), 231.

26. Ibid., 237.

27. See, for example, the creation of the U.S. Civil Rights Commission and the publication of its first report, in 1947, *To Secure These Rights*.

28. Philip S. Foner, ed., *Paul Robeson Speaks* (Larchmont, New York: Brunner/Mazel, 1978), 537. Also Keppel, "The Work of Democracy" (Ph.D. diss., University of California, Los Angeles, 1992), 154.

29. Keppel, "The Work of Democracy," 155.

30. Ibid.

31. Urquhart, *Ralph Bunche*, 100.

32. Norman Thomas, quoted in *Denver Post*, May 5, 1949, box 45, Bunche Papers.

33. Speech by Walter White, January 24, 1951, box 161, Bunche Papers.

34. See box 45, Breakneck Conference folder, Bunche Papers.

35. The power of Bunche as a model also extended across racial lines to the young University of Virginia law student Robert F. Kennedy. Keppel, "The Work of Democracy," 141.

36. Ibid., 137.

37. Martin Luther King, Jr., *Why We Can't Wait* (New York: Signet, 1964), 31.

38. Keppel, "The Work of Democracy," 144. For a contemporary example of this phenomenon, see Sut Jhally and Justin Lewis, *Enlightened Racism: The Cosby Show, Audiences, and the Myth of the American Dream* (Boulder: Westview Press, 1992): "What we discovered, in essence, was that the social and cultural context that gives the show its meaning turns its good intentions upside down" (132).

39. Urquhart, *Ralph Bunche*, 247.

40. Urquhart reports that Bunche was reluctant to ask John P. Davis to appear because he had become a successful businessman, community leader, and family man whose Communist past might hurt his image. However, when asked, Davis readily appeared to testify at the hearing that Bunche was not a party member. Ibid., 253–54.

41. FBI memorandum, D. M. Ladd to the Director [J. Edgar Hoover], n.d., FBI files.

42. FBI memorandum, C. H. Stanley to Mr. Rosen, May 27, 1954, FBI files. When questioned on his Communist affiliations, Harris had taken the Fifth Amendment, against Bunche's advice. A group of three international jurists appointed to advise Lie had ruled that taking the Fifth Amendment constituted grounds for dismissal. See Urquhart, *Ralph Bunche*, 247.

43. Abner Berry's earlier praise in the *Daily Worker* of Bunche and his work had been a subject of FBI and conservative concern.

44. Hastie, who had roomed with Bunche at Harvard, also claimed to have suggested to Truman after the 1948 campaign that Bunche be appointed assistant secretary of state. Truman had asked Hastie what he could do to show his appreciation for the Black support he had received. Although Hastie did not ask for anything for himself, Truman nominated him for a seat on the Third Circuit of the U.S. Court of Appeals. See Gilbert Ware, *William Hastie: Grace Under Pressure* (New York: Oxford University Press, 1984), 225.

NOTES TO CHAPTER 11

1. Ralph Bunche to Ralph Bunche, Jr., July 8, 1960, box 125, Bunche Papers.

2. See Ralph Bunche, "The Gay Lecture Upon Medical Ethics" (Harvard Medical School, May, 8, 1961), 15–16, Bunche Papers; Brian Urquhart, *Ralph Bunche: An American Life* (New York: Norton, 1993), 308.

3. Roland Oliver and J. D. Fage, *A Short History of Africa* (Baltimore: Penguin, 1962), 186.

4. Washington Okumu, *Lumumba's Congo: Roots of Conflict* (New York: Ivan Obolensky, 1963), 9–10.

5. Mark Twain, *King Leopold's Soliloquy* (Boston: P. R. Warren, 1905), 12. The Americans who negotiated U.S. recognition of Leopold's association were led by Henry Shelton Sanford, sometime ambassador to Brussels. Many of the Americans appear to have been directly in Leopold's pay. See Robert I. Rotberg, *A Political History of Tropical Africa* (New York: Harcourt, Brace & World, 1965), 244.

6. George Washington Williams, quoted in John Hope Franklin, *George Washington Williams* (Chicago: University of Chicago Press, 1985), 267.

7. Okumu, *Lumumba's Congo*, 13.

8. Twain, *King Leopold*, 18.

9. R. H. Davis, quoted in Okumu, *Lumumba's Congo*, 19.

10. Newton Leroy Gingrich, "Belgian Education Policy in the Congo, 1945–1960" (Ph.D. diss., Tulane University, May 1971), 18.

11. Walter Rodney, *How Europe Underdeveloped Africa* (London: Bogle L'Ouverture, 1988), 153.

12. Gingrich, "Belgian Education Policy," 11–46.

13. Ibid., 33.

14. Okumu, *Lumumba's Congo*, 239.

15. Thomas Kanza, *Conflict in the Congo* (Harmondsworth, England: Penguin, 1972), 19–20.

16. Gingrich, "Belgian Education Policy," 263.

17. Kanza *Conflict in the Congo*, remarked that the Belgian foreign minister knew hardly any Congolese yet represented them to the world. The average Belgian accepted the notion of benevolent Belgian rule (16–17).

18. Ibid., 49–50.

19. The sixteen points essentially modeled the Congolese government after the Belgian system and established a date for independence and the future relations between the two countries. See ibid., 82.

20. Bunche, "The Gay Lecture," 14.

21. Kanza, *Conflict in the Congo*, 162–63.

22. Ibid., 32.

23. Ralph Bunche to Professor Gains J. Slosser, February 28, 1961, box 125, folder 3, Bunche Papers.

24. Alan P. Merriam, *Congo: Background of Conflict* (Evanston: Northwestern University Press, 1961), 127–28.

25. Henry F. Jackson, *From the Congo to Soweto: U.S. Foreign Policy Toward Africa Since 1960* (New York: Quill, 1984), 27.

26. Tshombe sought meetings with Kasavubu and Lumumba during the Independence Day ceremonies without success. See Kanza, *Conflict in the Congo*, 145–202.

27. Fortunately, the French ambassador in Leopoldville opposed this idea and nothing came of it. Urquhart, *Ralph Bunche*, 311.

28. Ibid., 313.

29. Madeleine G. Kalb, *The Congo Cables* (New York: Macmillan, 1982), 40.

30. Kanza, *Conflict in the Congo*, 142.

31. Ibid., 142–43.

32. Jackson, *From the Congo to Soweto*, 21.

33. Ibid., 23.

34. Ibid., 23–24.

35. Kanza, *Conflict in the Congo*, 335.

36. The local papers headlined Bunche's response; Lumumba was highly insulted and confronted Bunche personally about it. Urquhart, *Ralph Bunche*, 317.

37. Merriam, *Congo*, 219.

38. Ralph Bunche, speech (Circus Saints and Sinners dinner, New York City, September 27, 1960), box 53, Bunche Papers.

39. Urquhart, *Ralph Bunche*, 318.

40. Kwame Nkrumah, *Challenge of the Congo* (London: Nelson, 1967), 243.

41. Kalb, *The Congo Cables*, 27–29.

42. Kanza, *Conflict in the Congo*, 227.

43. Ibid., 228.

44. Ibid., 238.

45. Kalb, *The Congo Cables*, 37–39.

46. Ibid., 40.

47. Urquhart, *Ralph Bunche*, 322.

48. Ralph Bunche to Glenn D. Kent, January 23, 1963, box 125, folder 6, Bunche Papers.

49. Ralph Bunche, "The United Nations Operation in the Congo," in Andrew W. Cordier and Wilder Foote, eds., *The Quest for Peace* (New York: Columbia University Press, 1965), 129.

50. Urquhart, *Ralph Bunche*, 324.

51. Ibid., 325.

52. Ibid., 328.

53. Colin Legum, *Pan-Africanism* (London: Pall Mall Press, 1962), 48.

54. Rajeshwar Dayal, *Mission for Hammarskjöld* (Princeton: Princeton University Press, 1976), 13–14.

55. Urquhart, *Ralph Bunche*, 337.

56. Ralph Bunche, "Africa and the United Nations" (Colby College, April 18, 1960), box 53, Bunche Papers. In a tribute to Heinz Wieschhoff at the Bronxville Public School on October 25, 1961, Bunche said Wieschhoff had taught Nkrumah while at Lincoln University in Pennsylvania and later regretted it. Box 54, Bunche Papers.

57. Bunche, "The Gay Lecture," 13.

58. Kalb, *The Congo Cables*, 69–71.

59. Ibid., 83–97.

60. The vote was 53 yes, 24 no, and 19 abstentions. Kanza, *Conflict in the Congo*, 307.

61. Kennedy had asked Bunche to serve as a foreign policy adviser during his campaign. Bunche declined, citing his position at the United Nations. After taking office, Kennedy again tried to lure Bunche back to Washington.

62. Kalb, *The Congo Cables*, 128–33.

63. Ibid., 133–36.

64. Kanza, *Conflict in the Congo*, 307–11.

65. Kalb, *The Congo Cables*, 194–96. Henry F. Jackson dates Lumumba's assassination as January 17, 1961; see his *From the Congo to Soweto*, ch. 9, 37.

66. Souad Halila, "The Intellectual Development and Diplomatic Career of Ralph J. Bunche: The Afro-American, Africanist, and Internationalist" (Ph.D. diss., University of Southern California, 1988), 192.

67. Urquhart, *Ralph Bunche*, 339.

68. Hammarskjöld did add three Africans to the "Congo Club." Ibid., 340–41.

69. Ibid., 342.

70. Brian Urquhart, *Hammarskjöld* (New York: Knopf, 1972), 520.

71. Ralph Bunche to President John L. Davis of Chapman College, April 17, 1963, box 125, Bunche Papers. UN officials were also in danger in Katanga. Conor Cruise O'Brien, who had served as the UN representative in Katanga for a controversial three months, was replaced by Brian Urquhart, Bunche's assistant, in October. Urquhart was kidnaped from an official dinner in honor of U.S. Senator Thomas Dodd and badly beaten by Tshombe's supporters. O'Brien later published a book critical of UN actions in Katanga: *To Katanga and Back: A UN Case History* (New York: Grosset & Dunlap, 1966). Bunche said the book was self-serving and that O'Brien had been fired from the UN on a matter of personal indiscretion about two months after his return from Katanga. See Ralph Bunche, "The United Nations and the African Revolution, 1960–1969" *Nigerian Journal* 7, no. 1 (winter 1969): 32–33.

72. Urquhart, *Ralph Bunche*, 355.

73. Ibid., 356.

74. Ibid., 360.

75. The final UN forces were not withdrawn until June 1964.

76. Bunche, "The United Nations Operation in the Congo," 126.

77. Okumu, *Lumumba's Congo*, 139.

78. See, Legum, *Pan-Africanism*, 48–55.

79. Soviet Press Summary Report, March 21, 1964, box 56, Bunche Papers.

80. Jack Woddis, in Okumu, *Lumumba's Congo*, 142. Apparently Sweden did not count as a socialist country.

81. Ralph Bunche, "Africa Tests the UN" (speech, Oberlin College, March 24, 1961), Bunche Papers.

82. Hammarskjöld is quoted as saying it was extremely difficult to break Hitlers when the alternatives were Hindenbergs. Kalb, *The Congo Cables*, 82.

NOTES TO CHAPTER 12

1. See, for example, Bunche's denial of slave ancestry in his *Long Island Daily Press* interview with William Oates, July 17, 1959, box 123, Bunche Papers.

2. See Richard Weiss, *The American Myth of Success* (New York: Basic Books, 1969); Seymour Martin Lipset, *The First New Nation* (New York: Basic Books, 1963); Samuel P. Huntington, *American Politics: The Promise of Disharmony* (Cambridge: Harvard University Press, 1981); and Vincent Harding, "Ralph Bunche: The Man without a Country," Institute of the Black World Monthly Report, Atlanta, 1972. Rogers M. Smith contends that other characteristics may just as appropriately be seen as the embodiment of American culture: "Beyond Tocqueville, Myrdal, and Hartz: The Multiple Traditions in America," *American Political Science Review* 87, no. 3 (September 1993): 549–66.

3. Paul Gilroy, *The Black Atlantic* (Cambridge: Harvard University Press, 1993), 49.

4. See John Blassingame, *The Slave Community* (New York: Oxford University Press, 1970); Eugene Genovese, *Roll, Jordan, Roll* (New York: Vintage, 1976); Lawrence W. Levine, *Black Culture and Black Consciousness* (New York: Oxford University Press, 1977); Herbert G. Gutman, *The Black Family in Slavery and Freedom, 1750–1925* (New York: Pantheon, 1976); Albert J. Raboteau, *Slave Religion* (New York: Oxford University Press, 1978); Sterling Stuckey, *Slave Culture* (New York:: Oxford University Press, 1987).

5. See Kenneth M. Stampp, *The Peculiar Institution* (New York: Random House, 1966); and Stanley M. Elkins, *Slavery: A Problem in American Institutional and Intellectual Life* (Chicago: University of Chicago Press, 1959). Early works by the then less established scholars Herbert Aptheker, *American Negro Slave Revolts* (New York: Columbia University Press, 1943), and John Hope Franklin, *The Militant South, 1800–1860* (Cambridge: Harvard University Press, 1970), also challenged the conventional wisdom of slavery as a benevolent institution. See Wilson Jeremiah Moses' discussion of these schools of thought in *The Wings of Ethiopia* (Ames: Iowa State University Press, 1990), 45–63.

6. In perhaps an apocryphal story, it is said that White abolitionists were dismayed by Frederick Douglass's dignified and cultured appearance as a lecturer on the horrors of slavery, contending that no one would believe he had been a slave.

7. Jerry Gafio Watts, *Heroism and the Black Intellectual* (Chapel Hill: University of North Carolina, 1994), 17.

8. Kimberle Williams Crenshaw, "Race, Reform, and Retrenchment: Transformation and Legitimation in Antidiscrimination Law," *Harvard Law Review* 101, no. 7 (May 1988): 1331–87. bell hooks offers evidence supporting Crenshaw when she cites James Baldwin to the effect that there is little interest among postcolonial critics in representations of Whiteness in the Black imagination. See bell hooks, *Black Looks* (Boston: South End Press, 1992), 166.

9. Watts has eloquently described this approach in his analysis of Ralph Ellison. Ellison, Bunche's contemporary, shares a remarkable number of traits that characterize Bunche. Each was raised without a father in poor but upwardly mobile environments. Neither was from the Deep South and both believed in a meritocratic, fully integrated American society. Like Bunche, Ellison came to see the race problem as a psychological one, and both criticized Martin Luther King's attack on President Johnson's war policy in Vietnam. See Watts, *Heroism*, 20–48.

10. The most influential critique of individualism—heroic or otherwise—has come from Harold Cruse, who contended that although American mainstream society portrayed success as based on individual merit, in fact, American cultural norms were deeply embedded in ethnic pluralism. See Harold Cruse, *The Crisis of the Negro Intellectual* (New York: Morrow, 1967).

11. "Excerpts from telephone conversation between Mr. Bunche and Mr. Burgland of the West Side Tennis Club," July 6, 1959, box 123, Bunche Papers. Bunche apparently sent the transcript of the conversation to Leonard Lyons, a reporter with the *New York Post*, with a note asking Lyons not to quote Burgland verbatim because he did not know his statements were being taken down.

12. In addition to the *New York Post* piece, the *New York Times* ran articles on July 9 and 10, and the *New York World Telegraph* on July 10.

13. Philip Benjamin, "City Investigates Tennis Club Bias," *New York Times*, July 10, 1959. Ironically, Arthur Ashe, who would later challenge apartheid in South Africa on the tennis court, was playing for the first time at the West Side Tennis Club in the eastern junior championships at exactly this time. He was sixteen years old and the number-one seed. Ashe had earlier been barred from competing at the Congressional Club in Washington. See the *New York Daily News*, July 11, 1959. Note that Brian Urquhart, *Ralph Bunche: An American Life* (New York: Norton, 1993), mistakenly dates the West Side incident as occurring in 1957.

14. Ralph Bunche, Notes on the West Side Tennis Club incident, July 10, 1959, box 123, Bunche Papers.

15. Statement by the Board of Governors of the West Side Tennis Club, July 15, 1959, box 123, Bunche Papers.

16. Ralph Bunche, statement on West Side incident, July 8, 1959, box 123, Bunche Papers; published in a page-one story in the *New York Times* on the following day.

17. Urquhart, *Ralph Bunche*, 436.

18. Quoted in Souad Halila, "The Intellectual Development and Diplomatic Career of Ralph J. Bunche" (Ph.D. diss., University of Southern California, 1988), 91.

19. Ibid.

20. Urquhart, *Ralph Bunche*, 433.

21. Ralph Bunche, "The Power of Non-Violence" (panel discussion sponsored by the Women's International League for Peace and Freedom, 1935), box 43, Bunche Papers.

22. Ralph Bunche, "Realism and the Negro Problem" (Young People's Forum, Philadelphia, 1936), box 43, Bunche Papers.

23. Ralph Bunche to Alma Booker, May 4, 1950, box 43, Bunche Papers. Booker responded by objecting to Bunche's use of the terms *man* and *brotherhood* and his focusing on female rights in Palestine rather than the United States.

24. Ralph Bunche, "Man, Democracy and Peace" (University of Chicago, April 13, 1950), 6–7, box 46, Bunche Papers.

25. Ralph Bunche, "Address" (42nd annual meeting of NAACP, Atlanta, July 1, 1951), box 47, Bunche Papers. Bunche succeeded Charles Houston on the NAACP Board of Directors upon the latter's death (May 8, 1950).

26. Ralph Bunche, "Address" (45th annual meeting of NAACP, Dallas, July 4, 1954), 3, box 50, Bunche Papers.

27. In *Stride Toward Freedom* (New York: Harper & Row, 1958), King expresses his faith in the goodwill of most White Southerners. By 1963, he has become more cynical about their support in "Letter from a Birmingham Jail," in his *Why We Can't Wait* (New York: Harper & Row, 1963). In his last book, *Where Do We Go From Here? Chaos or Community* (New York: Harper & Row, 1967), he attacks Northern White liberals as well for their lack of support. King's writings and those of his biographers like Stephen Oates document King's great admiration of Bunche.

28. Telegram, Bunche to King, February 22, 1956, box 127, Bunche Papers.

29. "Introduction" (NAACP Legal Defense Fund Dinner, May 17, 1956), box 52, Bunche Papers.

30. Ralph Bunche to Eleanor Roosevelt, April 20, 1956, box 127, folder 38, Bunche Papers.

31. James J. Kilpatrick, "A Humanitarian's Record," *Richmond New Leader*, February 22, 1963, 12.

32. Ralph Bunche, speech (Virginia Council on Human Relations, February 23, 1963), box 56, Bunche Papers. See also FBI documents of the same date, FBI files. Atlanta hotels were also a problem for Josephine Baker when she was invited to entertain at the annual NAACP meeting in 1951. Walter White wrote to Bunche and Eleanor Roosevelt asking that they intervene with the secretary of state to see what the State Department could do and that they call Baker and encourage her to come regardless of the type of accommodations. See Walter White to Ralph Bunche and Eleanor Roosevelt, June 8, 1951, box 47, Bunche Papers.

33. Ibid.

34. Ralph Bunche interview by Associated Press reporter William Oates, June 9, 1963, box 58, Bunche Papers.

35. See original Bunche interview by Oates, May 31, 1963, box 58, Bunche Papers.

36. Ralph Bunche, press statement, *New York Post*, June 17, 1963.

37. Ralph Bunche, "The UN in 1963," October 23, 1963, box 56, Bunche Papers. Bunche also indicated in his speech that his daughter Joan was involved in

voter-registration efforts in the South. He mentioned his son's involvement in the West Side Tennis Club incident in 1959 and added that he had encountered discrimination when he tried to enroll his daughter in a private Quaker school in Pennsylvania.

38. See Barnett's reaction in the *New York Times*, October 26, 1963, box 56, Bunche Papers.

39. "Introduction" (NAACP Legal Defense Fund Dinner, May 28, 1964), 3–4, box 56, Bunche Papers.

40. "March on Montgomery from Selma," March 25, 1965, box 57, Bunche Papers.

41. Ibid.

42. Bunche to Margaret Allen and Agnes Cross, March 10, 1965, box 127, Bunche Papers. Bunche always stressed that he did not consider himself a leader and that there were too many "self-appointed" Negro leaders. Still, he believed that his views represented those of a large majority of Black Americans.

43. Ralph Bunche, "Prejudice in World Perspective" (Fountain Street Church, Grand Rapids, Mich., April 24, 1954), 17–18, box 50, Bunche Papers.

44. Ibid., 19.

45. Ibid.

46. Louis Lomax, "The American Negro's New Comedy Act," *Harper's Magazine*, June 1961, 44.

47. Ralph Bunche, "Remarks before the Periclean Club" (Birmingham, Ala., February 13, 1959), box 50, Bunche Papers.

48. On this or another trip to the Deep South in which he denounced segregation, Bunche arrived at a distant airport due to bad local weather. He was escorted by the all-White highway patrol at breakneck speeds in order to deliver his talk on time.

49. "Many Negroes Back Segregation, Says Bunche," *Jet*, April 23, 1953, 3–4.

50. For a discussion of these traditions, see Cornel West, "The Dilemma of the Black Intellectual," in Cornel West and bell hooks, *Breaking Bread* (Boston: South End Press, 1992).

51. In a 1956 speech in which he described himself as a "back slider," Bunche said he believed that religion is far more a matter of the conscience and the heart, of doing right and of being right, than of dogma or ritual. "I respect all faiths," he said, "but I respect even more the individual who quietly governs his daily relations with his fellow-men by religious precepts, whatever his faith may be." Remarks at a testimonial dinner in honor of Bruce Hoblitzell and Joseph Rauch, Kentucky Region of National Conference of Christians and Jews, Louisville, January 10, 1956, Bunche Papers.

52. More recently, Derrick Bell has argued that racism is a permanent characteristic of American society. See *Faces at the Bottom of the Well*, (New York: Basic Books, 1992).

53. Urquhart, *Ralph Bunche*, 433.

54. James MacGregor Burns and Stewart Burns, *A People's Charter* (New York: Knopf, 1991), 345.

NOTES TO CHAPTER 13

1. Joe R. Feagin and Harlan Hahn, *Ghetto Revolts* (New York: Macmillan, 1973), ch. 1.

2. Ralph Bunche, "Statement on Watts," August 17, 1965, box 127, folder 58, Bunche Papers.

3. Ralph Bunche, "Some Crises and Prospects at the UN Today" (San Francisco, February 11, 1964), 3–4, Bunche Papers.

4. Ralph Bunche, "Upheavals in the Ghettos," unpublished paper, 7, Urquhart Files.

5. Ibid., 10.

6. Ibid., 14.

7. See Charles P. Henry, "An Event-Oriented Approach to the Civil Rights Movement" (Ph.D. diss., University of Chicago, 1974).

8. Bunche, "Upheavals," 17.

9. Brian Urquhart, *Ralph Bunche: An American Life* (New York: Norton, 1993), 450.

10. Ralph Bunche, "Notes on the Black Revolution," 1, Urquhart Files.

11. Ibid., 3.

12. Ibid. In a speech at the University of California, Los Angeles, Bunche defined Black Power as follows: "In essence, whatever other attributes it may have Black Power means the black man banding together to fight for his own good, to kick off the shackles of discrimination and inferiority and to achieve a better life for himself. This is realistic, sound and indispensable to the Negro cause." See "Two Critical Dilemmas: Vietnam and the Ghetto" (University of California, Los Angeles, February 21, 1968), 18, Urquhart Files.

13. Ibid., 4.

14. Ibid.

15. Ralph Bunche, "A Framework for a Course in Negro History" (Hunter College, 1940), Bunche Papers.

16. Bunche, "Notes on the Black Revolution," 5–6.

17. Ralph Bunche, "On Race: The Alienation of Modern Man," in Benjamin Rivlin, ed., *Ralph Bunche: The Man and His Times* (New York: Holmes & Meier, 1990), 254.

18. Ibid., 257–58.

19. Ralph Bunche, "The World the UN Seeks" (Howard University, May 14, 1964), 8, Bunche Papers.

20. In his biography, Urquhart argues that Bunche always opposed the war in

Vietnam. My reading of Bunche's statements suggests a good deal of ambiguity in the early sixties. See Urquhart, *Ralph Bunche*, 381.

21. Lawrence P. Neil, "Black Power in the International Context," in Floyd B. Barber, ed., *The Black Power Revolt* (New York: Collier, 1968), 159.

22. Urquhart, *Ralph Bunche*, 389.

23. Ibid., 391–92.

24. Rivlin, *Ralph Bunche*, 259.

25. Ralph Bunche, interview, *Issues and Answers*, ABC, December 28, 1969, 12, Urquhart Files.

26. Ralph Bunche, interview, *Today Show*, NBC, February 20, 1969, roll 4, 22, Urquhart Files.

27. Ibid., 1.

28. Ralph Bunche, "The Psychology of Humanity: A Conversation with Ralph Bunche and Mary Harrington Hall," *Psychology Today*, April 1969, 56.

29. Urquhart, *Ralph Bunche*, 447–49.

30. Charles P. Henry, "Big Philanthropy and the Funding of Black Organizations," *Review of Black Political Economy*, winter 1979.

31. Urquhart, *Ralph Bunche*, 454.

NOTES TO THE EPILOGUE

1. Walter Allen reports that of all Blacks in Africa and the Diaspora, African Americans identify most strongly with their ethnic group (61 percent), followed by Zimbabweans, who identify more strongly in nationalistic terms (55 percent), and Beninese, who identify strongest of all groups in Pan-Africanist terms (40 percent). "Ethnicity—Problem for the 21st Century?" *Voices of the African Diaspora* (Ann Arbor: University of Michigan, Center for African American Studies), spring 1992, 14. Among the general population, Tom W. Smith reports that Blacks are the easiest to evaluate in terms of images, and that Blacks and Latinos rank last in every positive characteristic. NORC, University of Chicago, "Ethnic Images," GSS Topical Report 19, December 1990, 4.

2. bell hooks, *Black Looks: Race and Representation* (Boston: South End Press, 1992), 3.

3. In her family history, Bunche's aunt Ethel reported that her brother Charlie died of pneumonia rather than suicide. Later, for several months, Ralph would deny that his daughter Jane committed suicide, insisting that she was murdered.

4. Benjamin Keppel, "The Work of Democracy" (Ph.D. diss., University of California, Los Angeles, 1993), 21.

5. Ralph Bunche, "The Fourth Dimension of Personality," in Benjamin Rivlin, ed., *Ralph Bunche: The Man and His Times* (New York: Holmes & Meier, 1990), 223.

6. Given the strong influence of Nana on her grandson, it is remarkable that he accepts so many of her principles but rejects their religious base. Older schol-

ars like Kelly Miller and even the younger Du Bois retained strong traces of Black religiosity.

7. Stuart Hall and Martin Jacques, eds., New Times (London: Verso, 1990), 120.

8. Kimberle Williams Crenshaw, "Race, Reform, and Retrenchment: Transformation and Legitimation in Antidiscrimination Law," Harvard Law Review 101, no. 7 (May 1988): 1358–59.

9. See W. Ofuatey-Kodjoe, "Ralph Bunche: An African Perspective," in Rivlin, Ralph Bunche, 102.

10. Ibid., 103.

11. Martin Luther King, Jr., Where Do We Go from Here: Chaos or Community? (Boston: Beacon Press, 1967), 188.

12. Colin Powell's popularity seems to follow the Bunche model. Enjoying the highest prestige among U.S. public figures, his support cuts across the entire spectrum of American voters, including those who are extremely conservative on racial issues. See Jeannete Belliveau, "A Look At . . . The Colin Powell Factor," Washington Post, January 8, 1995, C3.

13. Ralph Bunche, "Notes on the Black Revolution," 401, Urquhart Files.

Index

About the Author

Charles P. Henry is a Professor of African American Studies at the University of California, Berkeley. He is the author/editor of five books and numerous articles. He is also a former Chair of Amnesty International USA and has worked in the U.S. State Department.